CANTONESE

**Basic Course
Volume 1**

ELIZABETH LATIMORE BOYLE and ASSOCIATES

An Audio-Cassette Course   Specially created to accompany this book are 8 instructional audio cassettes. They are available from the publisher.

FOREIGN SERVICE INSTITUTE
DEPARTMENT OF STATE

audio·forum
A Division of Jeffrey Norton Publishers, Inc.
Guilford, CT 06437

Cantonese Basic Course Vol. 1

ISBN 0-88432-020-0 text and cassettes
ISBN 0-88432-799-X text only

This printing was produced by Audio-Forum,
a division of Jeffrey Norton Publishers, Inc.,
On-The-Green, Guilford, CT 06437 USA.

Printed in the United States of America

PREFACE

Cantonese is the principal language of Kwangtung province in Southeast China, parts of neighboring Kwangsi province, and Hong Kong and Macau on China's southeast periphery. In addition Cantonese is spoken by ethnic Chinese in Vietnam, Cambodia, Laos, Singapore and Malaysia, with the number of speakers in Southeast Asia being between 45 and 50 million altogether. Americans of Chinese descent in the U.S. are almost entirely of Cantonese origin.

Among the many dialects of Cantonese, the prestige variety spoken in Canton is standard, by definition, and is imitated over a wide area which includes Hong Kong. It is this dialect which is represented in the two-volume FSI **Cantonese Basic Course** and the related tape recordings.

The course, intended to provide a syllabus for an intensive course of about 400 classroom hours in spoken Cantonese, was prepared by Elizabeth Latimore Boyle with special assistance from Pauline Ng Delbridge. The direct costs were borne by the U.S. Office of Education. The Foreign Service Institute sponsored the project and underwrote the indirect costs.

The project profited considerably from the help of Cheong Kwong-yu of the National Taiwan University, who was one of the teachers in the earliest try-out of the course and who subsequently served as advisor on pronunciation and usage. Of additional help were the suggestions of Mr. Lung Sing, Cantonese instructor in the American Consulate General in Hong Kong, and the critiques of experienced instructors under Mr. Liu Ming in Hong Kong. Liu Ming, who is director of the Chinese Language Center at New Asia College, also assisted in assembling a staff to voice the text.

Professor John McCoy of Cornell read the manuscript in an early version and made helpful suggestions. Professor James E. Dew of the University of Michigan commented on the first five lessons and contributed two sections of pronunciation drills.

Miss Telia Thweatt had a unique sequence of service in the project, participating first as a student in the try-out of the course in Taipei, then as typist and general

iii

assistant for the present version. Mrs. Lily Lu prepared most of the final typescript. Linda Birkner of the FSI secretarial staff assisted in readying the camera copy for publication.

A Cantonese-English glossary appears at the end of each volume, three columns presenting respectively a romanization, the appropriate characters, and the gloss. A fourth column indicates where the item first occurs in the text. The characters for Volume I were written by Cheong Kwong-yu, and for Volume II by George Lin, Cantonese instructor at FSI..

The U.S. Information Agency cooperated by contributing recording studio time and technical personnel in Hong Kong and Taipei to make the tape recordings which accompany these volumes. N.C. Hon in Hong Kong and Y.T. Yu in Taipei were helpful both in their patience and in the care with which they made the recordings.

The Cantonese voices on the tapes are Pauline Delbridge, Chik Hon-man, Chow Wai-ming and Lung Yue-ching for the Basic Sentences and the Conversations for Listening. For the Drills, they are Cheong Kwong-yu and Ho Suk-ching. All grew up in Hong Kong with the exception of Miss Ho. Users of the tapes should be aware that Miss Ho, the female voice in all Drills in the FSI recording of this text, portrays a few deviations from the textbook standard. Particularly noticeable will be her use of [a] before [ŋ] where [ɔ] is standard in Canton and Hong Kong.

James R. Frith, Dean
School of Language Studies
Foreign Service Institute

CANTONESE BASIC COURSE

TABLE OF CONTENTS

	page
INTRODUCTION	vi
SYMBOLS USED IN THE TEXT	xvi
LESSON 1	1
LESSON 2	31
LESSON 3	56
LESSON 4	82
LESSON 5	104
LESSON 6	127
LESSON 7	152
LESSON 8	188
LESSON 9	200
LESSON 10	222
LESSON 11	241
LESSON 12	265
LESSON 13	289
LESSON 14	309
LESSON 15	330
APPENDIX 1: CONVERSATIONS FOR LISTENING	350
APPENDIX 2: GRAMMATICAL INDEX	366
CUMULATIVE VOCABULARY	371

INTRODUCTION

Scope of the text:

     This Cantonese Basic Course is a course in spoken Cantonese. It uses all the basic grammatical structures of the language and a vocabulary of approximately 950 words. The subject matter of the course deals with daily life in Hong Kong. The course was designed to be taught in an intensive language program of 25-30 class hours a week. Students are expected to spend additional time outside of class listening to tapes of the lessons. There are 30 lessons in the course, and the rate of progress in an intensive class is expected to be approximately 2 lessons per week, including time for review and testing. Each lesson contains five sections: I) a Basic Conversation to be memorized, II) Notes, III) Pattern Drills, structural drills of the type in which the teacher's cue is the stimulus for the students' response, IV) Conversations for Listening, a listening comprehension section, and V) Say it in Cantonese, English to Cantonese practice, much of it in conversational question-answer form, in which students activate what they have learned in the lesson. The early lessons in addition contain explanation and practice drills on pronunciation points, and some classroom phrases for the students to learn to respond to when used by the teacher.

Method of Instruction:

     Ideally, but perhaps not typically, instruction is by a team consisting of a native speaking Cantonese as instructor and a native speaking American as linguist, with the instructor teaching by voicing the Cantonese sentences of the text for the students to imitate and the linguist giving explanations in English when required. A good 80-90% of class time will then be spent with the native speaking instructor drilling the students in recitations, during which time the language in use is entirely Cantonese. Students will read the notes of each lesson outside of class, and questions they have on the text will be answered in English by the linguist during periods set aside for that purpose. Questions in English are not asked during drill sessions with the instructor. Psychologically this establishes the habit of using only Cantonese in classes with the instructor. Class time is concentrated on learning the language by imitation, repetition,

and transformation, according to spoken cues. The instructor speaks
at natural speed, and the students learn to comprehend and speak at
the same natural speed. If there is no linguist to explain students'
questions, special periods are set aside for students to ask questions
of the instructor. It is recommended that the rhythm of the drills not
be interrupted by questions in English.

Pace:

Although the course is projected as a 16 week course if studied
on an intensive program, the time plan is to be viewed as a rough
guide only. The number of students in the class, their language
learning aptitude, their amount of previous experience with related
languages, the amount of time available for outside study, the
excellence of the teacher--all these are variable factors which could
affect the pace of learning.

An earlier version of the course was tested out on a pilot class
of five students during the summer of 1967, and the proposed pace of
two lessons a week seemed about right. However the students in that
course had been selected on the basis of a roughly the same language
aptitude score on the Modern Language Aptitude Test, and they had all
previously studied Mandarin Chinese, a closely related language.
Also, the present version incorporates pronunciation practices which
the earlier version did not have, and additional Conversations for
Listening and Say It in Cantonese sections.

It is therefore suggested that the teacher rely on his own
judgment in regard to the pace of the lessons, rather than follow a
set pace rigidly. The text has been devised so that the crucial
grammatical structures are covered in the first 26 lessons. By
covering the first 26 lessons well students will gain a firm structural
control of the spoken language. We firmly feel that confident mastery
of the first 26 lessons is preferable to hesitant control of the entire
text, if a choice must be made between the two. The rule of thumb
should be that before going on to a new lesson students should be able
to recite the old lesson's Basic Conversation fluently and with
expression and should be able to do the Pattern Drills without looking
at the book and without marked hesitation.

Objectives of the course:

      The objectives of the course are to teach students to speak
Standard Cantonese in the locales where Cantonese is spoken, to speak
it fluently and grammatically, with acceptable pronunciation, within
the scope of topics of daily life. The course was not designed to
lay the groundwork for learning the written language. At the end
of the course students will be able to buy things; talk on the
telephone; ask and give directions; handle money; discuss events past,
present, and future; make comparisons; talk about themselves and their
families; tell time; order simple meals; talk with the landlord,
doctor, servant, bellboy, cabdriver, waiter, sales-clerk; discuss
what, when, where, why, who, how, how much. They will not be able
to discuss politics or their jobs or other topics of a specialized
nature.

Reliability of the material:

      All the conversations and drills in this book were written by
native Cantonese speakers working under the direction of an American
linguist who specified which grammatical points to cover and what
situations were required. The design of the text--what to cover,
what sequence to use in introducing new material, what limits to set
on vocabulary--, the write-ups of structure notes, types and layouts
of pattern drills, and the contents of the English-to-Chinese
translation sections, were done by the American linguist.

      What we have done to handle the problem of limited structures and
vocabulary is to plan the lessons so that certain topics and forms
don't come up until rather late in the course. The words 'yesterday,'
'today,' and 'tomorrow,' for example, don't occur until Lesson 16.
Meanwhile the student has built up the grammatical structure and
vocabulary to talk fluently on some subjects which don't involve
these expressions and the complexities of verb structures that are
involved with time-related sentences. For this reason the present
text is not appropriate for use of students whose needs are for just
a few phrases of Cantonese--it takes too long from that point of view
to get to some of the phrases which a tourist, for example, wants to
use right away. But the student who can study hard on an intensive
program for 4 months and cover at least 26 of the 30 lessons, will

then speak natural-sounding and grammatical Cantonese, and will be able
to cope with most daily life situations in the language.

Procedure:

Basic Conversation. Each lesson begins with a Basic Conversation
covering a daily life situation, organized around one or more grammatical points. The conversation is presented first in build-up form,
then in recapitulation.

The buildup is partly a device to isolate new words and phrases
for pronunciation and identification, partly a device to enable
students to gain smooth delivery and natural sentence rhythm by
starting with a small segment of a sentence then progressively adding
to it to build a full sentence.

The recommended procedure for the buildup is as follows: Students
open their books to the new lesson and look at the English equivalents
as the teacher voices the Cantonese. The teacher voices the first
item six times--three times for the students to listen only, three
times for them to repeat after the teacher. (The teacher may voice
the items more times, but it is recommended that he not do less.)
The teacher then moves on to the next item and repeats the same procedure. When the entire buildup has been performed this way, the
students close their books, and the teacher leads them through the
buildup again giving each item one time, the students this time
watching the teacher and imitating his behavior both vocal and
kinetic--his lip movements, facial expressions, and body gestures.
If the students have particular trouble with a portion of the buildup,
the teacher may give it a few more repetitions than the rest, but if
the difficulty persists, he drops it for the time being and marks
it to return to later. Repetitions under pressure are quite tension-
producing, and it works better to return to a difficult passage in a
more relaxed mood.

In the recapitulation section the conversation is repeated in
full sentence form. The teacher voices each sentence at least two
times, with pauses after each sentence for students to repeat. The
first goal is for the students to be able to say the conversation
after the teacher at natural speed and with natural sentence rhythm.

Details of pronunciation are spotlighted in another section--the first goal for the conversation is sentence rhythm and natural speed.

The second goal is for the students to memorize the Basic Conversation, so they can say it independently without the teacher's model to follow, maintaining natural speed and rhythm. Students will find the tape recorder a valuable aid to memorizing. The tape recorder is tireless in furnishing a model for students to imitate, and enables them to procede at the pace best suited to their needs.

The purpose of memorizing the Basic Conversations is twofold. Memorizing situational material gives students tip-of-the-tongue command of useable Cantonese. Secondly, since the basic conversations are organized on grammatical principles, students by memorizing the conversations will be learning the grammatical framework of the language, on which they can construct other sentences.

The second day on the lesson, when students have memorized the conversation, it is recommended that the teacher have them act out the conversational roles. Later, after moving on to a new lesson, the teacher has them act out the Basic Conversation of an earlier lesson as a form of review.

Pronunciation Practice:

In general, the Pronunciation Practices concentrate on giving limited explanation and fuller practice drills on new sounds encountered in a lesson, plus comparison drills with sounds previously learned and sometimes comparisons with American close counterparts. Instead of giving many examples, using items unknown to the students the pronunciation drills stick to examples from material they have met in the Basic Conversation or Pattern Drills. The exception to this is Lesson One, which presents an overview of all the tones, consonant initials, and vocalic finals of the language, in addition to giving an introduction to intonation and stress. Students who absorb pronunciation best thouugh mimicking the model and who find the linguistic description of sounds confusing or boring or both, should concentrate on mimicking the model and skimp or skip the explanations.

Notes:

There are two kinds of Notes--Structure (grammar) Notes and Culture Notes. These are to be read outside of class.

The structure notes summarize the structures used in the Basic Conversations and practiced in the Pattern Drills, and are for those students who want a general explanation of how the language works. The students who absorb language structures better through learning model sentences and drilling variations of the model can concentrate on the Basic Conversations and Pattern Drills, and skimp on the Structure Notes.

The Culture Notes comment on some Cantonese life patterns which differ from our own.

Pattern Drills:

There are six kinds of Pattern Drills in Cantonese Basic Course. The purpose of the drills is to make the vocabulary and sentence structures sink in and become speech habits, so that the student understands spoken Cantonese without having to translate mentally and speaks fluently and grammatically at natural speed without awkward hesitation and groping for words.

The Pattern Drills give students practice in structures and words which have been introduced in the Basic Conversations. In addition, there are other vocabulary items which appear first in the drill sections. A plus sign marks each occurrence of a new word in this section, and the English equivalent is given.

Each drill begins with an example giving a model of the teacher's cue and the students' response. Then there follow 8 to 10 problems to be done on this pattern. The teacher gives the cue, and the student responds to the new cue following the pattern set in the example. The response is thus predictable, controlled by the pattern and the cue. In the book the cues are given in the left hand column and the responses on the right, with the example above.

Students will find that going over the drills in a session with the tape recorder before performing them in class with the teacher aids their grasp of the material and smooths their delivery. In class students look at their books to check the example for each drill, to learn what their task is. Then they perform the drill with books closed, relying on the pattern of the example sentence and the cues provided to know what to say. A drill is mastered when the student can respond to the cues promptly, smoothly, and without reference to the book.

The types of drills follow:

1. Substitution Drills.

The teacher voices a pattern sentence, then voices a word or phrase (called a cue) to be substituted in the original sentence. The student notes the substitution cue and substitutes it in the appropriate place to make a new sentence.

> Example: T (for Teacher): Good morning, Mrs. Brown. /Jones/
>
> S (for Student): Good morning, Mrs. Jones.

2. Expansion Drills.

There are two kinds of expansion drills. One could be called a listen-and-add drill, using vocabulary and structures familiar to the students. The teacher says a word or phrase and the students repeat it. Then the teacher voices another word or phrase and the students add that word to the original utterance, expanding it. The teacher adds another cue, and the students incorporate it, and so on, making each time a progressively longer utterance.

> Example: T: Hat
>
> S: Hat
>
> T: Blue
>
> S: Blue hat
>
> T: Two
>
> S: Two blue hats.
>
> T: Buy
>
> S: Buy two blue hats.

This type of expansion drill is handled a little differently if it includes new vocabulary. In that case it is performed as a listen-and-repeat drill, the students echoing the teacher.

> Example: T: Hat
>
> S: Hat
>
> T: Blue hat

S: Blue hat
T: Two blue hats
S: Two blue hats

In the second type of expansion drill the example sentence gives the model to follow and the students expand the subsequent cue sentences according to the pattern set by the example.

Example: T: I'm not Mrs. Lee. /Chan/
S: I'm not Mrs. Lee--my name is Chan.

3. Response Drills.

The response drills involve 1) question stimulus and answer response, or 2) statement stimulus and statement response, or 3) statement stimulus and question response.

Ex. 1: T: Is your name Chan? /Lee/
S: No, it's Lee.
Ex. 2: T: He speaks Cantonese. /Mandarin/
S: He speaks Mandarin too.
Ex. 3: T: He speak Cantonese. /Mandarin/
S: Does he speak Mandarin too?

4. Transformation Drills.

In transformation drills the students transform the grammatical form of the cue sentences from positive to negative to question, according to the pattern set in the example. A positive to negative transformation would be:

Ex: T: Her name is Lee.
S: Her name isn't Lee.

5. Combining Drills.

In combining drills the students make one long sentence from two short cue sentences, according to the pattern set in the example.

Ex: T: It's nine o'clock.
We study Chinese.
S: We study Chinese at nine o'clock.

6. Conversation Drills.

In conversation drills students carry on a conversation following the pattern set by the example. The book or the teacher furnishes cues to vary the content while retaining the structure.

```
Ex:  A:  Good morning, Mrs. Lee.
     B:  Excuse me, I'm not Mrs. Lee.  My name is Chan.
     A:  Oh, excuse me, Miss Chan.
     B:  That's all right.
```

A.........Miss Smith.	A. Good morning, Miss Smith.
B.............Brown.	B. Excuse me, I'm not Miss Smith, My name is Brown.
A...................	A: Oh, excuse me, Miss Brown.
B.................	B: That's all right.

Conversations for Listening.

The Conversations for Listening, recorded on tapes, give the students a chance to listen to further conversations using the vocabulary and sentence patterns of the lesson under study. These can be listened to outside of class and replayed in class, with the teacher then asking questions (in Cantonese of course) on the selections and the students answering. Usually several replays are needed before the students' comprehension of the conversation is complete. After they understand a conversation in its entirety, it is recommended that they play it through two or three more times, listening especially for the expressive elements of intonation and final particles, as these occur primarily in conversation and not as natural features of pattern sentences which the students practice in the drill sections.

After Lesson 10, there will be new vocabulary in the Conversations for Listening, to help the story along. These words and phrases are glossed in Cantonese and English at the foot of each conversation in the printed text, but students will not be held responsible for learning them.

Say It in Cantonese.

The Say It in Cantonese section gives situations and sentences in English, and students are to give Cantonese equivalents. This section is to be performed in class for the linguist or the teacher, though the students may prepare it beforehand if they like. Students should recognize that there is often more than one acceptable way to 'say it in Cantonese.'

Vocabulary Checklist.

At the end of each lesson is a vocabulary checklist, giving the new vocabulary for that lesson, the part of speech for each entry (noun, verb, etc.), and the English translation.

Suggestions for Further Practice.

The Say it in Cantonese section is the final working section of each lesson. After doing that section the teacher is encouraged to allow time for the students to carry on conversation practice using the material in the lesson. The teacher should be referee for this part, and make sure all students get a chance to participate. Some students are by nature more talkative than others, and the teacher must see to it, by asking a few questions of the more retiring students, that participation in free conversation is fairly evenly distributed and that the naturally talkative students don't do all the talking.

Repeating the dialogue of the Basic Conversations of earlier lessons is a good way to keep those vocabularies and sentences fresh in the students' minds. Also, selections from earlier dialogues can often be used during free conversation practice of the lesson under study.

System of Romanization Used.

The system of romanization used in the text is a modification of the Huang-Kok Yale romanization. It is described in detail in Lesson 1. In comparing Cantonese and Mandarin sentence structures the system of romanization used for the Mandarin is Yale romanization.

SYMBOLS USED IN THIS TEXT

adj	adjective	QV	quod vide (Latin for 'which see')
adj.s.	adjective suffix	QW	question word
adv	adverb	S	subject
Aux V	auxiliary verb	sp	specifier
bf	boundform, boundword	SPr	sentence prefix
Cj	conjunction	SP	subject-predicate sentence
CoV	co-verb	SVO	subject-verb-object sentence
ex	exclamation; example	ss	sentence suffix
lit.	literally	sen.suf.	sentence suffix
m, M	Measure	sur	surname
MA	moveable adverb	t	title
n,N	noun	TA	term of address
NP	noun phrase	TW	timeword
nu	number	v,V	verb
P	predicate	VO	verb-object construction
PAdv	paired adverb	VP	verb phrase
PCj	paired conjunction	Vsuf	verb suffix
Ph	phrase	var	variant
PhF	phrase frame	(-)	= doesn't occur
PW	placeword	[ ]	= 1. re pronunciation = phonetic transcription.
prep	preposition		2. in cumulative vocabulary list, following noun entries = M for the N
pro	pronoun		3. within the text of English gloss = literal translation of the Cantonese term.

CLASSROOM PHRASES

The instructor will address you in Cantonese from the first day of class. The following are some instructions which you should learn to respond to. Look at your books while the instructor reads the phrases the first time. Then close your books, and the teacher will give the phrases several more times, using gestures to help you understand. Repeat the phrases after him, mimicking his movements as well as his voice, to help you absorb the rhythm and meaning.

1. Yìhgā néihdeih tèngjyuh ngóh góng.

   Now you (plu.) listen while I speak. (i.e., listen, but don't repeat.)

2. Yìhgā ngóh góng, néihdeih gànjyuh ngóh góng.

   Now I'll speak and you repeat after me.

3. Kámmàaih bún syù. or
   Kámmàaih dī syù.

   Close the book. or
   Close the books.

4. Dáhòi bún syù. or
   Dáhòi dī syù.

   Open the book. or
   Open the books.

5. Yìhgā yāt go yāt go góng.

   Now recite one by one.

6. Yātchàih góng.

   Recite all together. (i.e., in chorus)

7. Yìhgā yātchàih gànjyuh ngóh góng.

   Now all together repeat after me.

8. Joi góng yāt chi.

   Say it again.

9. M̀hhóu tái syù.

   Don't look at your book(s).

1

I. BASIC CONVERSATION

  A. **Buildup:**

          (At the beginning of class in the morning)

hohksāang	student

Hohksāang

Hòh	Ho, surname
Sàang	Mr.
Hòh Sàang	Mr. Ho
jóusàhn	"good morning"
Hòh Sàang, jóusàhn.	Good morning, Mr. Ho.
sīnsàang	teacher

Sīnsàang

Léih	Lee, surname
Táai	Mrs.
Léih Táai	Mrs. Lee
Léih Táai, jóusàhn.	Good morning, Mrs. Lee.

Hohksāang

deuiṁhjyuh	excuse me
ngóh	I
haih	am, is, are
ṁh-	not
ṁhhaih	am not, is not, are not
Ngóh ṁhhaih Léih Táai.	I'm not Mrs. Lee.
Deuiṁhjyuh, ngóh ṁhhaih Léih Táai.	Excuse me, I'm not Mrs. Lee.
sing	have the surname
Chàhn	Chan
Ngóh sing Chàhn.	My name is Chan.

Sīnsàang

síujé	Miss; unmarried woman
Chàhn Síujé	Miss Chan
A	Oh, Ah, a mild exclamation
A, deuiṁhjyuh, Chàhn Síujé.	Oh, excuse me, Miss Chan.

Hohksāang

| Ṁhgányiu. | That's all right. OR It doesn't matter. |

(At the end of the day, the students are leaving class.)

Hohksāang

Joigin.   Goodbye.

Sīnsàang

Joigin.   Goodbye.

─────────────

B. Recapitulation:

(At the beginning of class in the morning:)

Hohksāang

Hòh Sàang, jóusàhn.   Good morning, Mr. Ho.

Sīnsàang

Léih Táai, jóusàhn.   Good morning, Mrs. Lee.

Hohksāang

Deuimhjyuh, ngóh mhhaih Léih Táai.   Excuse me, I'm not Mrs. Lee.
 Ngóh sing Chàhn.   My name is Chan.

Sīnsàang

A, deuimhjyuh Chàhn Síujé.   Oh, excuse me, Miss Chan.

Hohksāang

Mhgányiu.   That's all right.

(At the end of the day, the students are leaving class:)

Hohksāang

Joigin.   Goodbye.

Sīnsàang

Joigin.   Goodbye.

+ + + + + + + + + + + + +

Introduction to Pronunciation:

A. Tones:

You have probably heard that Chinese languages are tone
languages, and know this means that sounds which are the same except
for rise and fall of the voice mean different things. This sometimes leads to confusion and/or merriment when a foreigner gets a
tone wrong in a phrase, and says 'lazy' when he means 'broken,'
'sugar' when he means 'soup,' 'ghost' when he means 'cupboard,'
and so on--and on and on.

3

In Cantonese there are seven tones, that is seven variations in voice pitch having the power to combine with an otherwise identical syllable to make seven different meanings. This is best illustrated by examples, which your teacher will read to you:

sì	思	think	(High falling tone)
sí	史	history	(High rising tone)
si	試	try	(Mid level tone)
sī	詩	poem	(High level tone)
sìh	時	time	(Low falling tone)
síh	市	a market	(Low rising tone)
sih	事	a matter; business	(Low level tone)

Below is a practice exercise on the seven tones. Close your books and concentrate on listening to the teacher or tape. Repeat loud and clear during the pause after each syllable or group of syllables.

(This practice section on the basic tones was prepared by Prof. James E. Dew.)

1. sì, sì____; sí sí____; si si____; sī sī____; sìh sìh____;
    síh síh____; sih sih____.

2. sì sì sì____; sí sí sí____; si si si sī____; sì sì si sī____;
    sìh sìh sìh____; síh síh sih____.

3. sì sí____; sí sí____; sìh síh____; síh síh____; si sih____;
    si sih____.

4. sì sìh____; sí síh____; si sih____; sī sìh____; sī si sih____;
    sī si sih____.

5. fàn fán fan____; fàn fán fan____; fàn fán fan fān____;
    fàhn fáhn fahn____; fàhn fáhn fahn____.

6. fàn fán____; fàhn fáhn____; fan fān fahn____; fān fan fahn____;
    fàn fàhn____; fán fáhn____; fàn fán fan fān____;
    fàhn fáhn fahn____.

7. bà bá ba____; bà bá ba____; màh máh mah____; màh máh mah____;
    bà bá ba màh máh mah_____.

8. bìn bín bin____; bìn bín bin____; bìn bín bin bīn____;
    mìhn míhn mihn____; mìhn míhn mihn____.

9. bīt bit miht____; bìn bín bin bit bīt____; mìhn míhn mihn
    miht____; bìn bín bin bit bīt____; mìhn míhn mihn miht____.

4

10. sì, fàn, bà, bìn____; sí fán bá bín____; si, fan, ba, bin____;

     sǐ, fān, bǐn, bǐt____; sìh, fàhn, màh, mìhn____; síh fáhn,

     máh, míhn____; sih, fahn, mah, mihn____; sí sǐ si sǐ,

     sìh síh sih____; bìn bǐn bin bit bǐt, mìhn míhn mihn miht____.

Discussion of Tones:

     There are seven tones in Standard Cantonese. Their designations,
together with examples of each tone, are:

         1. high level   sǐ 詩   fān 分

         2. high falling   sì 思   fàn 婚

         3. high rising   sí 史   fán 粉

         4. mid level   si 試   fan 訓

         5. low falling   sìh 時   fàhn 焚

         6. low rising   síh 市   fáhn 憤

         7. low level   sih 事   fahn 份

You will note that the tones have three contours--level, rising,
and falling.

     There are three level tones: high level, mid level, and low
level.

         ex: hl: sǐ 詩

             ml: si 試

             ll: sih 事

There are two rising tones: high rising and low rising.

         ex: hr: sí 史

             lr: síh 市

There are two falling tones: high falling and low falling.

         ex: hf: sì 思

             lf: sìh 時

     Following a chart devised by Y. R. Chao, we graph the tones of
Cantonese on a scale of one to five, thus:

high level	:55	sǐ 詩	
mid level	:33	si 試	
low level	:22	sih 事	
high rising	:35	sí 史	
low rising	:23	síh 市	
high falling	:53	sì 思	
low falling	:21	sìh 時	

In present day Standard Cantonese as spoken in Hong Kong the
high falling tone seems to be dying out. Many people do not have a
high falling tone in their speech, and use high level tone in place
of high falling. These people then have just six tones in their
speech. In this book we mark seven tones, but your teacher may
only have six, and the tapes accompanying the text include the
speech of some speakers with only six tones. Copy what you hear.
High falling and high level tones are given in the examples below.
If you do not hear a difference, your teacher doesn't differentiate.

Ex: high-falling, high-level contrasts:

Ex: 1. sàam   three   三
        sāam   clothing   衫
     2. fàn   divide   分
        fān   minute   分
     3. Hòh Sàang   Mr. Ho   何生
        hohksāang   student   學生
     4. sì   think   思
        sī   poetry   詩

Tonal Spelling:

The system of tonal spelling we will use in this book is a
modified form of the Huang-Kok Yale romanization. This system
divides the tones into two groups, an upper register group and a
lower register one. The lower register tones are marked by an <u>h</u>
following the vowel of the syllable. This <u>h</u> is silent and simply
indicates lower register. The upper register group doesn't have
the <u>h</u>:

Ex: Upper register tones: sī   詩
                             si   思
                             sí   史
                             si   試

Ex: Lower register: sìh   時
                        síh   市
                        sih   事

The rising, falling, and level contours of the tones are
indicated by the presence or absence of diacritics over the vowel

of each syllable. The diacritics are: ` , ´ , ¯ , representing
falling, rising, and level respectively.

Ex: à   falling

á   rising

ā   level

The absence of a diacritic represents level tone.

Ex: a

Using three diacritics and the low register symbol <u>h</u>, we spell
the seven tones thus:

ā   high level

a   mid level

ah   low level

à   high falling

àh   low falling

á   high rising

áh   low rising

The low register symbol <u>h</u> follows the vowel of the syllable.
If the syllable ends with a consonant, the <u>h</u> still follows the
vowel, but comes before the final consonant.

Ex.   sahp   ten

sèhng   whole, entire

Traditionally Chinese recite Cantonese tones in upper register-
lower register sequence, in the order falling, rising, level, thus:

sì	思	53
sí	史	35
si	試	33
sìh	時	21
síh	市	23
sih	事	22

This is the way Cantonese themselves recite tones. You will
note that the high level tone is not recited traditionally. There
are historical reasons for this which we won't go into here.

In a few words the consonants <u>m</u> and <u>ng</u> occur as vowels, and
in these cases the diacritics are placed above the <u>n</u> of <u>ng</u> and the
<u>m</u>.

7

Ex: m̀h   'not'

        ńgh   'five'

Tones in Sequence:

Tone Sandhi. Changes in the basic sound of tones when syllables are spoken in sequence is called tone sandhi. The high falling tone in Cantonese undergoes tone sandhi in certain position, as follows:

1. When high falling tones occur in succession without intervening pause, all but the final one are pronounced as high level.

Ex: hf + hf becomes hl + hf

烧 豬   1. sīu   jỳu ------ sīujỳu   烧豬
         roast   pig   roast pork

傷 風   2. sēung   fùng ---- sēung fùng   傷風
         hurt   wind   to catch cold

傷 風 添 3. sēung fùng tìm! --sēung fūng tìm! 傷風添
         hurt   wind !   caught cold!

2. When a high falling tone occurs before a high level tone without intervening pause, it is pronounced as high level.

Ex: hf + hl becomes hl + hl

租 屋   1. jòu   ūk -------jōu ūk   租屋
         rent   house   to rent a house

西 餐   2. sài   chāan --- sāichāan   西餐
         west   meal   western food

In this book high falling tone has been written high level only when the tone sandhi is within word boundaries. For separate words, the high falling will be marked with its usual diacritic.

Ex.	Separate forms		Combined forms	
先 生	sìn	sàang	-------	sīnsàang	先生
	first	born		man, teacher, Mr.	
張 生	Jèung	Sàang	-------	Jèung Sàang	張生
	Cheung	Mr.		Mr. Cheung	

Tones not 'sung.'

That Cantonese is a tone language does not mean that sentences in it are sung as you would sing a musical phrase. Music has sustained notes and strict rhythmic scheme, the spoken language does not. At first you may feel that Cantonese sounds sing-song,

8

but practice will bring familiarity and soon it will sound natural
to you.

B. Intonation:

    A sentence may be said different ways, to stress different
points in the sentence and also to express what the speaker feels
about what he is saying. To give an English example, the sentence
'So glad you could come,' may be said:

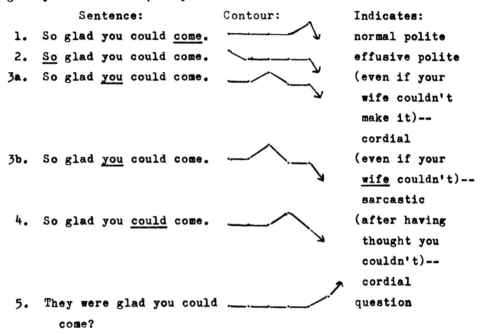

	Sentence:	Contour:	Indicates:
1.	So glad you could <u>come</u>.		normal polite
2.	<u>So</u> glad you could come.		effusive polite
3a.	So glad <u>you</u> could come.		(even if your wife couldn't make it)-- cordial
3b.	So glad <u>you</u> could come.		(even if your <u>wife</u> couldn't)-- sarcastic
4.	So glad you <u>could</u> come.		(after having thought you couldn't)-- cordial
5.	They were glad you could come?		question

The graphs of the sentence contours above represent the rise
and fall of the voice pitch throughout the length of the sentence.
This rise and fall over sentence length we call an "intonation."

    You will note that the question sentence (#5) rises in pitch
at the end, and the statement sentences (#1 - 4) all end with falling
pitch, although within their contours rise and fall occurs at
different points. In English sentence-final fall is the norm, and
sentence-final rise expresses doubt.

    Intonation also has another job within a sentence--it can
express how the speaker feels about what he is saying. By expressive
rise and fall of his voice, by varying his "tone of voice," the
speaker can indicate that he is angry or happy, doubtful or certain,
being polite or rude, suggesting or demanding.

Cantonese sentences too exhibit intonation contours. Sentence-final contours in particular are much more varied in Cantonese than in English, and capable of expressing quite a range of emotional implications.

You may wonder how intonation affects the tone situation in Cantonese, each syllable having as it does its characteristic tone. How the tone contours operate in the framework of sentence contour has been compared to the action of ripples riding on top of waves. Each ripple relates to the one before it and behind it, whether in the trough of the wave or on the crest.

Sentence Stress:

In speaking of sentence stress we mean relative prominence of syllables in a sentence--loud or soft (heavy or light), rapid or slow. Consider the stress pattern of the following English sentences:

1. I'm John Smith.   (In response to "Which one of you is John Smith?")

2. I'm John Smith.   (In response to "I was supposed to give this letter to Tom Smith.")

In the sentences above the stressed syllables (those underlined) give prominence to the information requested in the stimulus sentences.

In certain sentences stress differences alone indicate difference in message content. The pair of sentences often quoted in illustration of this is:

1. Ship sails today.   (The ship will sail today.)

2. Ship sails today.   (Please ship the sails today.)

Another example, from a headline in a newspaper:

Boy Scratching Cat Is Caught, Destroyed

How do you stress that one?

Sentence Pause:

Another feature important in establishing natural sentence rhythm is pause--the small silences between groups of syllables. Note the following English sentences:

10

In considering him for the job he took

into account his education, previous

experience, and appraised potential.

There is a pause between "job" and "he" in the sentence above, and
if you read it instead pausing after "took," you find the sentence
doesn't make sense--you have to go back and read it again putting a
pause in the right place.

We will not discuss Cantonese stress and pause features in this
Introduction, other than to say that Cantonese sentences, like
English ones, do exhibit stress and pause phenomena, as well as
intonational ones. What this effectively means for you as a student
is that you must not concentrate solely on learning words as
individual isolated units; but in imitating the teacher's spoken
model, you should be alert to his delivery of phrase-length segments
and whole sentences, and should mimic the stress, pause, and intonation of the phrases you repeat.

C. Consonants and Vowels

We regard the syllable in Cantonese as being composed of an
initial and a final. The initials are consonants. The finals are
vowels, or vowels plus consonants. Tones are also included as part
of the final.

The practices that follow include all the initials and finals
in Cantonese. They were prepared by James E. Dew.

Initials. Repeat after each syllable in the pause provided.
Concentrate on the initial sound of each syllable.

1. bò   bò   , pò   pò   , mò   mò   , fò   fò
2. dò   dò   , tò   tò   , nò   nò   , lò   lò
3. jà   jà   , chà   chà , sà   sà   , yà   yà
4. gà   gà   , kà   kà   , ngà   ngà , hà   hà
5. gwà   gwà , kwà   kwà , wà   wà

Finals. Listen carefully and repeat in the pauses provided.
Concentrate on the finals--the vowels and vowel+consonant combinat-
ions. (Tones are not marked.)

a	e	eu	i	o	u	yu
ga 架	je 借	heu 靴	ji 至	go 個	wu 惡	jyu 註
gaai界 gai計	gei記	geui句		goi蓋	fui悔	
gaau敎 gau夠			giu叫	gou告		
gaam監 gam柑			gim劍			
gaan澗 gan艮		deun敦	gin見	gon幹	gun冠	gyun絹
gaang gang更	geng鏡	geun羌	ging敬	gong鋼	gung供	
gaap甲 gap鴿			gip扱			
baat八 bat筆		cheut出	git結	got割	fut闊	kyut決
baak百 bak北 kek劇		geuk腳	gik	gok覺	guk焗	

The Mechanics of Producing speech sounds:

In speaking we make use of 1) air, 2) the vibration of the vocal chords (i.e. the voice), and 3) the position of the tongue and other members of the mouth to produce speech sounds. The air originates in the lungs and is released through the mouth, the vocal chords vibrate to produce voiced sounds, and the position of the tongue and other members affect the shape of the vocal instrument and thus the sounds it produces.

Consonants:

1) **Air:**

Air flow, originating in the lungs and released through the mouth, is required for all speech sounds, but different manner of air release produces different sounds. The manner of release is particularly important for consonant sounds. For consonant sounds friction is created at some point in the oral passageway by resistance to the flow of air. The point of resistance to the air flow and the manner of release from this resistance are important contributing factors in how consonants are made. There are several routes through which the air may be released:

A. **Nasal release:** Air can be released through the nose, producing nasal sounds. Try prolonging the English sounds m and n. mmmmm, nnnnn. While you are prolonging these sounds, hold your nose and you notice you can't say m or n. That's because the air flow is released through the nose in saying m and n.

12

B. **Lateral release:** The air release can be over the surface of the side of the tongue. Prolong the English sound l. lllll. Then breathe in and out through your mouth without moving your tongue from its l position. Can you feel that the air passes laterally out one or both sides of your mouth? For me, the air release for l is from both sides. Do you release the air to the right, or to the left, or from both sides?

C. **Stop and Release, with and without Aspiration:** Another manner of air release is for the air flow to be blocked at some point in the mouth and then released, letting the air flow through. When you make the English sounds p-, t-, k-, you notice that the air flow is first blocked at different points, and then released.

The stop releases can be either aspirated or unaspirated. In reference to language sounds 'aspirated' means released with a puff of air. Compare the English sounds p-, t-, k-, and b-, d-, g-. If you put your hand close to your mouth as you say p-, t-, k-, you will notice that you feel your breath against your hand. Say b-, d-, g-, and you find you do not feel your breath against your hand, or at least not as much so. The p-, t-, k- sounds are aspirated, the b-, d-, g- ones unaspirated.

Try:

p-	b-
t-	d-
k-	g-

D. **Spirant release:** When air is released through a narrow passage under pressure, a hissing sound is produced, as in s- sssss, and h- hhhhh. We refer to this type of air release as spirant release.

2) **Voicing:**

Voiced and Voiceless Consonants: The vocal chords vibrate to produce some sounds--which we refer to as voiced sounds--and do not vibrate in the production of other sounds--which are refered to as voiceless. For example, in English the 'z' sound is a voiced sound and the 's' sound is a voiceless one.

13

Prolong the buzzing sound of 'z'--zzzzz. You can hear the voicing, and if you put your hand on your throat over the Adam's apple, you can feel the vibration of the vocal chords. Prolong the hissing sound of 's'--sssss. Notice that voicing ceases, the vocal chords do not vibrate. In Cantonese the only consonants that are voiced are the nasals--m, n, and ng.

3) Position of tongue and other members: Different position of the tongue and other members of the mouth forms the third element in producing speech sounds. Note for example how the difference in tongue position produces different sounds in the English words 'tea' and 'key.' For 't,' the tip of tongue touches the roof of the mouth at the gum ridge behind the upper teeth. Try it: t-, t-, t-, tea. For 'k,' the back of the tongue touches the roof of the mouth at the back: k-, k-, k-, key.

We will describe the consonants of Cantonese in terms of air release, voicing, and position of tongue and other members of the vocal aparatus. We will concentrate primarily on those sounds which are problems for Americans.

Vowels:

Production of vowels, like production of consonants, is a matter of air flow, voicing, and positioning.

1. Air Flow:

Whereas in making a consonant sound friction is created by resistance at some point in the passageway to the flow of air, in making vowels the passageway does not resist the flow of air, and the sound produced is therefore frictionless. The presence or absence of friction is a factor distinguishing consonants and vowels.

2. Vibrating of vocal chords (Voicing):

Vowels are voiced sounds. Under certain circumstances, such as whispering, vowels may be de-voiced, but voicing for vowels is taken as a given, and when exceptions occur, they are specifically noted.

A feature of voicing which is potentially significant for vowels is vowel length. In some languages different vowel

length in an otherwise identical syllable can produce different
words.

> Example: In German, the following two words differ in
> pronunciation only in the length of their vowels:
>> staat [šta˚t]   'state'
>> statt [štaˇt]   'place'

3. **Positioning:**

In positioning for vowel sounds the important contributing
factors are how the lips and tongue are placed.

The lips, in making vowel sounds, are described in terms
of whether they are rounded or unrounded (spread). For example,
in English, the 'i' of 'pit' is a vowel said with lips spread,
and the 'u' of 'put' is said with lips rounded. There are
vowels which are produced with lips neither markedly rounded or
spread, such as 'a' in 'father.' This type is not described
in terms of lip position. If a vowel is not described as being
rounded or spread, you can assume that the lip position is
midway between rounded and spread. We will use the terms
'unrounded' and 'spread' interchangeably.

Tongue position for vowels is described in vertical terms
and in horizontal terms. On the vertical we speak of the
tongue height of a vowel. For example, take the vowels of
'pit,' 'pet,' and 'pat' in English. You notice that the forward part of the tongue is relatively high towards the roof
of the mouth in saying the 'i' of 'pit,' that it drops somewhat to say the 'e' of 'pet,' and drops still lower to say the
'a' of 'pat.' These positions might also be described in
terms of how wide the lower jaw opens in making the sounds--
narrow for the 'i,' medium for the 'e,' and wide for the 'a.'
However, since description in terms of tongue height has
become standard, we will adopt the standard description here,
and speak of vowels in terms of high, mid, and low in reference
to tongue height. Deviations from these cardinal positions are
described in terms of higher-mid, lower-mid, etc.

Horizontally, tongue position is described in terms of
front, central, and back. In English the vowels of 'pit,'

'pet,' and 'pat' are all front vowels, with the points of
reference for 'front' being the blade of the tongue and the
dental ridge. 'Pit,' 'pet,' and 'pat' are high front, mid
front, and low front respectively. For the central vowels
the points of reference in the oral passageway are the center
surface of the tongue and the hard palate. In English the
vowels of 'putt' and 'pot' are central vowels. For the back
vowels the points of reference in the passageway are the back
surface of the tongue and the soft palate. In English the
vowels of 'put,' 'pole,' and 'paw' are back vowels. Deviations
are described in terms of being fronted or backed from the
cardinal positions.

Pronunciation Practice:

1. ch, as in Chàhn

     ch is an initial consonant in Cantonese. We describe the ch
sound in terms of voicing, air flow, and position of tongue against
the roof of the mouth. Like the American ch sound in "chance," the
Cantonese ch is voiceless. In terms of air air flow the American and
Cantonese ch's are alike--both are stops with aspirated release. The
tongue pressing against the roof of the mouth stops the flow of air
entirely, then lets go and allows the air to flow through again,
accompanied by a puff of air. The tongue position for the American ch
and Cantonese ch differs. For the Cantonese ch sound, the tongue
rests flat against the dental ridge (the ridge just behind the upper
teeth) and the blade part of the tongue, that part just back from the
tip, blocks the air passage at the dental ridge. The blade of the
tongue is pressed flat against the ridge: [tɕ] The American ch the
contact point is the tip of the tongue, not the blade of the tongue;
the tongue is grooved, not flat; and the contact point on the roof
of the mouth is a little farther back on the dental ridge than for
the Cantonese ch sound.

          Compare--Listen and repeat: (Read across)

English:	chance	ch	ch	ch	chance	
Cantonese:	Chàhn	ch	ch	ch	Chàhn	陳
	chàn	ch	ch	ch	chàn	親

16

2.   j, as in joigin, jousàhn, Jèung, siujé

J is an initial consonant in Cantonese. We describe the j sound
in terms of voicing, air flow, and position of the tongue against the
roof of the mouth. Unlike the American j sound (in 'joy'), the Cantonese j sound is voiceless. In terms of air flow the American and
Cantonese j's are alike--both are stops with unaspirated release.
The tongue, pressing against the roof of the mouth, stops the flow of
air entirely, then lets go and allows the air to flow through again,
without aspiration (accompanying puff of air). The tongue position
for the Cantonese j is the same as that for the Cantonese ch, different
from that of the American counterpart. For the Cantonese j sound the
blade of the tongue, resting flat against the dental ridge, blocks
the air passage: [tɕ] For the American j the tip of the tongue,
grooved, blocks the air passage at a point a little farther back on
the dental ridge than for the Cantonese j. When air is released, it
flows over a grooved tongue surface for the American sound, a flat
tongue surface for the Cantonese sound.

Compare English and Cantonese similar syllables:
Listen and repeat: (Read across)

English	Cantonese	
1. Joe (3 times)	jóu (3 times)	早
2. joy (3 times)	joi (3 times)	再
3. Jess (3 times)	jé (3 times)	姐

The Cantonese j sound is said with lips rounded before rounded
vowels, and spread before unrounded vowels. (Rounded vowels are those
pronounced with the lips rounded, unrounded vowels those that are
not.)

Watch the teacher, listen and repeat: (read across)

Ex:	rounded	unrounded
1.	Jóu 早 (3 times)	jé 姐 (3 times)
2.	joi 再 (3 times)	jé 姐 (3 times)

Some speakers of Standard Cantonese use slightly different tongue
positions for the j sound, depending on whether it comes before a
rounded or unrounded vowel. Other speakers use the tongue position
described for j above throughout. Those that use different positions

17

before rounded and unrounded vowels use the position described above
before unrounded vowels. Before rounded vowels they retract their
tongue a bit and use the tip of the tongue instead of the part just
behind the tip as contact point for making j. Listen and see if your
teacher's j sounds the same or different before rounded and unrounded
vowels.

      Listen: (Watch the teacher:)

rounded		unrounded	
jó	左	je	借
joi	再	ja	榨
jóu	早		

What has been said in regard to lip-rounding for the j applies
also to ch sounds in Cantonese, but we will not practice this feature
in relation to ch until it comes up in the Basic Conversations.

3. ng, as in ngóh

ng is a voiced nasal initial consonant in Cantonese. In
position, the back surface of the tongue presses against the roof of
the mouth at the soft palate, in the same position as for the English
word "sing." We refer to this position as velar, making an adjective
of the word velum, the technical term for soft palate. ng is a velar
nasal consonant, which in Cantonese may occupy initial position in
a syllable.

      Listen and repeat:
          ngóh 我 (6 times)

The only reason this sound may be hard for English speakers is
that we don't have any words beginning with ng in English, though we
have many ending with the same sound.

If you have trouble, try saying "sing on" in English, and then
say the si part of "sing" silently, beginning to voice on the -ng
part:

          sing on

          (si)ng on

          ----ng on

Now try initial ng again:
      Listen and repeat:
          ngóh 我 (5 times)

4. o, and in Hòh, ngóh

    o is a final in Cantonese. It is a mid back rounded vowel--[ɔ].
The closest American sound is the vowel sound of general American
"dog," but with more rounding of the lips than in English. In Cantonese a rounded vowel has a rounding effect on a consonant preceding
it in a syllable. Watch your teacher and note that in syllables with
an o vowel, he rounds his lips for the preceding consonant too.

    Listen, watch the teacher, and repeat:

        ngóh 我 (5 times)

        Hòh 何 (5 times)

5. yu, as in deuimhjyuh

    yu is a single vowel spelled with two letters. yu is a high
front rounded vowel--[ü], occuring as a final in Cantonese. There is
no counterpart vowel in American English with a similar sound, but
you can produce the sound by protruding your lips while you sustain
the "ee" [i] sound of the English letter "E." The "long e" [i] sound
in English is a high front unrounded vowel. Rounding the lips produces a high front rounded vowel.

    Listen, watch the teacher, and repeat:

        1. deuimhjyuh jyuh jyuh

        2. jyuh 住 (3 times)

        3. yú 魚 (fish) (3 times)

6. eu

    eu is a single vowel spelled with two letters. eu is a mid front
rounded vowel--[ø], occuring as a final in Cantonese only in a very
few words. There is no counterpart vowel in American English with a
similar sound, but you can produce the sound by protruding your lips
while you sustain the "e" [E] sound of the English word "less." This
"short e" [E] sound in English is a mid front unrounded vowel.
Rounding the lips makes it a rounded vowel. In Cantonese a rounded
vowel has a rounding effect on a consonant preceding it in a syllable.

    Watch your teacher, listen, and repeat:

        lēu   'spit out'

        hēu 靴   'boot'

        dēu   'tiny bit'

7. <u>eung</u>, as in Jèung

  <u>eung</u> is a two-part final composed of the mid front rounded vowel
<u>eu</u> [ø] plus the velar nasal consonant <u>ng</u>. There is no close English
counterpart. As a rounded final, <u>eung</u> has a rounding effect on a
consonant preceding it in a syllable.

  Watch the teacher, listen, and repeat:

    Jèung 張 (5 times)

  The <u>eu</u> portion of <u>eung</u> is not nasalized. In English, a vowel
before a nasal final is nasalized--that is, part of the air release
for the vowel goes through the nose. To illustrate the English
situation, hold your nose and say the following English words:

    sue

    soon

    see

    seem

    sit

    sing

  You notice that the vowels of the words with nasal finals (-<u>n</u>,
-<u>m</u>, and -<u>ng</u>) are partially blocked when the nose is blocked, thus
revealing that for such vowels some of the air is normally released
through the nose. The vowels of the words which do not end in a
nasal are unaffected by clocking the nasal passage. They are 'open'
vowels, not 'nasalized' vowels.

  In Cantonese, a vowel before a nasal final is <u>not</u> nasalized--
All of the air is released through the mouth for the vowel portion.
Test whether you can keep the vowel open before nasal final by
stopping you nose as you say:

    Jèung   (5 times)

  To practice the open vowel before a nasal final, try saying the
following pairs of words in which -<u>eu</u> and -<u>eung</u> are contrasted. To
make the -<u>eung</u> sound, pretend through the -<u>eu</u> part that you are going
to say -<u>eu</u>, then add the -<u>ng</u> as an after-thought. You will then
have an open <u>eu</u> followed by the nasal <u>ng</u> sound.

    -<u>eu</u>   -<u>eung</u>

  1. hēu 靴 boot   hèung 香 fragrant

2. lēu   to spit out   léuhng 兩 two

3. geu 鋸 to saw   gèung 羌 ginger

4. jeuk 著 to wear   Jèung 張 surname Cheung

8. **eui**, as in <u>deuimhjyuh</u>

       eui is a two-part final composed of the mid front rounded vowel **eu** plus the high front rounded vowel **yu** [ü]. (We spell the second part of this two-part final with **i** instead of **yu**--**eui** instead of **euyu**, the latter being extremely awkward-looking.) The major force of the voice falls on the **eu** part, with the **yu** (spelled **i**) part an offglide.

       Listen and repeat:

       1. deuimhjyuh 對唔住 (3 times)

       2. deui 對 (3 times)

The tongue position for **eu** before **i** is slightly lower and more backed than it is for **eu** before **ng**. **eui** = [œü]; **eung** = [øŋ].

       Listen and watch for differences in **eu** sound: (Read across)

       1. Jèung 張 Jèung   Jèung   Jèung

       2. deui 對 deui   deui   deui

       3. Jèung 張 deui 對 (4 times)

       4. deui 對 Jèung 張 (4 times)

9. **an**, as in <u>Chàhn</u>, <u>jóusàhn</u>, <u>mhgányiu</u>

       an is a two-part final composed of the backed mid central vowel **a** [ə'] plus the dental nasal consonant **n**. Tongue height for the Cantonese **a** [ə'] is lower than that for American vowel in "cup," higher than that for American vowel in "cop," and more backed than either of the American counterparts. Before the nasal final the Cantonese vowel is not nasalized, as an American vowel before a nasal final would be. The Cantonese vowel is shorter and tenser than the American counterparts.

       Listen, watch the teacher, and repeat:

       1. Chàhn   (4 times)   陳

       2. jóusàhn   (4 times)   早晨

       3. mhgányiu   (4 times)   唔緊要

Compare English and Cantonese syllables:

Listen and repeat: (Read across)

       English   Cantonese

       1. John   John   Chàhn   Chàhn   陳

2. sun   sun   san   sàn 中

10. m as in m̀h

The bilabial nasal consonant m occurs as a vowel, in that the consonant m is syllabic in the syllable m̀h.

Listen and repeat:

1. m̀hhaih   (2 times)

2. haih m̀hhaih a?   (2 times)

11. Tone practice with words in Lesson 1:

Listen and repeat:

1. Jèung, jóu, sing ; Hòh, Léih, haih .

2. Jèung, jóu, sing ; Hòh, Léih, haih .

3. Jèung, Jèung ; Hòh, Hòh .

4. jóu, jóu ; Léih, Léih .

5. jóu, Léih ; Léih, jóu .

6. sing, sing ; haih, haih .

7. sing, haih ; haih, sing .

8. Jèung, Hòh ; jóu, Léih ; sing, haih .

9. Hòh, Jèung ; Léih, jóu ; haih, sing .

II. Notes:

A. Culture Notes

1. Surname and titles.

a. Titles follow surnames: (Drills 1-6)

Léih Sàang   'Mr. Lee'

Léih Táai   'Mrs. Lee'

Léih Síujé   'Miss Lee'

b. Sàang/Sīnsàang and Táai/Taaitáai

Sàang and Sīnsàang, Táai and Taaitáai are alternate forms for 'Mr.' and 'Mrs.' respectively.

Léih Sīnsàang   'Mr. Lee'

Léih Taaitáai   'Mrs. Lee'

Native speakers differ in respect to their use of Sàang and Sīnsàang, and Táai and Taaitáai as titles to surnames. Some say that the full forms denote more respect and the short forms are used in informal situations only. Others say that as title to

surnames the longer forms are used only in letters and that in
speech, Sàang and Táai are used even for subordinates speaking to
superiors. Everyone seems to agree that on the telephone both
long forms and the short forms are common. In this book we have
used the short forms almost exclusively, but you--when you get
into a Cantonese speaking situation--keep your ears peeled and
imitate what your Cantonese peers are saying. Incidentally, you
will notice that what people say and what they say they say do
not always coincide exactly. Also, different people may disagree
vehemently about what is 'right.' This is confusing to the
beginning student. Be advised, however, that the area of dis-
agreement is on peripheral matters. If your teachers disagree
about two forms, you may safely conclude that both forms are
used. taaitáai basically = 'married woman;' sĪnsàang = 'man.'

c. SĪnsàang as 'teacher'

   SĪnsàang meaning 'teacher' may be used with or without a
surname attached. A woman teacher named Wong may be addressed
as SĪnsàang or as Wòhng SĪnsàang.

d. SÍujé, 'unmarried woman,' used as title

   In addressing a woman whose name you do not know, it is
appropriate to address her as SÍujé, no matter how old she is,
and even if you know she is married. In addressing a woman by
her maiden name, the appropriate title is SÍujé. Ex: Wòhng
SÍujé. It is the custom for Chinese women to use their maiden
names in business life, so it often turns out that someone
addressed as SÍujé is married.

e. It is inappropriate to refer to oneself by title in a social
   situation. Avoid saying "Ngóh haih Smith Sàang." Say instead
   "Ngóh sing Smith." (See Drill 5).

2. sing, V/N to have the surname of; surname

   Sing is the surname one is born with. For married women,
equivalent to the English née. The English and American custom
is for a woman's surname to change at the time of marriage to
that of her husband. The Cantonese sing does not change upon
marriage. When you ask a woman her surname, ordinarily she

gives her maiden name in response. If it is a social gathering,
she might add something like "Ngóh sīnsàang sing..., My husband
has the surname...."

B. Structure Notes

1. Relationship of Cantonese to other Chinese languages.

   Cantonese is traditionally called a dialect of Chinese. The
major dialect of Chinese being Mandarin, and other important dialects in addition to Cantonese, are Shanghai, Fukkienese (also
called Hokkienese or Amoy), and Hakka. Mandarin is considered the
major dialect because it is spoken by the greatest number of people
and, more importantly, because it has been prompted as the national
standard language by both the Communist Chinese government on
Mainland China and the Nationalist Chinese government on Taiwan.

   Although historically descended from a single mother tongue,
the various Chinese dialects are today different languages. A
person who speaks only Cantonese cannot understand a person who
speaks only Mandarin, Shanghai, Fukkienese, or Hakka. However,
if two speakers of two different Chinese languages can read, they
can communicate, since Chinese has a uniform writing system which
is not based on sound. (A Western comparison can be made in the
number system, in which '2' is intelligible without reference to
pronunciation.)

   The languages of the Chinese family group are different--and
similar--on three levels: vocabulary, grammatical sentence structure, and phonological sound system. The level of greatest similarity is in that of the grammatical sentence structure. Students who
have studied another Chinese language will find that in great measure they already 'know' the sentence patterns of Cantonese. In
preparing this book we at first planned to make a Cantonese-Mandarin
grammatical appendix to list the grammatically different structures,
the idea being that they were listable, being so few of them. To
draw a parallel we wrote out the Basic Conversations of the first
15 lessons in Mandarin translation and found to our surprise quite
a lot more differences than we had expected. The differences, however, were mostly in the nature of 'You could say it that way--that
sentence pattern exists in Cantonese--but actually that's not the
way we say it, we say it this way.' We therefore didn't make the
appendix, but for the benefit of students who have previously
studied Mandarin, we have used the Notes section to draw attention
to basic grammatical differences where they come up in the text.

   On the level of vocabulary there are greater differences than

24

on the level of grammatical structure, but still a great deal of
similarity. A rough check of the first 10 lessons of this book re-
veals that more than 55% of the Cantonese expressions have identical
Mandarin counterparts.

In pronunciation, differences are greater still, but there are
systematic correspondences. For example, <u>ai</u> in Mandarin is <u>oi</u> in
Cantonese. In total, though, the phonological correspondences are
quite complex, as witnessed by a series of articles on the subject
in a Japanese linguistic journal which runs 26 pages long.

2. <u>Sentence Types--full sentences and minor sentences.</u>

   a. <u>Full sentences</u> have two parts--subject and predicate, in that
      order. Examples from the Basic Conversation of Lesson One are:

         1. Ngóh m̀hhaih Léih Táai.   I am not Mrs. Lee.

         2. Ngóh sing Chàhn.   I am surnamed Chan.

   In these sentences <u>Ngóh</u> is the subject and the remainder of
   each sentence is the predicate.

   b. <u>Minor sentences</u> are not in subject-predicate form. Minor
      sentences are common as responses, commands, exclamations.
      In Lesson One there are several minor sentences in the Basic
      Conversation:

         1. Hòh Sàang, jóusàhn.   Good morning, Mr. Ho.

         2. Joigin.   Goodbye.

         3. M̀hgányiu.   That's all right. [literally:
                              Not important.]

3. <u>Verbs.</u>

In Cantonese, words which can be preceded by the negative
m̀h are regarded as verbs. There are a few cases in which this rule
doesn't work, but basically, you can test whether a new word you
hear is a verb by asking whether you can say m̀h (new word).
Is <u>ngóh</u> a verb? Ask the teacher whether it's OK to say m̀h <u>ngóh</u>.
Is <u>haih</u> a verb? Ask the teacher whether it's OK to say m̀h <u>haih</u>.

4. <u>Adverbs.</u>

In Cantonese an adverb is a word or word group which forms
a construction with a verb. In most cases in Cantonese adverbs
precede the verb they belong with. An example from Lesson 1 is
m̀h-, 'not,' which precedes a verb to form the negative.

5. <u>Phrases.</u>

We give the name 'phrase' to a group of words which has a

specialized meaning as a group. For example, in English, spill +
water = spill the water, and spill + beans = spill the beans.
Spill the water is a simple Verb + Object construction. Spill the
beans may be, but it may also be a phrase whose meaning differs from
the added together meaning of the individual words. This type of
phrase is often called an idiom, or an idiomatic expression. In
this lesson M̀hgányiu, 'It doesn't matter; That's all right; Never
mind,' is such a phrase.

  We also give the name 'phrase' to another kind of construction—
a group of words whose total meaning may be the same as the added
together meaning of the individual words, but which we don't feel
is necessary for you to analyze and learn separately in the first
stage of learning Cantonese. It may even be that the fact that
the construction is grammatically a word group and not a single
word may not be apparent, since the construction may be written
as a single word. Examples are m̀hhóu 'don't' in the Classroom
Phrases of Lesson 1 and sèsiu 'a little' in Lesson 3.

6. Lead Sentences and Follow Sentences.
   a. It's a pretty day today.
   b. How about you?
   c. Where?

a, b and c are all sentences, and all are intelligible, but in b
and c as stated it is not clear what is happening. Without drawing
too rigid lines, we are going to distinguish between lead sentences—
sentences that are intelligible as self-contained units, and follow
sentences, ones which depend upon information supplied by a preceding sentence or the context for full intelligibility.

III. DRILLS

 1. Substitution Drill: Substitute joigin in the position of jóusàhn
   following the pattern of the example sentence.
    Ex: T: Léih Táai, jóusàhn. T: Good morning, Mrs. Lee.
     S: Léih Táai, joigin.   S: Goodbye, Mrs. Lee.

  1. Chàhn Táai, jóusàhn.   1. Chàhn Táai, joigin.

+ 2. Làuh Sàang, jóusàhn.   2. Làuh Sàang, joigin.
    (Good morning, Mr. Lau.)

+ 3. Jèung Síujé, jóusàhn   3. Jèung Síujé, joigin.
    (Good morning, Miss Cheung.)

+ 4. Máh Sàang, jóusàhn.   4. Máh Sàang, joigin.
    (Good morning, Mr. Ma.)

  5. Léih Táai, jóusàhn.   5. Léih Táai, joigin.

---

2. Substitution Drill: Substitute the cue in the appropriate position
   following the pattern of the example sentence.

        Ex: T: Léih Táai, jóusàhn.   T: Good morning, Mrs. Lee.
            /Chàhn/   /Chan/

            S: Chàhn Táai, jóusàhn.   S: Good morning, Mrs. Chan.

  1. Chàhn Táai, jóusàhn. /Léih/   1. Léih Táai, jóusàhn.

+ 2. Léih Táai, jóusàhn. /Wòhng/   2. Wòhng Táai, jóusàhn.
     (Wong)

  3. Wòhng Táai, jóusàhn. /Hòh/   3. Hòh Táai, jóusàhn.

  4. Hòh Táai, jóusàhn. /Jèung/   4. Jèung Táai, jóusàhn.

  5. Làuh Táai, jóusàhn. /Chàhn/   5. Chàhn Táai, jóusàhn.

---

3. Substitution Drill: Substitute the cue in the appropriate position,
   following the pattern of the example sentence.

        Ex: T: Wòhng Sàang, jóusàhn. T: Good morning, Mr. Wong.
            /Táai/   /Mrs./

            S: Wòhng Táai, jóusàhn.   S: Good morning, Mrs. Wong.

  1. Wòhng Táai, jóusàhn. /Síujé/   1. Wòhng Síujé, jóusàhn.

  2. Wòhng Síujé, jóusàhn. /Làuh/   2. Làuh Síujé, jóusàhn.

  3. Làuh Síujé, jóusàhn. /joigin/   3. Làuh Síujé, joigin.

  4. Làuh Síujé, joigin. /Sàang/   4. Làuh Sàang, joigin.

  5. Làuh Sàang, joigin. /Táai/   5. Làuh Táai, joigin.

27

4. Expansion Drill: Expand the cue sentence as indicated in the
   example.

   Ex: T: Ngóh m̀hhaih Wòhng   T: I'm not Mr. Wong.
          Sàang.

       S: Deuim̀hjyuh, ngóh   S: I beg your pardon, I'm not
          m̀hhaih Wòhng Sàang.   Mr. Wong.

   1. Ngóh m̀hhaih Léih Síujé.   1. Deuim̀hjyuh, ngóh m̀hhaih
                                          Léih Síujé.

   2. Ngóh m̀hhaih Chàhn Sàang.   2. Deuim̀hjyuh, ngóh m̀hhaih
                                          Chàhn Sàang.

   3. Ngóh m̀hhaih Jèung Táai.   3. Deuim̀hjyuh, ngóh m̀hhaih
                                          Jèung Táai.

   4. Ngóh m̀hhaih Hòh Sàang.   4. Deuim̀hjyuh, ngóh m̀hhaih Hòh
                                          Sàang.

   5. Ngóh m̀hhaih Wòhng Táai.   5. Deuim̀hjyuh, ngóh m̀hhaih
                                          Wòhng Táai.

   _____

5. Expansion Drill: Expand the cue sentences to conform with the
   pattern of the example.

   Ex: T: Ngóh m̀hhaih Léih   T: I'm not Mrs. Lee. /Cheung/
          Táai. /Jèung/

       S: Ngóh m̀hhaih Léih   S: I'm not Mrs. Lee, my name is
          Táai, ngóh sing   Cheung.
          Jèung.

   1. Ngóh m̀hhaih Hòh Táai. /Chàhn/   1. Ngóh m̀hhaih Hòh Táai, ngóh
                                          sing Chàhn.

   2. Ngóh m̀hhaih Chàhn Síujé. /Máh/ 2. Ngóh m̀hhaih Chàhn Síujé,
                                          ngóh sing Máh.

   3. Ngóh m̀hhaih Máh Sàang. /Wòhng/ 3. Ngóh m̀hhaih Máh Sàang, ngóh
                                          sing Wòhng.

   4. Ngóh m̀hhaih Wòhng Táai. /Jèung/ 4. Ngóh m̀hhaih Wòhng Táai,
                                          ngóh sing Jèung.

   5. Ngóh m̀hhaih Léih Táai. /Hòh/   5. Ngóh m̀hhaih Léih Táai, ngóh
                                          sing Hòh.

   _____

6. Conversation Drill: Carry on the suggested conversation following the model of the example.

Ex: A: Chàhn Sàang, jóusàhn.	A: Good morning Mr. Chan.
B: Deuimhjyuh, ngóh mhhaih Chàhn Sàang. Ngóh sing Jèung.	B: I beg your pardon, I'm not Mr. Chan. My name is Cheung.
A: A, deuimhjyuh, Jèung Sàang.	A: A, excuse me, Mr. Cheung.
B: Mhgányiu.	B: That's OK.

1. A: Chàhn Síujé........
   B: ....
   ....
   ....Wòhng.
   A: ....
   B: ....

1. A: Chàhn Síujé, jóusàhn.
   B: Deuimhjyuh, ngóh mhhaih Chàhn Síujé. Ngóh sing Wòhng.
   A: A, deuimhjyuh, Wòhng Síujé.
   B: Mhgányiu.

2. A: Jèung Síujé ....
   B: ....
   ....
   ....Léih.
   A: ....
   B: ....

2. A: Jèung Síujé, jóusàhn.
   B: Deuimhjyuh, ngóh mhhaih Jèung Síujé. Ngóh sing Léih.
   A: A, deuimhjyuh, Léih Síujé.
   B: Mhgányiu.

3. A: Hòh Sàang ....
   B: ....
   ....
   ....Wòhng.
   A: ....
   B: ....

3. A: Hòh Sàang, jóusàhn.
   B: Deuimhjyuh, ngóh mhhaih Hòh Sàang. Ngóh sing Wòhng.
   A: A, deuimhjyuh, Wòhng Sàang.
   B: Mhgányiu.

4. A: Jèung Sàang ....
   B: ....
   ....
   ....Léih.
   A: ....
   B: ....

4. A: Jèung Sàang, jóusàhn.
   B: Deuimhjyuh, ngóh mhhaih Jèung Sàang. Ngóh sing Léih.
   A: A, deuimhjyuh, Léih Sàang.
   B: Mhgányiu.

5. A: Chàhn Síujé ....
   B: ....
   ....
   ....Làuh.

5. A: Chàhn Síujé, jóusàhn.
   B: Deuimhjyuh, ngóh mhhaih Chàhn Síujé. Ngóh sing Làuh.

A: ....   A: A, deuimhjyuh, Làuh
                                 Síujé.

B: ....   B: Mhgányiu.

─────────────

Vocabulary Checklist for Lesson 1

  1. A   ex: Oh
  2. Chàhn   sur: Chan
  3. deuimhjyuh   ph: Excuse me; I beg your pardon; I'm sorry.
  4. haih   v: is, am, are, were, etc.
  5. Hòh   sur: Ho
  6. hohksāang   n: student
  7. Jèung   sur: Cheung
  8. Joigin   Ph: Goodbye
  9. Jóusàhn   Ph: Good morning
 10. Làuh   sur: Lau
 11. Léih   sur: Li
 12. Máh   sur: Ma
 13. mh-   adv: not
 14. Mhgányiu   Ph: That's all right; It doesn't matter; Never mind.
 15. ngóh   pro: I, me, my
 16. Sàang   t: Mr.
 17. sīnsàang   n: man (see notes); teacher
 18. Sīnsàang   t: Mr. (see notes)
 19. sing   v: have the surname
 20. síujé   n: unmarried woman; woman, lady (see notes)
 21. Síujé   t: Miss
 22. Táai   t: Mrs.
 23. taaitáai   n: married woman (see notes)
 24. Taaitáai   t: Mrs. (see notes)
 25. Wòhng   sur: Wong

30

CLASSROOM PHRASES

A. Learn to respond to the following classroom instructions:

1. Yìhgā ngóh mahn néih, néih daap ngóh.
   1. Now I'll ask you, and you answer me.

2. Yìhgā néihdeih jihgéi mahn, jihgéi daap.
   2. Now you yourselves ask and answer.

3. Gaijuhk.
   3. Continue. (i.e., Do the next one, Keep going.)

4. Néih jouh __A__, néih jouh __B__.
   4. You do A, you do B.

B. The following are some comments that the teacher may make on your recitations.

5. Ngāam laak. OR Āam laak.
   5. That's it. (After student succeeds in saying something right.)

6. Haih gám laak.
   6. That's it. Now you've got it.

7. Haih laak.
   7. That's it. Now you've got it.

8. Hóu jéun.
   8. Just right. Quite accurate.

9. Góngdāk hóu.
   9. Good, spoken well.

10. Góngdāk m̀hhóu.
    10. No, that won't do. Not spoken right.

11. Chàmhdō.
    11. Approximately. (i.e., Good enough for now, but not perfect.)

12. Yiu suhk dī.
    12. Get it smoother. (When a student's recitation is halting.)

13. Daaihsēng dī.
    13. Louder.

31

I. BASIC CONVERSATION

A. Buildup:

(At a party in Hong Kong)

sīnsàang	man

Sīnsàang

gwaising	your surname (polite)
a	sentence suffix, to soften abruptness
síujé	woman
Síujé gwaising a?	What is your surname, Miss?

Síujé

Ngóh sing Wòhng.	My name is Wong.

Sīnsàang
(bowing slightly)

Wòhng Síujé.	Miss Wong.

Síujé

nē?	sentence suffix for questions
Sīnsàang nē?	And you? (polite)

Sīnsàang

síusing	my name (polite)
Síusing Làuh.	My name is Lau.

Síujé
(bowing slightly)

Làuh Sàang	Mr. Lau.

Sīnsàang
(Indicating a young lady standing beside Miss Wong)

mātyéh or mēyéh or mīyéh	what?
sing mēyéh a?	have what surname?
pàhngyáuh	friend
néih	your
néih pàhngyáuh	your friend
Néih pàhngyáuh sing mēyéh a?	What is your friend's name?

Síujé

sing Màh	has the name Ma

32

ge	noun-forming boundword. <u>ge</u> suffixed to a Verb Phrase makes it grammatically a Noun Phrase.
sing Máh ge	is a named-Ma one
kéuih	he, she, it
Kéuih sing Máh ge.	Her name is Ma.

<u>Sīnsàang</u>

Gwóngdùng	Kwangtung
yàhn	person
Gwóngdùngyàhn	Cantonese person, a person from Kwangtung province
haih m̀haih a?	is/not-is? a question formula
Kéuih haih m̀haih Gwóngdùngyàhn a?	Is she Cantonese?

<u>Síujé</u>

Seuhnghói	Shanghai
Seuhnghóiyàhn	Shanghai person
M̀haih a. Kéuih haih Seuhnghóiyàhn.	No, she's from Shanghai.

<u>Sīnsàang</u>

gám,...	'Well then, ...', 'Say', ... sentence prefix, resuming the thread of previous discussion.
Gám, néih nē?	And you?

<u>Síujé</u>

dōu	also
dōu haih Seuhnghóiyàhn	also am Shanghai person
Ngóh dōu haih Seuhnghóiyàhn.	I'm also from Shanghai.

B. <u>Recapitulation</u>:

(At a party in Hong Kong)

<u>Sīnsàang</u>

Síujé gwaising a?	What is your (sur)name, Miss?

33

Síujé

Ngóh sing Wòhng.   My name is Wong.

Sīnsàang
(bowing slightly)

Wòhng Síujé.   Miss Wong.

Síujé

Sīnsàang nē?   And you?

Sīnsàang

Síusing Làuh.   My name is Lau.

Síujé
(bowing slightly)

Làuh Sàang.   Mr. Lau.

Sīnsàang

(Indicating a young lady standing beside Miss Wong)

Néih pàhngyáuh sing mēyéh a?   What is your friend's name?

Síujé

Kéuih sing Máh ge.   Her name is Ma.

Sīnsàang

Kéuih haih m̀haih Gwóngdùngyàhn   Is she Cantonese?
   a?

Síujé

M̀haih a. Kéuih haih Seuhnghóiyàhn.   No, she's from Shanghai.

Sīnsàang

Gám, néih nē?   And you?

Síujé

Ngóh dōu haih Seuhnghóiyàhn.   I'm also from Shanghai.

+ + + + + + + + + + + + +

Problem sounds in Lesson Two: Initials

1. b, d, g, and j (phonetically [p], [t], [k], and [tɕ].

     b, d, g, and j sounds in Cantonese are voiceless, in contrast
to the voiced English sounds spelled with the same letters.
Positioning for Cantonese b and g sounds is the same as for English.
For the d sound the tongue tip is more forward in Cantonese than in
English--against the base of the upper teeth for Cantonese, on the
dental ridge for English. Position for the j sound has been dis-

34

cussed in Lesson One. The sounds are unaspirated, as are their
English counterparts, but the Cantonese and English sounds contrast
with respect to tenseness--the Cantonese initial consonants being
tense and the English lax in isolated words and in stressed position
in a sentence.

Compare: (left to right, then right to left.)

	English		Cantonese		
b:	bean		bīn go	邊個	who
	beau		bou	布	cloth
	buoy		būi	杯	cup
	bun		bān	賓	guest
	buy		baai	拜	worship
d:	doe		dou	到	arrive
	die		daai	帶	bring
	ding		dīng	丁	surname Ting
	deem		dim	店	shop (Noun)
g:	gay		gei	記	record (Verb)
	gum		gam	喋	so
	guy		gaai	界	border
	guava		Gwóngdùng	廣東	Kwangtung
j:	joy		joi	再	again
	gee		ji	至	until, to
	Jew		jiu	照	reflect
	Joe		jou	灶	stove

2. p, t, k, and ch. As initials, phonetically [p´], [t´], [k´], and
[tɕ´].

     Cantonese p, t, k, and ch sounds are similar to English counter-
part p, t, k, ch sounds in that they are voiceless and aspirated.
Positioning for p and k is the same as for English. For the t
sound the tongue tip is more forward in Cantonese than in English--
against the base of the upper teeth for Cantonese, on the dental
ridge for English. The positioning for ch has been discussed in

Lesson One. The Cantonese consonants are tenser than the American counterparts.

Compare: (left to right, then right to left)

	English		Cantonese		
p:	pingpong		pàhngyáuh 朋友	friend	
	pay	pèi	披	to throw over the shoulders	
	pie	paai	派	send	
	Poe	pou	鋪	shop (N)	
	putt	pāt	匹	M for horses	
t:	tie	tāai	呔	necktie	
	team	tìm	添	additional	
	top	taap	塔	pagoda	
	tong	tong	烫	iron (Verb)	
k:	cow	kaau	靠	lean on	
	Kay	kei	冀	hope	
	cut	kāt	咳	cough	
	cup	kāp	級	step (Noun)	
ch:	chuck	chāk	測	guess	
	chew	chìu	超	exceed	
	chow	chau	臭	bad smell	
	chip	chip	妾	concubine	

3. un, as in Yahtbún, Yahtbúnyàhn

Un is a two-part final composed of the high back rounded vowel u [u] followed by the velar nasal consonant n.

u is a high back rounded vowel, which before n has a slight offglide to high central position: u + n = [u:ⁱn]. The vowel is open, not nasalized, before the nasal final. The Cantonese un is roughly comparable to the oon in general American "boon."

Compare Cantonese and English:

1. bún 本 boon   (3 times)
2. boon bún 本 (3 times)

4. __eui__ practice

    Listen and repeat--remember to keep the lips rounded throughout, remember that the __-i__ of __eui__ represents the rounded high front vowel __yu__ [ü].

kéuih	(5 times)	佢
deuiṁhjyuh	(5 times)	對唔住
deui	(5 times)	對

5. __iu__

    __iu__ is a two-part final composed of the high front unrounded vowel __i__ [i] plus the high back rounded vowel __u__ [u]. In this sequence the __i__ is pronounced as an onglide, with the main force of voicing on the __u__ portion of the syllable--[^{i}u].

    Listen and repeat:

    1. síujé   (3 times)

    2. síu   (3 times)

6. __Tone practice__

    1. dōu dōu   , sing sing   , haih haih   .

    2. dōu sing haih   , haih sing dōu   .

    3. dōu sing   , sing haih   , dōu haih   ,
       haih dōu   .

    4. dōu dōu   , Jèung Jèung   .

    5. Jèung, dōu   , dōu Jèung   .

    6. síu síu   , néih néih   .

    7. síu néih   , néih síu   .

    8. haih yàhn   , yàhn haih   .

II. Notes

  A. Culture Notes:

    1. A __Gwóngdùngyàhn__ is a person from Kwangtung province. In English such a person is usually referred to as 'Cantonese,' the English name deriving from the city of Canton in Kwangtung province. People from Hong Kong are also included in the term __Gwóngdùngyàhn__.

    2. __Polite forms in social conversation:__

      a) __Sīnsàang__ and __síujé__ are polite formal substitutes for __néih__-- 'you' as terms of direct address.

1. Sīnsàang gwaising a?   What is the gentleman's (i.e., your) name?

2. Síujé gwaising a?   What is the lady's (i.e., your) name?

(See Drill 11)

b) Síujé is the general polite substitute for néih when addressing a woman, even if she is a married woman.

Ex:

Mr. Lee (to Mrs. Chan):

Síujé haih m̀haih Gwóng-   Is the lady (i.e., Are you)
dùngyàhn a?   from Kwangtung?

(See Drill 14)

c) Surname and title as polite formal substitute for néih as term of address.

Ex:

Mr. Lee (to Miss Chan):

Chàhn Síujé haih m̀haih   Is Miss Chan (i.e., Are you)
Gwóngdùngyàhn a?   from Kwangtung?

(See Drill 14)

d) gwai- and síu-

1. gwai- is a polite form meaning "your," referring to the person you are talking to.

Ex: gwaising = your name. The literal meaning of gwai- "precious, valuable."

2. síu- is a polite form used in referring to oneself when talking with another person. It means "my." Ex: síusing = my name. The literal meaning of síu- is "small."

(See Drill 11)

3. Ngóh sing seems more commonly used than síusing, but gwaising is more common than Néih sing mēyéh a? in social conversation. At a doctor's office, or in registering for school 'What is your name' would be more apt to be asked as 'Sing mēyéh?' than as 'Gwaising a?'

B. Structure Notes.

Some people in speaking about Cantonese and other Chinese languages, say "Cantonese has no grammar." In this they are referring

to the fact that words in Cantonese (and other Chinese languages) do
not undergo the changes of form which English words experience in
relation to tense: see, saw, seen; to number: boy, boys; to case: I,
me, my, mine; to word class: photograph, photographer, photography,
photographic; to subject-verb concord: He sits, They sit.

1. <u>Verb form</u>: Absence of Subject-Verb concord.

There is no subject-verb concord in Cantonese. Whereas
the English verb changes form in concord with the subject--
I am, You are, He is--, the Cantonese verb remains in one
form regardless of the subject.

Ex:

Subject	Verb		
Ngóh	haih	Chàhn Síujé.	I am Miss Chan.
Néih	haih	ngóh pàhngyáuh.	You are my friend.
Kéuih	haih	Gwóngdùngyàhn.	He is Cantonese.
Kéuihdeih	haih	Seuhnghóiyàhn.	They are Shanghai people.

(See Drill __3__)

2. <u>Noun form</u>: Absence of Singular/Plural Distinction.

There is no distinction in Chinese nouns between singular
and plural. One form is used for both single and plural
objects, with other parts of the sentence, or sometimes simply
the situational context, giving information regarding number.

Ex: yàhn = person, people
Yìnggwokyàhn = 'Englishman, Englishmen.'

<u>Singular/Plural</u>

(a) Kéuih   haih Yìnggwokyàhn.   He is an Englishman.
(b) Kéuihdeih haih Yìnggwokyàhn.   They are Englishmen.

(See Drill __3__)

3. <u>Pronoun forms</u>.

1. Cantonese has three personal pronouns:

1. ngóh = I, me, my
2. néih = you, your (singular)
3. kéuih = he, she, it, him, her

2. Plurality is marked in personal pronouns by the plural
suffix <u>-deih</u>:

1. ngóh = I

   ngóhdeih = we (both inclusive and exclusive)

2. néih = you (sing.)

   néihdeih = you (plu.)

3. kéuih = he, she, it

   kéuihdeih = they

(See Drill __3_)

4. <u>Modification structures: Noun modification</u>:

In Cantonese a modifier precedes the noun it modifies:

   Example: <u>Modifier</u> + <u>Noun head</u>

   <u>Ngóh</u>   <u>pàhngyáuh</u> haih Yìnggwokyàhn.

   <u>My</u>   <u>friend</u>   is an Englishman.

We will refer to this modifier-modified noun structure as a
Noun Phrase (NP), consisting of modifier and head.

(See Drills <u>5a, 12, 13</u>)

5. <u>Sentence suffixes</u>.

   What we call sentence suffixes are also called "final
particles" and "sentence finals."

   Sentence suffixes are used in conversation, and are a
means by which the speaker signals the listener what he feels
about what he's saying--that he is doubtful, definite, surprised, sympathetic, that he means to be polite, or sar-
castic.

   Some sentence suffixes have actual content meaning. For
example, mē, which you will learn in Lesson 3, has interrogative meaning, and suffixed to a statement sentence makes
it a question. But others operate primarily as described
above--to add an emotion-carrying coloration to the sentences
they attach to. As such they have been called also "in-
tonation-carrying particles," intonation here used in its
"tone of voice" sense.

   Two sentence suffixes appear in the Basic Conversation
of this lesson:

   1. Sentence suffix <u>a</u>

      The sentence suffix <u>a</u> has the effect of softening the

sentence to which it is attached, making it less
abrupt than it would otherwise be.

    Examples from this lesson:

        1. Kéuih haih m̀hhaih   Is she a Cantonese?
            Gwóngdùngyàhn a?

        2. M̀hhaih a.   No.

In English a courteous tone of voice is perhaps the
best counterpart to the a sentence suffix.

    (See Basic Conversation (BC), and Drill __7__)

2. Sentence suffix nē

    nē in a follow sentence of structure Noun + nē? is
    an interrogative sentence suffix, meaning 'how
    about...?,' 'And...?' In such a sentence nē is
    interrogative on its own:

        Example:

            Ngóh haih Gwóngdùng-   I am a Cantonese; how
                yàhn; néih nē?   about you?

    Sentence suffix a is not substitutable for nē in
    this type of sentence, a not having an interrogative
    sense of its own.

    (See BC, and Drill __14__)

We have used tone marks in writing the sentence suffixes,
but perhaps it would have been better to use other symbols,
maybe arrows pointing up for high, diagonally for rising, to
the right for mid, down for falling. Since some finals can
be said with different pitch contours with the effect of
changing the coloration of what is said but not the content,
they are not truly tonal words. For example, sentence suffix
a, encountered in this lesson, we have described as having
the effect of softening an otherwise rather abrupt sentence.
This final can also be said at high pitch: ā, without changing the sentence-softening aspect, but adding liveliness to
the response.

    Ex: A: Néih haih m̀hhaih   Are you a Cantonese?
            Gwóngdùngyàhn a?

B: M̀hhaih ā. Ngóh haih   No, siree, I'm a Shanghai man.
   Seuhnghóiyàhn.

Beginning students, even advanced students, often have a
lot of difficulty with sentence suffixes, because they don't
fit into categories which we recognize in English. Partly
this is because most of us haven't analyzed the English we
use. How would you explain, for example, the English
"sentences suffixes" in the following:

   1. What do you mean by that, pray?

   2. Hand me that pencil, will you?

   3. Cut that out, hear?

   4. He's not coming, I don't think.

Our advice to students in regard to sentence suffixes is
absorb them as you can, don't get bogged down in trying to
plumb their "real" meanings--in doing so, you spend more time
on them than they warrant.

6. Choice-type Questions.

   Questions which in English would be answered by yes or
no, are formed in Cantonese by coupling the positive and
negative forms of a verb together, and requiring an echo
answer of the suitable one. This question form we call the
Choice-type Question.

   Example:
   Question: Kéuih haih m̀hhaih   Is he an American?
             Méihgwokyàhn a?   [He is-not is American-
                                   person a?]
   Responses: Haih.   Yes. [Is.]
              M̀hhaih.   No. [Not-is]
       (See BC and Drills 6, 9, 13, 14)

7. Question-word Questions.

   Question-word Questions are question sentences using
the Cantonese question-word equivalents of what, when, where,
why, how, how much, how many, who. mēyéh? 'what?' (variant
pronunciations mātyéh? and mīyéh?) is an example of a
question-word.

42

In Cantonese question-word (QW) questions pattern like statement sentences--they have the same word order as statement sentences, with the question-word occupying the same position in the
sentence which the reply word occupies in the statement.

    Example: Kéuih sing meyéh a?   [He is surnamed what?] What
                                       is his name?

              Kéuih sing Wòhng .   [He is surnamed Wong.] His
                                       name is Wong.

        (See BC and Drill 12, 13)

8. -ge, noun-forming boundword

    ge attaches to the end of a word or phrase which is not
a noun and makes it into a noun phrase. In such cases it
usually works to translate -ge into English as 'one who' or
'such a one.' When we say ge is a boundword we mean it is
never spoken as a one-word sentence, but always accompanies
some other word.

    Example: 1. Kéuih sing Wòhng ge. She is one who has the
                                     surname Wong. or
                                     She's a person named
                                     Wong.

        (See BC and Drills 9, 10, 12, 13)

    ga is a fusion of ge + sentence suffix a

    Example: A: Kéuih haih m̀hhaih   Is he named Wong?
                sing Wòhng ga?

          B: M̀hhaih--kéuih   No, he's not named Wong.
              m̀hhaih sing Wòhng   His name is Ho.
              ge. Kéuih sing
              Hòh.

        (See Drill 9)

9. mātyéh, mēyéh, and mīyéh = variant pronunciations for 'what?'
    mātyéh is occasionally used in conversations as an
    emphatic form; normally the spoken pronunciation is mēyéh or
    mīyéh, some people favoring mēyéh, others mīyéh. We have
    written mēyéh uniformly in the text, but on the tapes you
    will hear all three forms.

III. DRILLS

1. Transformation Drill: Make negative sentences following the
   pattern of the example. Student should point to himself in ngóh
   sentences, to another student in kéuih and néih sentences.

      Ex: T: Kéuih haih Seuhng-   T: He (or she) is from Shanghai.
             hóiyàhn.   (Shanghai person)

          S: Kéuih m̀hhaih   S: He (or she) is not from
             Seuhnghóiyàhn.   Shanghai.

   1. Kéuih haih Seuhnghóiyàhn   1. Kéuih m̀hhaih Seuhnghóiyàhn.

 + 2. Kéuihdeih haih Gwóngdùngyàhn.   2. Kéuihdeih m̀hhaih Gwóngdùng-
      (They are Cantonese.)   yàhn.

 + 3. Ngóh haih Jùnggwokyàhn.   3. Ngóh m̀hhaih Jùnggwokyàhn.
      (I am a Chinese.)

 + 4. Ngóhdeih haih Jùnggwokyàhn.   4. Ngóhdeih m̀hhaih Jùnggwokyàhn.
      (We are Chinese.)

 + 5. Néih haih Yìnggwokyàhn.   5. Néih m̀hhaih Yìnggwokyàhn.
      (You are an Englishman.)

 + 6. Néih haih Méihgwokyàhn.   6. Néih m̀hhaih Méihgwokyàhn.
      (You are an American)

 + 7. Néihdeih haih Méihgwokyàhn.   7. Néihdeih m̀hhaih Méihgwok-
      (You (plu.) are Americans.)   yàhn.

 + 8. Ngóh haih Yahtbúnyàhn.   8. Ngóh m̀hhaih Yahtbúnyàhn.
      (I am a Japanese.)

 + 9. Ngóh haih Tòihsāanyàhn.   9. Ngóh m̀hhaih Tòihsāanyàhn.
      (I am a Toishan man.)

2. Substitution Drill: Substitute the cue word to make a new sentence, following the pattern of the example.

      Ex: T: Kéuihdeih haih   T: They are Cantonese.
             Gwóngdùngyàhn   /Shanghai people/
             /Seuhnghóiyàhn/

S: Kéuihdeih haih
  Seuhnghóiyàhn.

S: They are Shanghai people.

1. Kéuihdeih haih Seuhnghóiyàhn.
  /Méihgwokyàhn/

1. Kéuihdeih haih Méihgwokyàhn.

2. Kéuihdeih haih Méihgwokyàhn.
  /Yìnggwokyàhn/

2. Kéuihdeih haih Yìnggwokyàhn.

3. Kéuihdeih haih Yìnggwokyàhn.
  /Yahtbúnyàhn/

3. Kéuihdeih haih Yahtbúnyàhn.

4. Kéuihdeih haih Yahtbúnyàhn.
  /Jùnggwokyàhn/

4. Kéuihdeih haih Jùnggwokyàhn.

5. Kéuihdeih haih Jùnggwokyàhn.
  /Gwóngdùngyàhn/

5. Kéuihdeih haih Gwóngdùngyàhn.

---

3. Mixed Substitution Drill: Substitute the cue word in the appropriate position, following the pattern of the example.

   Ex: T: Ngóh haih Seuhng-
       hóiyàhn. /néihdeih/

   I am from Shanghai.
   /you (plu.)/

   S: Néihdeih haih Seuhng-
      hóiyàhn.

   You (plu.) are from Shanghai.

   T: Néihdeih haih Seuhng-
      hóiyàhn.
      /Jùnggwokyàhn/

   You (plu.) are from Shanghai.
   /Chinese/

   S: Néihdeih haih Jùng-
      gwokyàhn.

   You (plu.) are Chinese.

1. Kéuih haih Yìnggwokyàhn.
  /kéuihdeih/

1. Kéuihdeih haih Yìnggwokyàhn.

2. Kéuihdeih haih Yìnggwokyàhn.
  /néihdeih/

2. Néihdeih haih Yìnggwokyàhn.

3. Néihdeih haih Yìnggwokyàhn.
  /Méihgwokyàhn/

3. Néihdeih haih Méihgwokyàhn.

4. Néihdeih haih Méihgwokyàhn.
  /ngóh/

4. Ngóh haih Méihgwokyàhn.

5. Ngóh haih hohksàang.
  /sìnsàang/

5. Ngóh haih sìnsàang.

---

4. Expansion Drill: Expand the cue sentences as indicated in the
   example. Students should gesture to indicate pronouns.

   Ex: T: Kéuih m̀haih Léih
       Táai.

   She is not Mrs. Lee.

S: Kéuih m̀hhaih Léih   She is not Mrs. Lee, I am.
Táai, ngóh haih.

1. Kéuih m̀hhaih Jèung Sàang.   1. Kéuih m̀hhaih Jèung Sàang;
ngóh haih.

2. Kéuih m̀hhaih Chàhn Síujé.   2. Kéuih m̀hhaih Chàhn Síujé;
ngóh haih.

3. Kéuih m̀hhaih Hòh Sàang.   3. Kéuih m̀hhaih Hòh Sàang;
ngóh haih.

4. Kéuih m̀hhaih Léih Táai.   4. Kéuih m̀hhaih Léih Táai;
ngóh haih.

5. Kéuih m̀hhaih Chàhn Sàang.   5. Kéuih m̀hhaih Chàhn Sàang;
ngóh haih.

---

5. Transformation Drill: Respond according to the pattern of the example. Students gesture pronouns.

Ex: T: Ngóh haih Méih-   T: I am an American.
gwokyàhn.

S: Néih haih m̀hhaih   S: Are you an American?
Méihgwokyàhn a?

1. Ngóh haih Gwóngdùngyàhn.   1. Néih haih m̀hhaih Gwóngdùngyàhn a?

2. Ngóh haih Wòhng Sàang.   2. Néih haih m̀hhaih Wòhng
Sàang a?

3. Kéuih haih Léih Sàang.   3. Kéuih haih m̀hhaih Léih
Sàang a?

4. Ngóh haih Méihgwokyàhn.   4. Néih haih m̀hhaih Méihgwokyàhn a?

5. Ngóhdeih haih Yahtbúnyàhn.   5. Néihdeih haih m̀hhaih
Yahtbúnyàhn a?

6. Kéuih haih Jùnggwokyàhn.   6. Kéuih haih m̀hhaih Jùnggwokyàhn a?

a. Do the above sentences as an expansion drill, expanding
with pàhngyáuh thus:

T: Ngóh haih Gwóngdùngyàhn.

S: Ngóh pàhngyáuh haih Gwóngdùngyàhn.

46

6. Response Drill: Respond according to the pattern of the example.

Ex: T: Jèung Síujé haih   T: Is Miss Cheung an American?
       m̀hhaih Méihgwokyàhn   /English-person/
       a? /Yìnggwokyàhn/

    S: M̀hhaih. Kéuih haih   S: No, she's English.
       Yìnggwokyàhn.

1. Néih haih m̀hhaih Yìnggwokyàhn   1. M̀hhaih. Ngóh haih Méih-
   a? /Méihgwokyàhn/   gwokyàhn.

2. Néih haih m̀hhaih Seuhng-   2. M̀hhaih. Ngóh haih Gwóng-
   hóiyàhn a? /Gwóngdùngyàhn/   dùngyàhn.

3. Jèung Sàang haih m̀hhaih   3. M̀hhaih. Kéuih haih Seuhng-
   Gwóngdùngyàhn a?   hóiyàhn.
   /Seuhnghóiyàhn/

4. Máh Táai haih m̀hhaih Yìng-   4. M̀hhaih. Kéuih haih Méihgwokyàhn a? /Méihgwokyàhn/   gwokyàhn.

5. Kéuih haih m̀hhaih Seuhng-   5. M̀hhaih. Kéuih haih Tòih-
   hóiyàhn a? /Tòihsāanyàhn/   sāanyàhn.

———————————

7. Conversation Exercise: Carry on the suggested Conversations
   following the pattern of the example.

Ex: A: Néih haih m̀hhaih   A: Are you Miss Cheung?
       Jèung Síujé a?

    B: M̀hhaih. Ngóh sing   B: No, my name is Chan.
       Chàhn.

1. A: .... Chàhn Sàang a?   1. A: Néih haih m̀hhaih Chàhn
                                         Sàang a?

   B: .... Hòh.   B: M̀hhaih a. Ngóh sing Hòh.

2. A: .... Léih Síujé a?   2. A: Néih haih m̀hhaih Léih
                                         Síujé a?

   B: .... Jèung.   B: M̀hhaih a. Ngóh sing
                                     Jèung.

3. A: .... Chàhn Táai a?   3. A: Néih haih m̀hhaih Chàhn
                                         Táai a?

   B: .... Hòh.   B: M̀hhaih a. Ngóh sing Hòh.

4. A: .... Léih Sàang a?   4. A: Néih haih m̀hhaih Léih
                                         Sàang a?

   B: .... Jèung.   B: M̀hhaih a. Ngóh sing
                                     Jèung.

5. A: .... Hòh Síujé a?   5. A: Néih haih m̀hhaih Hòh
                                         Síujé a?

47

B: .... Chàhn.   B: M̀hhaih a. Ngóh sing Chàhn.

7a. Continue, with student A using a name at random and student B using his own name in response.

---

8. Response Drill: Respond according to the pattern of the example:

Ex: T: Kéuih sing Wòhng. /Jèung/   T: Her name is Wong. /Cheung/

S: Kéuih m̀hhaih sing Wòhng, sing Jèung.   S: Her name is not Wong, it's Cheung.

1. Kéuih sing Jèung. /Hòh/   1. Kéuih m̀hhaih sing Jèung, sing Hòh.

2. Kéuih sing Hòh. /Chàhn/   2. Kéuih m̀hhaih sing Hòh, sing Chàhn.

3. Kéuih sing Chàhn. /Léih/   3. Kéuih m̀hhaih sing Chàhn, sing Léih.

4. Kéuih sing Léih. /Làuh/   4. Kéuih m̀hhaih sing Léih, sing Làuh.

5. Kéuih sing Máh. /Wòhng/   5. Kéuih m̀hhaih sing Máh, sing Wòhng.

---

9. Response Drill

Ex: T: Kéuih haih m̀hhaih sing Chàhn ga? /Hòh/   Is her name Chan? /Ho/

+

S: M̀hhaih. Kéuih sing Hòh ge.   No, her name is Ho.

1. Kéuih haih m̀hhaih sing Léih ga? /Chàhn/   1. M̀hhaih. Kéuih sing Chàhn ge.

2. Kéuih haih m̀hhaih sing Máh ga? /Hòh/   2. M̀hhaih. Kéuih sing Hòh ge.

3. Kéuih haih m̀hhaih sing Jèung ga? /Léih/   3. M̀hhaih. Kéuih sing Léih ge.

4. Kéuih haih m̀hhaih sing Chàhn ga? /Máh/   4. M̀hhaih. Kéuih sing Máh ge.

5. Kéuih haih m̀hhaih sing Hòh ga? /Jèung/   5. M̀hhaih. Kéuih sing Jèung ge.

Comment:

a. Sentence suffix ga is a fusion of ge + a = ga.

48

b. In the choice-type question form, <u>sing</u> is preceded by
<u>haih m̀haih</u> to make the question.

———————

10. Expansion Drill:

Ex: T: Néihdeih haih Méih-   You are Americans. /we/
gwokyàhn.
/ngóhdeih/

S: Néihdeih haih Méih-   You are Americans; we are also
gwokyàhn; ngóhdeih   Americans.
dōu haih Méihgwok-
yàhn.

1. Kéuihdeih haih Yìnggwokyàhn.   1. Kéuihdeih haih Yìnggwokyàhn;
/ngóhdeih/   ngóhdeih dōu haih Yìnggwokyàhn.

2. Ngóhdeih haih Seuhnghóiyàhn.   2. Ngóhdeih haih Seuhnghóiyàhn;
/kéuihdeih/   kéuihdeih dōu haih Seuhnghóiyàhn.

3. Wòhng Táai haih ngóh pàhng-   3. Wòhng Táai haih ngóh pàhngyáuh. /kéuih/   yáuh; kéuih dōu haih ngóh
pàhngyáuh.

4. Kéuihdeih haih Gwóngdùngyàhn.   4. Kéuihdeih haih Gwóngdùngyàhn;
/néihdeih/   néihdeih dōu haih Gwóngdùngyàhn.

5. Ngóhdeih haih sing Chàhn ge.   5. Ngóhdeih haih sing Chàhn ge;
/kéuihdeih/   kéuihdeih dōu haih sing
Chàhn ge.

———————

11. Conversation Exercise

Example:
1. A: Síujé gwaising a?   (To a woman) What is your name?
   B: Síusing Hòh.   My name is Ho.
   A: Hòh Síujé.   Miss Ho.

2. A: Sīnsàang gwaising a?   (To a man) What is your name?
   B: Síusing Làuh.   My name is Lau.
   A: Làuh Sàang.   Mr. Lau.

1. A: Sīnsàang ....?   1. A: Sīnsàang gwaising a?
   B: ....Léih.   B: Síusing Léih.
   A: ....   A: Léih Sàang.

49

2. A: Sīnsàang ....?
   B: ....Chàhn.
   A: ....

2. A: Sīnsàang gwaising a?
   B: Síusing Chàhn.
   A: Chàhn Sàang.

3. A: Sīnsàang ....?
   B: ....Jèung.
   A: ....

3. A: Sīnsàang gwaising a?
   B: Síusing Jèung.
   A: Jèung Sàang.

4. A: Síujé ....?
   B: ....Wòhng.
   A: ....

4. A: Síujé gwaising a?
   B: Síusing Wòhng.
   A: Wòhng Síujé.

5. A: Síujé ....?
   B: ....Hòh.
   A: ....

5. A: Síujé gwaising a?
   B: Síusing Hòh.
   A: Hòh Síujé.

---

12. Conversation Drill

   Ex: A: Néih pàhngyáuh sing
         mēyéh a?

      What is your friend's name?

      B: Kéuih sing Wòhng ge.

      His name is Wong.

1. A: ....?

   B: ......Hòh........

1. A: Néih pàhngyáuh sing
      mēyéh a?

   B: Kéuih sing Hòh ge.

2. A: ....?

   B: ......Làuh........

2. A: Néih pàhngyáuh sing
      mēyéh a?

   B: Kéuih sing Làuh ge.

3. A: ....?

   B: ......Wòhng......

3. A: Néih pàhngyáuh sing
      mēyéh a?

   B: Kéuih sing Wòhng ge.

4. A: ....?

   B: ......Jèung......

4. A: Néih pàhngyáuh sing
      mēyéh a?

   B: Kéuih sing Jèung ge.

5. A: ....?

   B: ......Léih........

5. A: Néih pàhngyáuh sing
      mēyéh a?

   B: Kéuih sing Léih ge.

---

13. Conversation Drill

Ex: A: Néih pàhngyáuh sing
       mēyéh a?

    B: Kéuih sing Wòhng ge.

    A: Kéuih haih m̀hhaih
       Gwóngdùngyàhn a?

    B: M̀hhaih. Kéuih haih
       Yahtbúnyàhn.

A: What is your friend's name?

B: His name is Wong.

A: Is he a Cantonese?

B: No, he's a Japanese.

1. A: ....?

   B: ....Hòh.

   A: ....Yìnggwokyàhn a?

   B: ......Méihgwokyàhn.

1. A: Néih pàhngyáuh sing
      mēyéh a?

   B: Kéuih sing Hòh ge.

   A: Kéuih haih m̀hhaih
      Yìnggwokyàhn a?

   B: M̀hhaih. Kéuih haih
      Méihgwokyàhn.

2. A: ....?

   B: ....Léih.

   A: ...Seuhnghóiyàhn a?

   B: ......Tòihsāanyàhn.

2. A: Néih pàhngyáuh sing
      mēyéh a?

   B: Kéuih sing Léih ge.

   A: Kéuih haih m̀hhaih
      Seuhnghóiyàhn a?

   B: M̀hhaih. Kéuih haih
      Tòihsāanyàhn.

3. A: ....?

   B: ....Chàhn.

   A: ....Méihgwokyàhn a?

   B: ......Yìnggwokyàhn.

3. A: Néih pàhngyáuh sing
      mēyéh a?

   B: Kéuih sing Chàhn ge.

   A: Kéuih haih m̀hhaih Méih-
      gwokyàhn a?

   B: M̀hhaih. Kéuih haih
      Yìnggwokyàhn.

4. A: ....?

   B: ....Máh.

   A: ...Gwóngdùngyàhn a?

   B: .....Seuhnghóiyàhn.

4. A: Néih pàhngyáuh sing
      mēyéh a?

   B: Kéuih sing Máh ge.

   A: Kéuih haih m̀hhaih Gwóng-
      dùngyàhn a?

   B: M̀hhaih. Kéuih haih
      Seuhnghóiyàhn.

5. A: ....?

   B: ....Wòhng.

5. A: Néih pàhngyáuh sing
      mēyéh a?

   B: Kéuih sing Wòhng ge.

A: .....Yahtbúnyàhn a?

B: ......Jùnggwokyàhn.

6. A: ....?

B: ....Jèung.

A: ...Seuhnghóiyàhn a?

B: ....Yahtbúnyàhn.

A: Kéuih haih m̀hhaih Yahtbúnyàhn a?

B: M̀hhaih. Kéuih haih Jùnggwokyàhn.

6. A: Néih pàhngyáuh sing
mēyéh a?

B: Kéuih sing Jèung ge.

A: Kéuih haih m̀hhaih Seuhnghóiyàhn a?

B: M̀hhaih. Kéuih haih Yahtbúnyàhn.

---

14. Conversation Drill: Carry on the suggested conversations following
the pattern of the example.

Ex: A: Sīnsàang haih m̀hhaih
Méihgwokyàhn a?

B: M̀hhaih--ngóh haih
Yìnggwokyàhn.
Síujé nē?

A: Ngóh haih Gwóngdùng-
yàhn.

Is the gentleman (i.e. Are you)
an American?

No, I'm an Englishman. And
the lady (i.e. you)?

I am a Cantonese.

1. A: (Woman): Sīnsàang .....
....Gwóngdùngyàhn.

B: (Man) : ....Seuhnghóiyàhn.

A: (Woman): .....Yahtbúnyàhn.

A: Sīnsàang haih m̀hhaih
Gwóngdùngyàhn a?

B: M̀hhaih. Ngóh haih Seuhnghóiyàhn. Síujé nē?

A: Ngóh haih Yahtbúnyàhn.

2. A: (Man) : Síujé ....
......Yahtbúnyàhn...

B: (Woman): ....Jùnggwokyàhn...

A: (Man) : .....Méihgwokyàhn..

A: Síujé haih m̀hhaih Yahtbúnyàhn a?

B: M̀hhaih. Ngóh haih Jùng-
gwoyàhn. Sīnsàang nē?

A: Ngóh haih Méihgwokyàhn.

3. A: (Man) : Sīnsàang ....
......Yìnggwokyàhn

B: (Man) : .....Méihgwokyàhn.

A: (Man) : .....Gwóngdùngyàhn.

A: Sīnsàang haih m̀hhaih
Yìnggwokyàhn a?

B: M̀hhaih. Ngóh haih Méihgwokyàhn. Sīnsàang nē?

A: Ngóh haih Gwóngdùngyàhn.

4. A: (Woman): Máh Sīnsàang ....
.....Yahtbúnyàhn.

A: Máh Sīnsàang haih m̀hhaih
Yahtbúnyàhn a?

B: (Man) : ..... Jùnggwokyàhn.   B: Mhhaih. Ngóh haih Jùng-
          ....Chàhn Síujé...?   gwokyàhn. Chàhn Síujé
                                              nē?

A: (Woman): .....Yìnggwokyàhn.   A: Ngóh haih Yìnggwokyàhn.

    a. Continue, students using their own situation to carry
       on the suggested conversations.

IV. CONVERSATIONS FOR LISTENING

    The text of these conversations is written out in Appendix 1.

    Listen to the tape with your book closed, checking the text
afterward, if necessary.

V. SAY IT IN CANTONESE:

    In this section you get directed practice in using some of the
Cantonese you have learned, using the English sentences to prompt
you. This is not to be thought of as a translation exercise--the
English is just to get you going. Try to put the ideas into Cantonese,
saying it the way the Cantonese would. Often there will be quite a
few ways to say the same thing.

A. Ask the person sitting next   And he answers:
   to you:

   1. What is your name?   1. My name is _____.

   2. Are you an Englishman?   2. No, I'm an American.

   3. Is your friend also an   3. Yes, he is.
      American?

   4. Is Miss Ho from Shanghai?   4. No, she's from Toishan.

   5. Is Mr. Lau a Toishan man?   5. Yes, he is.

   6. What is your friend's name?   6. His name is Lee.

   7. Are you Mr(s). Wong?   7. I'm not Mr(s). Wong, my name
                      is _____.

   8. Are you a student?   8. No, I'm not a student, I'm a
                      teacher.

53

B. At a party:

1. Mr. Wong asks Mr. Ho his name.

2. Mr. Ho replies that his name is Ho, and asks Mr. Wong his name.

3. Mr. Wong gives his name, and asks Mr. Ho if he is a Kwangtung man.

4. Mr. Ho answers that he is. He asks Mr. Ho if he also is from Kwangtung.

5. Mr. Wong says no, that he is a Shanghai man.

———————

C. A and B, two new students, wait for the teacher to come to class:

1. A asks B what his name is. (students use actual names)

2. B replies and inquires A's name.

3. A gives his name, and asks B if he is Japanese.

4. B replies, and asks A if he is an Englishman.

5. A replies, and asks B what C's name is.

6. B replies, adding that C is Chinese.

———————

Vocabulary Checklist for Lesson 2

1. a	ss:	sen. suf., to soften abruptness
2. dōu	Adv:	also
3. ga	ss:	sen. suf., fusion of ge + a = ga
4. Gám	sp:	'Well then, ...' 'Say,...' sen. prefix resuming the thread of previous discussion
5. -ge	bf:	noun-forming boundword; -ge added to a Verb Phrase makes it a Noun Phrase
6. gwaising?	Ph:	what is (your) surname? [polite]
7. Gwóngdùng	pw:	Kwangtung, a province in SE China
8. Gwóngdùngyàhn [go]	n:	Cantonese person, person from Kwangtung Province
9. Jùnggwokyàhn	n:	Chinese person
10. kéuih	Pro:	he, him, his
11. kéuihdeih	Pro:	they, them, their
12. mātyéh?	QW:	what?

13. Méihgwokyàhn   n: American
14. mēyéh?   QW: what?
15. mīyéh?   QW: what?
16. nē   ss: sen. suf. for questions
17. néih   Pro: you, your
18. néihdeih   Pro: you, your (plu.)
19. ngóhdeih   Pro: we, our, us
20. pàhngyáuh [gò]   n: friend
21. Seuhnghói   pw: Shanghai
22. Seuhnghóiyàhn   n: person from Shanghai
23. Sīnsàang   n: "Sir," term of direct address
24. sīnsàang   n: man
25. síujé   n: 'Miss,' Madame, term of direct address
26. síusing   Ph: my surname is (polite)
27. Tòihsāan   pw: Toishan, a county in southern Kwangtung
                                about 100 miles west of Hong Kong.
28. Tòihsāanyàhn   n: person from Toishan
29. yàhn   n: person
30. Yahtbúnyàhn   n: Japanese person
31. Yīnggwokyàhn   n: Englishman, person from England

CLASSROOM PHRASES

Learn to respond to the following classroom instructions. First look at the English equivalents as the teacher reads the Cantonese instructions. Then close your books and listen to the teacher and watch his gestures to help you understand. Check your book if you have difficulty. The teacher will say each sentence several times to help you become familiar with the instructions. Your goal is to be able to respond to the Cantonese without doing mental translations into English. Knowing the scope of what to expect will make the details stand out clearly.

1. Ngóh jídou bīngo, bīngo jauh góng.
    1. I'll point to someone, and that person should speak.

2. Yìhgā ngóh duhk, néihdeih sīn tèng.
    2. Now I'll read aloud and you (plu.) first listen.

3. Yìhgā néihdeih m̀hhóu tái syù, gànjyuh ngóh duhk.
    3. Now don't look at your books, and recite after me.

4. Yìhgā néihdeih gànjyuh laihgeui gám jouh.
    4. Do (the problems) according to the pattern set in the example sentence.

5. Yìhgā ngóhdeih tái daih yāt go lihnjaahp.
    5. Now we'll look at the first exercise.

6. Yìhgā ngóhdeih tái daih yāt geui.
    6. Now we'll look at the first sentence.

7. Yáuh móuh mahntàih?
    7. Are there any questions? OR Do you have any questions?

    Responses:
    Yáuh.

    Have. (i.e., Yes, I have a question)

    Móuh.

    Don't have. (i.e., No, I don't have any questions.)

8. Nihng táu.
    8. Shake the head.

9. Ngahp táu.
    9. Nod the head.

I. BASIC CONVERSATION

A. Buildup:

(Three colleagues, returning from lunch, are waiting
for the elevator in their office building. Next to
them two other businessmen are engaged in conversations)

Wòhng Síujé

wá	language
mēyéh wá a?	what language?
góng	speak
góng mēyéh wá a?	speak what language?
Kéuihdeih góng mēyéh wá a?	What language are they speaking?
jī or jīdou	know
jī m̀hjī a?	know/not know?
Néih jī m̀hjī kéuihdeih góng mēyéh wá a?	Do you know what language they are speaking?
Gwokyúh	Mandarin
góng Gwokyúh	speak Mandarin
Haih m̀hhaih góng Gwokyúh a?	Are they speaking Mandarin?

Chàhn Sàang

M̀hhaih.	(They) are not.
Seuhnghóiwá	Shanghai dialect
Kéuihdeih góng Seuhnghóiwá.	They're speaking the Shanghai dialect.

Jèung Síujé

sīk	know (how)
sīk góng Seuhnghóiwá	know how to speak Shanghai dialect, be able to speak Shanghai dialect.
mē?	sentence suf., indicating surprised question
Néih sīk góng Seuhnghóiwá mē?	You can speak Shanghai dialect?!

Chàhn Sàang

sèsíu	a little, somewhat

57

jē   sentence suf., indicating
                            'merely', 'only', 'that's
                            all'

Sīk sèsíu jē.   I know a little, that's all.

Wòhng Síujé

tùhng   and
Seuhnghóiwá tùhng Gwokyúh   Shanghai dialect and
                            Mandarin

dōu   both
kéuih dōu sīk góng   he speaks both
Seuhnghóiwá tùhng Gwokyúh   he speaks both Shanghai
    kéuih dōu sīk góng   dialect and Mandarin.
ga   sen. suf. for matter of
                            fact assertion.

Seuhnghóiwá tùhng Gwokyúh kéuih   He speaks both Shanghai dialect
    dōu sīk góng ga.   and Mandarin.

Jèung Síujé

Yìngmán or Yìngmàhn   English language
Gám, néih sīk mhsīk Yìngmán a?   Well, do you know English?

Chàhn Sàang

sīk góng sèsíu   can speak a little
sé   write
mhsīk sé   can't write
daahnhaih   but
daahnhaih mhsīk sé   but can't write
Sīk góng sèsíu, daahnhaih mhsīk   I can speak a little, but I
    sé.   can't write.

Jèung Síujé

hohk   study, learn
séung   wish to, want to, would
                            like to

séung hohk   would like to learn
séung hohk Yìngmán   would like to learn English
dī   a little, some
séung hohk dī Yìngmán   would like to learn a
                            little English

58

Ngóh séung hohk dī Yīngmán--	I'd like to learn a little English--
dím a?	how?
dím góng a?	how (do you) say?
Yīngmán, dím góng a?	how is it said in English?
yāt yih sàam sei ńgh	one two three four five
Yāt yih sàam sei ńgh, Yīngmán dím góng a?	How do you say 'one two three four five' in English?

<u>Chàhn Sàang</u>

One two three four five.	One two three four five.

<u>Jèung Síujé</u>

chīngchó	clear
m̀hchīngchó	not clear
Ngóh tèng m̀hchīngchó.	I didn't hear clearly.
yāt chi	one time, once
góng yāt chi	say (it) one time
joi	again
joi góng yāt chi	say (it) once again
m̀hgòi néih	Would you please ...
M̀hgòi néih joi góng yāt chi.	Would you please say it once again?

B. Recapitulation:

<u>Wòhng Síujé:</u>

Néih jī m̀hjī kéuihdeih góng mēyéh wá a? Haih m̀hhaih góng Gwokyúh a?	What language are they speaking? Are they speaking Mandarin?

<u>Chàhn Sàang:</u>

M̀hhaih. Kéuihdeih góng Seuhnghóiwá.	(They) are not. They're speaking the Shanghai dialect.

<u>Jèung Síujé:</u>

Néih sīk góng Seuhnghóiwá mē?	You can speak the Shanghai dialect?

<u>Chàhn Sàang:</u>

Sīk sèsíu jē.	I know a little, that's all.

Wòhng Síujé:

Seuhnghóiwá tùhng Gwokyúh kéuih dōu sīk góng ga.	He speaks both Shanghai dialect and Mandarin.

Jèung Síujé:

Gám, néih sīk mhsīk Yīngmán a?	Well, do you know English?

Chàhn Sàang:

Sīk góng sèsíu, daahnhaih mhsīk sé.	I can speak a little, but I can't write.

Jèung Síujé:

Ngóh séung hohk dī Yīngmán-- Yāt yih sàam sei ńgh, Yīngmán dím góng a?	I'd like to learn a little English--How do you say 'one two three four five' in English?

Chàhn Sàang:

One two three four five.	One two three four five.

Jèung Síujé:

Ngóh tèng mhchìngchó. Mhgòi néih joi góng yāt chi.	I didn't hear clearly. Would you please say it once again.

+ + + + + + + + + + + + +

Pronunciation

1. Open vowels before nasal consonants:

Practice the open vowel before a nasal final in the syllables of that structure you have had thus far in the text. Hold your nose, listen, and repeat:

-m: gám 敢 gám , sàam 衫 sàam .

-n: Yahtbún 日本 Yahtbún ,
Chàhn 陳 Chàhn , jóusàhn 早晨 jóusàhn .

-ng: séung 想 séung , Jèung 張 Jèung ,
góng 講 góng , sīnsàang 先生 sīnsàang ,
sing 姓 sing , gwaising 貴姓 gwaising .

2. Nasalized vowel following nasal consonant:

Vowels following nasal consonants in the same syllable are nasalized in Cantonese, whereas in English a vowel following a nasal consonant in the same syllable is open.

Listen to your teacher as he holds his nose and says:

ngóh 我

néih 你

nē 呢

Máh 馬

Yìngmán 英文

You notice that the vowels are partially blocked when the nose is blocked, revealing that some air is normally released through the nose. Repeat the above words after your teacher, holding your nose to test if you are nasalizing the vowel.

If you can't quite say these right your pronunciation will sound foreign accented, but it won't make any significant different because what you say won't have some other meaning, as it might if you got the tone wrong.

3. eung practice:

   1. séung   séung   séung

   2. Jèung   Jèung   Jèung

4. eui practice: (Remember that the -i here represents the lip-rounded yu sound.)

   1. kéuih   kéuih   kéuih

   2. deuimhjyuh   deui   deui

5. eui/oi contrast practice:

   1. deui   deui   deui

   2. joi   joi   joi

   3. deui   joi   , deui   joi   , deui   joi   .

   4. joi   deui   , joi   deui   , joi   deui   .

6. ok, as in hohk, Jùnggwok

   -k: k in final position is produced by the back of the tongue pressing against the roof of the mouth, stopping the air flow at the junction of the hard and soft palates. In final position k is un-released--[k˺].

   o: o before k has the same value as o elsewhere--mid back rounded vowel: [ɔ].

   Listen and repeat:

   1. hohk 學 (5 times)

   2. Jùnggwok 中國 (5 times)

   3. ngóh hohk 我學 , ngóh hohk   , ngóh hohk   .

   4. joi hohk 再學, joi hohk   , joi hohk   .

61

5. hohk 學 góng 講 , hohk   góng   , hohk   góng   .

7. <u>ng</u> as in <u>ńgh</u>

The velar nasal consonant <u>ng</u> occurs as a vowel, in that the consonant <u>ng</u> is syllabic in the syllable <u>ńgh</u>. (There are also two surnames using the syllable <u>ng</u>.)

Listen and repeat:

想　五　1. séung séung   , ńgh ńgh   .

我　五　2. ngóh ngóh   , ńgh ńgh   .

一二三四五 3. yāt yih sàam sei ńgh   .

II. <u>NOTES</u>

A. <u>Culture Notes</u>:

1. Chinese languages

Gwóngdùngwá: The language spoken in the area roughly coinciding
with Kwangtung Province in SE China is called <u>Gwóng-</u>
<u>dùngwá</u> 'Kwangtung - speech.' In English it is referred
to as 'Cantonese,' named after the major city in
which it was spoken when Westerners arrived in China
and began to learn it.

There are many dialects of <u>Gwóngdùngwá</u>, of which
the recognized standard is the language of Canton and
Hong Kong. This book will not concern itself with the
many dialects, but will concentrate solely on Standard Cantonese. (The dialect of Cantonese spoken by
most American Chinese is <u>Tòihsāanwá</u>, spoken in
Toishan county in Southern Kwangtung, from whence
most American Chinese emigrated.)

Gwokyúh:　[national-language] called in English 'Mandarin,' is
the native language of the greater part of north and
northwest China. Mandarin has been promoted as the
national language by both the Communist Chinese and
the Nationalists and is the language of instruction
in the school systems of both China and Taiwan.

Seuhnghóiwá: 'Shanghai dialect' spoken in the area around Shanghai
on the East Coast of China.

2. Dialect differences in Standard Cantonese: initial <u>n</u> <u>l</u>

In Standard Cantonese as spoken in Hong Kong there exist variations in pronunciation which cannot be called substandard, since they are used by educated persons. One such variation is to substitute an <u>l</u> sound for an <u>n</u> sound in words and syllables which begin with <u>n</u>. Some educated speakers do not have initial <u>n</u> in their speech, and substitute <u>l</u> wherever <u>n</u> occurs. This is quite common in Hong Kong.

Ex: néih   ⟶   léih   'you (sing.)'

néihdeih ⟶ léihdeih   'you (plu.)'

B. Structure Notes:

1. Uninflected verb forms in Cantonese:

Verbs in English have compulsory differences in form (inflections) to represent action in progress (is eating), intended action (going to eat), past action (ate), general statement (eats), and others.

Broadly speaking, Cantonese verbs do not have the same compulsory differences in form. One form may cover action in progress, intended action, past action, general statement. For example: Kéuih gaau Gwóngdùngwá can mean: He is teaching Cantonese, He taught Cantonese, He teaches Cantonese.

(See Drill 1, 6)

Additional elements <u>may</u> be used by the speaker to particularize action in progress, repeated action, accomplished action, etc., but their use is not the compulsory feature of the language that it is in English.

2. Verbs in series: affirmative, negative, and question forms.

1. When two verbs occur together in series, it is the first verb which forms a set with the negative and the choice-type question.

Example: Kéuih <u>sīk góng</u> Gwokyúh.   He can speak Mandarin.

Kéuih <u>mhsīk góng</u> Gwokyúh. He can't speak Mandarin.

Kéuih <u>sīk mhsīk góng</u>   Can he speak Mandarin?

Gwokyúh a?

2. <u>haih</u> is frequently used in series with action verbs in the
negative and in choice questions, but not normally in the
affirmative or in question-word questions.

      (QWQ): Kéuihdeih <u>góng</u> mēyéh   What language are they
            wá a?   speaking?

      (CHQ): <u>Haih m̀hhaih góng</u>   Are they speaking Mandarin?
            Gwokyúh a?

      (Neg): <u>M̀hhaih góng</u> Gwokyúh--   (They're) not speaking
                                  Mandarin--

      (Aff): Kéuihdeih <u>góng</u> Seuhng-   They're speaking Shanghai
            hóiwá.   dialect.

                (See BC)

3. Sentence suffix mē

    <u>mē</u> is an interrogative sentence suffix indicating surprised
question. <u>mē</u> makes a question sentence of the statement sentence
it attaches to, with the force of "What?! I can hardly believe
it!"

    Ex: Néih sīk góng Seuhnghóiwá mē?!   What?! You can speak Shang-
                                        hai dialect?!

                (See BC and Drill 2)

4. Sentence suffix jē.

    <u>jē</u> has the force of "merely," "only," "that's all." Alternate
pronunciations are <u>ja</u>, or <u>je</u>.

    Ex: Sīk góng sèsíu jē.   I can speak just a bit,
                                 that's all.

5. Sentence suffix ga

    1. Sentence suffix <u>ga</u> (usually pronounced [ka], similar to the <u>gu</u>
sound in the English word "Gus") attaches to a sentence,
giving a matter-of-fact connotation to the sentiment expressed.

    Ex. (from Basic Conversation):

      Seuhnghóiwá tùhng Gwokyúh   Shanghai dialect and Manda-
         Kéuih dōu sīk góng ga.   rin, he can speak both,
                                   that's a fact.

The implication is that there's nothing extraordinary about
it, that's simply the way it is.

2. Matter-of-fact _ga_ and NP forming _ge_.

These two are sometimes difficult to differentiate. A test is that a NP _ge_ sentence either uses the verb _haih_ or can be expanded with _haih_, but a matter-of-fact _ga_ sentence can't always be expanded with _haih_.

Ex: 1. Kéuih haih gaau Yìng-   He is someone who teaches
         mán ge.   English.
         (See Drill 18)
     2. Kéuih (haih) sing   He is someone named Wong.
         Wòhng ge.
     3. Seuhnghóiwá tùhng   Shanghai dialect and Manda-
         Gwokyúh kéuih dōu sīk   rin, he can speak both,
         góng ga.   that's a fact.

6. **Loose relationship of Subject-Predicate in Cantonese**: Subject + Predicate as Topic + Comment.

We described full sentences above in Lesson One as being composed of Subject and Predicate, in that order.

Below are examples of Subject-Predicate sentences:

	Subject	Predicate
1.	Ngóh	sing Chàhn.
2.	Kéuih	sīk góng Seuhnghóiwá mē?!
3.	Néih pàhngyáuh	góng mēyéh wá a?
4.	Síujé	gwaising a?
5.	Yìngmán	dím góng?
6.	Yāt yih sàam	Yìngmán dím góng a?
7.	Seuhnghóiwá tùhng Gwokyúh	kéuih dōu sīk góng ga.
8.	Néih jī m̀hjī	kéuihdeih góng mēyéh wá a?

You will note from the sentences above that Subject in Cantonese does **not cover the same territory** that Subject in English does. For example, Sentence No. 7 above might be rendered in English: "Shanghai dialect and Mandarin—he can speak both." The subject of that sentence is "he." If you were to say "Shanghai dialect and Mandarin are both spoken by him," the subject would be "Shanghai dialect and Mandarin." In English the subject of

65

the sentence is that which governs the verb. But in Cantonese the
subject doesn't govern the verb--there is no subject-verb concord
(He speaks, They speak, It is spoken), and the ground rules are
different. In Cantonese the subject comes first in a sentence,
and is what is being talked about; the predicate follows, and is
what is said about the subject. The subject is thus the topic
of the sentence, and the predicate is the comment. In Seuhnghóiwá
tùhng Gwokyúh kéuih dōu sīk góng ga, the subject, or topic,--
what is being talked about--is Seuhnghóiwá tùhng Gwókyúh "Shanghai
dialect and Mandarin," the predicate or comment,--what is said
about the topic--is "kéuih dōu sīk góng ga," "he knows how to
speak both."

In Sentence No. 5 above, Yìngmán dím góng a? the topic is
Yìngmán, "English," and the comment dím góng a? "how say?" Ex-
tended, in Sentence No. 6, to "Yāt yih sàam Yìngmán dím góng a?"
the subject, or topic, is Yāt yih sàam, the predicate, or comment,
is Yìngmán dím góng a?

The relationship of Subject and Predicate in Cantonese is
looser than that of Subject and Predicate in English. In English
Subject and Predicate are tied together by the verb of the predicate being governed by the status of the Subject. In Cantonese
Subject and Predicate are bound together by simple juxtaposition.

7. Types of Predicates

a. Verbal Predicate. The most common predicate is the verbal
predicate, consisting of a verb phrase (VP). A Verb Phrase
consists of a verb alone, a verb and preceding modifier(s), or
a verb and its following object(s), or a combination of these.

Ex: Subject   Predicate
                (modifier) Verb (Object)

Ngóh   jìdou.   I know.
Ngóh   m̀h   jì.   I don't know.
Kéuih   góng Gwokyúh. He's speaking Mandarin.

b. Nominal Predicate. Another type of predicate is the nominal
predicate, consisting of a nominal expression. Examples are:

Subject	Predicate		
	Nominal Expression		
Síusing	Hòh.	My name (is) Ho.	
Síujé	gwaising a?	Miss	your name?

c. <u>Sentence Predicate</u>. The predicate can be in itself a full
Subject-Predicate sentence.

Ex:
Subject	Predicate	
Ngóh m̀hjī	kéuihdeih góng mēyéh wá?	I don't know what language they are speaking.
Yāt yih sàam	Yìngmán dím góng a?	How do you say, one two three in English?
Yāt yih sàam	kéuih dōu m̀hsīk góng.	He can't even say one two three.

8. <u>Subject-Verb-Object (SVO) Sentence</u>.

A Subject-Predicate sentence in which the predicate contains
a verb and its object is a very frequent sentence type in Cantonese.
We take Subject-Verb-Object (SVO) as the base form of the Cantonese
sentence.

Ex: Subject: Predicate:

    subject   verb   object

    Kéuihdeih góng Seuhnghóiwá.

9. <u>Absence of pronoun object</u>.

Compare Cantonese and English:

1A. Néih sīk m̀hsīk Yìngmán a?   1A. Do you know English?

  B. Ngóh sīk góng, m̀hsīk sé.   B. I can speak (it), can't write (it).

  2. M̀hgòi néih joi góng yāt chi.   2. Please say (it) once again.

Note that English requires a pronoun object, and Cantonese
does not.

10. <u>Subjectless sentence</u>. The predicate sentence with no subject is
a very common sentence type in Chinese.

Ex: Sīk sèsíu jē. = (I) know just a little.

Note that the counterpart English sentence requires stated
subject. (We are referring here to statement sentences ('I study'),
not to imperative sentences ('study!'), which we will take up in
Lesson 5.)

11. tùhng and yauh

  1. tùhng, 'and,' links nominal expressions.

        Seuhnghóiwá tùhng Gwokyúh kéuih dōu sīk góng ga.

          He knows how to speak both Shanghai dialect and Mandarin.

        (See Drills 10, 11)

  2. yauh, 'and,' links verbal expressions. It is classed as an
    adverb because it is always linked to a verb, preceding it.

        Kéuih sīk góng yauh sīk sé.

        He can speak and write.

        (See Drill 9)

  3. yauh can be in a set with a second yauh, with the force of
    'both... and ...'

        Kéuih yauh sīk góng yauh sīk sé.

        He can both speak and write.

        (See Drill 9)

12. dōu 'also,' 'both,' 'all'; 'even'

    dōu is classed as an adverb, because it appears always linked
    to a verb, preceding it.

      Ex: 1. Ngóh dōu haih Seuhng-   I am also a Shanghai
          hóiyàhn.   person.

         2. Kéuih dōu sīk góng   He also can speak
           Gwokyúh.   Mandarin.

         3. Seuhnghóiwá tùhng   He can speak both Shanghai
           Gwokyúh kéuih   dialect and Mandarin.
           dōu sīk góng ga.

13. dōu, 'even'

    In the Subject-Predicate pattern X dōu negative Verb, dōu
    translates into English as 'even'.

      Ex: Yāt yih sàam (kéuih)   (He) can't even say 'one
         dōu m̀hsīk góng.   two three.'

        (See Drill 14)

14. Auxiliary verbs.

    Auxiliary verbs take other verbs as their objects. Two
    auxiliary verbs appear in Lesson Three: sīk, 'know (how),' and
    séung 'want to, plan to, be considering, have (it) in mind to ...'

    Ex: 1. Néih sīk góng Seuhnghóiwá mē?!

        You know how to speak Shanghai dialect?!

2. Ngóh séung hohk dí Yìngmán.

I want to learn a little English.

(See BC and Drill 2, 3, 4, 7)

15. sīk 'know (how),' 'be acquainted with'; 'know (someone)'

sīk operates both as an auxiliary verb and as a main verb.

1. As an auxiliary verb:

Ex: Kéuih sīk góng Gwokyúh.   He can speak Mandarin.

(See Drill __2__)

2. As a main verb:

Ex: 1. Kéuih mhsīk Seuhnghóiwá. He is unacquainted with

Shanghai dialect.

(See Drill __2a__)

2. Ngóh mhsīk kéuih.   I don't know him.

(See Drill __13__)

III. DRILLS

1. Transformation Drill: Transform the sentences from question to statement, following the pattern of the example.

Ex: T: Kéuih góng mēyéh   T: What language is he speaking?
+   wá a? /Gwóngdùngwá/   /Cantonese/
     (Cantonese)

S: Kéuih góng Gwóng-   S: He's speaking Cantonese.
   dùngwá.

1. Kéuih góng mēyéh wá a?   1. Kéuih góng Seuhnghóiwá.
/Seuhnghóiwá/

2. Kéuih góng mēyéh wá a?   2. Kéuih góng Gwokyúh.

3. Kéuih góng mēyéh wá a?   3. Kéuih góng Yìngmàhn.
Yìngmàhn/

+ 4. Kéuih góng mēyéh wá a?   4. Kéuih góng Yahtbúnwá.
/Yahtbúnwá/   He's speaking Japanese.
(Japanese spoken language)

5. Kéuih góng mēyéh wá a?   5. Kéuih góng Gwóngdùngwá.
/Gwóngdùngwá/

Comment: The examples in this drill could also serve as general statements:

T: What language(s) does he speak?

S: He speaks Cantonese.

69

2. Substitution Drill

      Ex: T: Kéuihdeih sīk góng   T: They can speak Cantonese.
             Gwóngdùngwá.   /Shanghai dialect/
             /Seuhnghóiwá/

            S: Kéuihdeih sīk góng   S: They can speak Shanghai
             Seuhnghóiwá.   dialect.

    1. Kéuih sīk góng Yìngmàhn.   1. Kéuih sīk góng Gwóngdùngwá.
        /Gwóngdùngwa/

    2. Wòhng Sàang sīk góng   2. Wòhng Sàang sīk góng
        Gwóngdùngwá.   Gwokyúh.

    3. Hòh Táai sīk góng Gwokyúh   3. Hòh Táai sīk góng Seuhng-
        /Seuhnghóiwa/   hóiwá.

    4. Hòh Sīnsàang sīk góng   4. Hòh Sīnsàang sīk góng
        Seuhnghóiwá. /Yìngmán/   Yìngmán.

    5. Chàhn Síujé sīk góng Yìngmán.   5. Chàhn Síujé sīk góng
        /Yahtbúnwá/   Yahtbúnwá.

       a. Repeat, omitting góng:

          T: Kéuihdeih sīk Gwóng-   They know Cantonese.
            dùngwá. /Seuhng-   /Shanghai dialect/
            hóiwá/

          S: Kéuihdeih sīk   They know Shanghai dialect.
            Seuhnghóiwá.

       b. Repeat, adding mē:

          T: Kéuihdeih sīk góng   They know Cantonese.
            Gwóngdùngwá.

          S: Kéuihdeih sīk góng   They know Cantonese?!?
            Gwóngdùngwá mē!?

----

3. Transformation Drill

      Ex: T: Méihgwokyàhn m̀hsīk   Americans can't speak Cantonese.
             góng Gwóngdùngwá.

            S: Méihgwokyàhn sīk   Can Americans speak Cantonese?
             m̀hsīk góng Gwóng-
             dùngwá a?

    1. Kéuih m̀hsīk góng Yìngmán.   1. Kéuih sīk m̀hsīk góng Yìng-
                                   mán a?

    2. Hòh Síujé sīk góng Seuhng-   2. Hòh Síujé sīk m̀hsīk góng
        hóiwá.   Seuhnghóiwá a?

3. Kéuihdeih sīk góng Gwokyúh.

+ 4. Méihgwokyàhn m̀hsīk sé
     Jùngmàhn.
     Americans can't write
     Chinese.

+ 5. Kéuih sīk gaau Yahtbúnwá.
     He knows how to teach
     spoken Japanese.

3. Kéuihdeih sīk m̀hsīk góng
   Gwokyúh a?

4. Méihgwokyàhn sīk m̀hsīk sé
   Jùngmàhn a?
   Do Americans know how to
   write Chinese.

5. Kéuih sīk m̀hsīk gaau Yahtbúnwá a?

---

4. Response Drill

Ex: T: Kéuih hohk Gwóng-
       dùngwá.
       /Seuhnghóiwá/

    S: Gám, kéuih hohk
       m̀hhohk Seuhnghóiwá
       a?

T: He studies Cantonese.
   /Shanghai dialect/

S: Well, then, does he study
   Shanghai dialect?

1. Kéuih sīk Yìngmán. /Jùngmàhn/

2. Kéuih gaau Gwóngdùngwá.
   /Gwokyúh/

3. Kéuih sīk góng Gwokyúh.
   /Seuhnghóiwá/

4. Kéuih sīk sé Jùngmàhn.
   /Yìngmán/

5. Kéuih sīk gaau Yìngmán.
   /Gwóngdùngwá/

1. Gám, kéuih sīk m̀hsīk Jùngmán
   a?

2. Gám, kéuih gaau m̀hgaau Gwokyúh a?

3. Gám, kéuih sīk m̀hsīk góng
   Seuhnghóiwá a?

4. Gám, kéuih sīk m̀hsīk sé
   Yìngmàhn a?

5. Gám, kéuih sīk m̀hsīk gaau
   Gwóngdùngwá a?

Comment: gám is a sentence prefix with the connotation of
         continuing from before, resuming the thread of pre-
         vious discourse. The closet English approximations
         would be 'In that case,...', 'Then,...', 'Well,
         then,...' but these don't always fit. Gam is very
         frequent in Cantonese, but if translated in counter-
         part English sentences is not usually idiomatic. We
         will usually not translate gám in the English
         sentences. In the above examples gám is translated
         as 'Well, then,' suggesting continuation from the
         previous statement.

---

5. Transformation Drill

Ex: T: Wòhng Sàang hohk
       Gwóngdùngwá.

T: Mr. Wong is studying Cantonese.

71

S: Wòhng Sàang haih   S: Is Mr. Wong studying Cantonese?
   m̀hhaih hohk
   Gwóngdùngwá a?

1. Léih Táai gaau Gwokyúh.   1. Léih Táai haih m̀hhaih gaau
                      Gwokyúh a?

2. Hòh Sàang góng Yìngmán.   2. Hòh Sàang haih m̀hhaih góng
                      Yìngmán a?

3. Chàhn Síujé sé Jùngmàhn.   3. Chàhn Síujé haih m̀hhaih sé
                      Jùngmàhn a?

4. Jèung Sàang sīk góng   4. Jèung Sàang haih m̀hhaih sīk
   Yahtbúnwá.   góng Yahtbúnwá a?

5. Làuh Táai sīk gaau Gwóng-   5. Làuh Táai haih m̀hhaih sīk
   dùngwá.   gaau Gwóngdùngwá a?

---

6. Question and Answer Drill

Ex: T: Wòhng Sàang sé   Mr. Wong is writing English
     Yìngmàhn.   (right now). /Japanese/
 +   /Yahtmàhn/ (or)
     Yahtmán/

S₁: Wòhng Sàang haih   Is Mr. Wong writing Japanese?
    m̀hhaih sé Yahtmán a?

S₂: M̀hhaih. Kéuih m̀hhaih   No, he's not writing Japanese,
    sé Yahtmán; kéuih   he's writing English.
    sé Yìngmàhn.

1. Jèung Táai góng Gwokyúh.   1. S₁: Jèung Táai haih m̀hhaih
   /Seuhnghóiwá/   góng Seuhnghóiwá a?

                          S₂: M̀hhaih. Kéuih m̀hhaih
                            góng Seuhnghóiwá,
                            kéuih góng Gwokyúh.

2. Wòhng Táai gaau Gwóngdùngwá.   2. S₁: Wòhng Táai haih m̀hhaih
   /Yìngmàhn/   gaau Yìngmàhn a?

                            S₂: M̀hhaih. Kéuih m̀hhaih
                            gaau Yìngmàhn; kéuih
                            gaau Gwóngdùngwá.

3. Léih Sàang hohk Yìngmàhn.   3. S₁: Léih Sàang haih m̀hhaih
   /Yahtbúnwá/   hohk Yahtbúnwá a?

                            S₂: M̀hhaih. Kéuih m̀hhaih
                            hohk Yahtbúnwá; kéuih
                            hohk Yìngmàhn.

Comment: The above sentence may also be translated 'He writes'
     instead of 'He is writing,' etc. For example:
     sé Yìngmàhn, 'writes English'--not knows how to,

but does it as a habit, custom or general rule. For
instance, He writes English at the office. Likewise
for sentences with main verb hohk, gaau, and góng.
The situational context, not the structural form
of the Cantonese verb, makes the meaning clear.

---

7. Expansion Drill

 Ex: T: Ngóh sīk góng Gwokyúh. I can speak Mandarin.
    /Seuhnghóiwá/   /Shanghai dialect/

   S: Ngóh sīk góng Gwokyúh, I can speak Mandarin, but not
    daahnhaih m̀hsīk góng the Shanghai dialect.
    Seuhnghóiwá.

1. Ngóh sīk góng Gwóngdùngwá. 1. Ngóh sīk góng Gwóngdùngwá,
 /Seuhnghóiwá/   daahnhaih m̀hsīk góng
            Seuhnghóiwá.

2. Kéuih sīk góng Yìngmán.   2. Kéuih sīk góng Yìngmán,
 /Gwokyúh/   daahnhaih m̀hsīk góng
            Gwokyúh.

+ 3. Kéuihdeih sīk góng Tòihsāanwá. 3. Kéuihdeih sīk góng Tòihsāan-
  They can speak Toishan   wá, daahnhaih m̀hsīk góng
  dialect. /Yìngmán/   Yìngmán.

4. Hòh Táai sīk góng Gwokyúh. 4. Hòh Táai sīk góng Gwokyúh,
 /Gwóngdùngwá/   daahnhaih m̀hsīk góng
            Gwóngdùngwá.

5. Chàhn Táai sīk góng Yìngmán. 5. Chàhn Táai sīk góng Yìng-
 /Yahtbúnwá/   mán, daahnhaih m̀hsīk góng
            Yahtbúnwá.

---

8. Expansion Drill

 Ex: T: Ngóh sīk góng Yìng- I can speak English. /Cantonese/
    màhn. /Gwóngdùngwá/

   S: Ngóh sīk góng Yìngmàhn; I can speak English; (and I)
    dōu sīk góng Gwóng- can also speak Cantonese.
    dùngwá.

1. Ngóh sīk góng Gwóngdùngwá. 1. Ngóh sīk góng Gwóngdùngwá
 /Seuhnghóiwá/   dōu sīk góng Seuhnghóiwá.

2. Kéuih sīk Gwokyúh. /Yìngmán/ 2. Kéuih sīk góng Gwokyúh;
            dōu sīk góng Yìngmán.

3. Léih Sàang sīk góng Seuhng- 3. Léih Sàang sīk góng Seuhnghóiwá. /Gwokyúh/   hóiwá; dōu sīk góng Gwokyúh.

73

4. Chàhn Táai sīk góng Yìngmán.
   /Gwóngdùngwá/

4. Chàhn Táai sīk góng Yìngmán; dōu sīk góng Gwóngdùngwá.

5. Hòh Síujé sīk góng Seuhnghóiwá.
   /Gwóngdùngwá/

5. Hòh Síujé sīk góng Seuhnghóiwá; dōu sīk góng Gwóngdùngwá.

------

9. Expansion Drill

    Ex: T: Kéuih sīk góng Gwóng-   He can speak Cantonese.
           dùngwá. /Gwokyúh/   /Mandarin/

    + S: Kéuih (yauh) sīk góng   He can speak Cantonese and
          Gwóngdùngwá, yauh   Mandarin. or
          sīk góng Gwokyúh.   He can speak both Cantonese
          [(both) ... and ...]   and Mandarin.

1. Kéuih hohk Yahtmàhn./Yìngmán/

1. Kéuih yauh hohk Yahtmán,
   yauh hohk Yìngmán.
   He's studying written
   Japanese and English.

2. Ngóh gaau Jùngmàhn. /Yìngmán/

2. Ngóh yauh gaau Jùngmán,
   yauh gaau Yìngmán.

3. Kéuih sīk sé Yìngmàhn.
   /Yahtmàhn/

3. Kéuih yauh sīk sé Yìngmàhn,
   yauh sīk sé Yahtmàhn.

4. Kéuih m̀hhaih Méihgwokyàhn.
   /Yìnggwokyàhn/

4. Kéuih yauh m̀hhaih Méihgwokyàhn, yauh m̀hhaih Yìnggwokyàhn.

5. Ngóh m̀hhohk góng Gwokyúh.
   /Seuhnghóiwá/

5. Ngóh yauh m̀hhohk góng Gwokyúh, yauh m̀hhohk góng
   Seuhnghóiwá.

------

10. Expansion Drill

    Ex: T: Léih Sàang haih Seuhng- Mr. Lee is from Shanghai
          hóiyàhn. /Léih Táai/   /Mrs. Lee/

      S: Léih Sàang tùhng Léih   Mr. [Lee] and Mrs. Lee are
          Táai dōu haih Seuhng-   both from Shanghai.
          hóiyàhn.

1. Wòhng Táai sīk góng Gwokyúh.
   /Chàhn Síujé/

1. Wòhng Táai tùhng Chàhn Síujé
   dōu sīk góng Gwokyúh.

2. Kéuih sīk Wòhng Sàang. /ngóh/

2. Kéuih tùhng ngóh dōu sīk
   Wòhng Sàang.

3. Jèung Síujé hohk Gwóngdùngwá.
　/kéuih pàhngyáuh/

3. Jèung Síujé tùhng kéuih
　pàhngyáuh dōu hohk Gwóng-
　dùngwá.

4. Ngóh haih sing Jèung ge.
　/kéuih/

4. Ngóh tùhng kéuih dōu haih
　sing Jèung ge.

5. Hòh Táai sīk sé Yahtmàhn.
　/Chàhn Síujé/

5. Hòh Táai tùhng Chàhn Síujé
　dōu sīk sé Yahtmàhn.

---

11. Expansion Drill

　　Ex: T: Kéuih sīk góng Gwokyúh.　He can speak Mandarin. /Canton-
　　　/Gwóngdùngwá/　　　　　ese/

　　　S: Kéuih sīk góng Gwokyúh　He can speak Mandarin and
　　　　tùhng Gwóngdùngwá.　　Cantonese.

1. Kéuih hohk Yìngmán. /Yahtmán/

1. Kéuih hohk Yìngmán tùhng
　Yahtmán.

2. Kéuihdeih gaau Jùngmàhn.
　/Yìngmán/

2. Kéuihdeih gaau Jùngmàhn
　tùhng Yìngmán.

3. Léih Táai sīk sé Yahtmàhn.
　/Jùngmán/

3. Léih Táai sīk sé Yahtmán
　tùhng Jùngmàhn.

+ 4. Ngóh sīk Léih Sàang. /Léih
　Táai/ (know (someone))

4. Ngóh sīk Léih Sàang tùhng
　Léih Táai.
　I know Mr. and Mrs Lee.

---

12. Substitution Drill

　+ Ex: T: Bīngo gaau Gwóng-
　　　dùngwá a?
　　　/Léih Sàang/

Who teaches Cantonese?

　　　S: Léih Sàang gaau Gwóng-
　　　dùngwá.

Mr. Lee teaches Cantonese.

1. Bīngo góng Seuhnghóiwá a?
　/Hòh Táai/

1. Hòh Táai góng Seuhnghóiwá.

2. Bīngo hohk Gwokyúh a?
　/Wòhng Sàang/

2. Wòhng Sàang hohk Gwokyúh.

3. Bīngo gaau Yìngmàhn a?
　/Chàhn Síujé/

3. Chàhn Síujé gaau Yìngmàhn.

4. Bīngo sīk góng Yahtbúnwá a?
　/Jèung Sàang/

4. Jèung Sàang sīk góng Yaht-
　búnwá.

5. Bīngo sīk gaau Gwóngdùngwá
   a? /Léih Táai/

5. Léih Táai sīk gaau Gwóngdùngwá.

---

13. Response & Expansion Drill

Ex: 1.T: Néih sīk m̀hsīk
         Wòhng Sàang a?
         /nod/

    T: Do you know Mr. Wong?

    S: Ngóh sīk kéuih.
       Kéuih haih ngóh
       pàhngyáuh.

    S: Yes, he is a friend of mine.

    2.T: Néih sīk m̀hsīk
         Wòhng Sàang a?
         /shake/

    T: Do you know Mr. Wong?

    S: Ngóh m̀hsīk kéuih.
       Kéuih haih bīngo
       a?

    S: No, who is he?

1. Néih sīk m̀hsīk Hòh Táai a?
   /nod/

1. Ngóh sīk kéuih. Kéuih haih
   ngóh pàhngyáuh.

2. Néih sīk m̀hsīk Chàhn Sàang a?
   /shake/

2. Ngóh m̀hsīk kéuih. Kéuih haih
   bīngo a?

3. Néih sīk m̀hsīk Jèung Síujé a?
   /nod/

3. Ngóh sīk kéuih. Kéuih haih
   ngóh pàhngyáuh.

4. Néih sīk m̀hsīk Léih Sàang a?
   /shake/

4. Ngóh m̀hsīk kéuih. Kéuih haih
   bīngo a?

---

14. Response Drill

Ex: T: Néih sīk m̀hsīk góng
        Yahtbúnwá a?
        /shake/

    T: Do you know how to speak
       Japanese? /shake/

    S: M̀hsīk. Yahtbúnwá
  +   ngóh yāt geui dōu
       m̀hsīk góng.

    S: No. I don't even know one
       <u>sentence</u> in Japanese.

    T: /nod/

    S: Sīk sèsíu jē.

    S: (I) know just a little.

1. Néih sīk m̀hsīk góng Gwóngdùngwá a? /shake/

1. M̀hsīk. Gwóngdùngwá ngóh
   yāt geui dōu m̀hsīk góng.

2. Néih sīk m̀hsīk góng Gwokyúh a?
   /shake/

2. M̀hsīk. Gwokyúh ngóh yāt geui
   dōu m̀hsīk góng.

3. Néih sīk m̀hsīk góng Seuhnghóiwá a? /nod/

3. Sīk sèsíu jē.

4. Néih sīk m̀hsīk góng Yìngmàhn a?
   /nod/

4. Sīk sèsíu jē.

5. Néih sīk m̀hsīk góng Yahtbúnwá
   a? /shake/

5. M̀hsīk. Yahtbúnwá ngóh yāt
   geui dōu m̀hsīk góng.

---

15. Expansion Drill

Ex: T: Kéuihdeih góng
      mēyéh wá a?

T: What language are they speaking?

S: Néih jī m̀hjī kéuih-
   deih góng mēyéh
   wá a?

S: Do you know what language
   they're speaking?

1. Kéuih sing mēyèh a?
   What is his name?

1. Néih jī m̀hjī kéuih sing
   mēyèh a?
   Do you know what his name
   is?

2. Kéuih gaau mēyèh wá a?
   What language does he teach?

2. Néih jī m̀hjī kéuih gaau
   mēyèh wá a?

3. Kéuih sé mēyèh a?
   What is he writing?

3. Néih jī m̀hjī kéuih sé mēyèh
   a?

4. Kéuih haih bīngo a?
   Who is he?

4. Néih jī m̀hjī kéuih haih
   bīngo a?

5. Kéuih haihm̀hhaih sing Hòh
   ga?
   Is her name Ho?

5. Néih jī m̀hjī kéuih haih
   m̀hhaih sing Hòh ga?
   Do you know if her name
   is Ho?

---

16. Translation Drill

Ex: T: "Pàhngyáuh" Yìngmán
      dím góng a?

T: How do you say "friend" in
   English

S: Friend

S: Friend.

1. "Hohk," Yìngmán dím góng a?

1. "Learn".

2. "Gaau," Yìngmán dím góng a?

2. "Teach!"

3. "Daahnhaih," Yìngmán dím góng
   a?

3. "But."

4. "Sèsíu," Yìngmán dím góng a?

4. "A little!"

5. "Gwokyúh," Yìngmán dím góng a?

5. "Mandarin!"

6. "Jídou", Yìngmán dím góng a?

6. "Know" (something)."

7. "Sīk", Yìngmán dím góng a?

7. "Know how to or know (a person)."

8. "Sé", Yìngmán dím góng a?

8. "Write."

9. "Hohksāang, "Yìngmán dím góng a?

9. "Student."

---

17. Translation Drill

Ex: T: "Two" Gwóngdùngwá dím góng a?

T: How do you say "two" in Cantonese?

S: "Yih".

S: "Yih".

1. "Three" Gwóngdùngwá dím góng a?

1. "Sàam."

2. "Teach" Gwóngdùngwá dím góng a?

2. "Gaau."

3. "They" Gwóngdùngwá dím góng a?

3. "Kéuihdeih."

4. "Who" Gwóngdùngwá dím góng a?

4. "Bīngo."

5. "Know how" Gwóngdùngwá dím góng a?

5. "Sīk."

6. "But" Gwóngdùngwá dím góng a?

6. "Daahnhaih."

7. "Please say it again" Gwóngdùngwá dím góng a?

7. "Mhgòi néih joi góng yāt chi."

8. "I don't know" Gwóngdùngwá dím góng a?

8. "Ngóh mhjí."

9. "Teacher" Gwóngdùngwá dím góng a?

9. "Sīnsàang."

10. "Four" Gwóngdùngwá dím góng a?

10. "Sei."

11. "Five" Gwóngdùngwá dím góng a?

11. "Ńgh."

---

18. Response Drill:

Ex: T: Kéuih haih bīngo a?
      /gaau Yìngmán/

T: Who is he?
      /teach English/

S: Kéuih haih gaau Yìngmán ge.

S: He's someone who teaches English.

78

1. Kéuih haih bīngo a?
   /sing Wòhng/

2. Kéuih haih bīngo a?
   /gaau Gwóngdùngwá/

3. Kéuih haih bīngo a?
   /gaau Yīngmán/

4. Kéuih haih bīngo a?
   /hohk Gwokyúh/

1. Kéuih haih sing Wòhng ge.

2. Kéuih haih gaau Gwóngdùngwá ge.

3. Kéuih haih gaau Yīngmán ge.

4. Kéuih haih hohk Gwokyúh ge.

    a. Repeat, teacher cueing with right hand column, students responding with correspond <u>haih m̀hhaih</u> question sentence, thus:

        T: Kéuih gaau ngóh Yīngmán ge.

        S: Kéuih haih m̀hhaih gaau néih Yīngmán ga?

IV. CONVERSATIONS FOR LISTENING

    (On tape. Listen to tape with book closed.)

V. SAY IT IN CANTONESE:

A. Ask your neighbor:

1. if he can speak the Shanghai dialect.

2. who teaches him to speak Cantonese.

3. if Mrs. Wong teaches Cantonese.

4. if his friend can speak Cantonese.

5. how to say 'Good morning' in Cantonese.

6. if he can write Chinese.

7. if Mr. Chan can speak the Taishan dialect.

8. if Mr. Cheung can speak Japanese and English.

B. And he answers:

1. that he can't, but that he can speak Mandarin.

2. that Mr. Cheung does.

3. that she doesn't; she teaches English.

4. that he can't say even one sentence.

5. that he didn't hear you (hear clearly)--would you repeat.

6. that he can't write it, but can speak a little.

7. that he can speak Taishan dialect and also can speak Shanghai dialect.

8. Yes, he can speak both Japanese and English.

79

9. if he knows what language
they are speaking.

9. they're speaking English.

10. whether his student is
American.

10. No, he's not an American, he's
an Englishman.

Vocabulary Checklist for Lesson 3

1.	bĭngo?	QW:	who?
2.	chi	m:	time, occasion
3.	chĭngchó	adj:	clear
4.	daahnhaih	cj:	but
5.	dĭ	m:	a little, some
6.	dĭm?	QW:	how?
7.	dōu	adv:	both
8.	gaau	v:	teach
9.	ga/ge/g	ss:	sen. suf. for matter of fact assertion
10.	geui	m:	sentence
11.	góng	v:	speak
12.	Gwokyúh	n:	Mandarin spoken language
13.	Gwóngdùngwá	n:	Cantonese spoken language
14.	hohk	v:	study, learn
15.	jē	ss:	sen. suf. only, merely; that's all
16.	jĭ(dou)	v:	know (something)
17.	joi	adv:	again
18.	Joi góng yātchi	Ph:	Say it again.
19.	Jùngmàhn	n:	Chinese (written) language
20.	mē	ss:	sen. suf. for question indicating surprise
21.	M̀hgòi néih...	Ph:	Please..., Would you please.... sen. pre. preceding a request
22.	ńgh	nu:	five
23.	sàam	nu:	three
24.	sé	v:	write
25.	sèsĭu	Ph:	a little
26.	sei	nu:	four
27.	Seuhnghóiwá	n:	Shanghai dialect (spoken language)

28. séung	aux v:	wish to, want to, would like to, am considering, be of a mind to
29. sīk	v:	to know someone
30. sīk	aux v/v:	know how (to do something)
31. tèng	v:	hear, listen
32. Tòihsāanwá	n:	Toishan dialect
33. tùhng	cj:	and (connects nouns)
34. wá	n:	spoken language, dialect
35. Yahtbúnwá	n:	Japanese (spoken) language
36. Yahtmán	n:	Japanese (written) language
37. Yahtmàhn	n:	Japanese (written) language
38. yāt	nu:	one
39. yāt chi	Ph:	once [one-time]
40. yauh	adv:	also (connects Verb Phrases)
41. yauh V, yauh V.	PAdv:	both..., and ....
42. yih	nu:	two
43. Yìngmàhn	n:	English language
44. Yìngmán	n:	English language

CLASSROOM PHRASES

Learn to respond to the following classroom instructions. First look at the English equivalents as the teacher reads the Cantonese instructions. Then close your books and listen to the teacher and watch his gestures to help you understand. Check your book if you have difficulty. The teacher will say the sentences several times to help you become familiar with them. Your goal is to be able to respond to the Cantonese without needing to do mental translations into English.

1. Yìhgā néihdeih tái daih
   __1__ yihp.

2. Dáhòi néih bún syù, daih
   __1__ yihp.

3. Yìhgā ngóhdeih duhk daih __4__
   fo gèibún wuihwá.

4. Yìhgā ngóhdeih wānjaahp daih
   __3__ fo.

5. Kàhmyaht gaaudou bīndouh a?

6. Seuhng chi gaaudou bīndouh a?

7. Kàhmyaht gaaudou daih __2__
   yihp, daih __2__ fo, daih
   __2__ go, lihnjaahp, daih
   __2__ geui.

8. Dāk meih?
   Responses:
        Dāk laak.
        Meih dāk a. or Meih dāk.

1. Now look at page __1__.

2. Open your book to page ____.

3. Now we'll read aloud Lesson __4__,
        Basic Conversation.

4. Now we'll review Lesson __3__.

5. Where did we get to [lit. teach to] yesterday?

6. Where did we get to last time?

7. Yesterday we got to page __2__,
        Lesson __2__, Drill __2__,
        Sentence __2__.

8. Are you ready yet?

        Ready.
        Not ready yet.

82

I. BASIC CONVERSATION

A. Buildup:

Léih Baak-chìu appears at the door of Làuh Gwok-jūng's office. The two had planned to have lunch together, and Mr. Léih has come to get Mr. Làuh.

Léih:

dāk meih?	ready?
Baak-chìu, dāk meih?	Baak-chìu, are you ready?

Làuh:

meih	not yet
Meih a.	Not yet.
dímjūng or dím	hour, o'clock
géidím or géidímjūng?	what time?
Géidím a?	What time is it?

Léih:

yìhgā	now
daahp yāt	five after the hour
yāt dím daahp yāt	five after one
Yìhgā ... (he looks at his watch) yāt dím daahp yāt.	It's ...five after one.

Làuh:

wá?	sentence suffix 'what did you say?'
Géidím wá?	What time did you say?

Léih:

yāt go jih	five minutes
Yāt dím yāt go jih.	It's one oh five.

Làuh:

jéun	accurate
jéun m̀hjéun a?	accurate/not accurate
bīu	wristwatch, watch
go bīu	a watch
néih go bīu	your watch
Néih go bīu jéun m̀hjéun ga?	Your watch accurate one? (i.e. Is your watch accurate?)

Léih

Chàmhdō--   Approximately--

    faai   fast

    la   sentence suffix indicating
                         change from previous
                         condition: 'has become'.

    faai sèsíu la   gotten a bit fast

    lā = la + raised sentence   raised final intonation =
       final intonation   a sentence suffix indi-
                         cating casualness.

    waahkjé   maybe, or

Waahkjé faai sèsíu lā.   Maybe it's a little fast. <u>or</u>
                     Or a little fast.

Làuh

    fānjūng   minute(s)

    géi   several

    géi fānjūng   several minutes

    dáng   wait

    dáng géi fānjūng   wait a few minutes

    dáng ngóh géi fānjūng   wait for me a few minutes

    joi dáng ngóh géi fānjūng   again wait for me a few
                     minutes

    tìm   in addition, also, more

    lā   sentence suffix for
                     suggestion--polite
                     imperative.

Gám, joi dáng ngóh géi fānjūng   Well, wait for me a few minutes
   tìm lā.   more, please.

Léih

    hóu   OK, all right, fine

Hóu, ngóh dáng néih lā.   OK, I'll wait for you.

Làuh

    m̀hhóu yisi   I'm sorry. <u>or</u> It's
                     embarrassing. (used in
                     apologizing for social
                     gaffe.)

bo	sentence suffix, expressing certainty.
M̀hhóu yisi bo.	I'm sorry.

<u>Léih</u>

M̀hgányiu.	It's all right.

B. <u>Recapitulation</u>:

<u>Léih</u>

Baak-chíu, dāk meih?   Baak-chíu, are you ready?

<u>Làuh</u>

Meih a. Géidím a?   Not yet. What time is it?

<u>Léih</u>

Yìhgā ... (he looks at his   It's ... five after one.
watch) ... yāt dím daahp yāt.

<u>Làuh</u>

Géidím wá?   What time did you say?

<u>Léih</u>

Yāt dím yāt go jih.   It's one oh five.

<u>Làuh</u>

Néih go bíu jéun m̀hjéun ga?   Is your watch accurate?
                                    [Your watch accurate one?]

<u>Léih</u>

Chàahdō--waahkjé faai sèsíu lā.   Approximately--or a little fast.

<u>Làuh</u>

Gám, joi dáng ngóh géi   Well, wait for me a few minutes
fānjūng tìm lā.   more, please.

<u>Léih</u>

Hóu, ngóh dáng néih lā.   OK, I'll wait for you.

<u>Làuh</u>

M̀hhóu yisi bo.   I'm sorry.

<u>Léih</u>

M̀hgányiu.   That's all right.

+ + + + + + + + + + + + +

PRONUNCIATION PRACTICE

1. aa, (written in our text as a when it is in syllable-final position)
   as in yìhgā, Máh, wá

   aa as syllable final is a low back vowel [ɑ]. It is similar to the
   vowel in the American word "Pa," though the American vowel is less
   backed than the Cantonese one. (American [a]; Cantonese [ɑ].
   Some Americans have the backed vowel in their pronunciation of the
   English word "balm." [bɑm] Since the backed mid-central vowel in
   Cantonese [ə'] which we write with the letter a does not occur as a
   syllable final but only as the first part of a two-part final, we
   use a single a to write the lowback vowel aa [ɑ] when it is final
   in its syllable.

   > Listen and repeat:
   > 1. Máh   , Máh   , Máh   . 馬
   > 2. wá   , wá   , wá   . 話
   > 3. yìhgā , yìhgā , yìhgā . 而家

2. aap, as in daahp

   aap is a two-part final composed of the low back vowel aa [ɑ]
   plus the bilabial stop consonant p [p]. As a final p is unreleased:
   [p˥]. aa before p is produced the same way as aa finally, as a low
   back vowel, relatively long in an isolated syllable [ɑ·p˥]. The
   nearest American counterpart is the op in the American word "pop,"
   but the vowel portion is more backed than the American vowel.
   (American [a], Cantonese [ɑ]).

   > Listen and repeat:
   > daahp   , daahp   , daahp   . 踏

3. ap, as in sahp, '10'

   ap is a two-part final composed of the backed mid-central vowel
   a [ə'] plus the bilabial stop consonant p [p]. As a final p is
   unreleased: [p˥]. The a is relatively short in an isolated syllable: [ə˅p˥], but it can be attenuated in sentence context under
   certain conditions. The nearest American counterpart to ap is the
   mid-central vowel [ə] in the up of general American "cup," [kəp],
   but the Cantonese vowel is more backed than the American one
   (Cantonese [ə'], American [ə]).

Listen and repeat:

sahp   , sahp   , sahp   , sahp   . 拾

4. **ap/aap** contrasts

Listen and repeat:

1. sahp   , sahp   , sahp   . 拾
2. daahp   , daahp   , daahp   . 踏
3. sahp daahp   , sahp daahp   , sahp daahp 拾踏.
4. daahp sahp   , daahp sahp   , daahp sahp 踏拾.

5. **eung** practice

1. léuhng   (5 times) 雨
2. séung   (5 times) 想
3. Jèung   (5 times) 張

6. **eun**, as in **jéun**

eun is a two-part final composed of the lower mid-central
rounded vowel **eu** [œ] plus the dental nasal **n**. **eu** before **n** is
lower and more backed than the same vowel before **ng**. **eun** = [œ n];
eung = [∅ ŋ] The vowel **eu** before **n** is relatively long: [œ :n].
The vowel is an open vowel before the nasal final. The rounded **eu**
has a rounding effect on a consonant preceding and following it.
There is no close counterpart in English.

Listen and repeat: (Watch the teacher, copy his lip
                    position)

準準準   1. jéun, jéun, jéun   ; jéun, jéun, jéun   .
準唔準听? 2. jéun m̀hjéun a?   , jéun m̀hjéun a?   ,
            jéun m̀hjéun a?   .

7. **eun/eung** contrast

1. jéun   (3 times)   , séung   (3 times)   .
2. jéun   (3 times)   , Jèung   (3 times)   .
3. jéun   (3 times)   , léuhng   (3 times)   .
4. séung, Jèung, léuhng   , jéun jéun jéun   ;
5. jéun, jéun, jéun   , séung, Jèung, léuhng   .

8. **eun/eui** contrast

1. jéun jéun deui deui
2. jéun deui   , deui jéun   , jéun deui   ,
       deui jéun   .

87

9. uk, as in luhk, 'six'

uk is a two-part final composed of the high back rounded
vowel u plus the velar stop consonant k. k as a final is unreleased: [kꜛ] Before k, the tongue position for u is considerably
lowered in regard to tongue height from cardinal high position to
upper-mid position: [o]. The vowel is relatively short before k:
[o k]. The closest American counterpart is the ook of "look," but
the Cantonese vowel is lower than the American one. (Cantonese
[oˇk], American [Uk].)

            Listen and repeat:
                1. luhk luhk luhk
                2. luhk   , luhk   , luhk   . 六

10. ung, as in tùhng

ung is a two-part final composed of the high back rounded vowel
u plus the velar nasal consonant ng: [ŋ]. The tongue position
for u before ng is the same as that of u before k--lowered from
cardinal high back position to upper mid position: [oŋ]. The
vowel is an open vowel before the nasal final. Lips are rounded.

            Listen and repeat:
                1. tùhng tùhng tùhng
                2. tùhng   , tùhng   , tùhng   . 同

11. ung/uk contrast

                1. luhk tùhng   , luhk tùhng   , luhk tùhng   .
                2. tùhng luhk   , tùhng luhk   , tùhng luhk   .
                3. luhk tùhng   , tùhng luhk   ,
                    tùhng luhk   , luhk tùhng   .

12. un/ung contrast [uᵻn]/[o ŋ]
            Compare: Listen and repeat:
                1. tùhng tùhng 同 , bun bun 半 .
                2. bun tùhng   , tùhng bun   .
                3. tùhng bun tùhng
                4. bun tùhng bun

II. NOTES

A. Culture Notes:

Greetings. When two Americans meet for the first time during the day they use some sort of greeting before ordinary talk begins. Hi, hello, good morning, good afternoon, whatever seems appropriate to the situation. In English it is a bit rude not to offer a greeting before getting down to the business at hand. But Cantonese doesn't have one to one correspondences with American greetings and uses greeting forms more sparingly than English does. A good all-purpose greeting is just to greet the addressee by name.

Ex: Mr. Chan (to Mr. Lee): Léih Sàang.

Mr. Lee: A, Chàhn Sàang.

In this connection notice the first lines of dialogue in the opening conversation.

Ex: When A comes to B's office to get him for lunch:

A: Bāk-chìu dāk meih?   Bāk-chìu, are you ready?

B: Meih a.   Not yet.

In an equivalent English situation, A would be likely to say "Hi" or some such greeting before saying "Ready yet?"

B. Structure Notes:

1. 'Dāk meih?'

Dāk means 'OK, all right' and meih, 'not yet,' Together they form a positive-negative question--'OK?, or not yet?,' i.e., "Ready yet?"

Responses to Dāk meih? are:

Dāk la. = Ready.

Meih dāk.= Not ready yet.

2. Time Expressions

1. The following time expressions are used in telling time in Cantonese:

dím or dímjūng = hour, o'clock

fānjūng   = minute (not used as much in Cantonese as in English)

gwāt   = quarter-hour sections of the hour (transliteration of English "quarter")

jih   = five-minute sections of the hour (jih

89

literally means "figure," here the 12
numbers on the clock dial.)

2. The above time-words combine as follows:

   1. yāt dím (jūng) = one o'clock
   2. yāt dím yāt fānjūng = one minute after one o'clock
   3. yāt dím yāt go jíh = five minutes after one
                (See Drill 7)
   4. yāt dím yāt go gwāt = a quarter after one
                (See Drill 6)
   5. yāt dím bun = half past one
                (See Drill 3)

3. daahp in time expressions

   daahp, literally "tread on" is used in reference to the
   number on the clock face to which the minute hand points to
   tell time:

        Ex: yāt dím daahp yāt = five minutes after one
            yāt dím daahp yih = ten minutes after one
            (See BC and Drills 4, 7)

4. géi? 'which number?' in time expressions

                        in time expressions operates as an
   interrogative number, and occupies the position in the sentence
   which the reply number occupies.

        Ex: 1. géi dím a? = what time is it? [What number o'clock?]
               Ńgh dím. = It's five o'clock.
            2. Yìhgā daahp géi a? = What time is it? [Now treads
                                    on what number?]
               Yìhgā daahp sei. = It's 20 after. [Now treads 4.]
            (See BC and Drills 1, 3, 4)

5. Positioning of time expressions in relation to main verbs:

   1. A time expression which precedes the verb in the sentence
      indicates the time that the action represented by the verb
      took/takes/will take place. We refer to the pre-verb time
      expression as a 'time when' expression.

        Ex: Kéuih sahp dímjùng gaau   He teaches Cantonese at
            Gwóngdùngwá.   10 o'clock.
            (See Drill 10)

2. A time expression which follows the verb indicates the length of time the action represented by the verb took/ takes/will take place. We refer to the post-verb time expression as a "time spent" expression.

>   Ex: Mhgòi néih joi dáng   Would you mind waiting for
>   ngóh géi fānjūng tìm   me a few more minutes.
>   lā.

>   (See Drill 12)

3. Sentence suffix wá?

>   wá is an interrogative sentence suffix attaching to question-word questions, asking for a repeat of the preceding sentence. It has the force of " ??? did you (or he, etc.) say?"

>   Ex: 1. Géidím wá?   What time did you say it was?
>   2. Bīngo gaau néih wá?   Who did you say taught you?
>   3. Kéuih sing mēyéh wá?   What did you say his name
>   was?

>   (See Drill 11)

4. Measures:

>   A Measure is a word in Cantonese which comes between a number (or a limited set of other entities) and a noun.

>   Ex: go   = representative of a class of words
>   called Measures.
>   Ngóh go bīu= my [Measure] watch = my watch
>   yāt go jih = one [Measure] figure = one figure, i.e.,
>   (in relation to time on the clock dial)
>   five minutes past the hour

>   Inasmuch as ordinary English nouns do not have a category of word standing between number (and certain other modifiers) and noun, Measures are usually not translatable in English equivalent sentences.
>   sàam go gwāt = 3 [M] quarters = three quarters
>   In follow sentences the Measure substitutes for the noun.
>   Ex: Kéuih go bīu jéun mhjéun   His [M] watch--is it
>   ga?   accurate?

Kéuih <u>go</u> m̀hjéun.   His one isn't accurate.

(See Drill <u>8</u>)

We defer fuller treatment of Measures to Lessons 6 and 7.

5. <u>Adjectives</u>:

Adjectives in Cantonese are descriptive words. Examples in this lesson are <u>jéun</u>, 'accurate,' <u>faai</u>, 'fast,' <u>maahn</u>, 'slow.'

Adjectives are classed with Verbs, since they can be preceded by the negative <u>m̀h</u>.

Ex: Néih go bīu jéun m̀h-
    jéun ga?   Is your watch accurate?

Ngóh go bīu m̀hjéun.   My watch isn't accurate.

(See BC)

Note that whereas in English an appropriate form of the verb "be" is needed when an adjective is used in the predicate, in Cantonese adjectives are used in the predicate without any other verb.

Compare:

Subject		Predicate
My	watch	is not accurate.
Ngóh go bīu		m̀hjéun.

This class of words which we call "adjectives," some other writers refer to as "stative verbs.'

Adjectives will be treated more fully in Lesson 8.

6. <u>Numbers</u>:

1. Simple numerals

  a. From 1 to 10:

1. yāt	6. luhk
2. yih	7. chāt
3. sàam	8. baat
4. sei	9. gáu
5. ńgh	10. sahp

  b. From 11 to 19 Cantonese numbers use an adding formula: ten-one, ten-two, etc:

11. sahpyāt	13. sahpsàam
12. sahpyih	14. sahpsei

15. sahpn͆gh   18. sahpbaat
16. sahpluhk   19. sahpgáu
17. sahpchāt

2. **yih** and **léuhng** = "2"

yih and **léuhng** both represent "2."

yih is used in counting off: **yāt, yih, sàam,** 'one, two, three,' and in compound numbers: **sahpyih,** '12,' **yihsahp,** '20,' **yihsahpyih,** '22,' etc.

léuhng represents "2" usually, but not in every case, before Measures.

Ex: léung dím   = 2:00
     léuhng dím yāt go jih   = 2:05
     léuhng dím léuhng go jih = 2:10

(See Drills 1, 2, 5, 7)

We recommend that students not try to generalize at first about when to use **léuhng** and when to use **yih**, but simply learn them as vocabulary in the places where they occur.

7. <u>Sentence suffix la</u>

la is a sentence suffix indicating that the condition described in the sentence to which it is attached is changed from the way it used to be.

Ex: Ngóh go bīu faai   My watch has gotten a little
    sèsíu la.   fast.

More on sentence suffix **la** in Lesson 5.

8. <u>Raised final intonation.</u>

In the Basic Conversation of this lesson, raised final intonation transforms sentence suffix **la** into **lā** in the following:

Waahkjé faai sèsíu lā.   Maybe (it's) a little fast.

Raised final intonation here indicates uncertainty, doubt.

9. <u>Sentence suffix lā</u>

lā attaches to imperative sentences, with the effect of making the imperative a gentle one, definitely a suggestion politely intended rather than a command. (By imperative we

mean 'inciting to action,' including everything from per-
emptory commands to polite requests and also self-imperatives,
such as the equivalent of 'I'll do such and such.') Perhaps
the closest English equivalent for lā is a polite tone of
voice. The connotation is 'please,' 'Would you mind...' and
for the self-imperative, 'I'll...'

> Ex: 1. M̀hgòi néih dáng ngóh   Would you please wait for
>   géi fānjūng tìm lā.   me a few minutes more.
>
>   2. Hóu, ngóh dáng néih   OK, I'll wait for you.
>   lā.

(See BC)

10. Dialect variations: (ng)āam(ng)āam and others

   Words in Cantonese which begin with aa, o, and u have a
variant pronunciation in Standard Cantonese in which the
initial vowel is preceded by ng.

> Examples: āamāam, ngāamngāam 'exactly; just'
>
>   oi, ngoi   'want'
>
>   ūk, ngūk   'house'
>
>   (See Drill 5)

III. DRILLS

Preliminary Number Drill: 6-10

1. Students listen.
   Teacher counts off from one to
+ five, then from six to ten,
   gesturing with fingers.

   Yāt yih sāam sei ńgh (1 time)
   luhk chāt baat gáu sahp
   (six seven eight nine ten)
   (do 10 times)

2. Students in chorus count simul-
   taneously with teacher.
   Teacher counts from 6 to 10,
   using hand signals.

   luhk chāt baat gáu sahp
   (10 times)

3. Teacher silent, signals to an
   individual student to recite
   by himself.

   luhk chāt baat gáu sahp

4. Random order count: Teacher
   indicates one finger at a time
   in random order, signalling
   students either individually
   or in chorus to call out
   appropriate number.

   sahp, luhk, gáu. etc.
   (approximately 30 numbers)

1. Listen and repeat: number drill: clock hours. Teacher uses pointer
   and blackboard clock. The students repeat after the teacher in
   the pauses provided.

     1. yāt (pause)   yāt dím. (pause)   yāt dímjūng. (pause)   1, 1:00.

   + 2. yih (pause)   léuhng dím   léuhng dímjūng. (pause) 2, 2:00.
                       (pause)

     3. sàam (pause)   sàam dím. (pause)   sàam dímjūng. (paus   3, 3:00.

     4. sei (pause)   sei dím. (pause)   sei dímjūng. (pause)   4, 4:00.

     5. ńgh (pause)   ńgh dím. (pause)   ńgh dímjūng. (pause)   5, 5:00.

     6. luhk (pause)   luhk dím. (pause)   luhk dímjūng. (pause)   6, 6.00.

     7. chāt (pause)   chāt dím. (pause)   chāt dímjūng. (pause)   7, 7:00.

     8. baat (pause)   baat dím. (pause)   baat dímjūng. (pause)   8, 8:00.

     9. gáu (pause)   gáu dím. (pause)   gáu dímjūng. (pause)   9, 9:00.

    10. sahp (pause)   sahp dím. (pause)   sahp dímjūng. (pause)   10, 10:00.

  + 11. sahpyāt   sahpyāt dím.   sahpyāt dímjūng.   11, 11:00.
        (pause)   (pause)   (pause)

  + 12. sahpyih   sahpyih dím.   sahpyih dímjūng.   12, 12:00.
        (pause)   (pause)   (pause)

    13. géi (pause)   géidím? (pause)   géidímjūng? (pause)
        Which   What o'clock?   What o'clock?
        number?

   a. Random order. Teacher silent, points to different numbers
      on clock dial in random order, students call out time.
      Individual or group response, or both.

   Comment: géi? 'which?' is an interrogative pronoun of number.

   _____

2. Expansion Drill: Props: A big clock drawn on blackboard. Teacher
   silent, gives visual cues by pointing to numbers on clock.

     Ex: T: (points to 7 on the clock dial)
         S: Yìhgā chāt dím.   It's seven o'clock. [Now
                                   seven o'clock.]

     1. (3)   1. Yìhgā sàam dím.
     2. (6)   2. Yìhgā luhk dím.
     3. (9)   3. Yìhgā gáu dím.
     4. (8)   4. Yìhgā baat dím.
     5. (2)   5. Yìhgā léuhng dím.

   a. Continue, teacher pointing to numbers on clock to cue
      students. Teacher signals for choral or individual response.

95

3. Expansion Drill: Props: A big clock drawn on blackboard. Teacher
   points to number and says cue word.

Ex: T: /yāt/   T: /one/

    S: Yīhgā daahp yat.   S: It's five after.

1. /sàam/	1. Yīhgā daahp sàam.
2. /baat/	2. Yīhgā daahp baat.
3. /gáu/	3. Yīhgā daahp gáu.
4. /sei/	4. Yīhgā daahp sei.
5. /chāt/	5. Yīhgā daahp chāt.
6. /yih/	6. Yīhgā daahp yih.
7. /sahpyat/	7. Yīhgā daahp sahpyāt.
+ 8. /bun/ <u>half</u>	8. Yīhgā daahp bun. It's half past.
9. /ńgh/	9. Yīhgā daahp ńgh.

---

4. Conversation Drill: Props: A big clock drawn on blackboard.
   Teacher provides visual cues only, by pointing to number on
   clock.

Ex: T: 1

    S₁: Yīhgā daahp géi a?   T: What time is it?

    S₂: Yīhgā daahp yāt.   S: It's five after.

1.	5	1. A. Yīhgā daahp géi a? B. Yīhgā daahp ńgh.
2.	7	2. A. Yīhgā daahp géi a? B. Yīhgā daahp chāt.
3.	11	3. A. Yīhgā daahp géi a? B. Yīhgā daahp sahpyāt.
4.	8	4. A. Yīhgā daahp géi a? B. Yīhgā daahp baat.
5. +	6	5. A. Yīhgā daahp géi a? B. Yīhgā <u>daahp bun.</u> (<u>daahp bun</u> = half past)
6.	2	6. A. Yīhgā daahp géi a? B. Yīhgā daahp yih.

5. Expansion Drill: Props: Blackboard clock. Teacher points first
   to hour number then to the half-hour number, as he voices the
   cue sentence.

> Ex: T: Yìhgā sàam dím bun.   T: It's half past three.
>   [Now three o'clock half.]
>
> + S: Yìhgā ngāamngāam   S: It's exactly half past three.
>   sàam dím bun.
>   (ng)āam(ng)āam =
>   exactly, just.

1. Yìhgā léuhng dím bun.	1. Yìhgā ngāamngāam léuhng dím bun.
2. Yìhgā ńgh dím bun.	2. Yìhgā ngāamngāam ńgh dím bun.
3. Yìhgā luhk dím bun.	3. Yìhgā ngāamngāam luhk dím bun.
4. Yìhgā baat dím bun.	4. Yìhgā ngāamngāam baat dím bun.
5. Yìhgā sahp dím bun.	5. Yìhgā ngāamngāam sahp dím bun.

---

6. Expansion Drill: Props: Blackboard clock. Teacher says cue then
   points to the quarter hour on the clock to signal students'
   response.

> Ex: T: Sahp dím.   T: Ten o'clock
>   S: Yìhgā sahp dím   S: It's a quarter after ten.
> +   yāt go gwāt.   [Now ten o'clock one quarter.]

1. yāt dím	1. Yìhgā yāt dím yāt go gwāt.
2. sei dím	2. Yìhgā sei dím yāt go gwāt.
3. chāt dím	3. Yìhgā chāt dím yāt go gwāt.
4. ńgh dím	4. Yìhgā ńgh dím yāt go gwāt.
5. sàam dím	5. Yìhgā sàam dím yāt go gwāt.
6. léuhng dím	6. Yìhgā léuhng dím yāt go gwāt.

Comment: gwāt 'quarter', a transliteration from English.
         Grammatically gwāt is a Noun, having the Measure go.
         It occurs in combination with numbers 1 and 3 to
         form time phrases marking the 2 quarter-hours:

> sàam dím yāt go gwāt - Three o'clock one quarter
>   = 3:15
>
> sàam dím sàam go gwāt - Three o'clock three quart-
>   ers = 3:45

7. Alteration Drill:

Ex: T: Yìhgā sàam dím   It's five after three.
    daahp yāt.   or It's three-oh-five.
                            [three touch one]

    S: Yìhgā sàam dím   It's five after three.
    yāt go jih.   or It's three-oh-five.
                            [Now three o'clock one figure.]

    (TO STUDENT: Take out paper & pencil and write a column
                 of numbers from 1 to 7. As you respond orally,
                 write down the times on paper (e.g. 3:05.)
                 After the exercise, the teacher will give
                 responses in English, and you correct your
                 paper.)

1. Yìhgā sàam dím daahp yih.   1. Yìhgā sàam dím léuhng go jih.

2. Yìhgā sàam dím daahp séi.   2. Yìhga sàam dím séi go jih.

3. Yìhgā sàam dím daahp chāt.   3. Yìhga sàam dím chāt go jih.

4. Yìhgā sàam dim daahp sàam.   4. Yìhgā sàam dím sàam go jih.

5. Yìhgā sàam dim daahp sahp.   5. Yìhgā sàam dím sahp go jih.

Comment: a. jih, 'figure'. Grammatically jih is a Noun, having
            the Meaaure go. It occurs in combination with the
            numbers 1 through 11 to form a series of time
            phrases marking the five-minutes subdivisions of the
            hour.

            yāt go jih = 5 after

            léuhng go jih = 10 after, etc.

         b. The go jih part of the above phrases may be omitted,
            with the meaning unchanged:

            sàam dím sàam go jih - sàam dím sàam = 3:15

---

8. Expansion Drill:

Ex: T: Léih Táai go bīu   Mrs. Lee's watch is a little
    faai sèsíu.   fast. /slow a little/
    /maahn sèsíu/

    B: Léih Táai go bīu faai   Mrs. Lee's watch is a little
    sèsíu; ngóh go   fast, mine's a little slow.
    maahn sèsíu.

1. Léih Táai go bīu maahn sèsíu.   1. Léih Táai go bīu maahn
   /faai sesiu/   sèsíu, ngóh go faai sèsíu.

2. Léih Táai go bīu faai yātgo-   2. Léih Táai go bīu faai yātgo-
   jih. /maahn yātgojih/   jih, ngóh go maahn yātgo-
                                      jih.

98

3. Léih Táai go bíu maahn
   yāt fānjūng /faai yāt fān-
   jūng/
   Mrs. Lee's watch is one
   minute slow.

3. Léih Táai go bíu maahn yāt
   fānjūng, ngóh go faai yāt
   fānjūng.

4. Chàhn Táai go bíu faai sèsíu.
   /maahn sèsíu/

4. Chàhn Táai go bíu faai sèsíu,
   ngóh go maahn sèsíu.

5. Chàhn Táai go bíu maahn léuhnggojih./faai yāt go gwāt/

5. Chàhn Táai go bíu maahn
   léuhng go jih, ngóh go
   faai yāt go gwāt.

---

9. Response Drill:

Ex: T: Kéuihdeih haih m̀hhaih
       Yīnggwokyàhn a?
       /Méihgwokyàhn/

Are they English?
/Americans/

S: Ngóh m̀hjī. Waahkjé
   haih Yīnggwokyàhn,
   waahkjé haih
   Méihgwokyàhn.

I don't know - They may be
English, may be Americans.

1. Kéuih haih m̀hhaih Gwóngdùngyàhn a? /Seuhnghóiyàhn/

1. Ngóh m̀hjī, waahkjé haih
   Gwóngdùngyàhn, waahkjé
   haih Seuhnghóiyàhn.

2. Kéuih haih m̀hhaih Méihgwokyàhn a? /Yīnggwokyàhn/

2. Ngóh m̀hjī, waahkjé haih
   Méihgwokyàhn, waahkjé
   haih Yīnggwokyàhn.

3. Kéuih haih m̀hhaih Seuhnghóiyàhn a? /Gwóngdùngyàhn/

3. Ngóh m̀hjī, waahkjé haih
   Seuhnghóiyàhn; waahkjé
   haih Gwóngdùngyàhn.

4. Kéuih haih m̀hhaih Jùnggwokyàhn a? /Yahtbúnyàhn/

4. Ngóh m̀hjī, waahkjé haih
   Jùnggwokyàhn; waahkjé
   haih Yahtbúnyàhn.

a. Repeat, Teacher giving the two fillers only, students
   taking both parts of conversation, thus:

   T: /Yīnggwokyàhn/ Méihgwokyàhn/

   S1: Kéuih haih m̀hhaih Yīnggwokyàhn a?

   S2: Waahkjé haih Yīnggwokyàhn, waahkjé haih Méihgwokyàhn.

---

10. Combining Drill:

Ex: T: Yīhgā sahp dím bun.   T: It's ten thirty.
       Kéuihdeih hohk   They study Cantonese.
       Gwóngdùngwá.

S: Kéuihdeih sahp dím   S: They study Cantonese at 10:30.
   bun hohk Gwóngdùng-
   wá.

1. Yìhgā gáu dímjūng.   1. Kéuih gáu dímjūng gaau
   Kéuih gaau bīngo a?   bīngo a?

2. Yìhgā léuhng dím yātgogwāt. 2. Bīngo léuhng dím yātgogwāt
   Bīngo hohk Yìngmàhn a?   hohk Yìngmàhn a?

3. Yìhgā sàam dím sàamgogwāt.   3. Léih Sàang sàam dím sàamgo-
   Léih Sàang hohk mēyéh a?   gwāt hohk mēyéh a?

4. Yìhgā sahpyāt dím bun.   4. Ngóhdeih sahpyāt dím bun
   Ngóhdeih hohk sé Jùngmàhn.   hohk sé Jùngmàhn.

5. Yìhgā sei dím bun.   5. Hòh Síujé sei dím bun gaau
   Hòh Síujé gaau Méihgwokyàhn   Méihgwokyàhn Gwokyúh.
   Gwokyúh.

6. Yìhgā baat dím sàamgogwāt. 6. Jèung Táai baat dím sàamgo-
   Jèung Táai gaau néih góng   gwāt gaau néih góng
   Gwóngdùngwá.   Gwóngdùngwá.

Comment: A time phrase which indicates the time that the
         action represented by the verb takes place, precedes
         the verb in the sentence.

---

11. Response Drill: Make a wá? question out of each statement, sub-
    stituting the appropriate question word for the expression
    underlined in the cue sentence.

    Ex: T: Yìhgā sahpdím bun.   T: It is now 10:30.

        S: Yìhgā géidím wá?   S: What time did you say it was
                                     now?

1. Kéuih sing Làuh.   1. Kéuih sing mēyéh wá?

2. Kéuih haih ngóh hohksàang. 2. Bīngo haih néih hohksàang
                                  wá?

3. Hòh Síujé gaau ngóh Seuhng- 3. Bīngo gaau néih Seuhnghói-
   hóiwá.   wá wá?

4. Chàhn Táai haih kéuih sīnsàang. 4. Bīngo haih kéuih sīnsàang
   Mrs. Chan is her teacher.   wá?

5. Léih Sàang haih Méihgwokyàhn. 5. Bīngo haih Méihgwokyàhn wá?

---

12. Substitution Drill: Repeat the first sentence, then substitute
    as directed.

1. Ńhgòi néih dáng ngóh géi   1. Ńhgòi néih dáng ngóh géi
   fānjūng.   fānjūng.

100

2. /géi go jih/   2. Ńhgòi néih dáng ngóh géi
                                     go jih.

3. /yāt go jih/   3. Ńhgòi néih dáng ngóh yāt
                                     go jih.

4. /léuhng fānjūng/   4. Ńhgòi néih dáng ngóh léuhng
                                     fānjūng.

5. /léuhng go jih/   5. Ńhgòi néih dáng ngóh léuhng
                                     go jih.

IV. CONVERSATIONS FOR LISTENING

  (On tape. Listen to tape with book closed.)

V. SAY IT IN CANTONESE.

  A. Ask your neighbor: B. And he replies:

   1. if his watch is accurate.   1. that it is a little slow.

   2. what time Mr. Chan teaches   2. that he is sorry but he doesn't
      English.   know.

   3. if Mr. Wong teaches English   3. no, he teaches English at
      at 2:15.   2:45.

   4. how to say 'five after   4. telling you two ways to say
      three' in Cantonese.   it.

   5. to wait for you 10 more   5. OK, he'll wait.
      minutes.

   6. if he's ready.   6. that he is.

   7. if he's ready.   7. that he's not--and asks you
                                        to wait a few minutes.

   8. what time he said it was.   8. 10:30.

   9. if Mr. and Mrs. Chan are   9. that Mr. Chan is from Shanghai
      from Shanghai.   but Mrs. Chan is from
                                        Taishan.

  10. what time his watch has,   10. that it's exactly 11:02.
      adding that your own
      might not be accurate.

101

Vocabulary Checklist for Lesson 4

1.	āamāam	adv:	exactly
2.	baat	nu:	eight
3.	bīu	n:	watch
4.	bo	ss:	sen. suf. for certainty
5.	bun	nu:	half
6.	chàmhdō	Ph:	approximately
7.	chāt	nu:	seven
8.	daahp	v:	tread on
9.	daahp bun	TW:	half past
10.	daahp géi?	TW:	how many five minutes past the hour?
11.	Dāk meih?	Ph:	Ready?
12.	dáng	v:	wait (for)
13.	dím(jūng)	m:	o'clock
14.	faai	adj:	fast
15.	fānjūng	m:	minute(s)
16.	gáu	nu:	nine
17.	géi	nu:	several
18.	géi?	QW:	which number?
19.	géidím(jūng)?	Ph:	What o'clock? What time?
20.	go	m:	M. for nouns
21.	gwāt	(bf)n:	quarter (hour)
22.	Hóu	adj:	OK. All right. (response used in agreeing with someone.)
23.	jéun	adj:	accurate, right
24.	jih	n:	written figure; word
25.	lā	ss:	sen. suf. la for change + raised intonation for doubt.
26.	lā	ss:	sen. suf. for polite suggestion
27.	la	ss:	sen. suf. indicating change from previous condition.
28.	léuhng	nu:	two
29.	luhk	nu:	six
30.	maahn	adj:	slow
31.	Meih	adv:	Not yet.

32. M̀hhóu yisi   Ph: I'm sorry; It's embarassing.

33. ngāamngāam   adv: exactly (see āamāam)

34. sàam go gwāt   Ph: three quarters after the hour

35. sahp   nu: ten

36. sahpyāt   nu: eleven

37. sahpyih   nu: twelve

38. tìm   ss: in addition, also, more

39. wá   ss: interrogative sen. suf. calling for repeat of
                        preceding sentence. i.e., ____ did you say?'

40. waahkjé   cj: maybe; or

41. yāt go gwāt   Ph: a quarter after the hour

42. yāt go jih   Ph: five minutes

43. yìhgā   TW: now

I. BASIC CONVERSATION

A. Buildup:

Mrs. Wòhng stops in to see her friend Mrs. Jèung at home.

jyúyàhn   host, hostess

Jyúyàhn

chóh   sit

chèuihbín   As you wish, at your
                                             convenience

Chèuihbín chóh lā.   Sit anywhere you like.

yàhnhaak   guest

Yàhnhaak

mhgòi   thank you

Hóu, mhgòi.   All right, thank you.

(The hostess extends a pack of cigarettes)

Jyúyàhn

yīn   tobacco

sihk   eat

sihk yīn   smoke tobacco, smoke

Sihk yīn lā.   Have a cigarette.

Yàhnhaak

haakhei   polite

mhsái   unnecessary, no need to

Mhsái haakhei.   You don't need to be polite.
                                             (i.e., no thanks)

Jyúyàhn

mhhóu   don't ... (as a command)
                                             [not good to ...]

Mhhóu haakhei a.   Don't be polite. (i.e., Do
                                             have one)

Yàhnhaak

Hóu, mhgòi.   All right, thanks.

Jyúyàhn

Mhsái mhgòi.   No need to thank. (i.e.,
                                             You're welcome.)

(A servant brings in tea and cakes.)

<u>Jyúhàhn</u>

chàh	tea
yám	drink
Yám chàh lā.	Have some tea.

<u>Yàhnhaak</u>

Mhgòi.	Thank you.

<u>Jyúyàhn</u>

béng	cake(s), cookie(s)
Sihk béng lā.	Have some cookies.

<u>Yàhnhaak</u>

laak	sentence suffix la indicating change or potential change + <u>k</u> = lively. <u>la</u> + <u>k</u> = <u>laak</u>.
Mhsái laak; mhgòi.	No thanks.

<u>Jyúyàhn</u>

si	try
Siháh lā.	Try a little.

<u>Yàhnhaak</u>

jànhaih	really
léh	sentence suffix for definiteness.
Jànhaih mhsái haakhei léh.	No thanks--really.

(They talk awhile, then the guest prepares to leave.)

<u>Yàhnhaak</u>

aiya!	exclamation of consternation
Aiya! Ngh dím la.	Oh--oh. It's five o'clock.
jáu	leave
yiu jáu	must go
Ngóh yiu jáu laak.	I must be going.

<u>Jyúyàhn</u>

faai	fast
gam	so
gam faai	so fast, so soon
gam faai jáu	go so soon

105

M̀hhóu gam faai jáu lā.	Don't go so soon!

<u>Yàhnhaak</u>

M̀hhaih a--	No--
Jànhaih yiu jáu laak.	I really must go.

B. Recapitulation:

Mrs. Wòhng stops in to see her friend Mrs. Jêung at home.

<u>Jyúyàhn</u>

Chèuihbín chóh lā.	Sit anywhere you like.

<u>Yàhnhaak</u>

Hóu, m̀hgòi.	All right; thanks.

(The hostess extends a pack of cigarettes.)

<u>Jyúyàhn</u>

Sihk yĭn lā.	Have a cigarette.

<u>Yàhnhaak</u>

M̀hsái haakhei.	You don't have to be polite. (i.e., No thanks.)

<u>Jyúyàhn</u>

M̀hhóu haakhei a.	Don't be polite. (i.e., Do have one.)

<u>Yàhnhaak</u>

Hóu, m̀hgòi.	All right, thanks.

<u>Jyúyàhn</u>

M̀hsái m̀hgòi.	No need to thank. (i.e., you're welcome.)

(A servant brings in tea and cakes.)

<u>Jyúyàhn</u>

Yám chàh lā.	Have some tea.

<u>Yàhnhaak</u>

M̀hgòi.	Thank you.

<u>Jyúyàhn</u>

Sihk béng lā.	Have some cookies.

<u>Yàhnhaak</u>

M̀hsái laak; m̀hgòi.	No thanks.

<u>Jyúyàhn</u>

Sìháh lā.   Try a little.

<u>Yàhnhaak</u>

Jànhaih m̀hsái haakhei lēh.   No thanks--really.

(They talk awhile, then the guest prepares to leave.)

<u>Yàhnhaak</u>

Aiya! Ńgh dím laak. Ngóh yiu   Oh--oh. It's five o'clock. I
jáu laak.   must be going.

<u>Jyúyàhn</u>

M̀hhóu gam faai jáu lā.   Don't go so soon!

<u>Yàhnhaak</u>

M̀hhaih a--   No--
Jànhaih yiu jáu laak.   I really must go.

+ + + + + + + + + + + + + +

Pronunciation:

1. <u>ai</u>

    <u>ai</u> is a two-part final composed of the backed mid central vowel
<u>a</u> [ə`] plus high front unrounded offglide <u>i</u> [ə`ⁱ]. The <u>a</u> portion is
quite short in an isolated syllable--[ə`ⁱ]. The syllable may be
lengthened when it occurs in stress position in a sentence, in which
case it is the <u>i</u> part that lengthens, not the <u>a</u> part.

         m̀hsái (5 times) 唔使

2. <u>aai</u>

    <u>aai</u> is a two-part final composed of the low back vowel <u>aa</u> [ɑ]
plus high front unrounded offglide <u>i</u>, which following <u>aa</u> is somewhat
lower than it is following <u>a</u>, [ɑI]. The <u>aa</u> portion is relatively
long in an isolated syllable--[ɑːI]. The <u>aai</u> syllable may be
lengthened when it occurs in stress position in a sentence, in which
case it is the <u>aa</u> part that lengthens, not the <u>i</u> part. The Cantonese
<u>aai</u> is similar to the <u>ie</u> of the American words 'fie,' 'die,' 'tie.'

         Listen and repeat:

             1. faai   (five times) 快
             2. táai   (five times) 太

3. <u>ai/aai</u> contrasts

         Listen and repeat:

107

1. m̀hsái, faai   . (5 times)
2. faai, m̀hsái   . (5 times)

4. <u>ang</u> in <u>dáng</u> (Lesson 4)

    <u>ang</u> is a two-part final composed of the backed mid central vowel
<u>a</u> [ə˞] plus the velar nasal consonant <u>ng</u>. The closest American
counterpart to the Cantonese vowel is the mid central vowel in the
English "dung." The Cantonese vowel is shorter than the American one,
more backed, and not nasalized before the nasal final.

              Compare English and Cantonese--Listen:
                dung dáng   (5 times) 凍 等
              Listen and repeat:
                dáng   (5 times) 等

5. <u>aang</u> in <u>cháang</u>

      <u>aang</u> is a two-part final composed of the low back vowel <u>aa</u> [ɑ]
plus the velar nasal consonant <u>ng</u>. The <u>aa</u> before <u>ng</u> is pronounced
the same way as <u>aa</u> before <u>p</u> and before <u>i</u>. The closest American
counterpart is the low central vowel of "dong" [a] in "ding dong,"
but the Cantonese <u>aa</u> [ɑ] is more backed and not nasalized before the
final nasal consonant.

              Compare English and Cantonese--Listen:
                dong cháang   (5 times)   橙
              Listen and repeat:
                cháang   (5 times) 橙
                sīnsàang   (5 times) 先生

6. <u>ang</u>/<u>aang</u> contrasts

              Listen and repeat:
                1. dáng   (3 times)
                2. cháang   (3 times)
                3. dáng cháang   (3 times)
                4. cháang dáng   (3 times)

7. <u>ak</u> in <u>dāk</u> (Lesson 4)

      <u>ak</u> is a two-part final composed of the backed mid central vowel
<u>a</u> [ə˞] plus velar stop consonant <u>k</u>. As a final <u>k</u> is unreleased--[k˺],
<u>a</u> is as elsewhere--short in an isolated unstressed syllable, more
backed than its closest American counterpart, which is the [ə] of
"duck." It is also tenser than the American counterpart.

Compare English and Cantonese:

    duck dāk   (5 times)

Listen and repeat:

    dāk   (5 times)

Compare the <u>a</u> before <u>k</u> with the <u>a</u> elsewhere:--

    Listen and repeat:

        1. dāk   (3 times)

        2. chāt   (3 times)

        3. sahp   (3 times)

        4. dāk chāt sahp   (3 times)

        5. gám   (3 times)

        6. Chàhn   (3 times)

        7. dáng   (3 times)

        8. gám, Chàhn, dáng

        9. m̀hsái

8. <u>aak</u> in <u>yàhnhaak</u>, <u>haakhei</u>

    <u>aak</u> is a two-part final composed of the low back vowel <u>aa</u> [ɑ] plus the velar stop <u>k</u>. As a final <u>k</u> is unreleased [k˺], <u>aa</u> is produced the same way as before <u>-ng</u>, <u>-p</u> and elsewhere. It is somewhat more backed than the vowel of "hock," the closest general American counterpart.

        Listen and repeat:

          1. yàhnhaak   (3 times) 人客

          2. haakhei   (3 times) 客氣

9. <u>ak</u>/<u>aak</u> contrasts

        Listen and repeat:

          1. meih dāk   (3 times) 未得

          2. yàhnhaak   (3 times) 人客

          3. meih dāk, yàhnhaak   (3 times)

          4. yàhnhaak, meih dāk   (3 times)

10. Fast speech forms.

        Listen to fast speech pronunciation:

          1. haakhei   客氣

          2. m̀hsái haakhei 唔使客氣

          3. m̀hhóu haakhei 唔好客氣

Comments: 1. You notice that there is a tendency for
the friction of the <u>h</u> consonant to dis-
appear in fast speech. This is particularly true in such ritual courtesy forms
as the above. We similarly abbreviate
courtesy forms in English without perhaps
noticing it. Ex: 'anksalot' = Thanks a
lot.

2. The <u>k</u> in syllable final but not word
final position has a tendency in fast
speech to be pronounced as a glottal
stop rather than as a velar stop. Listen:

1. waahkjé   (3 times)
2. Jùnggwokyàhn   (3 times)
3. haakhei   (3 times)
4. hohksāang   (3 times)

We are not going to give much specific
attention to fast speech forms in this
text. It is probably just as well for
you not to try to produce them, because
chances are you would notice some and not
others.

11. The <u>-k</u> final of sentence suffix <u>laak</u>.

We have used <u>k</u> to represent the final sound in the sentence
suffix <u>laak</u>. This sound is a glottal stop, rather than the velar stop
which is the sound <u>k</u> normally represents. Linguistically this is a
messy way to handle this situation, but in practice, restricted as
it is to sentence suffix position, it has not given previous students
difficulty.

The <u>laak</u> spelling derives thus:

<u>la</u> is initial <u>l</u> plus the low back <u>aa</u> vowel [α], which we
spell <u>a</u> when it is final in a syllable. (The mid central <u>a</u>
vowel [ə>] never occurs in syllable final position.)
Adding <u>k</u> as final makes the <u>aa</u> not final in its syllable,
so its spelling is represented as <u>aa</u>: <u>la</u> + <u>-k</u> = <u>laak</u>

110

Ex: Ngóh haih yàhnhaak.   I am a guest.
    Ngóh yiu jáu laak.   I must go now.

12. au as in jáu, gáu

au is a two-part final composed of the backed mid central vowel
a [ə˃] and the high back rounded vowel u [ʊ]. The a before u has
a tongue position slightly lower than in other positions (before
-i, -p, -k, etc.). The nearest American counterpart is general
American ow in "cow."

Listen and repeat:

1. jáu   (3 times) 酒
2. bējáu (3 times) 啤酒
3. gáu   (3 times) 九
4. jáu jái ("son")酒仔, jáu jái   , jáu jái   .

13. aau in gaau

aau is a two-part final composed of the low back vowel aa
and the high back rounded vowel u [ʊ]. In this position the aa
is more fronted [aˁ] than in other positions. The nearest American
counterpart is in the relatively fronted vowel of the Southern
Pronunciation of "cow," the vowel of which begins with the low front
a [æ] of "cat."

Listen and repeat:

gaau   (5 times)

14. au/aau

Listen and repeat, comparing au and aau:

1. jáu gaau   (3 times) 酒教
2. gaau jáu   (3 times) 教酒
3. gáu gaau   (3 times) 九教
4. gau ('enough') gaau (3 times) 夠教
5. gaau gau   (3 times) 教夠

111

II. NOTES

A. Culture Notes

1. Customs of polite behavior for host and guest.

In a host-guest situation in Cantonese, it is standard
courtesy for the host to offer some refreshment, for the guest
to politely decline, and for the host to urge the guest again to
have some, at which point the guest politely accepts or declines
as he wishes.

Since it is customary to decline offered refreshments, in
offering them it is best to avoid phrasing your offer in a choice-
type question, because your Cantonese friends will feel it pushy
to answer yes when asked this way. If the food is already at hand
it is better to use the polite suggestion form: Sihk béng lā.
'Have some cookies.' If the refreshments are not right at hand,
use the question-word question: Yám dī mēyéh a? [Drink a little
what?] 'What would you like to drink?

2. sihk faahn [eat rice] means 'to have a meal,' 'to eat.' It may
also mean to eat Chinese food, in contrast to eating Western
food.

3. yám chàh, 'drink tea.'

yám chàh also has a wider meaning, reflecting a distinctively
Cantonese custom. This is the custom of going to the teahouse in
the morning to drink tea and eat hot snacks, generally steamed
shrimp dumplings [hā gāau] and steamed dumplings of minced pork
and mushrooms [sīu màai]. This is called 'going out to yám chàh!'
It is on the whole a morning custom, though in Hong Kong, perhaps
influenced by the British custom of afternoon tea, some teahouse
also serve tea and snacks in the afternoon. yám chàh doesn't
correspond to the coffee break; instead it substitutes for a
regular meal, either breakfast or lunch. At a 'regular' meal you
have rice, but when you go to a teahouse to yám chàh, by tradition
you don't get rice. Now that custom too is breaking down, and you
may, though the chances are against it, get rice with a yám chàh
meal.

112

4. Aiya! is an exclamation of consternation. English equivalents are very much dependent on the speaker, ranging from "Oh, my!" to "Good Lord!" to "Oh my god!" etc.

    Aiya! is said to be used more by women than by men. Men use Wah! more often instead.

5. m̀hgòi, 'thank you' is appropriate for thanking someone for a service. When someone gives you some information or does you a favor, you thank them with m̀hgòi. There is another word, dòjeh, 'thank you,' which is appropriate for thanking someone for a gift. (We encounter this word is the text of Lesson 14.)

    In the Conversation which opens this lesson, the guest accepted a cigarette with m̀hgòi--viewing this as more of a courtesy than a gift.

(See BC and Drills 7, 8, 9)

B. Structure Notes

1. Sentence suffix laak.

    laak is a fusion of sentence suffix la indicating change-- (that change has occurred, or is about to occur, or may occur)-- plus k, which is suffixed to a few sentence suffixes, giving the sentence a lively air.

    Whether la or laak is used depends partly on the speaker-- some speakers habitually tend to use laak more than la--, partly on whether the conversation is spirited or matter-of-fact, laak tending to be used more in spirited than in matter-of-fact discourses.

    Because la/laak has to do with change, it works pretty well to translate it in English as "now," keeping in mind that it contrasts the present situation to some previous or future one.

    Examples from the Basic Conversation:

1. M̀hsái laak, m̀hgòi.   (In response to being offered some cookies:) Not [necessary] now, thanks. (It's not that I don't want your cookies, I might change and have some later, but not just now, thanks.)

2. Aiya! Ńgh dím laak!   Wow! It's five o'clock already (I didn't realize it had gotten so late.)

113

3. Ngóh yiu jáu laak.   I must be going now.

    (See BC and Drills 7, 8, 9)

2. -k for lively speech.

    -k is a glottal stop ending to certain sentence suffixes--
for example, la and a which adds liveliness.

    (See BC, Drills 7, 8, 9, and Structure Notes 1, 3)

3. Sentence suffix aak.

    aak is a fusion of sentence suffix a (which softens abrupt-
ness) and the final -k, giving a lively air.

    a + k = aak (cf: la + -k = laak)

        Example:

            Host: Sihk yīn lā.   Have a cigarette.

            Guest: Hóu aak, m̀hgòi.   OK, thanks.

                (See Drills 7, 8, 9)

4. Sentence suffix léh.

    léh is an emphatic sentence suffix, adding the connotation
that you are quite definite about what you say. (léh is probably
derived from sentence suffix la.) The tone of voice is polite.

        Example from the Basic Conversation:

            Jànhaih m̀hsái haakhei   (Declining cookies which the
              léh.   host has urged you twice to
                                          take) No thanks, really.

                (See BC and Drill 11)

5. Sentence suffix lā for polite suggestion.

    This lesson has many examples of sentence suffix lā, first
encountered in Lesson 4.

    lā is suffixed to command sentences, softening the command to
a polite suggestion.

            Ex: Sihk yīh lā.   Have a cigarette. (polite tone
                                          of voice.)

        (See BC and Drills 1, 2, 4, 5, 7, 8, 9)

6. Imperative sentences without sentence suffix.

    Without a softening sentence suffix an imperative sentence
has the force of a command rather than a suggestion.

        Example:

            M̀hhóu sihk béng.   Don't eat those cookies.

                (See Drill 5)

114

The above sentence might be one said by a father or mother to a child.

7. **-háh,** Verb suffix for casualness.

-hah is a verb suffix which gives a somewhat casual air to the verb it attaches to. In this lesson -háh attaches to the verb si, 'try.' Sìháh has the force of 'give it a try,'--a bit more casual than 'thr it.'

(See BC)

8. **yiu,** 'must,' and **m̀hsái,** 'mustn't;' 'needn't'

yiu used as an auxiliary verb preceding another verb can have the meaning 'must _V_,' ' have to _V_,' 'need to _V_.' The basic meaning of yiu is 'require,' and it can be used as a full verb, though in this lesson it is introduced only in its auxiliary verb use.

Ex: yiu jáu   =   must leave, have to be going
     Ngóh yiu jáu laak.   I must be going.

To express that you needn't do something, or to ask if something is necessary, Cantonese doesn't use the negative and question forms of yiu, but uses the negative and question forms of the verb sái, 'need,' 'have to.'

Ex: Ngóh yìhgā |yiu   hohk| Yìngmàhn.   I have to study English right now.

    Ngóh yìhgā| m̀hsái hohk| Yìngmàhn.   I don't have to study English right now.

    Néih yìhgā|sái m̀hsái hohk| Yìngmàhn a? Do you have to study English right now?

(See BC)

III. DRILLS

1. Substitution Drill

        Ex: T: Sihk béng lā.   T: Have a cookie [polite].
            /yǐn/   /tobacco/

                                        <u>or</u>
                                    Have some cookies [polite].

              S: Sihk yǐn lā.   S: Have a cigarette [polite].

+ 1. Sihk yǐn lā. /faahn/   1. Sihk faahn lā.
           (rice)   Dinner is ready; come eat.

+ 2. Sihk faahn lā. /pìhnggwó/   2. Sihk pìhnggwó lā.
             (apple)   Have an apple.

+ 3. /cháang/   3. Sihk cháang lā.
       (orange)   Have an orange.

  4. /béng/   4. Sihk béng lā.

  5. /yǐn/   5. Sihk yǐn lā.

+ 6. /jīu/   6. Sihk jīu lā.
      (banana)

------

2. Substitution Drill

+   Ex: T: Yám chàh lā! /<u>gafē</u>/ T: Have some tea! [polite] /<u>coffee</u>/
        S: Yám gafē lā!   S: Have some coffee!

  1. Yám chàh lā. /gafē/   1. Yám gafē lā.

+ 2. Yám gafē lā. /heiséui/   2. Yám heiséui lā.
         (soft drink)   Have a soft drink.

+ 3. Yám heiséui lā. /bējáu/   3. Yám bējáu lā.
         (beer)   Have a beer.

+ 4. Yám bējáu lā. /séui/   4. Yám séui lā.
         (water)   Have some water.

  5. Yám séui lā. /chàh/   5. Yám chàh lā.

+ 6. /ngàuhnáaih/   6. Yám ngàuhnáaih lā.
      (milk)

+ 7. /jáu/   7. Yám jáu lā.
   (alcoholic beverage)

------

3. Substitution Drill

    Ex: T: Yám m̀hyám heiséui a? T: Would you like a soft drink?
        /bējáu/   /beer/

      S: Yám m̀hyám bējáu a?   S: Would you like a beer?

1. /gafē/   1. Yám m̀hyám gafē a?
2. /heiséui/   2. Yám m̀hyám heiséui a?
3. /séui/   3. Yám m̀hyám séui a?
4. /bējáu/   4. Yám m̀hyám bējáu a?
5. /ngàuhnáaih/   5. Yám m̀hyám ngàuhnáaih a?

  Comment: The above sentences could also mean 'Do you drink?'
      (as a custom, as opposed to an intention)

  Social comment: Chinese custom makes one feel awkward to an-
      swer choice type question affirmatively.
      It is better to ask 'Yám dī mēyéh a?' 'You'll
      drink a little what?', i.e. "What'll you
      have to drink?"

---

4. Expansion Drill

    Ex: 1. T: chàh   T: tea
        S: Yám chàh lā!   S: Have some tea.
      2. T: béng   T: cookies
        S: Sihk béng lā!   S: Have a cookie.

                              <ins>or</ins>
                              Have some cookies.

1. gafē   1. Yám gafē lā!
2. heiséui   2. Yám heiséui lā!
3. faahn   3. Sihk faahn lā!
4. bējáu   4. Yám bējáu lā!
5. yīn   5. Sihk yīn lā!
6. pìhnggwó   6. Sihk pìhnggwó lā!
7. séui   7. Yám séui lā!
8. cháang   8. Sihk cháang lā!
9. béng   9. Sihk béng lā!
10. chàh   10. Yám chàh lā!
11. jáu   11. Yám jáu lā!
12. jīu   12. Sihk jīu lā!

5. Transformation Drill

Ex: T: Sihk yīn lā!   T: Have a cigarette. (polite
                                   invitation)

    S: M̀hhóu sihk yīn!   S: Don't smoke! (abrupt; note
                                   absence of lā)

1. Yám bējáu lā.   1. M̀hhóu yám bējáu!
2. Sihk yīn lā.   2. M̀hhóu sihk yīn!
3. Yám gafē lā.   3. M̀hhóu yám gafē!
4. Sihk béng lā.   4. M̀hhóu sihk béng!
5. Yám heiséui lā.   5. M̀hhóu yám heiséui!

   a. Repeat. as polite negative request, thus:

      T: Sihk yīn lā!   T: Have a cigarette.
      S: M̀hhóu sihk yīn lā.   S: Please don't smoke.

---

6. Expansion Drill

Ex: T: Kéuih yám chàh.   T: He drinks tea. /coffee/
       /gafē/

    S: Kéuih yám cháh,   S: He drinks tea, but he doesn't
       daahnhaih m̀hyám   drink coffee.
       gafē.
                              or

                              He drinks tea, but not coffee.

1. Kéuih yám heiséui. /bējáu/   1. Kéuih yám heiséui,
                                    daahnhaih m̀hyám bējáu.

2. Kéuih yám gafē. /chàh/   2. Kéuih yám gafē, daahnhaih
                                    m̀hyám chàh.

3. Kéuih sihk pìhnggwó. /cháang/ 3. Kéuih sihk pìhnggwó, daahn-
                                    haih m̀hsihk chàang.

4. Kéuih sihk béng. /yám chàh/   4. Kéuih sihk béng, daahnhaih
                                    m̀hyám chàh.

5. Kéuih sīk sé Jùngmàhn. /Yìng- 5. Kéuih sé Jùngmán, daahnhaih
      mán/   m̀hsīk sé Yìngmàhn.

118

7. Response Drill

    Ex: 1. T: Yám gafē lā?   T: Would you like some coffee?
               /nod/   /nod/

  +   S: <u>Hóu aak</u>. M̀hgòi.   S: <u>Yes</u>; thanks.

        2. T: Yám gafē lā?   T: Would you like some coffee?
               /shake/   /shake/

           S: M̀hyám laak,   S: No thanks, not right now.
               m̀hgòi.

  1. Yám chàh lā? /nod/   1. Hóu aak. M̀hgòi.
  2. Yám bējáu lā? /nod/   2. Hóu aak. M̀hgòi.
  3. Yám heiséui lā? /shake/   3. M̀hyám laak, m̀hgòi.
  4. Yám gafē lā? /shake/   4. M̀hyám laak, m̀hgòi.
  5. Yám séui lā? /nod/   5. Hóu aak. M̀hgòi.

    Comment: <u>aak</u> occurs in a set with <u>hóu</u> as a fixed phrase,
            followed by pause: Hóu aak. 'Agreed.', 'OK.' But
            <u>hóu</u>, when it introduces a comment, is not followed
            by <u>aak</u>. Compare the pausing of:

        Hóu, m̀hgòi.   OK, thanks.

        Hóu aak. M̀hgòi.   OK. Thanks.

---

8. Response Drill

    Ex: 1. T: Sihk béng   T: Have a cookie. /nod/
             lā! /nod/

           S: Hóu aak. M̀hgòi.   S: All right. Thanks you.

        2. T: Sihk béng lā!   T: Have a cookie. /shake/
               /shake/

           S: M̀hsihk laak;   S: Not just now, thanks.
               m̀hgòi.

  1. Sihk pìhnggwó lā! /nod/   1. Hóu aak. M̀hgòi.
  2. Sihk yīn lā! /nod/   2. Hóu aak. M̀hgòi.
  3. Sihk faahn lā! /shake/   3. M̀hsihk laak; m̀hgòi.
  4. Sihk cháang lā! /shake/   4. M̀hsihk laak; m̀hgòi.
  5. Sihk béng lā! /nod/   5. Hóu aak. M̀hgòi.
  6. Sihk jíu lā! /nod/   6. Hóu aak. M̀hgòi.

    Comment: If you don't smoke, the way to say so colloquially,
            when you are invited to have a cigarette, is:
            "Síu sihk", 'smoke very little', 'seldom smoke',
            <u>i.e.</u> "I don't smoke."

9. Response Drill: Respond appropriately, following patterns established in Drills 7 and 8. (For the negative use m̀hsihk and m̀hyám, although m̀hsái is equally appropriate.)

1. Yám chàh lā? /nod/	1. Hóu aak. M̀hgòi.
2. Yám bējáu lā? /shake/	2. M̀hyám laak. M̀hgòi.
3. Sihk yĭn lā! /nod/	3. Hóu aak. M̀hgòi.
4. Sihk béng lā! /shake/	4. M̀hsihk laak. M̀hgòi.
5. Yám gafē lā? /nod/	5. Hóu aak. M̀hgòi.
6. Sihk pìhnggwó lā! /nod/	6. Hóu aak. M̀hgòi.
7. Yám heiséui lā? /shake/	7. M̀hyám laak. M̀hgòi.
8. Sihk cháang lā? /shake/	8. M̀hsihk laak. M̀hgòi.

a. Repeat, teacher cueing nouns only, students doing Q&A, answering M̀hsái laak, m̀hgòi. 'No, thanks.'

---

10. Substitution Drill: Substitute in Subject or Object position as appropriate.

Ex: 1. T: Néih yám mēyéh a? /néih pàhngyáuh/

    T: What would you like to drink? /your friend/

    S: Néih pàhngyáuh yám mēyéh a?

    S: What would your friend like to drink?

    T: Néih pàhngyáuh yám mēyéh a? /heiséui/

    T: What would your friend like to drink? /soft drink/

    S: Néih pàhngyáuh yám heiséui.

    S: Your friend would like a soft drink.

1. Kéuih yám mēyéh a? /kéuih pàhngyáuh/	1. Kéuih pàhngyáuh yám mēyéh a?
2. /séui/	2. Kéuih pàhngyáuh yám séui.
3. /jáu/	3. Kéuih pàhngyáuh yám jáu.
4. /ngóhdeih pàhngyáuh/	4. Ngóhdeih pàhngyáuh yám jáu.
5. /néih pàhngyáuh/	5. Néih pàhngyáuh yám jáu.
6. /bĭngo/	6. Bĭngo yám jáu a?
7. /kéuih/	7. Kéuih yám jáu.
8. /mēyéh/	8. Kéuih yám mēyéh a?

Comment: Yám Object can mean (1) 'intend to yám object' and it can mean (2) in process of yám-ing object or could mean (3) 'customarily yám object'. The situation governs which interpretation is appropriate. This follows for all the sentences in this drill.

11. Conversation Drill

Ex: Host: Sihk béng lā?

Guest: Ṁhsái haakhei.

Host: Ṁhhóu haakhei a.

Guest: (shake) Ngóh jànhaih ṁhsihk léh.

<u>or</u>

Guest: (nod) Hóu aak. ṁhgòi.

Host: Ṁhsái ṁhgòi.

Host: Won't you have some cookies?

Guest: Ah, no, thank you.

Host: Oh, <u>do</u> have some.

Guest: No thanks, really not.

<u>or</u>

Guest: Well, all right, thanks.

Host: You're welcome. <u>or</u>
Not at all.

1. A. Sihk pǐhnggwó lā?
   B. ....
   A. ....
   B. (shake)

2. A. Yám gafē lā?
   B. ....
   A. ....
   B. (nod)
   A. ....

3. A. Sihk cháang lā?
   B. ....
   A. ....
   B. (shake)

4. A. Sihk yǐn lā?
   B. ....
   A. ....
   B. (shake)

5. A. Yám bējáu lā?
   B. ....
   A. ....
   B. (shake)

1. A. Sihk pǐhnggwó lā?
   B. Ṁhsái haakhei.
   A. Ṁhhóu haakhei a.
   B. Ngóh jànhaih ṁhsihk léh.

2. A. Yám gafē lā?
   B. Ṁhsái haakhei.
   A. Ṁhhóu haakhei a.
   B. Hóu aak, ṁhgòi.
   A. Ṁhsái ṁhgòi.

3. A. Sihk cháang lā?
   B. Ṁhsái haakhei.
   A. Ṁhhóu haakhei a.
   B. Ngóh jànhaih ṁhsihk léh.

4. A. Sihk yǐn lā?
   B. Ṁhsái haakhei.
   A. Ṁhhóu haakhei a.
   B. Ngóh jànhaih ṁhsihk léh.

5. A. Yám bējáu lā?
   B. Ṁhsái haakhei.
   A. Ṁhhóu haakhei a.
   B. Ngóh jànhaih ṁhyám léh.

12. Conversion Drill

Ex: Waiter: Yám mēyéh a?   A: What'll you have to drink?

Customer: Ngóh yám chàh.   B: I'll have tea.

Waiter: Síujé haih   A: Will the young lady have tea
          m̀haih dōu   too?
          yám chàh a?

Customer: M̀haih. Kéuih   B: No, she'll have coffee.
          yám gafē.

1. W. ....?   1. W. Yám mēyéh a?

   C. ...... bējáu.   C. Ngóh yám bējáu.

   W. Néih pàhngyáuh ......?   W. Néih pàhngyáuh haih
                                            m̀haih dōu yám bējáu a?

   C. ......gafē.   C. M̀haih. Kéuih yám gafē.

2. W. ....?   2. W. Yám mēyéh a?

   C. ......heiséui.   C. Ngóh yám heiséui.

   W. Kéuih ......?   W. Kéuih haih m̀haih dōu
                                            yám heiséui a?

   C. ...... bējáu.   C. M̀haih. Kéuih yám bējáu.

3. W. Sīnsàang ......?   3. W. Sīnsàang yám mēyéh a?
                                            What will you have to
                                            drink, sir?

   C. ...... chàh.   C. Ngóh yám chàh.

   W. Síujé ......?   W. Síujé haih m̀haih dōu
                                            yám chàh a?
                                            Will the young lady
                                            have tea too?

   C. ......heiséui.   C. M̀haih.Kéuih yám heiséui.

4. W. Hòh Sàang ......?   4. W. Hòh Sàang yám mēyéh a?
                                            What'll you have to
                                            drink, Mr. Ho?

   C. ...... bējáu.   C. Ngóh yám bējáu.

   W. Hòh Táai ......?   W. Hòh Táai haih m̀haih dōu
                                            yám bējáu a?
                                            Will Mrs. Ho have beer
                                            too?

   C. ......heiséui.   C. M̀haih.Kéuih yám heiséui.

Comment: In a different situation the Example conversation
         (and likewise those below) could also be appro-
         priately interpreted as:

         A. What's that you're drinking?

B: I'm drinking tea.

A: Is he drinking tea too?

A: No, he's drinking coffee.

----

13. Conversation Drill

Ex: Guest: Aiya! Yìhgā sahp dím daahp chāt. Ngóh yiu jáu laak.

     Guest: Oh-oh! It's 10:35. I must be going.

   Host: M̀hhóu gam faai jáu lā!

     Host: Oh don't go so soon!

   Guest: M̀hhaih a. Jànhaih yiu jáu laak.

     Guest: No. Really, I must go.

1.

1. A. Aiya! Yìhgā yāt dím daahp chāt. Ngóh yiu jáu laak.

   B. M̀hhóu gam faai jáu lā!

   A. M̀hhaih a. Jànhaih yiu jáu laak.

2.

2. A. Aiya! Yìhgā sàam dím sàamgogwāt. Ngóh yiu jáu laak.

   B. M̀hhóu gam faai jáu lā!

   A. M̀hhaih a. Jànhaih yiu jáu laak.

3.

3. A. Aiya! Yìhgā luhk dím daahp sahp. Ngóh yiu jáu laak.

   B. M̀hhóu gam faai jáu lā!

   A. M̀hhaih a. Jànhaih yiu jáu laak.

4.

4. A. Aiya! Yìhgā sahpyih dím daahp sei. Ngóh yiu jáu laak.

   B. M̀hhóu gam faai jáu lā!

   A. M̀hhaih a. Jànhaih yiu jáu laak.

5.   5. A. Aiya! Yìhgā baat dím yāt-
                                                           gogwāt. Ngóh yiu jáu
                                                           laak.

                                                        B. Ṁhhóu gam faai jáu lā!

                                                        A. Ṁhhaih a. Jànhaih yiu
                                                           jáu laak.

_____

IV. CONVERSATIONS FOR LISTENING

       (On tape. Listen to tape with book closed.)

_____

V. SAY IT IN CANTONESE

    A. Student A to Student B: B. Student B replies:

       1. offers him tea.   1. Thank you.

       2. Have some cookies.   2. No thanks.

       3. It's 6:30--I have to go.   3. Don't go so soon!

       4. Sit anywhere you like.   4. Thanks.

       5. (acting the part of a   5. I'll have beer.
          waiter:) What'll you have
          to drink?

       6. Don't go so soon!   6. No, I really have to go.

       7. (offering cookies to a guest   7. I really don't care for
          who has politely declined   any, thanks. [really not
          them already:)   eat]
          Do try some!

_____

124

Vocabulary Checklist for Lesson 5

1. aak   ss: sen. suf. a to soften abruptness + -k
                            for liveliness

2. Aiya!   ex: exclamation of consternation

3. bējáu   m: beer

4. béng   n: cake

5. cháang   n: orange

6. chàh   n: tea

7. chèuihbín   adv: As you wish, At your convenience

8. chèuihbín chóh lā. Ph: 'Sit anywhere you like.'

9. chóh   v: sit

10. faahn   n: rice (cooked)

11. gafē   n: coffee

12. gam   adv: so, such

13. haakhei   adj: polite

14. -háh   Vsuf: Verb suffix for casual effect

15. heiséui   n: soft drink

16. Hóu aak   Ph: OK. Agreed. Response indicating agreement.

17. jànhaih   adv: really, indeed

18. jáu   n: alcoholic beverage

19. jáu   v: leave, depart

20. jĩu   n: banana

21. jyúyàhn   n: host, hostess

22. -k   ss: a glottal stop ending to certain sentence
                            suffixes, giving sentence a lively air.

23. la   ss: sen. suf. indicating potential change

24. laak   ss: sen. suf. la (change) + sen. suf. -k
                            (liveliness)

25. léh   ss: sen. suf. for definiteness

26. M̀hgòi   Ph: Thank you (for service)

27. m̀hhóu   Ph: don't (as a command)

28. M̀hhóu haakhei   Ph: 'Don't be polite.'

29. M̀hsái   Ph: no need to, not necessary

30. M̀hsái la(ak)   Ph: No thanks (when offered something) [not
                            necessary now]

31. M̀hsái m̀hgòi.	Ph:	You're welcome. [not necessary] Polite response when someone thanks you for doing him a service
32. M̀hsái haakhei	Ph:	[don't need to be polite.] "No thanks." (to an offer) "You're welcome." (when someone thanks you.)
33. ngàuhnáaih	n:	milk
34. pìhnggwó	n:	apple
35. séui	n:	water
36. si	v:	try
37. siháh	Vsuf:	give it a try
38. sihk	v:	eat
39. sihk yīn	vo:	to smoke
40. Síu sihk	Ph:	'I don't smoke.' non-smoker's response in refusing a cigarette. [seldom-smoke]
41. yàhnhaak	n:	guest
42. yám	v:	drink
43. yīn	(bw)n:	tobacco; smoke
44. yiu	auxV:	must, need, have to

I. BASIC CONVERSATION

A. Buildup:

(Clerk and Customer in a department store)

sauhfoyùhn	sales clerk

Sauhfoyùhn

máaih	buy
Máaih mēyéh a?	Buy what? (i.e., May I help you?)
guhaak	customer

Guhaak

sēutsāam	shirt
gihn	measure for clothing
séung máaih	wish to buy, want to buy
Ngóh séung máaih gihn sēutsāam.	I want to buy a shirt.
chín	money
géidō?	how much?
géidō chín a?	how much money?
nī	this
nī gihn	this one (this 'measure')
Nī gihn géidō chín a?	How much is this one?

Sauhfoyùhn

mān	dollar
yahsei	twenty-four
yahsei mān	$24
Nī gihn yahsei mān.	This one is $24.

Guhaak

gó	that
gó gihn	that one (that 'measure')
gó léuhng gihn	those two
dōu haih yahsei mān	is also $24, are also $24.
haih ṁhhaih dōu haih yahsei mān a?	are (they) also $24? or is (it) also $24?
Gó léuhng gihn haih ṁhhaih dōu haih yahsei mān gihn a?	Those two, are they also $24 each?

Sauhfoyùhn

M̀hhaih; yihsahp màn jē.   No; twenty dollars only

M̀hhaih--yihsahp màn gihn jē.   No--Only $20 each.

Guhaak

béi   give

béi ngóh   give me

béi nī gihn ngóh   give this one (to) me

Hóu, béi nī gihn ngóh lā.   OK, give me this one.

Sauhfoyùhn

géidō gihn   how many ones

Yiu géidō gihn a?   How many do you want?

Guhaak

gau   enough

Yāt gihn gau laak.   One is enough.

Sauhfoyùhn

Gám, néih máaih m̀hmáaih gó   Are you going to buy those
  léuhng gihn a?   two?

Guhaak

M̀hmáaih laak.   Not buy.

B. Recapitulation:

Sauhfoyùhn

Máaih mēyéh a?   What would you like to buy?

Guhaak

Ngóh séung máaih gihn sēutsāam.   I'm looking for a shirt.
  Nī gihn géidō chín a?   How much is this one?

Sauhfoyùhn

Nī gihn yahsei màn.   This one is $24.

Guhaak

Gó léuhng gihn haih m̀hhaih   Are those two also $24 each?
  dōu haih yahsei màn gihn a?

Sauhfoyùhn

M̀hhaih; yihsahp màn gihn jē.   No; only $20 each.

Guhaak

Hóu, béi nī gihn ngóh lā.   OK, give me this one.

128

<u>Sauhfoyùhn</u>

Yiu géidō gihn a?   How many do you want?

<u>Guhaak</u>

Yāt gihn gau laak.   One is enough.

<u>Sauhfoyùhn</u>

Gám, néih máaih ṁhmáaih gó   Are you going to buy those two?
    léuhng gihn a?

<u>Guhaak</u>

Ṁhmáaih laak.   Not now, thanks.

+ + + + + + + + + + + + +

Pronunciation:

1. <u>at</u> in <u>chāt</u>, <u>bāt</u>, <u>maht</u>

    <u>at</u> is a two-part final composed of the mid central vowel <u>a</u> [əˠ],
plus the consonant stop <u>t</u>. To produce <u>t</u> the tongue tip stops the flow
of air at the dental ridge, close to the base of the lower teeth.
In final position the <u>t</u> is unreleased:--[tˀ]. The closest American
counterpart to the Cantonese <u>at</u> is the <u>ut</u> of general American "but,"
but the Cantonese syllable is shorter in an isolated syllable, more
backed, and tenser.

                Listen and repeat:
                    chāt   (3 times)   七
                    bāt   (3 times)   筆
                    maht   (3 times)   勿

2. <u>aat</u> in <u>baat</u>

    <u>aat</u> is two-part final composed of the low back unrounded vowel
<u>aa</u> [a], plus the consonant stop <u>t</u>. <u>t</u> is produced as described above,
with the tongue tip stopping the air flow at the dental ridge at the
base of the upper teeth, with the air unreleased. <u>aa</u> before <u>t</u> is
produced the same way as before the other final stops (-k and -p).
The nearest American counterpart to <u>aat</u> is the <u>ot</u> sound in general
American "hot," [a], but the Cantonese syllable is more backed, and
somewhat longer in the isolated syllable.

3. **at/aat** contrasts

      Listen and repeat:

         1. bāt baat   (3 times)

         2. baat bāt   (3 times)

         3. baat baat bāt bāt   (3 times)

         4. bāt bāt baat baat   (3 times)

         5. chāt baat baat chāt   .   (3 times)

         6. maht baat   (3 times)

         7. baat maht   (3 times)

         8. baat maht maht baat   (3 times)

         9. chāt baat maht   (3 times)

       10. maht baat chāt   (3 times)

4. **eui**

      Listen and repeat-(Remember that the **eui** final is rounded throughout, that the **i** part here represents that rounded **yu** [ü] sound, and that a rounded vowel has a rounding effect on a consonant preceding it in a syllable):

         1. chèuihbín   (3 times) 隨便

         2. chèuih   (3 times)   隨

         3. séui   (3 times)   水

         4. deuimhjyuh   (3 times) 對唔住

         5. deui   (3 times)   對

5. **au/aau** practice

      Listen and repeat: (Watch the teacher)

         1. gau , gau , gau .   狗

         2. gaau , gaau , gaau . 教

         3. gau gaau , gau gaau , gau gaau .

         4. gaau gau , gaau gau , gaau gau .

         5. gau gaau gaau gau

         6. gaau gau gau gaau

         7. mhgau唔狗, mhgaau唔教.

         8. gau mhgau a?   , gaau mhgaau a?   .

         9. Jáu gau mhgau a? 酒狗唔狗呀?

       10. Mhgau jáu.

6. <u>eut</u>, as in <u>sēutsāam</u>

      <u>eut</u> is a two-part final composed of the single vowel <u>eu</u> and the consonant stop <u>t</u>. <u>eu</u> before <u>t</u> is a lowered mid front rounded vowel [œ] produced the same way as before <u>n</u> and <u>i</u>. The <u>t</u> as final is produced as elsewhere as final, with the tongue tip stopping the flow of air at the dental ridge, near the base of the upper teeth, un-released--[t˺]. There is no close comparison in American English to the <u>eut</u> sound, though the "sēut" of "sēutsāam" is a transliteration into Cantonese of the English word "shirt."

      Listen and repeat: (Remember that the rounded vowel has a rounding effect on the consonant preceding it in a syllable)

    1. sēutsāam   (3 times) 恤衫
    2. sēut sēut sēut , sēut sēut sēut . 恤恤恤
    3. sēut séui   (3 times) 恤水
    4. séui sēut   (3 times) 水恤
    5. sēut jéun   (3 times) 恤準
    6. jéun sēut   (3 times) 準恤

7. <u>eu</u> before dentals in contrast to <u>eu</u> before velars: Notice the difference in tongue height of <u>eu</u> before the dentals <u>t</u>, <u>n</u>, and <u>yu</u> (spelled <u>i</u> following <u>eu</u>); and <u>eu</u> before the velar nasal <u>ng</u>. The <u>eu</u> is relatively lowered before the dentals, raised before the velar.

    1. sēut sēun séung séung
    2. sēut sēut léuhng léuhng
    3. séui séui séung séung
    4. deui deui Jèung Jèung
    5. jéun jéun Jèung Jèung
    6. jéun jéun séung séung

II. NOTES

1. <u>Numbers 20 - 99</u>

    a. 20 through 90. For the even 10's the Cantonese use a multiplying

        formula: two-ten's, three-ten's, etc.

20. yihsahp		60. luhksahp	
30. sàamsahp		70. chātsahp	
40. seisahp		80. baatsahp	
50. ńghsahp		90. gáusahp	

    b. 21 through 99. For these numbers which are not the even 10's, a

        combination of the multiplying and adding formula is used: two-

        ten's-one, two-ten's-two, etc.

        21. yihsahpyāt

        22. yihsahpyih

        23. yihsahpsàam etc., to

        99. gáusahpgáu

    c. Full forms and abbreviated forms:

        There is a full form and an abbreviated form for the numbers

    from twenty to ninety-nine. Both forms are used in everyday

    speech. The contracted form shortens the <u>sahp</u> element to <u>-ah-</u>.

Ex:	Full form	Abbreviated form
20	yihsahp	yah
21	yihsahpyāt	yahyāt
22	yihsahpyih	yahyih
30	sàamsahp	sà'ah
31	sàamsahpyāt	sà'ahyāt
40	seisahp	sei'ah
50	ńghsahp	ńgh'ah
60	luhksahp	luhk'ah
70	chātsahp	chāt'ah
80	baatsahp	baat'ah
90	gáusahp	gáu'ah
99	gáusahpgáu	gáu'ahgáu

                  (See Drill <u>6</u>)

2. Measures

In Lesson 4 we touched briefly on Measures, saying they were a class of word in Cantonese which comes between a number (or a limited set of other entities) and a noun.

Ex:	M	N	
ngóh	go	bīu	my watch
sàam	go	gwāt	three-quarters

In English some nouns are counted in terms of a measure of their volume or size or shape. For example, we do not ordinarily say 'a water,' but rather 'a glass of water,' 'a gallon of water,' 'a tub of water,' etc. In English 'glass, gallon, tub' type words are measures used in counting nouns perceived as a mass--(sand, bread, milk, tobacco, etc.) but not ordinarily in counting nouns perceived as individual units--(pencil, man, shirt, etc.)

In Chinese, however, a measure word precedes every noun when it is counted. For a mass-type noun the measure is variable--one cup, bowl, pound, etc. of rice, for example--but every individual-type noun has its own invariable measure which is by nature a pronoun standing in apposition to the noun.

a. Individual Measures

In Lesson Six you will encounter several new individual measures.

Ex:		M	Noun	
1.	yāt	tìuh	tāai	one [M] tie = one tie
2.	ngóh	bá	jē	my umbrella = my umbrella
3.	kéuih	gihn	sēutsāam	his [M] shirt = his shirt

The individual measures are in apposition to the noun that follows. Some individual measures have a degree of independent meaning apart from their structural function. For example, bá means 'handle,' and is a measure for objects having handles, tìuh means 'strip' and is a measure for objects which are long and narrow in shape. However, go, statistically the most frequent measure, has no independent meaning of its own.

What we have called individual measures some writers have called classifiers, indicating that nouns are classified according

to shape. We use the wider term 'measure' to cover individual
measures and other types of measure as well.

(See Drills <u>1, 2, 3, 4</u>)

b. Group Measures

    In addition to individual measures, there are other types of
measures. One type is the group measure. An example is <u>deui</u>, 'pair.'
Structurally group measures do not differ from individual measures--
they fill the same position in a sentence that individual measures
do, and combine with the same kinds of words. Semantically, of
course, a group measure differs from an individual measure.

Ex:

	Measure	+ Noun	
yāt	deui	hàaih	one pair shoes = one pair of shoes
yāt	jek	hàaih	one [M] shoe = one shoe

What we call group measures some writers have called
'collective' measures.

c. Standard Measures

    Another type of measure is the standard measure. In English
we talk of 'standard weights and measures'--pounds, inches, gal-
lons, etc. This is the type involved in the Cantonese category
of standard measure. The standard measure is of itself a meaning-
ful unit. Some examples which you have encountered so far are:

Number	+ Standard Measure	
yāt	mān	one dollar
yāt	dím	one o'clock (hour)
yāt	fānjūng	one minute

Standard measures, like all measures, may follow a number
directly. They differ from individual and group measures in that
they are not in apposition to a following noun, and do not depend
on a following noun to give them meaning. Thus they are measures
only in the grammatical sense; they behave like measures in that
they follow numerals directly. Semantically they are like nouns.

134

3. <u>Nouns</u>

      A word which requires a measure between a number and itself is classed as a noun in Cantonese.

      Ex: <u>Number</u> + <u>Measure</u> + <u>Noun</u>

léuhng	gihn	sēutsāam	two shirts
sàam	go	bīu	three watches
sei	go	jih	4 figures (in reference to time, 4 numbers on the clock dial, i.e. 20 minutes)

4. <u>Measure as substitute for noun.</u>

      In a follow sentence a measure substitutes for the noun it represents. In this way a measure operates like a pronoun.

      Ex: A. Ngóh máaih léuhng   I'm buying two [M] ties.
                tìuh tāai.

            B. Bīn léuhng <u>tìuh</u> a?   Which two [<u>ones</u>]?

            C. Nī léuhng <u>tìuh</u>.   These two [<u>ones</u>].

          (See BC and Drills <u>3</u>,4)

5. <u>Measure without preceding number.</u>

      We noted in Lesson 2 that nouns do not indicate singular and plural in Cantonese. (sēutsāam = shirt, shirts) The use of a measure without a number preceding it indicates singular number.

      Ex: 1. Kéuih séung máaih   1. He wants to buy some
            sēutsāam.   shirts. <u>or</u>
                                    He wants to buy a
                                    shirt.

           2. Kéuih séung máaih gihn   2. He wants to buy a
            sēutsāam.   shirt.

                (See BC)

6. <u>m̀hsái</u> not used in affirmative.

      The verb <u>sái</u> 'need,' 'have to,' is used in the negative and in choice-type question, but not in the affirmative.

      Ex: Q: Sái m̀hsái máaih luhk   Do you need to buy 6--
            gihn gàm dò a?   so many? (doubtful
                                   that it is necessary)

           A: M̀hsái máaih luhk gihn--   I don't need 6--3 are
            sàam gihn gau laak.   enough.

           (See Drills <u>1, 3, 12</u>)

135

To answer a sái m̀hsái? question affirmatively you use yiu 'require,' 'need,' 'have to.'

> Ex: Q: Sái m̀hsái máaih luhk   Do you need to buy so
>   gihn gàm dò a?   many as six?
>
>   A: Yiu máaih luhk gihn--   I need to buy six--
>   sàam gihn m̀hgau.   three aren't enough.

(See Drill _12_)

7. Free words and boundwords

     Words in Cantonese which can be spoken as one word sentences are _free words_, and ones which are never spoken as a one-word sentence, but always with some other word accompanying, are _boundwords_. Words which are always bound to an element which follows them we call right-bound (b-), and ones which are always bound to an element which precedes them we call left-bound (-b). Some boundwords can be bound in either direction.

8. nī, 'this,' and gó, 'that' classed as specifiers.

     nī, 'this,' and gó, 'that,' are boundwords functioning as modifier in a Noun Phrase (NP). They are right bound, bound to a _following_ element or elements, commonly a measure, or a number + measure:

> Ex: nī/gó   nu.   M
>   nī   gihn   = this one [this M]
>   gó   léuhng   go   = those two [that-two-M]

(See BC and Drills 2, 3, 11)

Note the word order of nī/gó constructions:

N/Pro.	nī/gó	Nu.	M	N	
1.		nī	léuhng	gihn	sēutsāam	these two shirts
2.		gó	sei	bá	jē	those 4 umbrellas
3. ngóh		nī	léuhng	tìuh	tāai	these two ties of mine

(See Drills 1, 11)

     nī and gó fill a position in a sentence that can be occupied by only a few words. bīn? 'which?' fills this same position. We use the class name _Specifier_ to refer to this small group.

     We call nī and gó 'this' and 'that' to give you memory-aid definitions. More specifically, nī refers to what is relatively near, and gó to what is relatively distant.

9. <u>Relative word order of direct and indirect object.</u>

Some verbs, such as <u>béi</u>, 'give,' take two objects: a direct object (thing), and indirect object (usually a person). In Cantonese the word order is Verb + Direct object + Indirect object.

Verb +	Direct obj +	Indirect obj		
Béi	nī gihn	ngóh	lā.	Give this one (to) me.
Béi	sàam mān	kéuih	lā.	Give $3 (to) him.

(See BC and Drills <u>11, 12, 15</u>)

10. <u>géi(dō)?</u>, 'how many, how much?' as an interrogative number.

<u>géidō?</u> and

occupying the position in a question-word sentence that a number occupies in the response sentence. In this frame <u>géi(dō)</u> is classed as an interrogative number. As a number it precedes a measure.

Ex:	<u>Number</u>	<u>Measure</u>		
Kéuih máaih	géi(dō)	gihn	a?	How many is he going to buy?
Kéuih máaih	sàam	gihn.		He's going to buy three.

(See BC and Drill <u>9</u>)

You will remember that <u>géi</u> has another meaning which you encountered in Lesson Four. <u>géi</u>, 'several' is an approximate number and is distinguished from <u>géi?</u>, 'how many?' in a sentence by the presence of the sentence suffix <u>a</u> in the question sentence but not in the statement sentence.

Ex: 1. Kéuih séung máaih géi gihn.	He's thinking of buying several.
2. Kéuih séung máaih géi gihn a?	How many is he thinking of buying?

11. <u>géidō?</u>, 'how many?' and <u>géi-?</u>, 'how many?' differentiated.

The difference between <u>géi-?</u> and <u>géidō?</u> is that <u>géi-?</u> is a boundword bound to a following Measure, and <u>géidō?</u> is a free word which can be bound to a following measure as modifier (in which case it is interchangeable with <u>géi-?</u>), but may also be head in a nominal construction, which <u>géi-?</u> cannot.

Ex: 1. Kéuih séung máaih {géi / géidō} gihn a?	1. How many [Ms] does he want?
2. Kéuih séung máaih géidō a?	2. How many does he want?

12. M̀hjì...{nē? / a?}, as polite question form: 'I wonder...?,' i.e., 'I wonder
    (if you could tell me)...?

    By extension m̀hjì, 'don't know,' may be taken to mean something like
'I wonder...?' 'Could you tell me...?' a polite way of making a question
without being abrupt. By adding the sentence suffix a or nē to the end
of the negative sentence, the negative is transformed to the polite
'I wonder...?' question.

Ex: M̀hjì yiu géidō chìn.	(I)don't know how much it costs.
M̀hjì yiu géidō chìn {nē / a} ?	(I) wonder how much it costs? (You assume that the person you're talking to <u>does</u> know and in this indirect way prompt him to tell you.)

III. DRILLS

1. Expansion Drill: (Students repeat sentence after the teacher.

+ 1. a. Máaih <u>yúhlāu</u>.
    b. Máaih gihn yúhlāu.
    c. Máaih ńgh gihn yúhlāu.
    d. Máaih nī ńgh gihn yúhlāu.
    e. Ngóh máaih nī ńgh gihn yúhlāu.

1. a. Buy a <u>raincoat/raincoats</u>.
    b. Buy a raincoat.
    c. Buy 5 raincoats.
    d. Buy these 5 raincoats.
    e. I'll take these 5 raincoats.

+ 2. a. Máaih <u>fu</u>.
    (<u>slacks</u>, <u>trousers</u>, <u>long-pants</u>)
+   b. Máaih tíuh fu.
    (<u>M. for trousers</u>)
    c. Máaih léuhng tíuh fu.
    d. Máaih nī léuhng tíuh fu.
    e. Máaih nī léuhng tíuh fu lā!

2. a. Buy slacks.
    b. Buy a pair of slacks.
    c. Buy two pairs of slacks.
    d. Buy these two pairs of slacks.
    e. Buy these two pairs of slacks!

+ 3. a. Máaih <u>maht</u>.
+   b. Máaih <u>deui</u> maht.
    c. Máaih sàam deui maht.
    d. M̀hsái máaih sàam deui maht.
    e. M̀hsái máaih sàam deui maht laak.

3. a. Buy <u>socks</u>.
    b. Buy a <u>pair</u> of socks.
    c. Buy three pairs of socks.
    d. You don't need to buy three pairs of socks.
    e. You don't need to buy 3 pairs of socks just now.

+ 4. a. Máaih <u>bāt</u>.
    (<u>writing implements</u>)
+   b. Máaih jì bāt.
    (<u>M. for bāt</u>)
+   c. Máaih jì <u>yùhnbāt</u>.
    d. Séung máaih jì yùhnbāt.
    e. M̀hséung máaih jì yùhnbāt.
    f. Séung m̀hséung máaih jì yùhnbāt a?

4. a. Buy pens (<u>or</u> pencils)
    b. Buy a pen (<u>or</u> pencil)
    c. Buy a <u>pencil</u>.
    d. Want to buy a pencil
    e. Don't want to buy a pencil.
    f. Do (you) want to buy a pencil?

    <u>or</u>
    Are you planning to buy a pencil?

or

Would you like to buy a
 pencil?

+ 5. a. <u>Jūng</u>.

    b. Máaih jūng.

    c. Máaih go jūng.

    d. Séung máaih go jūng.

    e. Séung máaih léuhng go
       jūng.

    f. Ngóh séung máaih léuhng
       go jūng.

+ 6. a. <u>Kwàhn</u>.

    b. Máaih kwàhn.

    c. Máaih tiuh kwàhn.

+   d. Máaih tiuh <u>dáikwàhn</u>
       (<u>slip</u>, <u>petticoat</u>)

    e. Máaih léuhng tiuh dái-
       kwàhn.

    f. Séung máaih léuhng tiuh
       dáikwàhn.

    g. Ngóh séung máaih léuhng
       tiuh dáikwàhn.

  7. a. Síujé

+   b. Go <u>wái</u> síujé

    c. Sīk go wái síujé.

    d. M̀hsīk go wái síujé.

    e. Ngóh m̀hsīk go wái síujé.

+ 8. a. <u>Jē</u>

+   b. Bá jē
       (<u>M. for umbrella</u>)

    c. Máaih nī bá jē.

    d. Máaih nī bá jē, géidō
       chín a?

+   e. Máaih nī bá jē <u>yiu</u> géidō
       chín a?
       (yiu + money expression =
       want <u>X</u> amount, costs <u>X</u>
       amount, i.e., the asking
       price)

5. a. Clock

    b. Buy clock(s)

    c. Buy a clock.

    d. Plan to buy a clock.

    e. Plan to buy two clocks.

    f. I plan to buy two clocks.

6. a. <u>Skirt</u>

    b. Buy skirt(s).

    c. Buy a skirt.

    d. Buy a slip.

    e. Buy two slips.

    f. Wish to buy two slips.

    g. I wish to buy two slips.

7. a. Lady

    b. That lady (<u>wái = polite
       M for person</u>)

    c. Know that lady

    d. Not know that lady.

    e. I don't know that lady.

8. a. <u>Umbrella</u>

    b. An umbrella

    c. Buy this umbrella.

    d. How much does this rain-
       coat cost?

    e. How much (do you) want
       for this raincoat?

f. Ngóh m̀hjī máaih nī bá jē
   yiu géidō chín.

f. I don't know how much
   this umbrella is.

+ g. Ngóh m̀hjī máaih nī bá jē yiu
     géidō chín a?
     [(Ngóh) m̀hjī...a? =
     I wonder...? i.e. polite
     question introduction]

g. I wonder how much this
   raincoat is?

2. Transformation Drill: Transform the sentences from affirmative to
   choice type question.

Ex: T: Nī gihn sēutsāam
       sahpsàam māan.

    S: Nī gihn sēutsāam
       haih m̀hhaih sahp-
       sàam māan a?

T: This shirt is thirteen dollars.

S: Is this shirt thirteen dollars?

1. Nī gihn sēutsāam sahpyāt māan.

1. Nī gihn sēutsāam haih m̀hhaih
   sahpyāt māan a?

+ 2. Gó tiuh tāai sei māan.
     That tie is four dollars.

2. Gó tiuh tāai haih m̀hhaih sei
   māan a?

3. Nī tiuh fu sahpsàam māan.

3. Nī tiuh fu haih m̀hhaih sahpsàam māan a?

+ 4. Gó deui hàaih yahńgh māan.
     That pair of shoes is
     twenty-five dollars.

4. Gó deui hàaih haih m̀hhaih
   yahńgh māan a?

5. Nī deui maht sàam māan.

5. Nī deui maht haih m̀hhaih
   sàam māan a?

6. Gó bá jē sahpyāt māan.

6. Gó bá jē haih m̀hhaih sahpyāt māan a?

7. Nī gihn yúhlāu sahpgáu māan.

7. Nī gihn yúhlāu haih m̀hhaih
   sahpgáu māan a?

8. Nī go bīu ńgh'ahgáu māan.

8. Nī go bīu haih m̀hhaih ńgh'ah-
   gāu māan a?

+ 9. Gó jī yùhnjíbāt yāt māan.
     That ball point pen is
     one dollar.

9. Gó jī yùhnjíbāt haih m̀hhaih
   yāt māan a?

3. Response Drill: Teacher should point to a spot near himself for
   nī-, students should point away for gó-, to link the words with
   the situation.

Ex: T: Nī gihn sahpyāt māan.

    S: Gó gihn dōu yiu
       sahpyāt māan.

T: This one is eleven dollars.

S: That one is eleven dollars.

1. Nī tiuh sahpsei mān.
2. Nī deui luhk mān.
3. Nī gihn sahpbaat mān.
4. Nī jì yāt mān.
5. Nī go yahgáu mān.
+ 6. Nī tiuh dáifu ńgh mān.
   (underpants, undershorts)

1. Gó tiuh dōu yiu sahpsei mān.
2. Gó deui dōu yiu luhk mān.
3. Gó gihn dōu yiu sahpbaat mān.
4. Gó jì dōu yiu yāt mān.
5. Gó go dōu yiu yahgáu mān.
6. Gó tiuh dáifu dōu yiu ńgh mān.

Comment: Note that in the sentences above, numbered money expressions stand as predicate without the inclusion of a verb. The inclusion of haih is, however, also permitted: Nī gihn haih sahpyāt mān. 'This one is $11'.

---

4. Expansion Drill

Ex: T: Nī gihn yúhlāu sahp mān.

S: Nī gihn yúhlāu sahp mān, gó gihn dōu haih sahp mān.

T: This raincoat is $10.

S: This raincoat is $10. That one is also $10.

1. Nī gihn sēutsāam sahpńgh mān.

1. Nī gihn sēutsāam sahpńgh mān, gó gihn dōu haih sahp-ńgh mān.

2. Nī deui hàaih yahluhk mān.

2. Nī deui hàaih yahluhk mān, gó deui dōu haih yahluhk mān.

3. Nī bá jē sahpchāt mān.

3. Nī bá jē sahpchāt mān, gó bá dōu haih sahpchāt mān.

4. Nī tiuh fu yahyih mān.

4. Nī tiuh fu yahyih mān, gó tiuh dōu haih yahyih mān.

5. Nī tiuh tāai baat mān.

5. Nī tiuh tāai baat mān, gó tiuh dōu haih baat mān.

---

5. Substitution Drill: Repeat the first sentence after the teacher, then substitute the cues as appropriate to make new sentences.

1. Ngóh séung máaih gihn yúhlāu.
   I want to buy a raincoat.

2. /gó go yàhn/

1. Ngóh séung máaih gihn yúhlāu.

2. Gó go yàhn séung máaih gihn yúhlāu.

That man wants to buy this
raincoat.

3. Gó go Yìnggwokyàhn.

3. Gó go Yìnggwokyàhn séung
máaih gihn yúhlāu.

4. deui maht

4. Gó go Yìnggwokyàhn séung
máaih deui maht.

+ 5. Gó go síujé
    (woman)

5. Gó go síujé séung máaih deui
maht.
That lady wants to buy a
pair of socks.

+ 6. Gó wái sīnsàang
    (man)

6. Gó wái sīnsàang séung máaih
deui maht.

7. tiuh fu

7. Gó wái sīnsàang séung máaih
tiuh fu.

_____

6. Transformation Drill: Transform the numbers from full form to
   abbreviated form.

   Ex: T: Nī tiuh sàamsahp mān. T: This one is thirty dollars.

       S: Nī tiuh sà'ah mān.   S: This one is thirty dollars.

1. Nī tiuh yihsahpsei mān.
   [24]

1. Nī tiuh yahsei mān.

2. Nī tiuh yihsahpchāt mān.
   [27]

2. Nī tiuh yahchāt mān.

3. Nī tiuh sàamsahpńgh mān.
   [35]

3. Nī tiuh sà'ahńgh mān.

4. Nī tiuh sàamsahpyih mān.
   [32]

4. Nī tiuh sà'ahyih mān.

5. Nī tiuh seisahpbaat mān.
   [48]

5. Nī tiuh sei'ahbaat mān.

6. Nī tiuh seisahpluhk mān.
   [46]

6. Nī tiuh sei'ahluhk mān.

7. Nī tiuh ńghsahpsei mān.
   [54]

7. Nī tiuh ńgh'ahsei mān.

8. Nī tiuh ńghsahpyih mān.
   [51]

8. Nī tiuh ńgh'ahyih mān.

9. Nī tiuh luhksahpńgh mān.
   [65]

9. Nī tiuh luhk'ahńgh mān.

10. Nī tiuh luhksahpgáu mān.
    [69]

10. Nī tiuh luhk'ahgáu mān.

_____

7. Response Drill: Teacher points away for gó-, students near for nī-.

      Ex: T: Gó tīuh fu sahp   T: That pair of trousers is ten
                mān. /baat mān/   dollars.

          S: NĪ tīuh baat mān jē.   S: This pair is only eight dollars.

    1. Gó deui haaih yahsāam mān.   1. NĪ deui yahyāt mān jē.
       /yahyāt mān/

    2. Gó deui maht luhk mān. /sei mān/   2. NĪ deui sei mān jē.

    3. Gó tīuh fu sahpyih mān.   3. NĪ tīuh sahp mān jē.
       /sahp mān/

    4. Gó go bīu sà'ahngh mān.   4. NĪ go yahchāt mān jē.
       /yahchāt mān/

    5. Gó gihn yúhlāu yihsahp mān.   5. NĪ gihn sahpgáu mān jē.
       /sahpgáu mān/

---

8. Response Drill

      Ex: T: NĪ gihn sahpluhk   T: This one is sixteen dollars.
                mān.

         S: Gám, gó gihn haih   S: Well, is that one sixteen
            m̄hhaih dōu haih   dollars too?
            sahpluhk mān a?

    1. NĪ bá sahpbaat mān.   1. Gám, gó bá haih m̄hhaih dōu
                          haih sahpbaat mān a?

    2. NĪ tīuh ńgh mān.   2. Gám, gó tīuh haih m̄hhaih
                          dōu haih ńgh mān a?

    3. NĪ gihn sahpsei mān.   3. Gám, gó gihn haih m̄hhaih
                          dōu haih sahpsei mān a?

    4. NĪ deui yahsàam mān.   4. Gám, gó deui haih m̄hhaih
                          dōu haih yahsàam mān a?

    5. Kéuih haih Gwóngdùngyàhn.   5. Gám, kéuih pàhngyáuh haih
       /kéuih pàhngyáuh/   m̄hhaih dōu haih Gwóng-
                           dùngyàhn a?

---

9. Response Drill

      Ex: T: Néih máaih géidō   T: How many do you want to buy?
                gihn a? /ńgh/   are you going to get?
                           /5/

         S: Ngóh máaih ńgh gihn.   S: I want five.

144

1. Néih máaih géidō bá a?
   /léuhng/

1. Ngóh máaih léuhng bá.

2. Néih máaih géidō tiuh a? /sàam/

2. Ngóh máaih sàam tiuh.

3. Néih máaih géidō deui a? /luhk/

3. Ngóh máaih luhk deui.

4. Néih máaih géidō gihn a? /sei/

4. Ngóh máaih sei gihn.

5. Néih máaih géidō jí a? /sei/

5. Ngóh máaih sei jí.

6. Néih máaih géidō go a? /
   /sahpyih/

6. Ngóh máaih sahpyih go.

a. Repeat, teacher cuing with Measure and number only, students giving question and answer, thus:

T: /gihn/ńgh/   T: /M:/5/

S1: Néih máaih géidō   S1: How many are you going to buy?
gihn a?

S2: Ngóh máaih ńgh   S2: I'm going to buy 5.
gihn.

---

10. Expansion Drill

Ex: T: Máaih sēutsāam.   T: Buy shirts.

S: Kéuih máaih gihn   S: She's buying a shirt.
sēutsāam.

Note that the measure is not cued, that student must supply it.

1. Máaih fu.   1. Kéuih máaih tiuh fu.

2. Máaih tāai.   2. Kéuih máaih tiuh tāai.

3. Máaih maht.   3. Kéuih máaih deui maht.

4. Máaih jē.   4. Kéuih máaih bá jē.

5. Máaih hàaih.   5. Kéuih máaih deui hàaih.

6. Máaih yúhlāu.   6. Kéuih máaih gihn yúhlāu.

7. Máaih sēutsāam.   7. Kéuih máaih gihn sēutsāam.

8. Máaih bíu.   8. Kéuih máaih go bíu.

9. Máaih cháang.   9. Kéuih máaih go cháang.

10. Máaih kwàhn.   10. Kéuih máaih tiuh kwàhn.

11. Máaih dáikwàhn.   11. Kéuih máaih tiuh dáikwàhn.

12. Máaih pìhnggwó.   12. Kéuih máaih go pìhnggwó.

13. Máaih bāt.   13. Kéuih máaih jí bāt.

14. Máaih yùhnbāt.   14. Kéuih máaih jí yùhnbāt.

15. Máaih yùhnjíbāt.   15. Kéuih máaih jí yùhnjíbāt.

16. Máaih bējáu.   16. Kéuih máaih jī bējáu.

17. Máaih jūng.   17. Kéuih máaih go jūng.

---

11. Expansion Drill: Expand the given sentence by adding the cue word
    in the appropriate place.

    Ex: T: Béi léuhng tiuh   T: Give me two ties. /this/
        tāai ngóh lā. /nī/

       S: Béi nī léuhng tiuh   S: Give me these two ties.
        tāai ngóh lā.

1. Béi bá ngóh lā. /nī/   1. Béi nī bá ngóh lā.

2. Béi tiuh fu ngóh lā. /gó/   2. Béi gó tiuh fu ngóh lā.

3. Béi deui maht ngóh lā. /luhk/   3. Béi luhk deui maht ngóh lā.

4. Béi sàam gihn ngóh lā. /gó/   4. Béi gó sàam gihn ngóh lā.

5. Béi sàam tiuh ngóh lā. /nī/   5. Béi nī sàam tiuh ngóh lā.

6. Béi léuhng tiuh ngóh lā. /tāai/ 6. Béi léuhng tiuh tāai ngóh
                                      lā.

7. Béi gó deui hàaih ngóh lā.   7. Béi gó léuhng deui hàaih
   /léuhng/   ngóh lā.

8. Béi léuhng gihn sēutsāam ngóh   8. Béi gó léuhng gihn sēutsāam
   lā. /gó/   ngóh lā.

9. Béi tiuh kwàhn ngóh lā. /gó/   9. Béi gó tiuh kwàhn ngóh lā.

---

12. Response Drill

    Ex: 1. T: Néih máaih m̀h-   T: Are you going to get this pair
        máaih nī deui   of shoes? Do you want this
        hàaih a? /nod/   pair of shoes?

       S: Hóu, béi nī deui   S: OK, give me that pair.
        ngóh lā.

      2. T: Néih máaih m̀h-   T: Do you want this pair of
        máaih nī deui   shoes?
        hàaih a? /shake/

       S: M̀hmáaih laak.   S: Not today, thanks. [not buy
                                      now.]

1. Néih máaih m̀hmáaih nī gihn   1. Hóu, béi nī gihn ngóh lā.
   sēutsāam a? /nod/

2. Néih máaih m̀hmáaih nī gihn   2. Hóu, béi nī gihn ngóh lā.
   yùhlāu a? /nod/

3. Néih máaih m̀hmáaih nī bá jē   3. M̀hmáaih laak.
   a? /shake/

4. Néih máaih m̀hmáaih nī tìuh   4. M̀hmáaih laak.
   fu a? /shake/

5. Néih máaih m̀hmáaih nī deui maht   5. Hóu, béi nī deui ngóh lā.
   a? /nod/

6. Néih máaih m̀hmáaih nī tìuh   6. M̀hmáaih laak.
   tāai a? /shake/

7. Néih máaih m̀hmáaih nī deui   7. Hóu, béi nī deui ngóh lā.
   hàaih a? /nod/

8. Néih máaih m̀hmáaih nī jī   8. M̀hmáaih laak.
   yùhnbāt a? /shake/

9. Néih máaih m̀hmáaih nī go bīu   9. Hóu, béi nī go ngóh lā.
   a? /nod/

Comment: In these sentences idiomatic English counterparts for
         máaih might be 'take,' 'get,' 'want,' as well as
         'buy.'

---

13. Expansion/Substitution Drill: Expand or substitute as appropriate
    with the cue provided.

        Ex: T: Máaih nī gihn.   T: Buy this one. /I/
            /ngóh/

            S: Ngóh máaih nī gihn.   S: I'll take this one.
                                        (said to clerk in store)

            T: /gó gihn/   T: That one.

            S: Ngóh máaih gó gihn.   S: I'll take that one.
                                        (said to clerk)

    1. Gó go yàhn máaih sēutsāam.   1. Gó go yàhn séung máaih
       /séung/   sēutsāam.
       That man is buying shirts.   That man wants to buy
                                        shirts.

    2. /gihn/   2. Gó go yàhn séung máaih gihn
                                        sēutsāam.

    3. /léuhng/   3. Gó go yàhn séung máaih
                                        léuhng gihn sēutsāam.

    4. /géidō/   4. Gó go yàhn séung máaih
                                        géidō gihn sēutsāam a?

    5. /sei/   5. Gó go yàhn séung máaih sei
                                        gihn sēutsāam.

    6. /m̀hséung/   6. Gó go yàhn m̀hséung máaih
                                        sei gihn sēutsāam.

147

7. /séung m̀hséung a?/

7. Gó gó yàhn séung m̀hséung máaih sei gihn sēutsāam a?

8. /léuhng tìuh tāai/

8. Gó go yàhn séung m̀hséung máaih léuhng tìuh tāai a?

---

14. Conversation Exercise:

Ex: A: M̀hsái máaih luhk gihn sēutsāam, sàam gihn gau laak.

A: You needn't buy 6 shirts; 3 is enough.

B: M̀hhaih. Sàam gihn m̀hgau; yiu máaih luhk gihn.

B: No, 3 isn't enough; I need to get 6.

1. A. ...sàam deui maht; Yāt deui ......

    B. ....

1. A. M̀hsái máaih sàam deui maht; yāt deui gau laak.

    B. M̀hhaih. Yāt deui m̀hgau; yiu máaih sàam deui.

2. A. ...léuhng bá jē; Yāt bá......

    B. ....

2. A. M̀hsái máaih léuhng bá jē; yāt bá gau laak.

    B. M̀hhaih. Yāt bá m̀hgau; yiu máaih léuhng bá.

3. A. ...sahp go cháang; Gáu go......

    B. ....

3. A. M̀hsái máaih sahp go cháang; gáu go gau laak.

    B. M̀hhaih. Gáu go m̀hgau; yiu máaih sahp go.

4. A. ...chāt jì bējáu; luhk jì......

    B. ....

4. A. M̀hsái máaih chāt jì bējáu; luhk jì gau laak.

    B. M̀hhaih. Luhk jì m̀hgau; yiu máaih chāt jì.

5. A. ...sei go béng; Léuhng go......

    B. ....

5. A. M̀hsái máaih sei go béng; léuhng go gau laak.

    B. M̀hhaih. Léuhng go m̀hgau; yiu máaih sei go.

---

15. Response Drill: Respond affirmatively or negatively as directed, following the pattern of the example.

Ex: 1. T: Yāt bá jē gau
         m̀hgau a? /nod/

    S: Gau laak. Yāt bá
       gau laak.

T: Is one umbrella enough?

S: Yes, one is enough.

    2. T: Yāt bá jē gau
          m̀hgau a? /shake/

    S: Yāt bá m̀hgau.
       m̀hgòi néih béi
       léuhng bá ngóh
       lā.

T: Is one umbrella enough?

S: One is not enough. Please give me two.

1. Léuhng jí yùhnjíbāt gau
   m̀hgau a? /nod/

1. Gau laak. Léuhng jí gau laak.

2. Yāt gihn yúhlāu gau m̀hgau a?
   /shake/

2. Yāt gihn m̀hgau. M̀hgòi néih béi léuhng gihn ngóh lā.

3. Luhk jí heiséui gau m̀hgau a?
   /nod/

3. Gau laak. Luhk jí gau laak.

4. Yāt deui hàaih gau m̀hgau a?
   /shake/

4. Yāt deui m̀hgau. M̀hgòi néih béi léuhng deui ngóh lā.

5. Sàam go pìhnggwó gau m̀hgau a?
   /shake/

5. Sàam go m̀hgau. M̀hgòi néih béi sei go ngóh lā.

6. Léuhng go bīu gau m̀hgau a?
   /nod/

6. Gau laak. Léuhng go gau laak.

7. Sahp go béng gau m̀hgau a?
   /shake/

7. Sahp go m̀hgau. M̀hgòi néih béi sahpyāt go ngóh lā.

IV. CONVERSATIONS FOR LISTENING

(On tape. Listen to tape with book closed.)

V. SAY IT IN CANTONESE

A. You ask your neighbor:

   1. What he wants to buy.

   2. How many (ties) he wants.

   3. How much these shoes cost.

   4. Whether those (shoes) are also $60.00 a pair.

B. And he replies:

   1. That he wants to buy a tie.

   2. He wants to buy two.

   3. They are $60 a pair.

   4. No, they are $65.

149

5. Whether three pairs of socks are enough.

6. How much that ballpoint pen is.

7. Whether 5 pencils are enough.

8. How much that petticoat costs.

9. Who that gentleman is.

10. Who that lady is.

5. That he doesn't need three pairs--two pairs are enough.

6. That it is $1--two sell for $1.90.

7. That five aren't enough-- he wants ten.

8. That it sells for $12.50.

9. That he doesn't know.

10. That her name is Chan--she teaches Cantonese.

Vocabulary Checklist for Lesson 6

1.	bá	m:	M. for things with handles, such as umbrellas
2.	bāt	n:	writing implement; pen or pencil
3.	béi	v:	give
4.	chín	n/m:	money
5.	dáifu	n:	underpants, undershorts
6.	dáikwàhn	n:	slip, petticoat
7.	deui	m:	pair; group measure for shoes, socks, chopsticks
8.	fu	n:	trousers
9.	gau	adj:	enough
10.	géi(dō)	QW/nu:	how much? how many?
11.	gihn	m:	M. for clothes
12.	gó	sp:	that
13.	go	m:	general M. for nouns
14.	guhaak	n:	customer (restricted use)
15.	hàaih	n:	shoes
16.	jē	n:	umbrella
17.	jí	m:	M. for pen, pencil, bottles
18.	jūng	n:	clock
19.	kwàhn	n:	skirt
20.	máaih	v:	buy
21.	maht	n:	socks

150

22. māan   m: dollar
23. M̀hjī(dou)...a?   Ph: I wonder...?
24. nī   sp: this
25. sauhfoyùhn   n: Salesclerk [sell-goods-personnel]
26. sēutsāam   n: shirt
27. sīnsàang   n: man
28. síujé   n: lady, woman
29. tāai   n: tie
30. tìuh   m: M. for trousers, ties, roads
31. wái   m: polite M. for persons
32. yàhn   n: person
33. yiu + money expression   v: wants X amount, costs X amount, (i.e.,
                                       the asking price is X amount.)
34. yúhlāu   n: raincoat
35. yùhnbāt   n: pencil
36. yùhnjíbāt   n: ball point pen

CLASSROOM PHRASES

Below are some sentences for students to say to the teacher. Don't try to memorize them all at once, but learn them as you find them useful.

1. Ngóh m̀hjì ____ dím gáai.
    I don't know what ____ means.
    [lit. I don't know how ____ is explained.]

2. M̀hgòi néih gáaisÍkháh.
    Please explain.

3. M̀hgòi néih géui go laih láih táiháh.
    Please give an example to demonstrate.

4. M̀hgòi néih yuhng ____ jouh yāt geui béi ngóh tèngháh.
    Please use ____ to make a sentence for me to hear.

5. Hái mēyéh sìhhauh sÍnji góng?
    When do you say that? (i.e., in what kind of situation?)

6. Hái mēyéh chìhngyìhng sÍnji góng?
    In what circumstances is that said?

7. _A_ tùhng _B_ yáuh móuh fànbiht?
    Is there any difference between _A_ and _B_?

8. _A_ tùhng _B_ yáuh mēyéh fànbiht?
    What is the difference between _A_ and _B_?

9. Ngóh nÍ geui yáuh dÍ mahntàih.
    I have a question about this sentence.

10. Ngóh nÍ go jih yáuh dÍ mahntàih.
    I have a question about this word.

11. Gám góng dāk m̀hdāk a?
    Is it OK to say it this/that way?

12. ____ hóu m̀hhóu tèng?
    Does ____ sound right?

13. ____ duhk mēyéh sÍng a?
    What tone is ____?

I. BASIC CONVERSATION

A. Buildup:

(Customer and clerk in a grocery store:)

Fógei

| fógei | clerk |
| Máaih mēyéh a? | What will you have? |

Guhaak

haih ... làih ge	is...(grammatical structure emphasizing enclosed noun.)
haih mēyéh làih ga?	is what?
dī	mass measure; plural measure
nī dī	this (mass); these (units)
Nī dī haih mēyéh làih ga?	What's this?

Fógei

ngàuhyuhk	beef
Nī dī haih ngàuhyuhk.	This is beef.
oi, or ngoi	want, want to possess, want to have
oi mhoi, or ngoi mhngoi	want/not want?
Néih oi mhoi nē?	Do you want some?

Guhaak

jyùyuhk	pork
dī jyùyuhk	some pork
Mhoi, ngóh séung oi dī jyùyuhk.	No, I don't; I want to get some pork.
gàn	catty (unit of measure = 600 gms. ca. 1 1/3 pounds)
Géidō chín gàn a?	How much is it per catty?

Fógei

sei go luhk	$4.60 [4 measure 6 (dimes)]
ngàhnchín	money [silver-money]
sei go luhk ngàhnchín	$4.60 [4 dollars 6 (dimes)]
sei go luhk ngàhnchín gàn	$4.60 per catty
Nī dī sei go luhk ngàhnchín gàn.	This is $4.60 per catty.

<u>Guhaak</u>

béi ngóh lā	give (it to) me please
léuhng gàn	two catties
Béi léuhng gàn ngóh lā.	Please give me two catties.

(They go over to the fruit section.)

<u>Guhaak</u>

maaih	sell
dím maaih nē?	how sell?
cháang dím maaih nē?	oranges--how sell?
Dí cháang dím maaih nē?	What do the oranges sell for?

<u>Fógei</u>

hòuh(jí)	dime
Ńgh hòuhjí go.	50¢ [5 dimes] each.

<u>Guhaak</u>

Dí pihnggwó nē?	And the apples?

<u>Fógei</u>

yātyeuhng	same
Yātyeuhng--ńgh hòuhji go.	The same--50¢ each.

<u>Guhaak</u>

tòhng	sugar
bohng tòhng	a pound of sugar
léuhng bohng tòhng	two pounds of sugar
A! Ngóh dōu séung máaih léuhng bohng tòhng.	Oh! I also want to buy two pounds of sugar.
géi chín a?	how much money?
Géidō chín bohng a?	How much is it per pound?

<u>Fógei</u>

luhk hòuh bun	65¢ [6 dimes + half]
luhk hòuh bun jí	65¢ [6 dimes half dime]
Luhk hòuh bun jí bohng.	65¢ per pound.

B. <u>Recapitulation:</u>

<u>Fógei</u>

Máaih mēyéh a?	What will you have?

<u>Guhaak</u>

Nī dī haih mēyéh làih ga?   What's <u>this</u>?

<u>Fógei</u>

Nī dī haih ngàuhyuhk. Néih oi   This is beef. Do you want
àhoi nē?   some?

<u>Guhaak</u>

Àhoi, ngóh séung oi dī jyùyuhk.   No, I don't; I want to get
Géidō chín gàn a?   some pork. How much is it
                                                         per catty?

<u>Fógei</u>

Nī dī sei go luhk ngàhnchín   This is $4.60 per catty.
gàn.

<u>Guhaak</u>

Béi léuhng gàn ngóh lā.   Please give me two catties.

(They go over to the fruit counter.)

<u>Guhaak</u>

Dī cháang dím maaih nē?   What do the oranges sell for?

<u>Fógei</u>

Ńgh hòuhjí go.   50¢ [5 dimes] each.

<u>Guhaak</u>

Dī pìhnggwó nē?   And the apples?

<u>Fógei</u>

Yātyeuhng--ńgh hòuhjí go.   The same--50¢ each.

<u>Guhaak</u>

A! Ngóh dōu séung máaih léuhng   Oh! I also want to buy two
bohng tòhng. Géidō chín   pounds of sugar. How much
bohng a?   is it per pound?

<u>Fógei</u>

Luhk hòuh bun jí bohng.   65¢ per pound.

_____

Note to teacher: In drill #2 of this lesson there are some
                                        visual props needed which you may want to
                                        assemble early.

+ + + + + + + + + + + + + +

Pronunciation

1. Tone practice:

    A. Tone practice with Measures: Repeat during the pauses provided:

        1. máh (= yard (in length)   (3 times)

        2. yāt jí , yāt bá , yāt go ; yāt tíuh , yāt máh ,
            yāt gihn .

        3. yāt jí, yāt bá, yāt go ; yāt tíuh, yāt máh, yāt gihn

        4. yāt jí, yāt tíuh , (3 times)

        5. yāt go, yāt gihn (3 times); yāt gihn, yāt go . (3 times)

        6. yāt bá, yāt máh (3 times); yāt máh, yāt bá . (3 times)

        7. yāt gihn, yāt tíuh (3 times)

        8. chēut (= M. for movie) . (3 times)

        9. yāt chēut, yāt go, yāt gihn ; yāt gihn, yāt go, yāt chēut .

        10. jí bá go chēut , tíuh máh gihn .

        11. jí bá go chēut tíuh máh gihn .

    B. Tone practice with Numbers:

        1. lìhng (= 'zero') . (3 times)

        2. sàam, gáu sei ; lìhng, ńgh, yih .

        3. sàam, gáu, sei, lìhng, ńgh, yih .

        4. sàam, gáu, sei, chāt ; lìhng, ńgh, yih .

        5. sàam, gáu, sei, chāt, lìhng, ńgh, yih .

        6. chāt sei , sei chāt ; yih sei , sei yih .

        7. gáu ńgh , ńgh gáu .

        8. lìhng yih , yih lìhng .

        9. chāt go, baat go, sahp go , sahp go, baat go, chāt go .

        10. sahp go, baat go; baat go, sahp go .

        11. chāt go, baat go , baat go, chāt go .

        12. gáu go, léuhng go , léuhng go, gáu go .

2. ai/aai contrasts

                    Listen and repeat: (Notice that ai is shorter and
                    tenser in an isolated syllable than is aai; that the
                    a of ai is a mid central vowel, whereas the aa of
                    aai is a low back vowel; that i after a is high
                    front unrounded, after aa is somewhat lower (i after
                    a is more like the ee sound of English "see," after

aa it is more like the i sound of English "is.")

1. gāi gāi gāi 雞 , tāai tāai tāai 大 .

2. gāi tāai   , tāai gāi   .

3. haih haih haih   , maaih maaih maaih   .

4. haih m̀hhaih a?   , maaih m̀hmaaih a?   .

5. haih m̀hhaih a?   , máaih m̀hmáaih a?   .

6. Gó wái taaitáai haih m̀hhaih máaih hàaih a?

7. Jánhaih m̀hsái máaih hàaih.

3. **maaih** and **máaih**

Listen and repeat:

1. maaih, maaih   , máaih, máaih   .

2. máaih, máaih   , maaih, maaih   .

3. máaih m̀hmáaih a?   , maaih m̀hmaaih a?   .

4. maaih m̀hmaaih a?   , máaih m̀hmáaih a?   .

5. m̀hséung maaih   , m̀hséung máaih   .

6. máaih léuhng go, máaih léuhng go   ,

   maaih léuhng go   , maaih léuhng go   .

4. **yuk** = **y** + **uk**

     yuk is a syllable composed of **y** as initial and **uk** as a two-part final, composed of the high back rounded vowel **u** plus the velar consonant stop **k**. The high front rounded **yu** [ü] plus velar stop consonant **k** doesn't occur as a two-part final in Cantonese. Therefore the spelling **yuk**, which on paper could be ambiguously interpreted as either **yu** + **k** or **y** + **uk**, can only be **y** + **uk**.

Listen and repeat:

1. jyùyuhk jyùyuhk   豬肉

2. yuhk yuhk   肉肉

3. luhk luhk   六肉

4. yuhk luhk   (2 times)肉六

157

1. NOTES

1. d**Ī** 'some,' as general plural measure for individual nouns

    a. Plurality unspecified in number is expressed by the plural measure

        d**Ī**, 'some.'

            1.   go pìhnggwó = the apple, an apple

                  dĪ pìhnggwó = the apples, some apples

            2. nĪ go pìhnggwó = this apple

                nĪ dĪ pìhnggwó = these apples

    b. Individual nouns have different individual measures, but d**Ī** serves

        as plural measure for all individual nouns.

        Ex: 1. bá jē   = the umbrella, an umbrella

              dĪ jē   = the umbrellas, some umbrellas

           2. tìuh tāai = the tie, a tie

              dĪ tāai   = the ties, some ties

           3. go cháang = the orange, an orange

              dĪ cháang = the oranges, some oranges

              (See BC and Drill __4__)

    c. In a follow sentence d**Ī** substitutes for the noun it represents,

        serving in such position as an impersonal pronoun.

        Béi gó dĪ cháang ngóh lā. = Give me those [M] oranges.

        Béi gó dĪ   ngóh lā. = Give me those. [distant ones]

    d. d**Ī** is not used as Measure following a number. When number is

        specified, the individual measure follows the number.

        Ex: sp+nu +m +n

            nĪ   dĪ jē   = these umbrellas

                sàam bá jē = three umbrellas

            nĪ sàam bá jē = these three umbrellas

        (-)   sàam dĪ jē   -- doesn't occur

        (-)nĪ sàam dĪ jē   -- doesn't occur

           (See BC and Drills _1.5, 1.6_)

158

2. <u>Mass Nouns</u>

  a. Mass nouns designate substances which are perceived in the mass rather than as discrete units. For example:

<u>tòhng</u>   -   'sugar'

<u>séui</u>   -   'water'

<u>jyùyuhk</u>   -   'pork'

  b. When counted, mass nouns do not use individual measures. Instead they are counted in terms of their length, weight, or some other standard; or in terms of a container of their volume; or in terms of a segment of their whole.

Ex: <u>Nu.</u> +   <u>M</u>   +   <u>N</u>

sàam	bohng	tòhng	= three pounds of sugar
sàam	máh	bou	= three yards of cloth
sàam	bùi	chàh	= three cups of tea
sàam	faai	pāi	= three pieces of pie

Certain individual nouns may also be counted in terms of weight or other standard; but they are not limited to being counted this way:

Ex: sàam   bohng   cháang   = three pounds of oranges

           sàam   go   cháang   = three oranges

  c. Similarities and differences between individual and mass measures.

The standard/container/segment measures used in counting mass nouns occupy the same position in the sentence that individual measures occupy. The measures for mass nouns, however, differ from individual measures in not being in apposition with the following noun. They also differ in having independent meaning.

3. <u>dī</u>, general measure for mass nouns.

When mass nouns are particularized but not counted by number, the plural measure <u>dī</u> serves as general mass measure for all mass nouns. It is translated in English as 'the' in subject position, 'some,' 'a little,' in object position. Incorporated into a <u>nī</u> or <u>gó</u> compound, it translates as 'this' or 'that' in both subject and object positions.

159

Ex: 1. Nīdī ngàuhyuhk yiu luhk   1. This beef costs $6.00
    màn gàn.   a catty.

    2. Dī faahn dungjó.   2. The rice has totten cold.

    3. Ngóh séung máaih dī   3. I'd like to buy some beef.
    ngàuhyuhk.

    4. Néih séung yám dī mēyéh   4. You'd like to drink a little
    a?   what? (i.e. What would
                                     you like to drink?)

(See BC and Drills 6, 7, 10, 11, 12 for
subject position examples: See BC and Drills
1, 2, 3 for object position examples.)

4. haih ..X.. làih ga?
                  ge.

    haih ..X.. làih ga? (& ge) is a phrase frame which has the effect
of emphasizing the noun it envelopes.

    Ex: Nī dī haih mēyéh a?   What's this?

        Nī dī haih mēyéh làih   What in the world is this?
        ga?

        Gó go haih bīngo làih   Who in the world is that?
        ga?

(See BC and Drill 14)

    Note that the question: Nī dī haih mēyéh làih ga? permits the
mass/plural dī regardless of whether the object referred to is unit
or mass, or whether, if unit, is singular or plural. If the item is
singular, using the singular pronoun is also permitted.

    Ex: Q: Nī jī haih mēyéh   What's this?
           làih ga?

        A: Nī jī haih yùhnbāt   It's a pencil.
           làih ge.

    or Q: Nī dī haih mēyéh   What's this?
          làih ga?

        A: Nī dī haih yùhnbāt   It's a pencil.
           làih ge.

5. Money Measures.

    The unit of currency in Hong Kong is the Hong Kong dollar.
HK$1.00 = US$0.16 2/3; US$1.00 = approximately HK$6.00 in 1970.

    a. The money measures used in counting money are the following:

        1. māṇ = measure for 'dollar,' used when the figure is a
           round number. The word is derived from the first syllable
           of the English word 'money.'

160

2. <u>go ngàhnchín</u> = measure + noun. The compound of the two is
   used to represent 'dollar' when the figure is a round
   number. This form less common than the mān form for
   round number dollar figures. The basic meaning of
   ngàhnchín is 'money,' [literally 'silver-money']

       Ex: sàam gò ngàhnchín = three dollars

3. <u>go</u> = measure for 'dollar' when the figure is not a round
   number.

       Ex: $3.10 = sàam go yāt = three dollars one (dime)
                     = $3.10

4. <u>hòuh(jí)</u> = measure for 'dime,' used when the amount is
   less than one dollar.

       Ex: sàam hòuh(jí) = three dimes, i.e. thirty cents
   Note (in #3 above) that when dimes are part of a money
   expression which is larger than a dollar the dime
   measure is not stated. That a number following the
   dollar measure would indicate the dime number is predictable on the basis of the decimal system used in
   counting money.

5. The penny measure is not used in Hong Kong, except perhaps
   in banking. 5¢ is expressed, however, thus:

       sei hòuh bun = 4 dimes (and) half = 45¢
   In fact <u>bun</u> following any measure is left-bound to that
   measure, and means 'plus half that measure.'

       Ex: sàam go bun = three dollars and a half

b. '$1.00 apiece,' '$1.00 a pound' type phrases.

    In 'one dollar apiece' expressions in Cantonese the order of
parts is irreversible with the money part coming first. (In
English the order is often reversible: '5 cents for two/two for
5 cents.'

    In the Cantonese phrase, the last number of the money
measure must not directly precede the noun measure.

    Ex: (read across)

Nu	M	Nu	M		Nu	M	
1. sei	go	sei	ngàhnchìn			bá	⎫ 4 dollars 4 dimes
2. sei	go	sei			yāt	bá	⎬ for one [M] =
3. sei	go	sei	ngàhnchìn		yāt	bá	⎭ $4.40 each.
(-) 4. sei	go	sei				bá	(not said this way)
5. sei	go	sei	ngàhnchìn		léuhng	bá:	4 dollars 4 dimes for two [M] = 2 for $4.40

(See BC and Drills 1, 6, 16.1)

c. Omission of yāt in certain 'one dollar' phrases.

When the dollar amount is one dollar and a fraction, the numeral yāt preceding the dollar measure go is ordinarily omitted in the spoken language.

Ex: go yāt = a dollar ten cents ($1.10)

go yāt ngàhnchìn bohng = a dollar ten cents a pound
or go yat yat bohng   ($1.10 per pound)

(See Drill 1.3)

Yāt is required, however, if the expression reaches a three-figure number.

Ex: yāt go baat hòuh bun jí bohng = $1.85 per pound
yāt go baat hòuh bun   = $1.85

6. Words belonging to more than one grammatical category.

Ex: ngàhnchìn = noun and measure: 'money' [silver-money]

nu + m + nu + m	(+ n)	+ nu + m.
1. sei go sàam ngàhnchìn		léuhng bohng = $4.30 for 2 pounds
2. sàam go	ngàhnchìn	léuhng bohng = $3.00 for 2 pounds
3. sàam mān		léuhng bohng = $3.00 for 2 pounds

In Sentence #1 above, ngàhnchìn is a measure, in #2 a noun. In comparison with English, there are relatively few words in Cantonese which belong to more than one grammatical category.

III. DRILLS

1. Expansion Drill: Repeat after the teacher:

1. a. Gàn.
   b. Géidō chín gàn a?
   c. Ngàuhyuhk géidō chín gàn a?
   d. Dī ngàuhyuhk géidō chín gàn a?
   e. Dī ngàuhyuhk maaih géidō chín gàn a?
   f. Gó dī ngàuhyuhk maaih géidō chín gàn a?
   g. Gó dī ngàuhyuhk maaih ńgh mān gàn.

+ 2. a. Yú
   b. Dī yú.
   c. Nī dī yú.
   d. Nī dī yú géidō chín gàn a?
   e. Nī dī yú sàam go sei ngàhnchín gàn.

3. a. Go yih.
      (go + number, in a money phrase = one dollar and X number dimes)
   b. Go yih ngàhnchín.
+ c. Go yih ngàhnchín bàau.
+ d. Yīnjái go yih ngàhnchín bàau.
   e. Dī yīnjái go yih ngàhnchín bàau.
   f. Nī dī yīnjái go yih ngàhnchín bàau.
   g. Kéuih wah nī dī yīnjái go yih ngàhnchín bàau.

+ 4. a. máh
   b. Géidō chín máh a?
+ c. Dī bou géidō chín máh a?
      [cloth, fabric, material]

1. a. Catty (1-1/3 pounds)
   b. How much per catty?
   c. How much is beef per catty.
   d. How much is the beef per catty?
   e. How much does the beef sell for per catty?
   f. How much does that beef sell for per catty?
   g. That beef sells for five dollars per catty.

2. a. Fish
   b. The fish (in the mass) or These fish.
   c. This fish (in the mass) or These fish.
   d. How much is this fish per catty? or ...are these fish.
   e. This fish is $3.40 per catty. or These are ...

3. a. $1.20
   b. $1.20
   c. $1.20 per pack(age)
   d. Cigarettes are $1.20 per pack.
   e. The cigarettes are $1.20 per pack.
   f. These cigarettes are $1.20 per pack.
   g. He says these cigarettes are $1.20 per pack.

4. a. yard (in length)
   b. How much per yard?
   c. How much is the cloth per yard?

163

d. Nĭ dĭ bou géidō chĭn máh a?

d. How much is this cloth per yard?

e. Nĭ dĭ bou géidō chĭn léuhng máh a?

e. How much is this cloth for 2 yards? How much is 2 yards of this cloth?

f. Nĭ dĭ bou yahgáu mān léuhng máh.

f. This cloth is $29 for 2 yards.

+ 5. a. <u>syù</u>

5. a. <u>book</u>

+   b. <u>bún syù</u> (<u>M. for book</u>)

b. a/the book

c. Nĭ bún syù

c. this book

d. Nĭ bún syù dĭm maaih a?

d. How much is this book? <u>or</u> How much does this book sell for?

e. Nĭ léuhng bún syù dĭm maaih a?

e. How much do these 2 books sell for?

f. Nĭ léuhng bún syù maaih yah mān.

f. These two books are $20.00.

g. Nĭ léuhng bún syù maaih yihsahp mān bún.

g. These two books are $20.00 each.

+ 6. a. <u>Gāi.</u>

6. a. <u>Chicken.</u>

+   b. <u>Jek gāi.</u> (<u>M. for chicken</u>)

b. A/the chicken.

c. Léuhng jek gāi.

c. 2 chickens

d. Nĭ léuhng jek gāi.

d. These 2 chickens.

e. Nĭ léuhng jek gāi sei mān gàn.

e. These 2 chickens are $4 a catty.

f. Nĭ léuhng jek gāi maaih sei mān gàn.

f. These 2 chickens sell for $4 per catty.

g. Nĭ léuhng jek gāi maaih sei go bun ngàhnchĭn gàn.

g. These 2 chickens sell for $4.50 per catty.

h. Kéuih wah nĭ léuhng jek gāi maaih sei go bun ngàhnchĭn gàn.

h. He says these 2 chickens sell for $4.50 per catty.

+ 7. a. <u>Hàaih.</u>

7. a. <u>Shoe</u>

b. Jek hàaih.

b. the/a shoe

c. Béi jek hàaih ngóh.

c. Give me the shoe.

d. Ńhgói néih béi jek hàaih ngóh.

d. Please give me the shoe.

Comment: <u>jek</u> is also the M. for <u>maht</u>, 'socks,' 'stockings.'

2. Response Drill

  Ex: T: Ngóh séung máaih T: I want to buy some beef.
     dī ngàuhyuhk.

    S: Kéuih dōu séung   S: He also wants to buy some beef.
     máaih dī ngàuhyuhk.

1. Ngóh séung máaih bá jē.   1. Kéuih dōu séung máaih bá jē.

2. Ngóh séung máaih dī jyùyuhk. 2. Kéuih dōu séung máaih dī jyùyuhk.

3. Ngóh séung máaih bāau yīnjái. 3. Kéuih dōu séung máaih bāau yīnjái.

4. Ngóh séung máaih dī tòhng. 4. Kéuih dōu séung máaih dī tòhng.

5. Ngóh séung máaih tìuh yú. 5. Kéuih dōu séung máaih tìuh yú.

6. Ngóh séung máaih jī bējáu. 6. Kéuih dōu séung máaih jī bējáu.

7. Ngóh séung máaih gihn sēutsāam. 7. Kéuih dōu séung máaih gihn sēutsāam.

---

3. Conversation Drill

  Ex: T: /dī jyùyuhk/   T: /some pork/

    S1: Máaih mēyéh a? S1: May I help you?

    S2: Ngóh séung máaih dī S2: I'd like to buy some pork.
     jyùyuhk.

1. /dī ngàuhyuhk/   1. A. Máaih mēyéh a?
            B. Ngóh séung máaih dī ngàuhyuhk.

2. /bāau yīnjái/   2. A. Máaih mēyéh a?
            B. Ngóh séung máaih bāau yīnjái.

3. /jek gāi/   3. A. Máaih mēyéh a?
            B. Ngóh séung máaih jek gāi.

4. /bohng tòhng/   4. A. Máaih mēyéh a?
            B. Ngóh séung máaih bohng tòhng.

5. /dī jyùyuhk/   5. A. Máaih mēyéh a?
            B. Ngóh séung máaih dī jyùyuhk.

6. /tìuh yú/   6. A. Máaih mēyéh a?

                                             B. Ngóh séung máaih tìuh yú.

7. /deui hàaih/   7. A. Máaih mēyéh a?

                                             B. Ngóh séung máaih deui
                                                hàaih.

---

4. Transformation Drill

    Ex: T: Nī gihn sēutsāam   How much is this shirt?
          géidō chín a?

      S: Nī dī sēutsāam géidō   How much are these shirts
        chín gihn a?   apiece?

1. Nī bāau yīnjái géidō chín a?   1. Nī dī yīnjái géidō chín
                                             bāau a?

2. Nī bá jē géidō chín a?   2. Nī dī jē géidō chín bá a?

3. Nī deui hàaih géidō chín a?   3. Nī dī hàaih géidō chín
                                             deui a?

4. Nī gihn yúhlāu géidō chín a?   4. Nī dī yúhlāu géidō chín
                                             gihn a?

5. Nī tìuh fu géidō chín a?   5. Nī dī fu géidō chín tìuh a?

6. Nī gihn sāam géidō chín a?   6. Nī dī sāam géidō chín gihn
                                             a?

    Comment: The individual Measures mean 'apiece,' 'each,'
        following a money phrase: Standard Measures mean
        'per M.'

        Ex: Nī dī gāi sei   These chickens are $4.00
           mān gàn.   per catty.

          Nī dī yùhnbāt   These pencils are 30¢ each.
          sāam hòuhjí jí.

          Nī dī yùhnbāt   These pencils are 60¢ for
          luhk hòuhjí   two.
          léuhng jí.

---

5. Substitution Drill

    Ex: T: jyùyuhk /gàn/   T: pork /catty/
      S: Nī dī jyùyuhk géidō   S: How much is this pork per
      chín gàn a?   catty?

1. /ngàuhyuhk /gàn/   1. Nī dī ngàuhyuhk géidō chín
                                             gàn a?

2. /sēutsāam/gihn/   2. Nǐ dǐ sēutsāam géidō chǐn
                                     gihn a?

3. /gāi/jek/   3. Nǐ dǐ gāi géidō chǐn jek a?

4. /bējáu/jǐ/   4. Nǐ dǐ bējáu géidō chǐn jǐ a?

5. /yǐnjái/bāau/   5. Nǐ dǐ yǐnjái géidō chǐn bāau
                                     a?

6. /tòhng/bohng/   6. Nǐ dǐ tòhng géidō chǐn
                                     bohng a?

7. /cháang/go/   7. Nǐ dǐ cháang géidō chǐn go a?

8. /pǐhnggwó/go/   8. Nǐ dǐ pǐhnggwó géidō chǐn
                                     go a?

9. /jǐu/gàn/   9. Nǐ dǐ jǐu géidō chǐn gàn a?

10. /dáifu/tǐuh/   10. Nǐ dǐ dáifu géidō chǐn tǐuh
                                     a?

---

6. Transformation Drill

Ex: T: Nǐ dǐ ngàuhyuhk   T: This beef is $3.60 per catty.
       sàam go luhk
       ngàhnchǐn gàn.

S1: Nǐ dǐ ngàuyuhk géidō   S1: How much is this beef per
    chǐn gàn a?   catty?

S2: Sàam go luhk $3.60 per catty.
    ngàhnchǐn gàn.

1. Nǐ dǐ jyùyuhk sei man gàn.   1. A. Nǐ dǐ jyùyuhk géidō chǐn
                                       gàn a?

                                    B. Sei māan gàn.

2. Nǐ dǐ ngàuhyuhk ńgh māan bohng.   2. A. Nǐ dǐ ngàuhyuhk géidō
                                           chǐn bohng a?

                                        B. Ńgh māan bohng.

3. Nǐ dǐ yǐnjái go yih ngàhnchǐn   3. A. Nǐ dǐ yǐnjái géidō chǐn
   bāau.   bāau a?

                                      B. Go yih ngàhnchǐn bāau.

4. Nǐ dǐ dáikwàhn léuhng māan tǐuh.   4. A. Nǐ dǐ dáikwàhn géidō
                                           chǐn tǐuh a?

                                        B. Léuhng māan tǐuh.

5. Nǐ dǐ dáikwàhn go yih ngàhnchǐn   5. A. Nǐ dǐ dáikwàhn géidō
   gihn.   chǐn gihn a?

                                      B. Go yih ngàhnchǐn gihn.

167

7. Alteration Drill

    Ex: T: Nǐ dǐ ngàuhyuhk   T: How do you sell this beef? or
           dǐm maaih a?   What does this beef sell for?

        S: Nǐ dǐ ngàuhyuhk géi-   S: How much is this beef per
           dō chǐn gàn a?   catty?

    1. Nǐ dǐ jyùyuhk dǐm maaih a?   1. Nǐ dǐ jyùyuhk géidō chǐn
       /gàn/   gàn a?

    2. Nǐ dǐ gāi dǐm maaih a? /gàn/   2. Nǐ dǐ gāi géidō chǐn gàn a?

    3. Nǐ dǐ yú dǐm maaih a? /gàn/   3. Nǐ dǐ yú géidō chǐn gàn a?

    4. Nǐ dǐ bējáu dǐm maaih a? /jǐ/ 4. Nǐ dǐ bējáu géidō chǐn jǐ a?

    5. Nǐ dǐ tòhng dǐm maaih a?   5. Nǐ dǐ tòhng géidō chǐn
       /bohng/   bohng a?

    6. Nǐ dǐ yǐnjái dǐm maaih a?   6. Nǐ dǐ yǐnjái géidō chǐn
       /bàau/   bāau a?

_____

8. Response Drill: Answer with '2' each time.

    Ex: T: Néih oi m̀hoi yǐnjái   T: Do you want cigarettes?
           a?

        S: Oi - Béi léuhng   S: Yes - Give me two packs
           bāau ngóh lā.   please.

    1. Néih oi m̀hoi bējáu a?   1. Oi - Béi léuhng jǐ ngóh lā.

    2. Néih oi m̀hoi yǐnjái a?   2. Oi - Béi léuhng bāau ngóh
                                         lā.

    3. Néih oi m̀hoi ngàuhyuhk a?   3. Oi - Béi léuhng gàn ngóh lā.

    4. Néih oi m̀hoi tòhng a?   4. Oi - Béi léuhng bohng ngóh
                                         lā.

    5. Néih oi m̀hoi heiséui a?   5. Oi - Béi léuhng jǐ ngóh lā.

    6. Néih oi m̀hoi yǐnjái a? /jǐ/   6. Oi - Béi léuhng jǐ ngóh lā.

            (M for one cigarette)

_____

9. Response Drill

    Ex: 1. T: Ńgh bohng gau   T: Is five pounds enough?
              m̀hgau a? /nod/

        S: Gau laak.   S: That's enough.

168

2. T: Ǹgh bohng gau   T: Is five pounds enough?
      m̀hgau a? /shake/

   S: M̀hgau. Ngóh oi luhk S: No, I want to get six pounds.
      bohng.

   Note: Answer with one more than the given number in
         response to the negative cue.

1. Sei bohng gau m̀hgau a? /nod/   1. Gau laak.

2. Léuhng bāau gau m̀hgau a? /shake/ 2. M̀hgau. Ngóh oi sàam bāau.

3. Luhk gàn gau m̀hgau a? /shake/   3. M̀hgau. Ngóh oi chāt gàn.

4. Sàam jí gau m̀hgau a? /nod/   4. Gau laak.

5. Yāt jek gau m̀hgau a? /shake/   5. M̀hgau. Ngóh oi léuhng jek.

6. Chāt gihn gau m̀hgau a? /nod/   6. Gau laak.

7. Ǹgh tìuh gau m̀hgau a? /nod/   7. Gau laak.

8. Baat deui gau m̀hgau a? /shake/   8. M̀hgau. Ngóh oi gáu deui.

9. Gáu go gau m̀hgau a? /shake/   9. M̀hgau. Ngóh oi sahp go.

---

10. Conversation Drill

   Ex: A: Nǐ dǐ yǐnjái dím   A. What do these cigarettes sell
         maaih a?   for?

       B: Go yih ngàhnchín   B. $1.20 per pack. How many packs
          bàau. Néih máaih   do you want?
          géidō bàau a?

       A: Yāt bāau gau laak.   A. One pack is enough.

1. A. Nǐ dǐ jyùyuhk ......?   1. A. Nǐ dǐ jyùhyuhk dím
                                         maaih a?

   B. Ǹgh go sei ngàhnchín gàn.   B. Ǹgh go sei ngàhnchín gàn.
                                      Néih máaih géidō gàn
                                      a?

   A. Yāt ....   A. Yāt gàn gau laak.

2. A. Nǐ dǐ bējáu ......?   2. A. Nǐ dǐ bējáu dím maaih a?

   B. Go baat ngàhnchín jí.   B. Go baat ngàhnchín jí.
                                      Néih máaih géidō jí a?

   A. Luhk ......   A. Luhk jí gau laak.

3. A. Nǐ dǐ fu ....?   3. A. Nǐ dǐ fu dím maaih a?

   B. Yahluhk go baat ngàhnchín   B. Yahluhk go baat ngàhnchín
      tìuh.   tìuh. Néih máaih géidō
                                      tìuh a?

   A. Yāt ....   A. Yāt tìuh gau laak.

169

4. A. Nī dī bou ....
   B. Sahpchāt mān máh ......

   A. Sàam ....

5. A. Nī dī tòhng ....?
   B. Luhk hòuhjí bohng....

   A. Yāt ....

6. A. Nī dī maht ....
   B. Léuhng go bun ngàhnchín
      deui ....

   A. Léuhng ....

4. A. Nī dī bou dím maaih a?
   B. Sahpchāt mān máh.
      Néih máaih géidō máh a?

   A. Sàam máh gau laak.

5. A. Nī dī tòhng dím maaih a?
   B. Luhk hòuhjí bohng.
      Néih máaih géidō bohng
      a?

   A. Yāt bohng gau laak.

6. A. Nī dī maht dím maaih a?
   B. Léuhng go bun ngàhnchín
      deui. Néih máaih géidō
      deui a?

   A. Léuhng deui gau laak.

---

11. Combining Drill

Ex: T: Nī dī haih tòhng.
      Béi sàam bohng
      ngóh lā.

    S: Béi sàam bohng nī
      dī ngóh lā.

T: This is sugar.
    Give me three pounds.

S: Give me three pounds of this.

1. Nī dī haih pìhnggwó.
   Béi luhk go pìhnggwó ngóh lā.

2. Nī dī haih bou.
   Béi léuhng máh bou ngóh lā.

3. Nī dī haih yùhnbāt.
   Béi sei jì yùhnbāt ngóh lā.

4. Nī dī haih syù.
   Béi bún syù ngóh lā.

5. Nī dī haih heiséui.
   Béi sàam jì heiséui ngóh lā.

6. Nī dī haih yú.
   Béi tìuh yú ngóh lā.

1. Béi luhk go nī dī ngóh lā.
   Give me six of these.

2. Béi léuhng máh nī dī ngóh
   lā.

3. Béi sei jì nī dī ngóh lā.

4. Béi bún nī dī ngóh lā.

5. Béi sàam jì nī dī ngóh lā.

6. Béi tìuh nī dī ngóh lā.

---

12. Response Drill

    Ex: T: Nī dī haih jē.   T: These are umbrellas.

        S: M̀hgòi néih béi bá   S: Please give me one.
           ngóh lā!

1. Nī dī haih bāt.   1. M̀hgòi néih béi jī ngóh lā!
2. Nī dī haih syù.   2. M̀hgòi néih béi bún ngóh lā!
3. Nī dī haih yùhnbāt.   3. M̀hgòi néih béi jī ngóh lā!
4. Nī dī haih pìhnggwó.   4. M̀hgòi néih béi go ngóh lā!
5. Nī dī haih béng.   5. M̀hgòi néih béi go ngóh lā!

---

13. Conversation Drill:

    Ex: T: géi jek jīu   a few bananas

       S1: M̀hgòi béi géi jek   Please give me a few bananas.
           jīu ngóh lā.

       S2: Béi géi jek mēyéh wá? Give a few whats, did you say?

       S1: Géi jek jīu.   A few bananas.

1. géi go pìhnggwó   1. S1: M̀hgòi béi géi go pìhng-
                          gwó ngóh lā.
                     S2: Béi géi go mēyéh wá?
                     S1: Géi go pìhnggwó.

2. géi tìuh tāai   2. S1: M̀hgòi béi géi tìuh tāai
                          ngóh lā.
                     S2: Béi géi tìuh mēyéh wá?
                     S1: Géi tìuh tāai.

3. géi go cháang   3. S1: M̀hgòi béi géi go cháang
                          ngóh lā.
                     S2: Béi géi go mēyéh wá?
                     S1: Géi go cháang.

4. géi jī yùhnjíbāt   4. S1: M̀hgòi béi géi jī yùhn-
                          jíbāt ngóh lā.
                     S2: Béi géi jī mēyéh wá?
                     S1: Géi jī yùhnjíbāt.

5. géi bāau yīn   5. S1: M̀hgòi béi géi bāau yīn
                          ngóh lā.
                     S2: Béi géi bāau mēyéh wá?
                     S1: Géi bāau yīn.

14. Question & Answer Drill: Teacher gives cue by pointing to objects,
    or pictures of them. Props required: apple, orange, ball point pen,
    etc.
        Ex: T: (pencil)
            S1: Nī dī haih mēyéh   S1: What's this?
                làih ga?

            S2: Yùhnbāt. Gó dī   S2: A pencil. That's a pencil. or
                haih yùhnbāt.   Pencils. Those are pencils.

            S1: Géidō jí nē? /4/   S1: How many? /unit/
                (holds up fingers)

            S2: Sei jí.   S2: 4.

    1. (apple)   1. A. Nī dī haih mēyéh làih ga?
                                     B. Pìhnggwó. Gó dī haih
                                        pìhnggwó.
                                     A. Géidō go nē? /3/
                                     B. Sàam go.

    2. (orange)   2. A. Nī dī haih mēyéh làih ga?
                                     B. Cháang. Gó dī haih cháang.
                                     A. Géidō go nē? /1/
                                     B. Yāt go.

    3. (ball point pen)   3. A. Nī dī haih mēyéh làih ga?
                                     B. Yùhnjíbāt. Gó dī haih
                                        yùhnjíbāt.
                                     A. Géidō jí nē? /6/
                                     B. Luhk jí.

    4. (pack of cigarettes)   4. A. Nī dī haih mēyéh làih ga?
                                     B. Yīnjái. Gó dī haih yīnjái.
                                     A. Géidō bāau nē? /2/
                                     B. Léuhng bāau.

    5. (book)   5. A. Gó dī haih mēyéh làih ga?
                                     B. Syù. Gó dī haih syù.
                                     A. Géidō bún nē? /1/
                                     B. Yāt bún.

———

15. Substitution Drill: Teacher writes numbers on the blackboard to
    cue the students.

        Ex: T: $12.40   T: $12.40

15. Substitution Drill: Teacher writes numbers on the blackboard to cue the students.

Ex: T: $12.40

S: Nī gihn sēutsāam maaih sahpyih go sei.

T: $12.40

S: This shirt sells for $12.40.

1. $12.20
2. $13.60
3. $13.20
4. $13.50
5. $15.90

1. Nī gihn sēutsāam maaih sahpyih go yih.
2. Nī gihn sēutsāam maaih sahpsàam go luhk.
3. Nī gihn sēutsāam maaih sahpsàam go yih.
4. Nī gihn sēutsāam maaih sahpsàam go bun.
5. Nī gihn sēutsāam maaih sahpńgh go gáu.

a. Continue, with other numbers.

16. Expansion Drill

1. a. ngàuhnáaih.
   b. Dī ngàuhnáaih.
   c. Dī ngàuhnáaih go baat ngàhnchín jī.
   d. Dī ngàuhnáaih yiu go baat ngàhnchín jī.

   a. milk
   b. the milk, or some milk
   c. The milk is $1.80 a bottle.
   d. The milk costs $1.80 a bottle.

2. a. jīu
   b. dī jīu.
   c. dī jīu ńgh hòuhjí gàn.
   d. Dī jīu maaih ńgh hòuhjí gàn.
   e. Dī jīu haih m̀haih maaih ńgh hòuhjí gàn a?

   a. bananas
   b. the bananas or some bananas
   c. the bananas are 50¢ a catty.
   d. The bananas sell for 50¢ a catty.
   e. Do the bananas sell for 50¢ a catty?

IV. CONVERSATIONS FOR LISTENING

    (On tape. Listen to tape with book closed.)

V. SAY IT IN CANTONESE

A. In a grocery store, the clerk asks:

  1. What do you want to buy?

  2. Is 5 pounds of sugar enough?

  3. Whether you'd like to buy some fish.

  4. How many packs (of cigarettes) do you want?

B. And the customer answers:

  1. I want some beef, and also some pork and milk.

  2. 5 pounds is not enough-- give me 10 pounds.

  3. Yes, I'd like to buy one fish.

  4. Two packs are enough.

C. In a grocery store, the customer asks:

  1. How much does the beef sell for?

  2. How much are these cigarettes?

  3. Is this fish $3.00 a catty?

  4. What is this?

  5. These bananas are 80¢ a catty, aren't they?

  6. These apples are 30¢ each, aren't they?

  7. How much is the sugar per pound?

D: And the clerk answers:

  1. It's $5.80 a catty.

  2. They're $1.20 a pack.

  3. No, this is $2.80 a catty-- those (pointing) are $3.00 a catty.

  4. That's pork--would you like some?

  5. Yes, 80¢ a catty.--how many catties would you like?

  6. No, the apples are 50¢ each-- the oranges are 30¢ each.

  7. It's 75¢ a pound.

Vocabulary Checklist for Lesson 7

1.	bàau	m:	package, M. for cigarette pack
2.	bohng	m:	pound
3.	bou	n:	cloth
4.	bún	m:	M. for book
5.	-bun	nu:	half
6.	dī	m:	some, the
7.	gāi	n:	chicken
8.	gàn	m:	catty, unit of weight ca 1 1/3 lb
9.	gó dī	sp+m:	those (in reference to unit nouns); that (in reference to mass nouns)
10.	haih...làih ge Ph:		is..(grammatical structure giving emphasis to enclosed noun)
11.	hòuh(jí)	m:	dime
12.	jek	m:	M. for chicken, shoe, sock, ship.
13.	jí	m:	M. for cigarette
14.	jyùyuhk	n:	pork
15.	...làih ge		see: haih...làih ge
16.	maaih	v:	sell
17.	máh	m:	yard (in length)
18.	ngàhnchín	n/m:	money [silver-money]
19.	ngàuhyuhk	n:	beef
20.	nī dī	sp+m:	these (in reference to unit nouns) this (in reference to mass nouns)
21.	ngoi	v:	var. of oi, want, want to have, want to possess
22.	oi	v:	want, want to have, want to possess
23.	syù	n:	book
24.	tòhng	n:	sugar
25.	yātyeuhng nuM/adj:		same
26.	yīnjái	n:	cigarette
27.	yú	n:	fish

I. BASIC CONVERSATION

A. Buildup:

(Buying socks at a department store:)

Guhaak

dyún	short
dyún maht	socks
baahk-	white
baahk dyún maht	white socks
yáuh	have; there is/are
móuh	not have; there is/are not
yáuh móuh?	have/not have? do you have? is there? are there?
yáuh móuh maht?	do (you) have socks?
yáuh móuh baahk dyún maht	do you have white socks? or are there any white socks?

Yáuh móuh baahk dyún maht maaih a? — Do you have white socks for sale?

Sauhfoyùhn

Yáuh. — Yes. [Have]

jeuk — wear (clothes)

Haih m̀haih néih jeuk ga? — Are they for you? [ones for you to wear?]

Guhaak

Haih. — That's right.

Sauhfoyùhn

houh	number; size
géi houh?	what size?

Jeuk géi houh a? — What size do you wear?

Guhaak

Gáu houh. — Number nine.

Sauhfoyùhn

pèhng	cheap
leng	pretty
yauh	also

yauh pèhng yauh leng   both cheap and pretty

Nī dī yauh pèhng yauh leng.   These are both cheap and
                                     pretty.

jùngyi   like; like to

jùng m̀hjùngyi a?   do you like (it/them)?

Néih jùng m̀hjùngyi a?   Do you like them?

Guhaak

hóu   good, nice

géi hóu   quite nice, pretty nice

daaih   big

m̀hgau daaih   not big enough

Géi hóu, daahnhaih m̀hgau daaih.   They're quite nice, but they're
                                     not big enough.

-dī   somewhat--, a little bit--

daaihdī   a little larger

daaihdī ge   larger one (or ones)

Yáuhmóuh daaihdī ge nē?   Do you have any little bit
                                     larger ones?

Sauhfoyùhn

-saai   completely

maaihsaai laak.   all sold out

Deuimhjyuh--daaihdī ge dōu   I'm sorry, the larger ones are
   maaihsaai laak.   all sold out.

hāak-   black

hāaksīk   black color

hóu m̀hhóu?   is (that) all right?

Hāaksīk, hóu m̀hhóu a?   Would black be all right?

Hāaksīk dōu hóu leng ga.   The black are also very pretty.

Guhaak

Hóu aak.   All right.

Sauhfoyùhn

Nī dī sàam mān, nīdī sàam go   These are three dollars, and
   bun.   these are three and a half.

bīn-?   which?

júng   kind, type

Néih ngoi bīn júng a?   Which ones do you want?

            <u>Guhaak</u>

    sàam go bun ge   the three-fifty ones (or
                        one)

Oi sàam go bun ge lā.   I'd like the $3.50 ones.

            <u>Sauhfoyùhn</u>

    dā   dozen
    máaih bun dā   buy half a dozen
    àh   sentence suffix adding force
                     of 'I suppose' to sentence
                     it attaches to.

Máaih bun dā àh.   You'll take a half a dozen, I
                     suppose.

            <u>Guhaak</u>

    dò   much, many
Ṁhsái gam dò.   (I) don't need that many.
Sàam deui gau laak.   Three pairs are enough.

B. <u>Recapitulation</u>:

            <u>Guhaak</u>

Yáuh móuh baahk dyún maht   Do you have white socks for
  maaih a?   sale?

            <u>Sauhfoyùhn</u>

Yáuh. Haih ṁhhaih néih jeuk ga?   Yes. Are they for you?

            <u>Guhaak</u>

Haih.   That's right.

            <u>Sauhfoyùhn</u>

Jeuk géi houh a?   What size do you wear?

            <u>Guhaak</u>

Gáu houh.   Number nine.

            <u>Sauhfoyùhn</u>

Nī dī yauh pèhng yauh leng.   These are both cheap and
  Néih jùng ṁhjùngyi a?   pretty. Do you like them?

            <u>Guhaak</u>

Géi hóu, daahṁhaih ṁhgau   They're quite nice, but they're

daaih.	not big enough.
Yáuh móuh daaihdĪ ge nē?	Do you have any larger ones?

<u>Sauhfoyùhn</u>

Deuimhjyuh--daaihdĪ ge	I'm sorry, the larger ones are
dōu maaihsaai laak.	all sold out.
HāaksĪk, hóu mhhóu a?	Would black be all right?
HāaksĪk dōu hóu leng ga.	The black are also very pretty.

<u>Guhaak</u>

Hóu aak.	All right.

<u>Sauhfoyùhn</u>

NĪ dĪ sàam mān, nĪ dĪ sàam	These are three dollars, these
go bun.	are $3.50.
Néih ngoi bĪn júng nē?	Which ones do you want?

<u>Guhaak</u>

Oi sàam go bun ge lā.	I'd like the three-fifty ones,
	please.

<u>Sauhfoyùhn</u>

Máaih bun dā àh.	Half a dozen, I suppose.

<u>Guhaak</u>

Mhsái gam dò. Sàam deui gau	I don't need so many. Three
laak.	pairs are enough.

+ + + + + + + + + + + + +

Pronunciation Practice:

1. <u>yun</u> as in <u>dyún</u>

    <u>yun</u> is a two-part final composed of the high front rounded vowel <u>yu</u> [ü], plus the dental nasal consonant <u>n</u>. The <u>yu</u> is an open vowel before the nasal final, and being a rounded vowel, has a rounding effect on a consonant preceding it in the same syllable, as well as the consonant following it.

    Listen and repeat:

短   1. dyún   , dyún   , dyún   .

鉛筆   2. yùhnbāt (5 times separately)

短鉛   3. dyún yùhn   , yùhn dyún   . 鉛短

鉛短   4. yùhn dyún   , dyún yùhn   . 短鉛

2. <u>yu</u>/<u>yun</u> contrasts

> Listen and repeat: (Watch the teacher)
>> 1. yú yú 魚 , dyún dyún 短 .
>> 2. dyún dyún   , yú yú   .
>> 3. dyún yú   , yú dyún   .

3. <u>euk</u> in <u>jeuk</u>, (ng)<u>āamjeuk</u>

> <u>euk</u> is a two-part final composed of the rounded mid front vowel
> <u>eu</u> plus the velar stop consonant <u>k</u>. In final position in a syllable,
> <u>k</u> is unreleased--[k˺]. Before <u>k</u>, the positioning for <u>eu</u> is the same
> as that for <u>eu</u> before <u>ng</u>--raised mid front rounded--[ø]. Lips are
> rounded for the vowel and also for consonants preceding and following
> it in a syllable.

> Listen and repeat: (Watch the teacher)
> 著 1. jeuk jeuk jeuk   ; jeuk   , jeuk   ,
>> jeuk   .
> 喘著 2. āamjeuk āamjeuk   .
>> 3. ngāamjeuk ngāamjeuk   .

4. <u>euk</u>/<u>eung</u> contrasts

> Listen and repeat: (Note that tongue and lip position
>> is the same for <u>eu</u> before <u>k</u> as it is for <u>eu</u> before
>> <u>ng</u>.)
>>> 1. jeuk, jeuk   , Jèung, Jèung   .
>>> 2. jeuk Jèung   , Jèung jeuk   .
>>> 3. jeuk séung   , jeuk léuhng   ,
>>> 4. jeuk chèuhng   , jeuk yātyèuhng   .

5. <u>euk</u>/<u>eut</u> contrasts

> Listen and repeat: (Note that the tongue position for
>> <u>eu</u> before the dental <u>t</u> is somewhat lower than its
>> position before the velar <u>k</u>.)
>>> 1. jeuk jeuk   , sēut sēut   .
>>> 2. jeuk sāam   , sēutsāam   .
>>> 3. sēutsāam   , jeuk sāam   .

6. <u>ek</u> as in <u>jek</u>

> <u>ek</u> is a two-part final composed of the mid front unrounded vowel
> <u>e</u> [E] plus the velar stop consonant <u>k</u>. In final position in a
> syllable, <u>k</u> is unreleased--[k˺]. The American counterpart of the

Cantonese ek is the eck in 'peck,' although in final position the
American k is not necessarily unreleased--it may or may not be, with
no significant difference.

Listen and repeat:

jek   (5 times) 隻

7. eng as in leng, pèhng, béng, tèng

eng is a two-part final composed of the mid front unrounded vowel
e [E] plus the velar nasal consonant ng. The e is like the e in the
American 'bet.' It is an open vowel before the nasal final.

Listen and repeat, comparing English and Cantonese:

(Read across)

	English	Cantonese	
1.	bet	béng	餅
2.	pet	pèhng	平
3.	let	leng	靚
4.	Tet	tèng	聽

8. ut as in fut, 'wide' (See Drill 3)

ut is a two-part final composed of the high back rounded vowel u
plus the dental stop consonant t. The tongue position for t is like
that for English words ending with t--the tip of the tongue stops the
flow of air at the dental ridge behind the upper teeth. In final
position the Cantonese t is unreleased--[t˺]. u before t is produced
the same as was u finally and u before n--as a high back rounded vowel
[u] with tongue position somewhat higher than for u before k and ng.
Before t the u is relatively long and has a slight offglide to high
central position--[u·ᵘ̇] [u·ᵘ̇t].

Listen and repeat:

濶 fut   , fut   , fut   , fut   , fut   .

9. u/ut contrasts

u before t is similar to u as a one-part final; both are high
back rounded vowels, but u before t has a slight offglide to high
central position [uᵘ̇t].

Listen and repeat:

褲 1. fu fu fu   , fu fu fu   .
濶 2. fut fut fut   , fut fut fut   .

181

3. fu fut   , fu fut   , fu fut   ,
    fut fu   , fut fu   , fut fu   .

10. ut/un contrasts

     u before t is pronounced the same as u before n, rather long, and
with a slight forward offglide before the final consonant--[u•ủt'],
[u:ủn].

                    Listen and repeat:
                    1. fut fut   , bun bun   .
                    2. fut bun   , bun fut   .
                    3. bun bun   , fut fut   .

11. ut/uk contrasts

     Tongue position for u before k is slightly lower than that for u
before t, and the vowel is relatively short before k and long before
t--[Uˇk'], [u:ủt'].

                    Listen and repeat:
                    1. fut fut   , luhk luhk   .
                    2. ngàuhyuhk yuhk, yuhk   , fut fut   .
                    3. fut yuhk   , fut luʰ ̣   , luhk yuhk fut
                        fut   .

12. ak/aak contrasts

                    Listen and repeat:
                    1. dāk dāk 得 , hāak hāak 黑 .
                    2. dāk hāak   , hāak dāk   .
                    3. jaak jaak ('narrow') 窄 , jaak dāk   .
                    4. hāak dāk   , jaak dāk   , baahk dāk   .
                    5. hāak hāak   , jaak jaak   , baahk baahk   ,
                        dāk dāk   .

II. NOTES

1. The verb ya̋uh, 'have,' 'there is/are'

   a. ya̋uh is irregular in that its negative is not 'm̀hya̋uh' but mőuh.
      It patterns like other verbs in the affirmative, negative
      and choice questions:

      Ex: aff: ya̋uh   = have; there is

          neg: mőuh   = don't have; there isn't

          q: ya̋uh mőuh ...? = do (you) have?; is there?

      (See BC and Drills <u>1.1, 1.3, 8</u>)

2. <u>Adjectives</u>

   a. Adjectives are descriptive words. Words like <u>daaih</u>, 'big,' and
      <u>dyűn</u>, 'short,' are adjectives.

   b. From the grammatical point of view an adjective is a word that
      fits into certain positions in a sentence. A word which may
      be preceded by the following words and word groups is classed
      as an adjective in Cantonese:

      | hőu | very |
      | géi | quite |
      | m̀hhaih géi | not very |
      | m̀hhaih hőu | not exceptionally |

      (See BC and Drills <u>4, 5</u>)

   c. A word which is an adjective in Cantonese may translate into
      another part of speech in English. For example, nga̅amjeuk
      'fits, fits well' is an adjective in Cantonese, because it
      patterns like an adjective, whereas the English equivalent
      expression 'fit' is a verb:

      Nῑ gihn se̅utsa̅am = This shirt fits well.
        hőu nga̅amjeuk.   [This shirt is very well-fitting.]

      <u>hőusihk</u> 'good to eat,' 'tasty,' and <u>hőuya̋m</u> 'good to
      drink,' 'tasty,' are also adjectives, since they pattern like
      adjectives. They can be modified with the set of words, 'géi,'
      'hőu,' etc. that modify adjectives.

      1. Nῑ go pῐhnggwő hőu   This apple is very tasty.
         hőusihk.   (i.e., tastes good.)

      2. Dῑ be̅jáu hőu hőuya̋m.   The beer is very tasty.
                                     (i.e., tastes good.)

      (See Drill <u>2</u>)

183

d. Adjectives in Cantonese, unlike English, do not require the
   equivalent of the verb 'is' to serve as the predicate.

   Compare:

Cantonese:		English:	
Subject	Predicate	Subject	Predicate
	Adj.		Verb + Adj.
NÍ gihn	daaih.	This one	is big.
NÍ dÍ	hóu leng.	Those	are very pretty.

Since adjectives share this characteristic of verbs, and
share also the characteristic of being able to be preceded
directly by m̀h, 'not,' we consider adjectives in Cantonese to be
a sub-category of verbs. Some writers call this category of word
'stative verb' rather than adjective.

e. Adjectives modified and unmodified.

   1. An adjective modified by géi 'quite' or hóu 'very' carries
      the force which an unmodified adjective does in English:

      Ex: NÍ gihn géi leng.

                                This one is pretty.
      NÍ gihn hóu leng.

   2. An unmodified adjective indicates an implied comparison in
      a Cantonese sentence with a single adjective as predicate.

      Ex: A: Néih wah bÍn gihn   Which one do you think is
             leng a?   pretty?

          B: NÍ gihn leng.   This one is pretty. (i.e.
                                   prettier than the other)

   3. With two adjectives in the predicate, a yauh...yauh...
      construction is required, and in such a case, the unmodified
      adjective is the norm.

      Ex: NÍ go pÍhnggwó yauh   This apple is both cheap
          pèhng yauh leng.   and good.
      (See BC and Drill 10)

   4. The choice-type question follows the verbal pattern of V m̀hV,
      yielding Adj m̀hAdj.

      Ex: NÍ gihn gwai m̀hgwai a? Is this one expensive?
          (See Drills 3, 11)

To say 'Is this one very expensive?' requires a <u>haih</u>
<u>m̀hhaih</u> question:

      Ex: Nĭ gihn haih m̀hhaih   Is this one very expensive?
         hŏu gwai a?

f. Adj + <u>ge</u> combination = noun phrase (NP).

    An adjective is frequently used to form a noun phrase by
adding the noun-forming suffix <u>ge</u>.

      Ex: 1. M̀hhaih daaih ge, haih   1. It's not the big one, it's
           sai ge.   the small one. <u>or</u>
                                They aren't the big ones,
                                they are the small ones.

         2. yiu daaihdĭ ge.   2. Want a large one (<u>or</u> ones).

        (See Drill <u>13</u>)

    Note that when an adjective combines with <u>ge</u> to form a noun
construction, it is necessary to add <u>haih</u> or another verb to form
a sentence.

3. <u>dĭ</u> as adj. suffix, 'a little,' 'Adj-er.'

    In Cantonese <u>Adj-dĭ</u> has a comparative sense, but the English
equivalents are translated variously, depending on context as:
'somewhat,' 'a little;' and also the comparative '-er.'

      Ex: Ngŏh go bĭu faaidĭ.   [My watch is a bit faster (than
                           the right time).]
                           My watch is a little fast.

      Nĭ gihn lāangsāam   [This sweater is a little
        daaihdĭ.   larger (than the size I
                           need).]
                           This sweater is a little too
                           large.

      Yáuh móuh saidĭ ge nē?   Do you have a smaller one?
                            (<u>or</u> smaller ones)

        (See BC and Drills <u>13, 15</u>)

4. Two syllable verbs and adjectives form the choice-type questions by
using only the first syllable before the <u>m̀h</u>, and the whole word
after:

    <u>V/Adj.</u>   <u>Choice question</u>
    jùngyi   like   jùng m̀hjùngyi a?   (do you) like (it)?
    ngāamjeuk well-fitting ngāam m̀hngāamjeuk a? (Does it) fit?

        (See BC)

5. <u>àh</u> sentence suffix, adding force of 'I suppose' to sentence it
   attaches to. It makes the sentence a rhetorical question. The
   speaker indicates with the <u>àh</u> final that he knows the response
   to his sentence will be in agreement with what he says. The
   intonation has the sentence-final fall characteristic of statement
   sentences.

   Ex: Máaih bún dā àh.   (You'll) buy a half dozen,
                                 I suppose.

   (See BC and Drill 9)

   Compare the two following English sentences, of which the
   second has a connotation similar to the Cantonese <u>àh</u> sentences:

       1. He's drinking tea, isn't he? (you're not sure)

       2. He's drinking tea, isn't he. (you're sure he is)

6. Further use of sentence suffix <u>nē</u>?

   A question sentence which continues a topic already being
   discussed often uses the sentence suffix <u>nē</u>?, with force of:
   '...then?;' '...And...?'

   Ex: Yáuh móuh daaihdī   Do you have any larger ones,
       ge nē?   then? (Having been shown
                                  smaller ones)

   (See BC and Drill 16)

   This <u>nē</u>? is the same final you encountered in Lesson 2 in the
   sentence composed of <u>Noun + nē</u>:

       Sīnsàang nē?   'And you, Sir?'

   The use of <u>nē</u> in this lesson is new in that it is here a
   final in a sentence which is itself a question. This use of <u>nē</u>
   is apparently used more frequently by women than by men, and its
   frequent use by men is said to give an effiminate cast to their
   speech. Sentence suffix <u>a</u> can be substituted for <u>nē</u> in all cases
   in which <u>nē</u> is a sentence suffix to a sentence which is itself
   a question.

186

7. Noun modification structures.

   a. Noun as modifier to a following noun head:

      1. Nouns as modifiers directly precede the noun they modify:

          Ex: Yìnggwok hàaih   English shoes

             Yahtbún bējáu   Japanese beer

             bou hàaih   cloth shoes

             pìhnggwó pāi   apple pie

      2. When the noun head is already established, <u>ge</u> may substitute

         for the noun head in a follow sentence, keeping modification

         structures intact:

          Ex: a. Ngóh yiu máaih jì   I want to buy a bottle of
              Yahtbún bējáu.   Japanese beer [Japan beer].
              Yáuh móuh a?   Do you have any?

             b. Móuh a. Máaih jì   No, we don't. How about
              Méihgwok ge, hóu   getting an American one?
              m̀hhóu a?   [America-one]

          (See Drill <u>8</u>)

   b. Adjectives as modifiers to a following noun head:

      1. A one syllable adjective as modifier directly preceeds the

         noun it modifies:

          Ex: 1. Néih gihn sàn   Your new shirt is pretty.
              sēutsāam hóu
              leng.

             2. Ngóh m̀hjùngyi   I don't like to wear shorts.
              jeuk dyún fu.   [short trousers]

      2. Adjectives that are pre-modified add <u>ge</u> when modifying a

         following noun:

          1. chèuhng yùhnbāt   long pencil

          2. hóu chèuhng ge yùhn- very long pencil
             bāt

          3. hóu gwai ge chèuhng very expensive long pencil
             yùhnbāt

          (See Drill <u>1.3</u>)

8. dò 'many'

1. dò, 'many,' patterns like an adjective in taking the adjective
   modifiers hóu, géi, etc. and the adjective suffix dĪ, but
   within the larger framework of the sentence it patterns
   differently from adjectives. dò is a boundword, bound either
   to a preceding adverb or a following measure; adjectives are
   free words. Adjectives when pre-modified add ge when modifying
   a following noun, but dò does not:

   Ex: hóu pèhng ge syù   very cheap books

       hóu dò syù   very many books

   A dò phrase patterns like a noun in that it can be the object
   of a verb without adding ge; but adjectives add ge when
   nominalized.

   Ex: Kéuih yáuh hóu dò.   He has many.

       Kéuih yáuh hóu   He has a big one (or ones.)
       daaih ge.

   dò also shares some characteristics with numbers and can be
   viewed as an indefinite number. It is, in fact, a case unto
   itself, and you will learn its various faces bit by bit.

9. bĪn- M ? = 'which M ?'

   bĪn-? is an interrogative boundword, bound to a following measure.
   It occupies the same position in a sentence as nĪ-, 'this' and gó-, 'that'
   and is classed with them as a specifier.

   Ex: A: Néih séung máaih bĪn gihn a?   Which one are you going to
                                          buy?

       B: Ngóh   máaih nĪ gihn laak.I'll buy this one.

                    (See BC and Drill 14)

III. DRILLS

1. Expansion Drill: Students repeat after the teacher.

+ 1. a. chèuhng.
    b. chèuhng fu.

    c. yáuh tìuh chèuhng fu.

    d. Yáuh tìuh hāak chèuhng fu.

    e. Yáuh tìuh hāak sīk ge
       chèuhng fu.

+ 2. a. gwai
+   b. géi gwai

+   c. m̀hhaih géi gwai

    d. Dī bou m̀hhaih géi gwai.

    e. Dī Yahtbún bou m̀hhaih
       géi gwai.

3. a. Jī yùhnbāt.
    b. Yáuh jī yùhnbāt.
    c. Ngóh yáuh jī yùhnbāt.
    d. Ngóh yáuh jī chèuhng yùhnbāt.
    e. Ngóh yáuh jī hóu gwai ge
       chèuhng yùhnbāt.

+ 4. a. Gihn lāangsāam.
+   b. Gihn sàn lāangsāam.
    c. Ngóh gihn sàn lāangsāam.
    d. Ngóh gihn sàn lāangsāam
       hóu gwai.
    e. Kéuih m̀hjīdou ngóh gihn sàn
       lāangsāam hóu gwai.

+ 5. a. gauh
    b. gauh bāt
    c. Jī gauh bāt.
    d. Jī gauh yùhnjíbāt.

1. a. long.
    b. slacks, trousers.
       [long trousers]

    c. Have a pair of slacks.

    d. Have a pair of black
       slacks.

    e. Have a pair of black
       coloured slacks.

2. a. expensive.
    b. rather expensive,
       quite expensive

    c. not very expensive, not
       expensive

    d. The cloth is not too
       expensive.

    e. The Japanese cloth is not
       expensive.

3. a. A (or The) pencil.
    b. Have a pencil.
    c. I have a pencil.
    d. I have a long pencil.
    e. I have a very expensive
       long pencil.

4. a. The (or a) sweater.
    b. The new sweater.
    c. My new sweater.
    d. My new sweater is very
       expensive.
    e. He does not know (that)
       my new sweater is very
       expensive.

5. a. old
    b. old pen.
    c. The old pen (or pencil).
    d. The old ball-point pen.

2. Substitution Drill: Adjectives

Ex: T: Nī dī géi daaih.   T: These are (or this (mass) is)
        /leng/   quite big. /pretty/

    S: Nī dī géi leng.   S: These are very pretty. or
                                    This (mass) is very pretty.

    1. Nī dī géi gwai. /pèhng/   1. Nī dī géi pèhng.

 + 2. /sai/   2. Nī dī géi sai.
        (small)   These are (or This (mass)
                                        is) quite small.

    3. /daaih/   3. Nī dī géi daaih.

 + 4. /hóuyám/   4. Nī dī géi hóuyám.
        (tasty, good to drink.)   These are (or This is)
                                        very tasty. - very good to
                                        drink.

 + 5. /hóusihk/   5. Nī dī géi hóusihk
        (tasty, good to eat.)   These are (or This is)
                                        very tasty. - very good
                                        to eat.

 + 6. /ngāamjeuk (or āamjeuk)   6. Nī dī géi ngāamjeuk.
        (well fitting, fits properly)   These fit well.

----

3. Expansion Drill: Fluency practice.

Ex: 1. T: Leng m̀hleng a?   Is it pretty?

    + S: Néih wah leng   Do you think it's pretty?
         m̀hleng a?
         (say, think)

    2. T: Hóu m̀hhóusihk a?   Is it tasty?

       S: Néih wah hóu   Do you think it's tasty?
          m̀hhóusihk a?

    1. Ngāam m̀hngāamjeuk a?   1. Néih wah ngāam m̀hngāam
                                        jeuk a?

    2. Gwai m̀hgwai a?   2. Néih wah gwai m̀hgwai a?

    3. Pèhng m̀hpèhng a?   3. Néih wah pèhng m̀hpèhng a?

    4. Sai m̀hsai a?   4. Néih wah sai m̀hsai a?

    5. Daaih m̀hdaaih a?   5. Néih wah daaih m̀hdaaih a?

    6. Hóu m̀hhóuyám a?   6. Néih wah hóu m̀hhóuyám a?

    7. Hóu m̀hhóusihk a?   7. Néih wah hóu m̀hhóusihk a?

    8. Leng m̀hleng a?   8. Néih wah leng m̀hleng a?

9. Gauh m̀hgauh a?   9. Néih wah gauh m̀hgauh a?

+ 10. <u>Fut</u> m̀hfut a? (<u>wide</u>)   10. Néih wah fut m̀hfut a?

+ 11. <u>Jaak</u> m̀hjaak a? (<u>narrow</u>) 11. Néih wah jaak m̀hjaak a?

---

4. Substitution Drill: Pre-modifiers of Adjectives

      Ex: T: Gó tìuh fu géi   Those slacks are quite cheap.
           pèhng. /hóu/   /very/

        S: Gó tìuh fu hóu pèhng.   Those slacks are very cheap.

1. Gó tìuh fu géi pèhng. /hóu/   1. Gó tìuh fu hóu pèhng.

2. Gó tìuh fu hóu gwai.   2. Gó tìuh fu m̀hhaih géi gwai.
   /m̀hhaih géi/   Those slacks aren't very
                                            expensive.

3. Gó tìuh fu m̀hhaih géi gwai.   3. Gó tìuh fu géi gwai.
   /géi/

4. Gó tìuh fu géi pèhng. /m̀h/   4. Gó tìuh fu m̀h pèhng.

+ 5. Gó tìuh fu m̀h pèhng.   5. Gó tìuh fu m̀hhaih hóu pèhng.
     /m̀hhaih hóu/ (<u>not very</u>)

---

5. Substitution Drill: Mixed: Nouns and Adjectives

      Ex: 1. T: Gó tìuh yú géi   That fish is pretty cheap.
             pèhng. /hóu/   /very/

         S: Gó tìuh yú hóu   That fish is very cheap.
           pèhng.

        2. T: Gó tìuh yú hóu   That fish is very cheap.
           pèhng. /go bìu/   /watch/

         S: Gó go bìu hóu   That watch is very cheap.
           pèhng.

1. Kéuih deui maht hóu leng.   1. Kéuih deui maht m̀hhaih géi
   /m̀hhaih géi/   leng.

2. /tìuh dyún fu/   2. Kéuih tìuh dyún fu m̀hhaih
                                     géi leng.

3. /hóu gwai/   3. Kéuih tìuh dyún fu hóu gwai.

4. /nì dì yìnjái/   4. Nì dì yìnjái hóu gwai.

5. /hóu hóusihk/   5. Nì dì yìnjái hóu hóusihk.

---

6. Substitution Drill: Adjectives as predicates

Ex: T: Nī gihn lāangsāam   T: This sweater is pretty.
hóu leng. /hóu
jaak/

S: Nī gihn lāangsāam   S: This sweater is narrow.
hóu jaak.

1. Nī gihn lāangsāam hóu jaak.   1. Nī gihn lāangsāam hóu
hóu ngāamjeuk.   ngāamjeuk.

2. Hóu gwai.   2. Nī gihn lāangsāam hóu gwai.

3. Gwaidī.   3. Nī gihn lāangsāam gwaidī.

4. Sai sèsíu.   4. Nī gihn lāangsāam sai sèsíu.

5. Daaihdī.   5. Nī gihn lāangsāam daaihdī.

6. Hóu pèhng.   6. Nī gihn lāangsāam hóu pèhng.

7. M̀hhaih géi gwai.   7. Nī gihn lāangsāam m̀hhaih
géi gwai.

8. M̀hhaih hóu leng.   8. Nī gihn lāangsāam m̀hhaih
Not very pretty.   hóu leng.

9. Hóu jaak.   9. Nī gihn lāangsāam hóu jaak.

---

7. Substitution Drill: Repeat the first sentence, then substitute
as directed.

1. Kéuih m̀hjùngyi jeuk dyún fu.   1. Kéuih m̀hjùngyi jeuk dyún fu.
She doesn't like to wear
shorts.

+ 2. /chèuhngsāam/(cheongsaam)   2. Kéuih m̀hjùngyi jeuk chèuhngsāam.
She doesn't like to wear
cheongsaams.

3. /dyún maht/(socks)   3. Kéuih m̀hjùngyi jeuk dyún
maht.

4. /chèuhng maht/(stockings)   4. Kéuih m̀hjùngyi jeuk chèuhng
maht.

5. /lāangsāam/   5. Kéuih m̀hjùngyi jeuk lāangsāam.

6. /chèuhng fu/(long pants)   6. Kéuih m̀hjùngyi jeuk chèuhng
fu.

Comment: A cheongsaam is the style of dress worn by Chinese
women, with a high collar and the skirt slit at
the sides.

192

8. Response Drill

      Ex: T: Yáuh móuh cháang   T: Are there oranges for sale
           maaih a?   [to sell] (here)? <u>or</u>
           /píhnggwó/   (Do you) have oranges for
                               sale? /apples?

         S: Deuimhjyuh, maaih-   S: Sorry, they're all sold out.
           saai laak. Píhng-   Would apples be OK?
           gwó hóu mhhóu a?

   1. Yáuh móuh Yinggwok hàaih maaih   1. Deuimhjyuh, maaihsaai laak.
+   a? /Méihgwok <u>ge</u>/   Méihgwok ge hóu mhhóu a?
     Do you have English shoes   I'm sorry, they're all
     for sale? /American ones/   sold out. Would American
     (<u>ge</u> as noun substitute)   ones be all right?

   2. Yáuh móuh Méihgwok yinjái   2. Deuimhjyuh, maaihsaai laak.
     maaih a? /Yinggwok ge/   Yinggwok ge hóu mhhóu a?

   3. Yáuh móuh jyùyuhk maaih a?   3. Deuimhjyuh, maaihsaai laak.
     /ngàuhyuhk/   Ngàuhyuhk hóu mhhóu a?

    Comment: <u>ge</u> can substitute for a noun in a follow sentence.
        The structure <u>modifier + ge</u> substitutes for
        <u>modifier + Noun</u>. See #1 and #2 above.

---

9. Response Drill

      Ex: 1. T: Néih yáuh móuh   1. T: Do you have ten dollars?
             sahp mān a?
             /nod/

            S: Yáuh. Néih yiu   S: Yes I do. You want it, huh.
                àh!

         2. T: Néih yáuh móuh   2. T: Do you have $10?
             sahp mān a?
             /shake/

            S: Móuh a. Deui-   S: No I don't, I'm sorry.
                mhjyuh laak.

   1. Néih yáuh móuh tòhng a?   1. Móuh a. Deuimhjyuh laak.
     /shake/

   2. Néih yáuh móuh yinjái a?   2. Móuh a. Deuimhjyuh laak.
     /shake/

   3. Néih yáuh móuh jē a? /shake/   3. Móuh a. Deuimhjyuh laak.

   4. Néih yáuh móuh go bun ngàhn-   4. Yáuh. Néih yiu àh.
     chìn a? /nod/

   5. Néih yáuh móuh yih sahp mān   5. Móuh a. Deuimhjyuh laak.
     a? /shake/

6. Néih yáuh móuh léuhng go bun   6. Yáuh. Néih yiu àh!
     ngàhnchín a? /nod/

7. Néih yáuh móuh yāt dā bējáu   7. Yáuh. Néih yiu àh!
     a? /nod/

Comment: Móuh a. and Móuh laak. compared as follow sentences to
     a yáuh móuh? question:

Móuh a. indicates simple negative 'Don't have any.'

Móuh laak. indicates that you used to have some, but
you don't have any any more.

---

10. Expansion Drill

Ex: T: Nī go píhnggwó hóu   T: This apple is cheap. /delicious/
     pèhng. /housihk/

S: Nī go píhnggwó yauh   S: This apple is both cheap and
     pèhng yauh hóusihk.   delicious.

1. Nī go cháang hóu gwai.   1. Nī go cháang yauh gwai yauh
     /m̀hhóusihk/   m̀hhóusihk.

2. Nī go bíu hóu pèhng. /jéun/   2. Nī dī bíu yauh pèhng yáuh
                                             jéun.

3. Gó dī béng hóu sai. /gwai/   3. Gó dī béng yauh sai yauh
                                             gwai.

4. Kéuih gihn sēutsāam hóu   4. Kéuih gihn sēutsāam yauh
     chèuhng. /daaih/   chèuhng yauh daaih.

5. Nī tìuh kwàhn hóu fut.   5. Nī tìuh kwàhn yauh fut yauh
     /daaih/   daaih.

6. Nī júng bāt hóu pèhng. /leng/   6. Nī júng bāt yauh pèhng yauh
                                             leng.

---

11. Transformation Drill

Ex: T: Kéuih gihn yúhlāu   T: Her raincoat is pretty.
     hóu leng.

S: Kéuih gihn yúhlāu   S: Is her raincoat pretty?
     leng m̀hleng a?

1. Kéuih gó tìuh fu hóu ngāam-   1. Kéuih gó tìuh fu ngāam
     jeuk.   m̀hngāamjeuk a?
     Those trousers of his fit
     very well.

2. Sahp māan m̀hgwai.   2. Sahp māan gwai m̀hgwai a?

3. Nī dī maht hóu pèhng.   3. Nī dī maht pèhng m̀hpèhng a?

4. Hāak sīk ge m̀hhaih géi leng. 4. Hāak sīk ge leng m̀hleng a?

5. Gó dī jyùuyuhk gei hóusihk.   5. Gó dī jyùuyuhk hóu m̀hhóu
                                    sihk a?

6. Gó tiuh saidī.   6. Gó tiuh sai m̀hsai a?

7. Nī gihn baahk sēutsāam daaihdī. 7. Nī gihn baahk sēutsāam daaih
                                       m̀hdaaih a?

8. Kéuih gihn sāam hóu leng.   8. Kéuih gihn sāam leng m̀hleng
                                    a?

9. Kéuih gó deui hàaih hóu jaak. 9. Kéuih gó deui hàaih jaak
                                    m̀hjaak a?

---

12. Transformation Drill: Transform the cue sentence into a <u>wá?</u> question
     sentence, following the pattern of the example.

        Ex: T: Kéuih sing Wòhng.   His name is Wong.

            S: Kéuih sing mēyéh wá?   You said his name was what?

1. Wòhng Sàang séung máaih   1. Wòhng Sàang séung máaih
   tiuh fu.   mēyéh wá?

2. Léih Síujé jùngyi ngóh.   2. Léih Síujé jùngyi bīngo wá?

3. Kéuih máaih nī gihn.   3. Kéuih máaih bīn gihn wá?
   She wants this one.   which one does she want?

4. Kéuih séung oi gó tiuh.   4. Kéuih séung oi bīn tiuh wá?
   He wants to have that one.   Which one does he want?

5. Kéuih sihk béng.   5. Kéuih sihk mēyéh wá?

6. Kéuih jeuk gáu houh.   6. Kéuih jeuk géidō houh wá?

7. Yìhgā daahp yāt.   7. Yìhgā daahp géi wá?

8. Yìhgā sāam dím bun.   8. Yìhgā géidímjùng wá?

9. Kéuih máaih sei deui.   9. Kéuih máaih géidō deui wá?

10. Kéuih yáuh sahp māan.   10. Kéuih yáuh géidō chín wá?

---

13. Expansion Drill

      Ex: T: Nī gihn yúhlāu   This raincoat is a bit small.
           saidī.

        S: Nī gihn yúhlāu saidī,   This raincoat is a bit small;
           yauh mōuh daaihdī   do you have any larger ones?
           ge nē?

1. Nī dī yú gwaidī.   1. Nī dī yú gwaidī, yáuh móuh
                                  pèhngdī ge nē?

2. Nī tiuh fu daaihdī.   2. Nī tiuh fu daaihdī, yáuh
                                móuh saidī ge nē?

3. Nī gihn lāangsāam chèuhngdī. 3. Nī gihn lāangsāam chèuhngdī,
                                  yáuh móuh dyúndī ge nē?

+ 4. Nī gihn <u>dáisāam</u> saidī.   4. Nī gihn dáisāam saidī, yáuh
    (<u>underwear</u>)   móuh daaihdī ge nē?

5. Nī tiuh fu jaak dī.   5. Nī tiuh fu jaak dī, yáuh
                                  móuh fut dī ge nē?

---

14. Response Drill

      Ex: T: Néih oi bīn gihn   Which shirt do you want?
           sēutsāam nē?   /white color/
           /baahk sīk/

        S: Ngóh oi baahk sīk   I want that (<u>or</u> the) white one.
           gó gihn.

1. Néih oi bīn deui maht nē?   1. Ngóh oi hāak sīk gó deui.
    /hāak sīk/

2. Néih oi bīn bá jē nē? /daaih- 2. Ngóh oi daaihdī gó bá.
    dī/

3. Néih oi bīn tiuh fu nē?   3. Ngóh oi chèuhngdī gó tiuh.
    /chèuhngdī/

4. Néih oi bīn bāau yīnjái nē? 4. Ngóh oi saidī gó bāau.
    /saidī/

5. Néih oi bīn jek gāi nē?   5. Ngóh oi gwaidī gó jek.
    /gwaidī/

CANTONESE BASIC COURSE   LESSON 8

15. Alteration Drill

       Ex: T: Ngóh ngoi gihn   I want a larger one.
              daaihdí ge.

          S: Béi gihn daaihdí   Give me a larger one.
             ge ngóh lā!

1. Ngóh ngoi tiuh futdí ge.   1. Béi tiuh futdí ge ngóh lā!
2. Ngóh ngoi deui jaakdí ge.   2. Béi deui jaakdí ge ngóh lā!
3. Ngóh ngoi bá lengdí ge.   3. Béi bá lengdí ge ngóh lā!
4. Ngóh ngoi jí saidí ge.   4. Béi jí saidí ge ngóh lā!
5. Ngóh ngoi go pèhngdí ge.   5. Béi go pèhngdí ge ngóh lā!
6. Ngóh ngoi géi gihn saidí ge.   6. Béi géi gihn saidí ge ngóh
                                      lā!
7. Ngóh ngoi géi tiuh chèuhngdí 7. Béi géi tiuh chèuhngdí ge
   ge.   ngóh lā!

---

16. Response Drill

       Ex: T: Ngóh séung máaih T: I want to buy two ties.
              léuhng tiuh tāai.

          S: Máaih bīn léuhng   S: Which two do you want?
             tiuh nē?

1. Ngóh séung máaih tiuh tāai.   1. Máaih bīn tiuh nē?
2. Ngóh séung máaih dí yùhnbāt. 2. Máaih bīn dí nē?
3. Ngóh séung máaih dí bou.   3. Máaih bīn dí nē?
4. Ngóh séung oi sàam deui   4. Oi bīn sàam deui nē?
   dyún maht.
   I want to get three pairs
   of socks.

IV. CONVERSATIONS FOR LISTENING

    (On tape. Listen to tape with book closed.)

V. SAY IT IN CANTONESE

A. In a store, the customer says:

1. These shoes are pretty--
    do you have (are there?)
    size eight for sale?

2. I don't like the black ones--
    are there white ones
    (do you have white ones)?

3. This sweater is a little
    too wide--I want a smaller
    one.

4. I'll take a dozen of these
    socks.

5. This sweater is pretty, but
    it doesn't fit--do you
    have larger one?

6. These shoes are a bit ex-
    pensive, do you have any
    cheaper ones?

7. How much do these shorts
    cost?

8. This one (sweater) is pretty
    and fits well, but it's a
    bit expensive--$30, OK?

B. And the clerk responds:

1. I'm sorry, size eight is
    all sold out.

2. Yes, what size do you want?

3. This one is narrower--try
    it.

4. Fine, what size do you wear?

5. Yes.

6. Yes, those are cheaper--do
    you like them?

7. This one is $15.00 and that
    one is $15.50--which one
    do you want?

8. OK.

Vocabulary Checklist for Lesson 8

1. āamjeuk	adj:	fits well, well-fitting
2. àh	ss:	sen. suf. with force of 'I suppose'
3. baahk	adj:	white
4. bīn?	QW:	which?
5. chèuhng	adj:	long (in length)
6. chèuhngsāam	n:	cheongsaam
7. dā	m:	dozen
8. daaih	adj:	large
9. daaihdī	Ph:	a little larger
10. dáisāam	n:	underwear
11. -dī	adj.s:	attaches to adjectives to mean 'a little Adj; somewhat adj; Adj--er.

198

12.	dò	bf:	much, many
13.	dyún	adj:	short
14.	fut	adj:	wide
15.	gauh	adj:	old (not new)
16.	-ge	bf:	one(s) = (noun substitute)
17.	géi	adv:	rather, quite
18.	gwai	adj:	expensive
19.	hāak	adj:	black
20.	hóu	adv:	very
21.	hóu	adj:	good
22.	Hóu m̀hhóu a?	Ph:	OK? Is (that) all right?
23.	houh	m:	number
24.	hóusihk	adj:	good to eat; tasty
25.	hóuyám	adj:	good to drink; tasty
26.	jaak	adj:	narrow
27.	jeuk	v:	wear; put on (clothes)
28.	júng	m:	type
29.	jùngyi	auxV/v:	like, prefer; like to
30.	lāangsāam	n:	sweater
31.	leng	adj:	pretty; good-looking; good, nice (for foods)
32.	Máaihsaai laak	Ph:	All sold out.
33.	m̀hhaih géi	adv:	not very..., not....
34.	m̀hhaih hóu	adv:	not very
35.	móuh	v:	not have, there isn't (aren't)
36.	ngāamjeuk	adj:	well fitting (for clothes), fits well (var. of āamjeuk)
37.	pèhng	adj:	cheap
38.	-saai	Vsuf:	completely
39.	sai	adj:	small
40.	sàn	adj:	new
41.	sīk	(bf)n:	color
42.	wah	v:	say, opine
43.	yáuh	v:	have, there is (are)

. BASIC CONVERSATION

A. **Buildup:**

gùngyàhn	servant

Gùngyàhn

Wéi.	Hello.
wán	look for, search
Wán bīnwái a?	Who are you calling?

Jèung Sàang

dihnwá	telephone
tèng	listen, hear
tèng dihnwá	talk [listen] on the telephone
giu	instruct, order, tell
giu kéuih tèng dihnwá	ask her to come to the phone
M̀hgòi néih giu Léih Táai tèng dihnwá.	Please ask Mrs. Lee to come to the phone.

Gùngyàhn

Wán bīnwái wá? Ngóh tèng m̀hchìngchó.	Who did you say you were looking for? I didn't hear.
daaihsēngdī	louder voice
M̀hgòi daaihsēngdī lā.	Please speak louder.

Jèung Sàang

Léih Taaitáai.	Mrs. Lee.

Gùngyàhn

heui gāai	go out [go street]
jó	Verb suffix, indicating fulfillment of an expectation.
heuijó gāai	has gone out, went out
Kéuih heuijó gāai bo.	She's gone out.
Gwaising wán kéuih a?	Who is calling please?

Jèung Sàang

Sing Jèung ge.	My name is Cheung.
fàanlàih	come back, return

géisìh (géisí)

Kéuih géisìh fàanlaih a?

when?

When will she be back?

Gùngyàhn

sahpyih dím

-lèhng-

12 o'clock

-and some odd. Added to a number phrase.

Waahkjé sahpyih dím lèhng lā.

sihk aan or sihk ngaan

yiu

Kéuih yiu fàanlàih sihk ngaan gé.

sih

yáuh sih

Probably a little after 12.

eat the midday meal

going to, intend to

She's going to come home for lunch.

business, affair, matter

have something to attend to; have errand, business

Yáuh mēyéh sih a?

What is it you want? (i.e., What matter are you calling about?)

Jèung Sàang

dá dihnwá

make a phone call, to telephone.

dá dihnwá béi ngóh

giu kéuih dá dihnwá béi ngóh

ṁhgòi néih giu kéuih dá dihnwá béi Jèung Sàang lā.

Gám, kéuih fàanlàih, ṁhgòi néih giu kéuih dá dihnwá béi Jèung Sàang lā.

telephone me

tell her to phone me

please ask her to phone Mr. Cheung.

Well, when she comes home, please ask her to call Mr. Cheung.

Gùngyàhn

néih ge dihnwá

géidō houh?

néih ge dihnwá géidō houh a?

your telephone

what number?

what is your telephone number?

Kéuih jì ṁhjì néih ge dihnwá géidō houh a?

Does she know your telephone number?

201

Jèung Sàang

Kéuih m̀hjì ga.   She doesn't know.

Ngóh ge dihnwá haih chāt   My telephone number is 7 8 ...
    baat ...

Gùngyàhn

   ló   fetch, go get

   dáng ngóh   let me; wait while I ...

   dáng ngóh ló jī bāt sìn   let me get a pen first.

Dáng ngóh ló jī bāt sìn lā.   Let me get a pen first ...

             (She returns with a pen:)

Gùngyàhn

Wéi, géidō houh wá?   Hello, what number did you say?

Jèung Sàang

   lìhng   zero

Chāt baat luhk lìhng n̍gh gáu.   786059

Gùngyàhn

Chāt baat luhk lìhng n̍gh gáu.   786059

   wah kéuih jì   tell her

   ngóh wah kéuih jì   I'll tell her

Hóu, kéuih fàanlàih, ngóh wah   All right--when she comes back,
    kéuih jì lā.   I'll tell her.

Jèung Sàang

Hóu, m̀hgòi.   Fine; thanks.

B. Recapitulation:

Gùngyàhn

Wéi. Wán bīnwái a?   Hello. Who are you calling?

Jèung Sàang

M̀hgòi néih giu Leih Táai tèng   Please ask Mrs. Lee to come
    dihnwá.   to the phone.

Gùngyàhn

Wán bīnwái wá? Ngóh tèng   Who did you say you
    m̀hchìngchó. M̀hgòi daaihsēng-   wanted? I couldn't hear.
    dī lā.   Please speak louder.

202

Jèung Sàang

Lèih Taaitáai.   Mrs. Lee.

Gùngyàhn

Kéuih heuijó gāai bo.   She's gone out. Who is calling
    Gwaising wán kéuih a?   please?

Jèung Sàang

Sing Jèung ge. Kéuih géisìh   My name is Cheung. When will
    fàanlàih a?   she be back?

Gùngyàhn

Waahkjé sahpyih dím lèhng lā.   Probably a little after 12.
    Kéuih yiu fàanlàih sihk aan   She's going to come home for
    gé. Yáuh mēyéh sih a?   lunch. What is it you want?

Jèung Sàang

Gám, kéuih fàanlàih, m̀hgòi   Well, (when) she comes home,
    néih giu kéuih dá dihnwá   please ask her to call Mr.
    béi Jèung Sàang lā.   Cheung.

Gùngyàhn

Kéuih jì m̀hjì néih ge dihnwá   Does she know your telephone
    géidō houh a?   number?

Jèung Sàang

Kéuih m̀hji ga. Ngóh ge dihnwá   She doesn't know. My tele-
    haih chāt baat ...   phone number is 7 8 ...

Gùngyàhn

Dáng ngóh ló jì bāt sìn lā.   Let me get a pen first.

                (She returns with a pen:)

Gùngyàhn

Wéi, géidō houh wá?   Hello, what number did you
                                       say?

Jèung Sàang

Chāt baat luhk lìhng ńgh gáu.   786059

Gùngyàhn

Chāt baat luhk lìhng ńgh gáu.   786059
Hóu, kéuih fàanlàih, ngóh   All right--when she comes back,
    wah kéuih jì lā.   I'll tell her.

Jēung Sàang

Hóu, m̀hgòi.   Fine; thanks.

+ + + + + + + + + + + + + +

Pronunciation Practice:

1. i as in si, chi, jí, dī, nī, sih, sih, hòuhjí

    i as syllable final is a high front unrounded vowel--[i].

        Listen and repeat:

            1. nī nī   .

            2. si si   .

            3. sih sih   .

            4. sih sih   .

            5. jí jí   .

2. ik as in sīk, sihk

    ik is a two-part final composed of the high front unrounded vowel
i plus the velar stop consonant k. Before k the tongue position for
i approaches higher-mid front unrounded [e], tenser and lower than
the American i in "sick,"--[I], closer to the French é in été,
'summer.' The tongue position of k following the front vowel is more
forward than that of k following the back vowels u, o, and a --
[Ik˥].

        Listen and repeat:

           1. sīk sīk sīk   . 識

           2. sihk sihk sihk   . 食

3. i/ik contrasts

    Note that in addition to the difference in tongue position for i
as a final and before k as described, there is also a length difference. i before k is shorter than i as final--[Iˇk] or [e ˇk], and
[i:].

        Listen and repeat:

           1. sih sih   , sihk sihk   .

           2. sih sihk   , sihk sih   .

4. ing as in lìhng, sing, pìhnggwó, chìngchó

    ing is a two-part final composed of the high front unrounded
vowel i and the velar nasal ng. The tongue position for i before ng
is similar to that of i before k--lowered from high front position.
The vowel is open before the nasal final.

Listen and repeat:

1. sing sing 姓 , lìhng lìhng 零 , chìng chìng 清 .
2. chìng sing lìhng   . 清姓零
3. lìhng lìhng 零 , pìhng pìhng 蘋 .

5. **ing/eng contrasts**

Listen and repeat:

1. lìhng lìhng 零 , pèhng pèhng 平 .
2. pìhng pìhng pìhnggwó   . 蘋蘋蘋果
3. pìhng pèhng 蘋平, pìhng pèhng   .
4. leng sing 靚姓, sing leng 姓靚.

6. **ing/ik contrasts**

Listen and repeat:

1. sìk sìk 識 , sing sing 姓 .
2. sihk sihk 食 , sing sing   .

7. **eu finals**

A. **eut**, **eun**, and **eui**

Listen and repeat:

1. chēut, sēut 出 恤
2. deui, heui 對 去
3. jéun, jéun 準 準

B. **eung** and **euk**

Listen and repeat:

1. Jèung chèuhng 張 長
2. séung, léuhng 想 雨
3. jeuk, jeuk 著 著

8. **s** as in sing, sihk, si, sé, sei, séung, sàang, sahp, séui.

   s is an initial consonant in Cantonese. Like the American **s** (as in 'see'), the Cantonese **s** is voiceless. In terms of air flow the American and Cantonese **s** sounds are the same--both are spirants, that is to say, the air is forced through a narrow passage under friction, producing a hissing sound. The tongue position for the Cantonese **s** differs from that of the American **s**. The friction points for the Cantonese sound are the blade of the tongue (that part just back from the tip) and the dental ridge. The flat surface of the blade of the tongue comes close to the dental ridge (the tip of the tongue is at rest, approximately near the base of the upper teeth) and air is forced through the passage thus provided. For the American s, the friction points are the tip of the tongue, not the blade, and the dental ridge. For the American s the grooved tip of the tongue approaches the dental ridge and air is forced through this passageway. For the Cantonese sound the lips are rounded before a rounded vowel and spread before an unrounded one.

1. Compare American and Cantonese s sounds:

American	Cantonese
1. see see see	si si si
2. sing sing sing	sing sing sing
3. set set set	sé sé sé
4. say say say	sei sei sei
5. son son son	sàn sàn sàn
6. soot soot soot	sēut sēut sēut

2. Listen and repeat:

1. si   , si   , si   .
2. sih   , sih   , sih   .
3. sé   , sé   , sé   .
4. sing   , sing   , sing   .
5. sēut   , sēut   , sēut   .

9. s/j/ch compared.

There are some similarities of tongue positioning among these sounds. To make s the blade of the tongue approaches close to the dental ridge at the point where the tongue touches the ridge to make the j and ch sounds. The flat surface of the blade is the friction point for all three sounds.

Listen and repeat:

1. ji 至 , chi 次 , si 試 .
2. jing 正 , chǐng 清 , sing 性 .
3. jē 姐 , chē 車 , sé 寫 .
4. jái 仔 , chàih 齊 , sai 細 .

II. NOTES

1. bo = sentence suffix expressing definiteness, conviction.

    Ex: Kéuih chēutjó gāai laak.   She's gone out. (change from
                                        former condition)

        Kéuih chēutjó gāai bo.   She's gone out, that's
                                         definite.

                       (See BC)

2. -jó verb suffix indicating accomplishment of intended action.

    This will be treated in detail in later lessons. At present
learn it in the set phrases you will be apt to need to say and comprehend over the telephone:

    Ex: Kéuih fàanjó gùng.   He's gone to work.
                                       [return-jó work]

        Kéuih h∘uijó gāai.   She's gone out (from her own
                                       house). [go-jó street]

        Kéuih fàanjó ngūkkéi.   He's gone home.
                                       [return-jó home]

        (See BC and Drills 1.3, 4, 5, 6, 7)

3. ge translated as possessive.

    ge is suffixed to personal nouns and pronouns to show ownership,
'belonging to,' referred to in grammatical terms as the possessive.
ge operates as possessive in noun phrases both in head and modifier
structures:

    a. In head structures:

        ge combines with a preceding personal noun (or pronoun)
          to form the head of a noun phrase.

        Ex: 1. Gó dī
             Gó bún syù haih Léih   Those   book(s) is/are
                                  That
           Síujé ge.   Miss Lee's.

           2. Nī dī
             Nī bún haih ngóh ge.   These   are   mine.
                                  This   one is

           3. Léih Síujé ge haih   Miss Lee's is a new one.
              sàn ge.   are   ones.

           4. Ngóh ge haih gauh ge.   Mine are   old ones.
                                        is an   one.

    In a head structure ge cannot be omitted from the N-ge combination.

        (See Drills 10, 11)

b. In modification structures:

ge combines with personal nouns (and pronouns) to form a
possessive modifier to a following noun head.

Ex: 1. Ngóh ge dihnwá haih   My telephone number is....
...houh.

2. Kéuihdeih ge néuih-   Their girlfriends have gone
pàhngyáuh fàanjó   home.
ngūkkéi laak.

3. Ngóh m̀hjùngyi Léih   I don't like Miss Lee's new
Síujé ge sàn   sweater.
lāangsāam.

(See BC)

4. ge/Measure overlap.

ge may replace the measure in a modification structure.

Ex: 1. Ngón go néui m̀hhái   My daughter is not here.
douh.

2. Ngóh dī néui m̀hhái   My daughters are not here.
douh.

3. Ngóh ge néui m̀hhái   My daughter(s) is (are) not
douh.   here.

5. Possessive modification without ge or Measure.

A few nouns accept modification by personal nouns and pronouns
directly. Pàhngyáuh, (ng)ūkkéi, and gùngyàhn are the only nouns
of this type we have studied so far.

Ex: Ngóh pàhngyáuh   My friend/friends

Léih Síujé (ng)ūkkéi   Miss Lee's home

But even for these nouns, ge must be used with bīngo ge, whose?
to differentiate from bīn go, which (M)?

Ex: Bīn go pàhngyáuh?   Which friend?

Bīngo ge pàhngyáuh?   Whose friend?

Compare:

bīngo ge pàhngyáuh?   whose friend?

bīn go pàhngyáuh?   which friend?

Léih Táai gaau bīngo   Whose friend does Mrs. Lee
ge pàhngyáuh?   teach?

Léih Táai gaau bīn go   Which friend does Mrs. Lee
pàhngyáuh?   teach?

The nouns that accept direct modification by personal noun/

208

pronoun will be treated as exceptions and noted as such. As a rule of thumb, such nouns must be of more than one syllable.

6. yiu..V..;séung..V.. differentiated.

    yiu..V.. = definitely intend to ..V..

    séung..V.. = plan to ..V.. (but maybe it won't happen)

    In English yiu can be translated as 'going to' if the sentence is one of future reference. Yiu contrasts with séung in such sentences in that with séung the implication is that it's iffy whether or not the action expressed by the following verb will actually take place, but with yiu the person has definitely made up his mind to do the action.

    Ex: 1. Kéuih wah ngóh jî   She told me she was planning
           kéuih séung faan-   to come home for lunch.
           làih sihk aan.

        2. Kéuih wah ngóh jî   She told me she was coming
           kéuih yiu fàanlàih   home for lunch.
           sihk aan.

7. séung..V.. and jùngyi..V..differentiated.

    séung = would like to ..V..; think I'll ..V..

    jùngyi = like (as a general statement)

    Ex: Ngóh séung yám dî chàh.   I'd like some tea.

        Ngóh séung sihk go   I'd like an apple.
          pìhnggwó.

        Ngóh hóu jùngyi yám chàh.   I like to drink tea.
                                I like tea.

    The differentiation of meaning between jùngyi and séung breaks down with a mēyéh question, where the jùngyi pattern is used as a polite way to ask what the addressee wishes. (The jùngyi mēyéh? question may also mean: What do you like?)

    Ex: Néih séung yám dî   What would you like to drink?
        mēyéh a?

        Néih jùngyi yám dî   What would you like to drink?
        mēyéh a?

                (See Drill _12_)

8. Omission of yāt in certain 'one o'clock' phrases.

   The numeral yāt is ordinarily omitted in the spoken language before the time measure dím, 'o'clock,' when dím is followed by géi, lèhng or bun.

   Ex: 1. dím géi jūng = sometime after one o'clock
       2. dím lèhng (jūng) = a little after one o'clock
       3. dím bun = half past one
                   (See Drill 7)

   In all other phrases concerning one o'clock, yāt cannot be omitted.

9. Omission of go jih in a time phrase.

   go jih is frequently omitted in the spoken language as the final element in a time phrase.

   Ex: sàam dím yāt = 3:05
       sàam dím sàam = 3:15
       sàam dím sei = 3:20

   Note in these abbreviated forms that the numeral following dím is in construction with an unspoken go jih, not with go gwāt. Thus sàam dím sàam is 3:15, not 3:45. X:30 is never stated as X dím luhk, but as X dím bún.

                   (See Drill 7)

   Although infrequent, X dím yih rather than (-) X dím léuhng is the abbreviated form for X dím léuhng go jih.

III. DRILLS

1. Substitution Drill: Repeat the first sentence, then substitute as directed.

1. M̀hgòi néih giu Léih Táai tèng dihnwá lā. Please call Mrs. Lee to the telephone.	1. M̀hgòi néih giu Léih Tāai tèng dihnwá lā.
2. Hòh Táai	2. M̀hgòi néih giu Hòh Táai tèng dihnwá lā.
3. Hòh Síujé	3. M̀hgòi néih giu Hòh Síujé tèng dihnwá lā.
4. Jèung Sàang	4. M̀hgòi néih giu Jèung Sàang tèng dihnwá lā.
5. Chàhn Táai	5. M̀hgòi néih giu Chàhn Táai tèng dihnwá lā.

------

2. Expansion Drill

Ex: T: Jèung Sàang, tèng dihnwá.	T: Mr. Cheung, telephone!
S: M̀hgòi néih giu Jèung Sàang tèng dihnwá.	S: Please ask Mr. Cheung to come to the phone.
1. Chàhn Sàang, tèng dihnwá.	1. M̀hgòi néih giu Chàhn Sàang tèng dihnwá.
2. Léih Táai, tèng dihnwá.	2. M̀hgòi néih giu Léih Táai tèng dihnwá.
3. Hòh Síujé, tèng dihnwá.	3. M̀hgòi néih giu Hòh Síujé tèng dihnwá.
4. Wòhng Sáang, tèng dihnwá.	4. M̀hgòi néih giu Wòhng Sáang tèng dihnwá.
5. Làuh Táai, tèng dihnwá.	5. M̀hgòi néih giu Làuh Táai tèng dihnwá.

------

3. Expansion Drill: telephone talk; listen and repeat:

+ 1. cho	**mistake, make a mistake**
+ cho sin (line, thread)	wrong line
+ Daap cho sin	Wrong number! [connected the wrong line]

211

2.	dáng	wait
+	dáng (yāt)jahn (var: (yāt)ján)	wait awhile
	M̀hgòi néih dáng yātjahn.	Just a moment, please. [Please wait awhile]
	M̀hgòi néih dáng yātjahn lā.	Just a moment, please!
+ 3.	fàan	go [return] to place you habitually go to.
+	fàan gùng	go [return] to work
	fàanjó gùng	has gone [or went] to work
	Kéuih fàanjó gùng.	(S)He's gone to work.
	Kéuih fàanjó gùng bo.	I am sorry, but he's gone to work.
+ 4.	chēut gāai	go out [out (to) street]
	chēutjó gāai	has gone [or went] out
	Kéuih chēutjó gāai.	(S)He's gone out.
	Kéuih chēutjó gāai bo.	I'm sorry, but she's gone out.
+ 5.	fàan (ng)ūkkéi	go [return] home
	fàanjó (ng)ūkkéi	has gone [or went] home
	Kéuih fàanjó (ng)ūkkéi	(S)He's gone home.
	Kéuih fàanjó (ng)ūkkéi bo.	I'm sorry, but he's gone home.
+ 6.	fàan hohk	go [return] to school
	fàanjó hohk	gone to school, left for school
	Kéuih fàanjó hohk la.	He's gone to school.
+ 7.	heui gāai	go out [go (to) street]
	heuijó gāai	has gone (or went) out
	Kéuih heuijó gāai.	(S)He's gone out.
	Kéuih heuijó gāai bo.	I'm sorry, but he's gone out.
+ 8.	joi dálàih	call back (on the phone)
	dángjahn joi dálàih	call back later
	Dángjahn joi dálàih lā.	Call back later.

a. Repeat the final sentence of each of the above problem
   sentences as a Listen and Repeat drill, students repeating
   after the teacher.

b. Repeat, teacher giving the English of the final sentences,
   students called on individually to give Cantonese equivalents.

4. Conversation Drill: Carry on the suggested conversations following the pattern of the example.

  Ex: 1. T: Néih wán mēyéh a? /jì yùhn-bāt/ T: What are you looking for? /a pencil/

     S: Ngóh wán jì yùhn-bāt. S: I'm looking for a pencil.

   2. T: Néih wán bīngo a? /Chàhn Sàang/ T: Who are you looking for? /Mr. Chan/

     S: Ngóh wán Chàhn Sàang. S: I'm looking for Mr. Chan.

1. Néih wán mēyéh a? /bàau yìnjái/ 1. Ngóh wán bàau yìnjái.

2. Néih wán mēyéh a? /bá jē/ 2. Ngóh wán bá jē.

3. Néih wán bīngo a? /Wòhng Táai/ 3. Ngóh wán Wòhng Táai.

4. Néih wán bīngo a? /Làuh Síujé/ 4. Ngóh wán Làuh Síujé.

5. Néih wán mēyéh a? /jì yùhnjíbāt/ 5. Ngóh wán jì yùhnjíbāt.

6. Néih wán bīngo a? /Jèung Sàang/ 6. Ngóh wán Jèung Sàang.

 a. Repeat as Conversation Drill, thus:

  1. T: /yùhnbāt/

   S1: Néih wán mēyéh a?

   S2: Ngóh wán jì yùhnbāt.

  2. T: /Chàhn Sàang/

   S1: Néih wán bīngo a?

   S2: Ngóh wán Chàhn Sàang.

---

5. Conversation Drill

  Ex: A: Ṁhgòi néih giu Wòhng Sàang tèng dihnwá lā. A: Please ask Mr. Wong to come to the phone.

   B: Kéuih chēutjó gāai bo. Gwaising wán kéuih a? B: I'm sorry but he's gone out. Who is calling please?

   A: Sing Jèung ge. A: My name is Cheung.

1. A. ......Hòh Táai ...... 1. A. Ṁhgòi néih giu Hòh Táai tèng dihnwá lā.

213

B. . . . .   B. Kéuih chēutjó gāai bo.
                                                     Gwaising wán kéuih a?

A. . . . . . . Léih . . . . . .   A. Sing Léih ge.

2. A. . . . . . . Jèung Sàang . . . . . .   2. A. Ṁhgòi néih giu Jèung
                                                        Sàang tèng dihnwá lā.

B. . . . .   B. Kéuih chēutjó gāai bo.
                                                     Gwaising wán kéuih a?

A. . . . . . . Máh . . . . . .   A. Sing Máh ge.

3. A. . . . . . . Chàhn Síujé . . . . . .   3. A. Ṁhgòi néih giu Chàhn
                                                        Síujé tèng dihnwá lā.

B. . . . .   B. Kéuih chēutjó gāai bo.
                                                     Gwaising wán kéuih a?

A. . . . . . . Wòhng . . . . . .   A. Sing Wòhng ge.

   a. Continue, using actual names of students.

   Comment: BĪnwái?, who? (polite) may be substituted for
            Gwaising thus:

            Gwaising wán kéuih a?

            BĪnwái wán kéuih a?   Who is calling her?

_____

6. Translation & Conversation Drill

   Ex: S1: Ṁhgòi néih giu   S1: Please ask Mr. Lee to come to
           Léih Sàang tèng   the phone.
           dihnwá lā.

       S2: Kéuih heuijó gāai   S2: I'm sorry, but he's gone out.
           bo.

   1. A. . . . .   1. A. Ṁhgòi néih giu Léih
                                               Sàang tèng dihnwá lā.

      T. Wrong number!

      B. . . . .   B. Daap cho sin.

   2. A. . . . .   2. A. Ṁhgòi néih giu Léih
                                               Sàang tèng dihnwá lā.

      T. Just a moment, please.

      B. . . . .   B. Ṁhgòi néih dáng yātján
                                               lā.

   3. A. . . . .   3. A. Ṁhgòi néih giu Léih
                                               Sàang tèng dihnwá lā.

214

T. He's gone to work.

B. ....

4. A. ....

T. He's gone out.

B. ....

5. A. ....

T. He's gone home.

B. ....

6. A. ....

T. He's gone to school.

B. ....

B. Kéuih fàanjó gùng bo.

4. A. M̀hgòi néih giu Léih
　　 Sàang tèng dihnwá lā.

B. Kéuih chēutjó gāai bo.

　　 or

Kéuih heuijó gāai bo.

5. A. M̀hgòi néih giu Léih
　　 Sàang tèng dihnwá lā.

B. Kéuih fàanjó ngūkkéi bo.

6. A. M̀hgòi néih giu Léih
　　 Sàang tèng dihnwá lā.

B. Kéuih fàanjó hohk bo.

---

7. **Expansion Drill:**

Ex: T: chāt dím

S: Yìhgā chāt dím
　　 gamseuhnghá lā.
　　 (approximately)

T: Nī tiuh dyúnfu sahp
　　 mān.

S: Nī tiuh dyúnfu sahp
　　 mān gamseuhnghá lā.

T: 7 o'clock.

S: It's about 7 o'clock.

T: These shorts are $10.

S: These shorts are about $10.

+ 1. dím bun.
　　 1:30 (time expression)

2. luhk dím sàam
　　 six-fifteen
　　 (short for luhk dim
　　 sàamgojih)

3. Nī gihn chèuhngsāam
　　 yahńgh mān.

4. Nī tiuh chèuhngfu sahpluhk
　　 mān.

5. Nī gihn lāangsāam sà'ahsei man.

1. Yìhga dím bun gamseuhnghá lā.
　　 It's about 1:30.

2. Yìhga luhk dím sàam
　　 gamseuhnghá lā.

3. Nī gihn chèuhng sàam yahńgh
　　 mān gamseuhnghá lā.

4. Nī tiuh chèuhngfu sahpluhk
　　 mān gamseuhnghá lā.

5. Nī gihn lāangsāam sà'ahsei
　　 man gamseuhnghá lā.

Comments: a. <u>gamseuhnghá</u> attaches to the end of a number expression, to make it an approximate number.

---

8. Expansion Drill

Ex: T: Léih Táai wah nī   T: Mrs. Lee says this one is ten
    gihn sahp mān.   dollars.

   S: Léih Táai wah ngóh   S: Mrs. Lee told me this one is
    jī nī gihn sahp mān   ten dollars.

1. Léih Sàang wah kéuih sahp   1. Léih Sàang wah ngóh jī
   dīm fàanlàih.   kéuih sahp dīm fàan-
                     làih.

2. Kéuih wah gó go yàhn haih   2. Kéuih wah ngóh jī gó go
   sing Wòhng ge.   yàhn haih sing Wòhng ge.

3. Chàhn Táai wah kéuih hohk   3. Chàhn Táai wah ngóh jī
   Gwóngdùngwá.   kéuih hohk Gwóngdùngwá.

4. Hòh Síujé wah kéuih go bīu   4. Hòh Síujé wah ngóh jī kéuih
   hóu pèhng.   go bīu hóu pèhng.

5. Kéuih wah kéuih sahpyih dīm   5. Kéuih wah ngóh jī kéuih
   yiu jáu laak.   sahpyih dīm yiu jáu laak.

Comment: <u>wah (Person jī)</u>,'tell someone', is interchangeable with
    <u>góng (Person) tèng</u>, <u>góng (Person) jī</u>, and <u>wah (Person)</u>
    <u>tèng</u>.

Learn to recognize the alternate ways when you hear
them.

---

9. Expansion Drill

Ex: T: Kéuih sihk faahn.   T: He is eating dinner.

   S: Giu kéuih sihk faahn   S: Tell him to come to dinner!
    lā!   (i.e. Dinner is on the
                   table-come eat.)

1. Léih Táai, tèng dihnwá.   1. Giu Léih Táai tèng dihnwá lā!
   Telephone for you, Mrs. Lee.   Tell Mrs. Lee to come to
                   the phone.

2. Kéuih yìhgā fàanlàih.   2. Giu kéuih yìhgā fàanlàih lā!
   He's coming back now.   Tell him to come back
                   right now.

3. Kéuih dáng jahn joi dá làih.   3. Giu kéuih dáng jahn joi
                       dá làih lā!

He'll call back in a little while.	Tell him to call back in a little while.

4. Kéuih léuhng dím làih wán ngóh.
   She's coming to see me [lit: look for me] at two o'clock.
+ (heui wán yàhn = go see someone)

4. Giu kéuih léuhng dím làih wán ngóh lā!
   Tell her to come see me at 2 o'clock.

5. Kéuih gaau ngóh góng Gwóngdùngwá.

5. Giu kéuih gaau ngóh góng Gwóngdùngwá lā!

---

10. Response Drill

Ex: T: Nī bún syù haih bīngo ga? /ngóh/

T: Whose book is this? /I/

+ S: Haih ngóh ge.
   (ge = possessive marker)

S: It's mine.

1. Gó bá jē haih bīngo ga? /ngóh gùngyàhn/

1. Haih ngóh gùngyàhn ge.

2. Nī dī bāt haih bīngo ga? /Léih Síujé/

2. Haih Léih Síujé ge.

3. Gó dī maht haih bīngo ga? /Wòhng Sàang/

3. Haih Wòhng Sàang ge.

4. Nī léuhng jī bējáu haih bīngo ga? /ngóh pàhngyáuh/

4. Haih ngóh pàhngyáuh ge.

5. Gó sàam go pìhnggwó haih bīngo ga? /gó go Yìnggwokyàhn/

5. Haih gó go Yìnggwokyàhn ge.

---

11. Response Drill

Ex: T: Bīn jī yùhnjíbāt haih néih ga? /hāak sīk/

T: Which ball point pen is yours?

S: Hāaksīk gó jī.

S: That (or the) black one.

1. Bīn gihn sēutsāam haih néih pàhngyáuh ga? /chèuhngdī/

1. Chèuhngdī gó gihn.

2. Bīn bá jē haih néih ga? /daaihdī/

2. Daaihdī gó bá.

3. Bīn bún syù haih néih ga? /saidī/

3. Saidī gó bún.

4. Bīn gihn làangsāam haih néih ga? /sa'ahsei houh/

4. Sa'ahsei houh gó gihn.

5. Bīn deui hàaih haih néih ga?   5. Baat houh gó deui.
   /baat houh/

6. Bīn tiuh fu haih néih ga?   6. Dyún gó tiuh.
   /dyún/

_____

12. Substitution Drill: Repeat the first sentence, then substitute as
    directed.

1. Ngóh hóu jùngyi yám bējáu.   1. Ngóh hóu jùngyi yám bējáu.
   I like to drink beer. =
   I like beer.

2. /kéuih/   2. Kéuih hóu jùngyi yám bējáu.
                                           He likes to drink beer.

3. /séung/   3. Kéuih séung yám bējáu.
                                           He'd like some beer.

4. /mēyéh/   4. Kéuih séung yám mēyéh a?
                                           What would he like to
                                           drink?

5. /jùngyi/   5. Kéuih jùngyi yám mēyéh a?
                                           What does he like ...?
                                           or (Polite)
                                           What does he want ...?

6. /gafē/   6. Kéuih jùngyi yám gafē.
                                           He likes coffee.

7. /m̀hjùngyi/   7. Kéuih m̀hjùngyi yám gafē.
                                           He does not like coffee.

8. /m̀hséung/   8. Kéuih m̀hséung yám gafē.
                                           He does not want any
                                           coffee.

9. /séung m̀hséung/   9. Kéuih séung m̀hséung yám gafē
                                           a?
                                           Would he like some coffee?

10. /hóu séung/   10. Kéuih hóu séung yám gafē.
                                            He'd like very much to
                                            have some coffee.

11. /hóu jùngyi/   11. Kéuih hóu jùngyi yám gafē.
                                            He likes coffee.

_____

IV. CONVERSATIONS FOR LISTENING

    (On tape. Listen to tape with book closed.)

_____

V.   SAY IT IN CANTONESE

A. On the telephone, you say:

   1. Hello, who are you calling?

   2. Mr. Chang is out--may I take a message [lit: What is your business?]

   3. What did you say your name was? Please speak louder.

   4. Mrs. Ma has gone to work.

   5. May I speak to Mr. Lee?

   6. Please ask Miss Ho to come to the phone.

   7. My phone number is _____.

   8. Hello, what number did you say?

   9. When is Mr. Lau coming home?

   10. When he comes back I'll tell him.

B. And the other person responds:

   1. Please ask Mr. Chang to come to the phone.

   2. My name is Wong. Please ask Mr. Chang to call me when he gets back.

   3. My name is _____. My phone number is _____.

   4. Will she be home for lunch?

   5. He's gone home.

   6. You have the wrong number.

   7. Just a minute, let me get a pen.

   8. _____.

   9. I don't know. Do you have a message?

   10. Thank you.

Vocabulary Checklist for Lesson 9

1.	aan (var: ngaan)	bf:	noon, midday
2.	chēut gāai	VO:	go out (from one's own house)
3.	cho	n/v:	mistake, make a mistake
4.	Daaihsèngdī	Ph:	Speak louder!
5.	dáng yātján (also dáng yātjahn)	Ph:	wait awhile
6.	Daap cho sin!	Ph:	Wrong number! [caught-mistake-line]
7.	dá	v:	hit
8.	dihnwá	VO:	make a telephone call
9.	dáng	v:	wait
10.	dáng Person Verb	v:	allow, let Person do something; wait while Person does something.
11.	dihnwá	n:	telephone
12.	dím bun	TW:	1:30 o'clock

219

13. fàan	v:	return (to/from a place you habitually go to)
14. fàan gùng	VO:	go [return] to work
15. fàan hohk	VO:	to to school
16. fàanlàih	v:	come back, return (here)
17. fàan (ng)ūkkéi	VO:	go [return] home
18. gamseuhnghá	Ph:	approximately
19. ge	bf:	mark of the possessive. joins with preceding personal noun (or pronoun) to form possessive.
20. géidō houh?	Ph:	what number?
21. géisi? or géisìh?	QW:	when?
22. giu	v:	instruct, tell, order, call
23. góng Person jì	Ph:	tell someone
24. góng Person tèng	Ph:	tell someone
25. gùngyàhn	n:	servant, laborer
26. heui gāai	VO:	go out (from one's own house)
27. -jó	Vsuf:	verb suf. indicating accomplishment of the action
28. joi dálàih	Ph:	call back (on the phone)
29. lèhng	nu:	'and a little bit' in a number phrase
30. lìhng	nu:	zero
31. ló	v:	fetch, to go get (something)
32. ngaan	bf:	noon, midday
33. ngūkkéi or ūkkéi	PW:	home
34. sih	v:	business, affair, matter
35. sihk (ng)aan	VO:	eat lunch
36. sìn	adv/ss:	first
37. sin	n:	line, thread
38. tèng	v:	hear, listen to
39. tèng dihnwá	VO:	talk [listen] on the telephone
40. ūkkéi or ngūkkéi	PW:	home
41. wah ngoh jì	Ph:	tell me
42. wah yàhn tèng	Ph:	tell someone
43. wah yàhn jì	Ph:	tell someone
44. wán	v:	look for, search
45. wán yàhn	VO:	look someone up

46. heui/làih wán yàhn   Ph: come/go see someone

47. Wéi!   ex: Hello! (Telephone greeting)

48. (Yáuh) mēyéh sih a?   Ph: What is it you want? (i.e.,(on the phone)
                                    May I take a message?)

49. yáuh sih   VO: have something to attend to; have errand,
                                    business

50. yiu   auxV: going to, intend to

I. BASIC CONVERSATION

  A. Buildup:

yàuhhaak	tourist

Yàuhhaak

bĭndouh?	where?
hái	location verb, variously translated. 'is located.'
hái bĭndouh a?	where is (it)?
jáudìm	hotel
Màhnwàh Jáudìm	Mandarin Hotel
Màhnwàh Jáudìm hái bĭndouh a?	Where is the Mandarin Hotel?
Chéng mahn ...?	May I ask ...? polite form used in asking questions, equivalent to English: Could you please tell me ...?
Chéng mahn, Màhnwàh Jáudìm hái bĭndouh a?	Could you please tell me where the Mandarin Hotel is?

Búndeihyàhn

búndeihyàhn	a native, person belonging to a place by ancestry and upbringing.
-bihn	side
gó bihn	over there, on that side
hái gó bihn	(it) is over there
Nē!	there! an exclamation accompanying pointing out something to somebody.
Nē!-hái gó bihn.	There!--over there.

Yàuhhaak

táidóu	see [look successfully = see]
táimhdóu	look, but don't see; don't see.

222

Deuihàyjyuh, ngóh táiàhdóu.   Excuse me, I don't see it. Over
  Gó bihn bĭndouh a?   there where?

<u>Búndeihyàhn</u>

    deuimihn   opposite, facing
    màhtàuh   pier, wharf
    màhtàuh deuimihn   opposite the pier
    Tĭnsĭng Màhtàuh   Star Ferry Pier
Hái Tĭnsĭng Màhtàuh deuimihn.   It's opposite the Star Ferry
                                Pier.

           <u>Yàuhhaak</u>

    gūngsĭ   department store
    yáuh móuh gūngsĭ a?   is there a department store?
    nĭjógán, (var: jógán)   hereabouts, close by
Nĭjógán yáuh móuh gūngsĭ a?   Is there a department store
                                near here?

           <u>Búndeihyàhn</u>

Yáuh.   Yes, there is.
    gàan   measure for buildings
Nē - gó bihn yáuh gàan.   There's one over there.
    ngàhnhòhng   bank
    gó gàan ngàhnhòhng   that bank
    gaaklèih   next to, adjacent
Hái gó gàan ngàhnhòhng gaaklèih.   Next to the bank.
           <u>Yàuhhaak</u>

A! Táidóu laak! Ñhgòi.   Oh, I see it! Thanks.

B. <u>Recapitulation</u>:
           <u>Yàuhhaak</u>

Chéng mahn, Màhnwàh Jáudim   Could you please tell me where
  hái bĭndouh a?   the Mandarin Hotel is?
           <u>Búndeihyàhn</u>

Nē!--hái gó bihn.   There!--over there.
           <u>Yàuhhaak</u>

Deuiàhjyuh, ngóh táiàhdóu.   Excuse me, I don't see it.
  Gó bihn bĭndouh a?   Over there where?

Búndeihyàhn

Hái Tīnsīng Máhtàuh deuimihn.   It's opposite the Star Ferry
                                                        Pier.

Yàuhhaak

Nījógán yáuh móuh gūngsī a?   Is there a department store
                                                        near here?

Búndeihyàhn

Yáuh. Nē - gó bihn yáuh gàan.   Yes, there is. There's one
Hái gó gàan ngàhnhòhng gaak-   over there. It's next to
lèih.   the bank.

Yàuhhaak

A! Táidóu laak! Mhgòi.   Oh, I see it! Thanks.

II. NOTES

A. Culture Notes: Restaurants:

   In this lesson we introduce two of the many names for different
types of restaurants: chāansāt, and chàhlàuh. Chāansāt is the generic
term for a restaurant serving Western food. (Western in contrast
to Chinese, that is.) chàhlàuh is the word for Cantonese teahouse,
mentioned in the notes for Lesson 5. In the teahouse you select what
you want to eat from trays of hot snacks that are circulated up and
down the aisles of the restaurant by vendor-girls. You don't have
to order, just point. Very convenient for beginning language students.
Of other names for restaurants, chāantēng refers to restaurants
serving Western food. (chāansāt is the generic term, chāantēng is
more elegant, used more frequently in restaurant names. Ex: Méih
Sām Chāantēng haih gàan chāansāt. 'Maxim's Restaurant is a restaurant
serving Western food.)

   Restaurants serving Chinese food are called jáugā, jáulàuh,
faahndim, choigwún, and faahngwún.

B. Structure Notes

   1. Placewords.

      Placeword is a name given to expressions which can, as the
final element in the sentence, follow the location verb hái. Placewords can occupy the positions of subject, object, and modifier.

There are several different kinds of placewords:

1. Geographic names:

    Hèunggóng = Hong Kong

    Kéuih yìhgā hái Hèunggóng. = He is in Hong Kong now.

Geographic names may also function as ordinary nouns,

though this is not their most common use.

    Ex: Bīngo wah yáuh   Who says there are two Hong

        léuhng go   Kongs?

        Hèunggóng a?

2. Locatives

Locatives are pronouns of place, whose meanings derive

from position in relation to another element:

    Ex: nīdouh   = 'here' [near-place]

                    in relationship to the speaker =
                    near the speaker

        gódouh   = 'there' [distant-place]

                    in relationship to the speaker =
                    distant from the speaker

        deuimihn = opposite, facing [facing-face]

                    in relationship to speaker or other
                    place element: facing the point of
                    reference.

    Kéuih hái nīdouh.   He is here.

    Kéuih hái gódouh.   He is there.

    Kéuih hái deuimihn.   He is facing (this way).

    (See BC and Drill _6_)

Locatives may be preceded by placeword nouns in modifi-

cation-head structure.

    Ex: Kéuih hái gaaklèih.   He is next door.
                             [adjacent]

        Kéuih hái ngàhnhòhng   He is next door to the
        gaaklèih.   bank.

    (See BC and Drill _7_)

3. Some ordinary nouns double as placewords.

    Ex: chàhlàuh = teahouse

    a. as an ordinary noun:

        Gó gàan chàhlàuh   That teahouse is very
        hóu gwai.   expensive.

225

b. as a placeword:

Wòhng Sàang hái   Mr. Wong is at the tea-
  chàhlàuh.   house.

(See Drill 2)

4. Nouns and pronouns which are not placewords (cannot
   follow hái as final element in sentence) form placeword phrases by suffixing a locative or the boundword
   -douh 'place.'

Ex: Bún syù hái ngóh   The book is (here) by me.
      (nī)douh.

    Bún syù hái Léih   The book is at Mr. Lee's.
      Sàang douh.

    Bún syù hái tói   The book is (there) on
      (gó)douh.   the table.

2. -douh, -syu = placeword formants

   -douh 'place,' is a boundform, left-bound to the verb hái,
or to one of the specifiers nī/gó/bīn, or to a noun or pronoun to
form a place phrase.

Ex: 1. Wòhng Táai hái m̀hhái   Is Mrs. Wong at home? or
         douh a?   here? or there? [i.e.,
                                  at the place where the
                                  listener is]

    Hái douh.   (She) is here.

    M̀hhái douh.   She's not here.

    2. Kéuih hái nīdouh.   She's at this place.

    3. Kéuih hái ngóh douh. She's at my place. (here
                             by me.)

   -syu, 'place,' is another boundword of place, which can be
substituted for -douh everywhere. In Hong Kong -douh seems favored
by most speakers, but -syu is occasionally heard also.

3. hái = location verb, requiring placeword object.

   a. hái occurs: (1) as the only verb in the sentence, and
                  (2) as one verb in a series of verbal expressions.

      (1) as the only verb in the sentence:

          aff: Kéuih hái Méihgwok.   He's in America.

          neg: Kéuih m̀hhái Méihgwok.   He isn't in America.

            q: Kéuih hái m̀hhái   Is he in America?
               Méihgwok a?

          (See BC and Drills 1, 2, 3, 4)

226

(2) as one verb in a series of verbal expressions:

aff: Kéuih hái ūkkéi dáng   She's waiting (or waited)
    ngóh.   for me at home.

neg: Kéuih m̀hhái ūkkéi   She's not waiting (or
    dáng ngóh.   didn't wait) for me at home.

q: Kéuih haih m̀hhaih   Is she waiting (or did she
    hái ūkkéi dáng néih a?   wait) for you at home?

(See Drill 9)

b. Translation of hái into English

When hái is the only verb in the sentence, it translates into English as the appropriate tense and person of the verb 'be,' with in/on/at/ added as necessary, according to the requirements of English grammar.

Ex: 1. Kéuih hái méihgwok.   He is/was in   America.

    2. Kéuih hái ūkkéi.   He is/was (at)   home.

    3. Kéuih hái séjihlàuh.   He is/was at   the office.

    4. Kéuih hái gódouh.   He is/was   there.

When hái is one verb in a series of verbs, it translates into English as a preposition-- 'at,' 'on,' or 'in.'

Ex: Kéuih hái Méihgwok   He waited/is waiting for
    dáng ngóh.   me in America.

4. Placeword yáuh Noun sentence type.

The Placeword yáuh Noun sentence is a form of SVO sentence, with yáuh as 'there is,' 'there are,' 'there exists.'

Ex: aff: 1. Gaaklèih yáuh (gàan)   Next door there is a bank.
    ngàhnhòhng.

neg: 2. Gaaklèih móuh   There's no bank next door.
    ngàhnhòhng.

q: 3. Gaaklèih yáuh móuh   Is there a bank next door?
    ngàhnhòhng a?

(See BC and Drills 11, 12, 13)

5. Pivotal constructions: PW yáuh SVO

The PW yáuh N sentence can be expanded to PW yáuh SVO, with the S of the SVO standing as the object of the first verb (yáuh) and the subject of the verb which follows it. Such a construction, in which the object of V_1 is the subject of V_2, we call a pivotal construction.

Ex: Gaaklèih yáuh yàhn sihk   Next door there are people
    faahn.   (or there is someone)
                         eating dinner.

(See Drill 14)

6. <u>-dóu</u> = verb suffix, indicating successful accomplishment of action of the verb.

   a. Verbs which take the suffix <u>-dóu</u> include the following:

Verb		V-dóu	
tái	look	táidóu	see [look successfully]
wán	search, look for	wándóu	find [search successfully]
máaih	buy	máaihdóu	buy [i.e. after overcoming obstacles]

   b. Illustrative examples:

     A. Tái m̀htáidóu gó gàan   A: Do you see that bank?
        ngàhnhòhng a?

     B. Táidóu.   B: Yes, I see it.

     C. Táim̀hdóu.   C: No, I don't see it.

     A. Nē, hái gó gàan jáudim   A: There--next to the hotel.
        gaaklèih.

     C. A, yìhgā táidóu laak.   C: Oh, now I see it.

   c. Verb forms of <u>V-dóu</u>:

       aff: táidóu

       neg: táim̀hdóu (<u>or</u> m̀htáidóu)

         q: tái m̀htáidóu? (<u>or</u> tái m̀htáidākdóu?)

     Of the negative forms <u>V-m̀hdóu</u> is more common, though <u>m̀htáidóu</u> also is said. Both question forms are common.

              (See BC and Drill <u>13</u>)

III. DRILLS

1. Expansion Drill: Students point nearby for nīdouh, away for gódouh.

    Ex: T: /Ngóh/Néih/Kéuih/   T: I, you, he.

  + S: Ngóh hái nīdouh.   S: I'm here;
  +   Néih hái gódouh.   you're there;
        Kéuih hái bīndouh a?   where's she?

1. /ngóhdeih/néihdeih/kéuihdeih/

  1. Ngóhdeih hái nīdouh;
    néihdeih hái gódouh;
    kéuihdeih hái bīndouh a?

2. /Chàhn Sàang/Chàhn Táai/Chàhn Síujé/

  2. Chàhn Sàang hái nīdouh;
    Chàhn Táai hái gódouh;
    Chàhn Síujé hái bīndouh a?

3. /tìuh fu/gihn sēutsāam/ deui hàaih/

  3. Tìuh fu hái nīdouh;
    gihn sēutsāam hái gódouh;
    deui hàaih hái bīndouh a?

4. /jī yùhnbāt/jī yùhnjíbāt/ bún syù/

  4. Jī yùhnbāt hái nīdouh;
    jī yùhnjíbāt hái gódouh;
    bún syù hái bīndouh a?

5. /dī pìhnggwó/dī cháang/dī jīu/

  5. Dī pìhnggwó hái nīdouh;
    dī cháang hái gódouh;
    dī jīu hái bīndouh a?

---

2. Conversation Drill: Carry on the suggested conversations following the pattern of the example.

    Ex: T: /jáudím/   hotel

      S1: Kéuih hái bīndouh a?   Where is (or was) he? /hotel/

      S2: Kéuih hái jáudim.   He is (or was) at the hotel.

  1. /ngàhnhòhng/

    1. S1: Kéuih hái bīndouh a?
       S2: Kéuih hái ngàhnhòhng.

+ 2. /chāansāt/
    (Western restaurant)

    2. S1: Kéuih hái bīndouh a?
       S2: Kéuih hái chāansāt.

+ 3. /chàhlàuh/
    (teahouse)

    3. S1: Kéuih hái bīndouh a?
       S2: Kéuih hái chàhlàuh.

  4. /jáudim/

    4. S1: Kéuih hái bīndouh a?
       S2· Kéuih hái jáudim.

+ 5. /séjihlàuh/
    (office)

    5. S1: Kéuih hái bīndouh a?
       S2: Kéuih hái séjihlàuh.

6. /gūngsĪ/

6. S1: Kéuih hái bĪndouh a?
   S2: Kéuih hái gūngsĪ.

+ 7. /tòuhsyùgwún/
     (library)

7. S1: Kéuih hái bĪndouh a?
   S2: Kéuih hái tòuhsyùgwún.

---

3. Expansion Drill:

Ex: T: Chàhn Táai m̀hhái
      ngūkkéi.
      /chāansāt/

T: Mrs. Chan is not at home.

S: Chàhn Táai m̀hhái
   ngūkkéi, hái
   chāansāt.

S: Mrs. Chan is not at home,
   she's at the restaurant.

1. Kéuih m̀hhái tòuhsyùgwún.
   /gūngsĪ/
   He's not at the library.
   /department store/

1. Kéuih m̀hhái tòuhsyùgwún,
   hái gūngsĪ.
   He's not at the library,
   he's at the department
   store.

2. Léih Sàang m̀hhái gūngsĪ.
   /jáudim/

2. Léih Sàang m̀hhái gūngsĪ,
   hái jáudim.

3. Léih SĪujé m̀hhái chāansāt.
   /séjihlàuh/

3. Léih SĪujé m̀hhái chāansāt,
   hái séjihlàuh.

4. Chàhn Sàang m̀hhái séjihlàuh.
   /chāansāt/

4. Chàhn Sàang m̀hhái séjihlàuh,
   hái chāansāt.

+ 5. Màhnwàh Jáudim m̀hhái Daaih
     Douh Jùng. /TĪnsĪng Máhtàuh
     deuimihn/
     The Mandarin Hotel is not on
     Queen's Road Central.
     /opposite the Star Ferry/

5. Màhnwàh Jáudim m̀hhái Daaih
   Douh Jùng, hái TĪnsĪng
   Máhtàuh deuimihn.

+ 6. Go chē jaahm m̀hhái deuimihn.
+   /nĪ bihn/
     The bus stop is not across
     the street. /this side/

6. Go chē jaahm m̀hhái deuimihn,
   hái nĪ bihn.
   The car stop is not across
   the street, it's on this
   side.

+ 7. Méihgwok Ngàhnhòhng m̀hhái nĪ
     bihn. /deuimihn/
     The Bank of America is not on
     this side.

7. Méihgwok Ngàhnhòhng m̀hhái
   nĪ bihn, hái deuimihn.
   The Bank of America is
   not on this side, it's in
   front.

+ 8. Kéuih gàan ngūk m̀hhái Hèunggóng
     nĪ bihn. /Gáulùhng gó bihn/
     His house is not here on the
     Hong Kong side. /there on the
     Kowloon side/

8. Kʹuih gàan ngūk m̀hhái Hèunggóng nĪ bihn, hái Gáulùhng
   gó bihn.

230

9. Hèunggóng chāansāt m̀hhái gó
   bihn. /nǐ bihn/

9. Hèunggóng chāansāt m̀hhái
   góbihn, hái nǐ bihn.

10. Tīnsīng Máhtàuh m̀hhái gaaklèih.
    /deuimihn/

10. Tīnsīng Máhtàuh m̀hhái
    gaaklèih, hái deuimihn.

+ 11. Méihgwok Jáudim m̀hhái (nǐ)
   jógán. (Jùngwàahn/
   The American Hotel is not
   hereabouts. /Central District/

11. Méihgwok Jáudim m̀hhái
    (nǐ) jógán, hái Jùngwàahn.

12. Gó gàan gūngsī m̀hhái nǐ jógán.
    /Daaih Douh Jùng/

12. Gó gàan gūngsī m̀hhái nǐ
    jógán, hái Daaih Douh
    Jùng.

Comments: (1) Méihgwok Jáudim, 'American Hotel' is the Hong Kong
              Hilton, also called 'Hèiyìhdeuhn Jáudim'

          (2) (ng)ūk 'house,' is not the one you live in.
              ngūkkéi, 'home,' 'house one lives in'

---

4. Alteration Drill

   Ex: T: Wòhng Sàang hái   T: Is Mr. Wong at home?
          m̀hhái ūkkéi a?

       S: Wòhng Sàang haih   S: Is Mr. Wong at home?
          m̀hhaih hái ūkkéi a?

   1. Kéuih hái m̀hhái séjihlàuh a?   1. Kéuih haih m̀hhaih hái
                                          séjihlàuh a?

   2. Chàhn Síujé bá jē hái m̀hhái   2. Chàhn Síujé bá jē haih
      nǐdouh a?   m̀hhaih hái nǐdouh a?
      Is Miss Chan's umbrella
      here?

   3. Hòh Táai gihn làangsāam hái   3. Hòh Táai gihn làangsāam
      m̀hhái néih ūkkéi a?   haih m̀hhaih hái néih
      Is Mrs. Ho's sweater at   ūkkéi a?
      your house?

   Comment: a location question of the choice type may be either
            hái m̀hhái Placeword? or haih m̀hhaih hái Placeword?

---

5. Substitution Drill: Repeat first sentence, then substitute as
   directed.
   1. Méihgwok Jáudim hái bǐndouh a?   1. Méihgwok Jáudim hái bǐndouh
      Where is the American Hotel?   a?

   2. /Màhnwàh Jáudim/   2. Màhnwàh Jáudim hái bǐndouh
                                          a?

3. /Méihgwok Ngàhnhòhng/

3. Méihgwok Ngàhnhòhng hái bindouh a?

4. /Daaih Douh Jùng/

4. Daaih Douh Jùng hái bindouh a?

5. /Néih ge séjihlàuh/

5. Néih ge séjihlàuh hái bindouh a?

+ 6. /Dākfuh Douh Jùng/
    Des Voeux Road Central

6. Dākfuh Douh Jùng hái bindouh a?

7. /Tīnsīng Máhtàuh/

7. Tīnsīng Máhtàuh hái bindouh a?

---

6. Expansion Drill

Ex: T: Làuh Síujé hái nīdouh. T: Miss Lau is (or was) here.

S: Wòhng Síujé wah ngóh S: Miss Wong told me Miss Lau
   jī Làuh Síujé hái   was here.
   nīdouh.

1. Làuh Síujé hái gódouh.

1. Wòhng Síujé wah ngóh jī Làuh Síujé hái gódouh.

2. Làuh Síujé hái nī bihn.

2. Wòhng Síujé wah ngóh jī Làuh Síujé hái nī bihn.

3. Làuh Síujé hái gó bihn.

3. Wòhng Síujé wah ngóh jī Làuh Síujé hái gó bihn.

4. Làuh Síujé hái deuimihn.

4. Wòhng Síujé wah ngóh jī Làuh Síujé hái deuimihn.

5. Làuh Síujé hái gaaklèih.

5. Wòhng Síujé wah ngóh jī Làuh Síujé hái gaaklèih.

6. Làuh Síujé hái nī jógán.

6. Wòhng Síujé wah ngóh jī. Làuh Síujé hái nī jógán.

+ 7. Làuh Síujé hái mùhnháu.
    Miss Làuh is at the door.
    (doorway)

7. Wòhng Síujé wah ngóh jī Làuh Síujé hái mùhnháu.

---

7. Expansion Drill

Ex: T: Gàan ngàhnhòhng T: The bank is on the opposite
      hái deuimihn.   side. /bus stop/
      /chē jaahm/

S: Gàan ngàhnhòhng hái S: The bank is opposite the bus
   chē jaahm deuimihn.   stop.

232

1. Gàan gūngsī hái deuimihn.
   /jáudim/

1. Gàan gūngsī hái jáudim
   deuimihn.

2. Gàan jáudim hái deuimihn.
   /gūngsī/

2. Gàan jáudim hái gūngsī
   deuimihn.

3. Gàan ngàhnhòhng hái nī jógán.
   /chē jaahm/
   The bank is near here.

3. Gàan ngàhnhòhng hái chē
   jaahm nī jógán.
   The bank is near the bus
   stop, here.

4. Go chē jaahm hái nī jógán.
   /ngàhnhòhng/
   The bus stop is nearby. /bank/

4. Go chē jaahm hái ngàhnhòhng
   nī jógán.
   The bus stop is near the
   bank.

5. Gàan gūngsī hái gaaklèih.
   /chāansāt/
   The department store is next
   door. /restaurant/

5. Gàan gūngsī hái chāansāt
   gaaklèih.
   The department store is
   next the restaurant.

6. Gàan chāansāt hái gaaklèih.
   /tòuhsyùgwún/

6. Gàan chāansāt hái tòusyùgwún
   gaaklèih.

7. Ngóh ge séjihlàuh hái nībihn.
   /jáudim/
   My office is on this side
   of the street. /hotel/

7. Ngóh ge séjihlàuh hái jáudim
   nī bihn.
   My office is this side
   of the street, on the side
   where the hotel is.

Comment on #7:

chàh-làuh	gūng-sī

jáu-dim	séjih-làuh	ngàhn-hòhng

Ngóh ge séjihlàuh hái jáudim nī bihn. Ngóh,
séjihlàuh, and jáudim are all on the same side
of the street. Above, in refering to the dept.
store, speaker would say: Gūngsī hái chàhlàuh
gó bihn. The dept. store is on that side (away
from me) where the teahouse is.

8. Response Drill

   Ex: T: Méihgwok Jáudim
          hái bindouh a?
          /Daaih Douh Jūng/

   T: Where's the Hilton Hotel?

   S: Méihgwok Jáudim hái
      Daaih Douh Jūng.

   S: The Hilton Hotel is on Queen's
      Road Central.

233

1. Néih ge séjihlàuh hái bīndouh
   a? /Dākfuh Douh Jùng/

          1. Ngóh ge séjihlàuh hái Dākfuh
   Douh Jùng.

2. Méihgwok Jáudim hái bīndouh a?
   /Daaih Douh Jùng/

          2. Méihgwok Jáudim hái Daaih
   Douh Jùng.

3. Daaih Douh Jùng hái bīndouh a?
   /Hèunggóng nī bihn/
   on the Hongkong side

          3. Daaih Douh Jùng hái
   Hèunggóng nī bihn.

+ 4. Màhnwàh Jáudim hái bīnbihn a?
   /deuimihn/ (which side?)

          4. Màhnwàh Jáudim hái deuimihn.

5. Tīnsīng Máhtàuh hái bīndouh a?
   /gó bihn/

          5. Tīnsīng Máhtàuh hái gó bihn.

6. Go chē jaahm hái bīndouh a?
   /ngàhnhòhng deuimihn/

          6. Go chē jaahm hái ngàhnhòhng
   deuimihn.

7. Tòuhsyùgwún hái bīndouh a?
   /gaaklèih/

          7. Tòuhsyùgwún hái gaaklèih.

Comment: People in Hongkong identify places as being 'on the
Hongkong side' or 'on the Kowloon side'. Kowloon and Hongkong are on opposite sides of the Hongkong Harbour.
Hèunggóng nī bihn 'on the Hongkong side' [Hongkong this
side] is said from the standpoint of a person who is on
the Hongkong side. To him the Kowloon side would be
Gáulùhng gó bihn 'on the Kowloon side' [Kowloon that side].

---

9. Combining Drill

     Ex: T: Kéuih hái Méihgwok
          Jáudim.
          Kéuih dáng ngóh.

     T: He is (or was) at the American
        Hotel.
        He is (or was) waiting
        (or He waited) for me.

     S: Kéuih hái Méihgwok
          Jáudim dáng ngóh.

     S: He is (or was) waiting, (or
        He waited) for me at the
        American Hotel.

1. Kéuih hái mùhnháu.
   Kéuih dáng pàhngyáuh.

          1. Kéuih hái mùhnháu dáng
   pàhngyáuh.

2. Kéuih hái Tīnsīng Máhtàuh.
   Kéuih dáng pàhngyáuh.

          2. Kéuih hái Tīnsīng Máhtàuh
   dáng pàhngyáuh.

3. Jèung Sàang hái Yahtbún.
   Jàung Sàang gaau Yahtmàhn.

          3. Jèung Sàang hái Yahtbún
   gaau Yahtmàhn.

4. Ngóh hái Hèunggóng.
   Ngóh hohk Gwóngdùngwá.

          4. Ngóh hái Hèunggóng hohk
   Gwóngdùngwá.

+ 5. Kéuih hái Méihgwok Ngàhnhòhng.
   Kéuih ló chín.
   He withdraws money.

          5. Kéuih hái Méihgwok Ngàhn-
   hòhng ló chín.
   He's at the Bank of
   America withdrawing money.

+ 6. Chèuhn Táai hái chē jaahm.
    Chèuhn Táai dáng chē.
    Mrs. Cheun is waiting for
    the bus. [vehicle]

6. Chèuhn Táai hái chē jaahm
   dáng chē.

7. Wòhng Síujé hái Jùnggwok
   Chàhlàuh.
   Wòhng Síujé sihk faahn.

7. Wòhng Síujé hái Jùnggwok
   Chàhlàuh sihk faahn.

---

10. Expansion Drill

Ex: T: Néih bá jē hái
       gódouh. /Làuh
       Táai/

    T: Your umbrella is over there.
       /Mrs. Lau/

    S: Néih bá jē hái Làuh
       Táai gódouh.

    S: Your umbrella is there by Mrs.
       Lau.

1. Jī yùhnbāt hái nīdouh. /ngóh/
2. Gihn yúhlāu hái gódouh.
   /Wòhng Táai/
3. Ngóh bāau yīnjái hái nīdouh.
   /Léih Sàang/
4. Tìuh kwàhn hái nīdouh. /ngóh/
5. Gihn sāam hái gódouh. /kéuih/

1. Jī yùhnbāt hái ngóh nīdouh.
2. Gihn yúhlāu hái Wòhng Táai
   gódouh.
3. Ngóh bāau yīnjái hái Léih
   Sàang nīdouh.
4. Tìuh kwàhn hái ngóh nīdouh.
5. Gihn sāam hái kéuih gódouh.

Comment: Nouns and pronouns which do not in themselves have any
        reference to place, can function in placeword ex-
        pressions when joined to a following locative.

---

11. Conversation Exercise

Ex: A: Nīdouh jógán yáuh
       móuh chāansāt a?

    A: Is there a western restaurant
       around here?

    B: Yáuh. Deuimihn yáuh
       gàan.

    B: Yes. There's one across the
       street.

1. A. ....?

   B. Yáuh. Gó bihn ......

1. A. Nīdouh jógán yáuh móuh
   chāansāt a?
   B. Yáuh. Gó bihn yáuh gàan.

2. A. ....?

   B. Yáuh. Gaaklèih ......

2. A. Nīdouh jógán yáuh móuh
   chāansāt a?
   B. Yáuh. Gaaklèih yáuh gàan.

3. A. ....?

3. A. Nīdouh jógán yáuh móuh
   chāansāt a?

B. Yáuh. Dāk Fuh Douh Jùng ...   B. Yáuh. Dāk Fuh Douh Jùng
                                           yáuh gàan.

4. A. ....?   4. A. Nĭdouh jógán yáuh móuh
                                    chāansāt a?

   B. Yáuh. Daaih Douh Jùng ...   B. Yáuh. Daaih Douh Jùng
                                       yáuh gàan.

5. A. ....?   5. A. Nĭdouh jógán yáuh móuh
                                    chāansāt a?

   B. Yáuh. Ngàhnhòhng gaaklèih.   B. Yáuh. Ngàhnhòhng gaaklèih
                                       yáuh gàan.

6. A. ....?   6. A. Nĭdouh jógán yáuh móuh
                                    chāansāt a?

   B. Yáuh. Gó gàan gūngsĭ   B. Yáuh. Gó gàan gūngsĭ
      deuimihn ...   deuimihn yáuh gàan.

---

12. Substitution Drill: Repeat the first sentence then substitute as
    directed.

   1. Chéng mahn, nĭdouh jógán yáuh   1. Nĭdouh jógán yáuh móuh
      móuh gūngsĭ a?   gūngsĭ a?
      Could you please tell me,
      is there a department store
      around here?

   2. /chē jaahm/   2. Chéng mahn, nĭ jógán yáuh
                                               móuh chē jaahm a?

   3. /jáudim/   3. Chéng mahn, nĭdouh jógán
                                               yáuh móuh jáudim a?

   4. /chāansāt/   4. Chéng mahn, nĭ jógán yáuh
                                               móuh chāansāt a?

   5. /ngàhnhòhng/   5. Chéng mahn, nĭdouh jógán
                                               yáuh móuh ngàhnhòhng a?

---

13. Conversation Drill

        Ex: T: /deuimihn/   T: opposite

      +   S1: Néih tái m̀htáidóu   S1: Can you see what there is
             deuimihn yáuh   opposite us?
             mēyéh a?

           T: /jáudim/   T: hotel

           S2: Deuimihn yáuh gàan   S2: Opposite us there's a hotel. or
             jáudim.   There's a hotel across the
                                             street.

236

1./gaaklèih/   1. A. Néih tái m̀htáidóu gaak-
                                          lèih yáuh mēyéh a?

   /gūngsī/   B. Gaaklèih yáuh gàan
                                        gūngsī.

2./gódouh/   2. A. Néih tái m̀htáidóu gódouh
                                          yáuh mēyéh a?

   /chāansāt/   B. Gódouh yáuh gàan chāansāt.

3./deuimihn/   3. A. Néih tái m̀htáidóu deui-
                                          mihn yáuh mēyéh a?

   /chē jaahm/   B. Deuimihn yáuh go chē
                                        jaahm.

4./gaaklèih/   4. A. Néih tái m̀htáidóu gaak-
                                          lèih yáuh mēyéh a?

   /ngàhnhòhng/   B. Gaaklèih yáuh gàan
                                        ngàhnhòhng.

6./nī bihn/   5. A. Néih tái m̀htáidóu nībihn
                                          yáuh mēyéh a?

   /jáudim/   B. Nī bihn yáuh gàan jáudim.

---

14. Alteration Drill

     Ex: T: Gó go yàhn dá dihn-   T: That man is making a phone
         wá. /gódouh/   call/there/

         S: Gódouh yáuh go   S: Over there there's a man
            yàhn dá dihnwá.   making a phone call.

   1. Gó go yàhn wán néih.   1. Mùhnháu gódouh yáuh go yàhn
      /mùhnháu gódouh/   wán néih.
                                       There's a man at the door
                                       looking for you.

   2. Gó wái sīnsàang dáng chē.   2. Chē jaahm gódouh yáuh wái
      /chē jaahm gódouh/   sīnsàang dáng chē.

   3. Gó go Yīnggwokyàhn sihk chāan. 3. Chāansāt gódouh yáuh go
      /chāansāt gódouh/   Yīnggwokyàhn sihk chāan.

+ 4. Gó go Méihgwokyàhn tái syù.   4. Séjihlàuh gódouh yáuh go
      /séjihlàuh gódouh/ ([read-   Méihgwokyàhn tái syù.
      book], read)
      That American is reading.

   5. Gó go yàhn maaih cháang.   5. Mùhnháu yáuh go yàhn maaih
      /mùhnháu/   cháang.

   6. Gó go yàhn dá dihnwá.   6. Gó bihn yáuh go yàhn dá
      /gó bihn/   dihnwá.

237

Comment: Note that in the left hand column sentences above, of the structure: <u>Noun Phrase Verb Phrase</u>, the nouns are

gó go yàhn = <u>that</u> person.

In the right hand column sentences, of the structure: <u>Placeword yáuh Noun Phrase Verb Phrase</u>, the nouns are un-specific:

go yàhn = '<u>a</u> person'.

This is characteristic of the <u>Placeword yáuh</u> ...... structure.

Compare: (1) Gó go yàhn hái gó bihn   That man is making a
           dá dihnwá.   phone call over there.

         (2) Gó bihn yáuh go yàhn dá   Over there, there's some-
             dihnwá.   one making a phone call.

IV. CONVERSATIONS FOR LISTENING

(On tape. Refer to wordlist below as you listen.)

Unfamiliar terms, in order of occurrence:

1) yātján = dángyātjahn = 'in a little while'

2) wán m̀hdóu = can't find it, search but not successful

V. SAY IT IN CANTONESE

A. You ask a pedestrian:

1. Could you please tell me where the Star Ferry is?

2. Could you please tell me where the Hilton Hotel is?

3. Is there a car stop around here?

4. Where is the Bank of America?

B. And he responds:

1. There! (pointing) It's over there.

2. There! It's across the street.

3. Yes, there's one opposite the library.

4. The Bank of America is in Central District.

C. You ask a friend:

1. Where is your umbrella?

2. Where is your office?

3. Can you make out (see successfully) what that is across the street?

D. And he replies:

1. It's here.

2. It's on Des Voeux Road Central.

3. Across the street there's a tea-house.

238

4. Who is over there waiting
   for you?

5. Where is Mr. Wong's office?

6. Is Mr. Wong in his office now?

7. There's a man over there
   making a phone call--
   do you know him?

4. It's my wife.

5. It's next to my office.

6. No, he's at home.

7. Yes, he's my student.

Vocabulary Checklist for Lesson 10

1.	bīnbihn?	PW:	which side?
2.	-bihn	bf:	side
3.	bīndouh?	QW:	where?
4.	búndeihyàhn	n:	a native of the place under discussion
5.	chāansāt	n/PW:	western style restaurant
6.	chàhlàuh	n/PW:	Cantonese style tea-house
7.	chē	n:	vehicle: car, bus, or tram
8.	chē jaahm	n/PW:	car stop (bus or tram stop)
9.	chéng mahn	Ph:	'May I ask...?'
10.	Daaih Douh Jùng	PW:	Queen's Road Central
11.	Dakfuh Douh Jùng	PW:	Des Veoux Road Central
12.	deuimihn	PW:	opposite side
13.	-dóu	vs:	verb suffix indicating successful accomplishment of the action of the verb.
14.	gàan	m:	M. for buildings
15.	gaaklèih	PW:	next door
16.	gódouh	PW:	there
17.	gó bihn	PW:	over there, on that side
18.	gūngsī	n/PW:	department store; office (of a commercial company)
19.	hái	v:	location verb, translated as: is in/at/on
20.	Hèunggóng	PW:	Hong Kong
21.	jaahm	n:	station, stop (as train station, bus stop)
22.	jáudim	n/PW:	hotel
23.	jógán	PW:	nearby, hereabouts
24.	Jùngwàahn	PW:	Central District

25. ló chín	VO:	withdraw money (from bank)
26. máhtàuh	n/PW:	pier
27. Màhnwàh Jáudim	PW:	Mandarin Hotel
28. mahn	v:	ask
29. Méihgwok Jáudim	PW:	'American Hotel,' (in HK, the Hong Kong Hilton)
30. Méihgwok Ngàhnhòhng	PW:	Bank of America
31. mùhnháu	n/PW:	doorway
32. Nē!	ex:	'There!' an exclamation used when pointing out something to someone
33. nībihn	PW:	this side
34. nīdouh	PW:	here
35. nījógán	PW:	closeby, hereabouts
36. ngàhnhòhng	n/PW:	bank
37. ngūk (or ūk)	n/PW:	house
38. séjihlàuh	n/PW:	office
39. táimhdóu	VP:	can't see
40. táidóu	VP:	see [look successfully]
41. tái mhtáidóu?	VP:	can [you] see?
42. tái syù	VO:	read (a book)
43. Tīnsīng Máhtàuh	PW:	Star Ferry Pier
44. tòuhsyùgwún	n/PW:	library
45. ūk (var: ngūk)	n/PW:	house
46. yàhnhaak	n:	tourist

BASIC CONVERSATION

A. Buildup:

(A brother and sister are sharing a taxi to work)

saimúi	younger sister

Saimúi

m̀hgeidāk	forgot, forget
daai	carry, take or bring along
m̀hgeidāk daai chín	forgot to bring money
tìm	sentence suffix, indicating taken by surprise
Ngóh m̀hgeidāk daai chín tìm!	I forgot to bring my money!
Aiya! Ngóh m̀hgeidāk daai chín tìm!	Aiya! I forgot to bring my money!
agō	elder brother

Agō

M̀hgányiu--ngóh yáuh.	Never mind--I have (some).

(He hands $3.00 to the driver)

jáaufàan	give back change (give change--return)
jáaufàan sàam hòuh	give back 30¢ change
dāk laak	that will be all right
Jáaufàan sàam hòuh dāk laak.	Give me 30¢ change, that'll be OK.
sígēi	driver, cab driver, chauffeur

Sígēi

móuhdāk	not have available
Ngóh móuhdāk jáau.	I don't have any change. [don't have (money) available to give change]
sàan ngán	small coins
Néih yáuh móuh sáan ngán a?	Do you have any small coins?

Agō

Yáuh, yáuh.	Yes, I have.

m̀hginjó	lose/lost (something), 'nowhere to be seen'
Yíı	exclamation of distress
Yíı m̀hginjó gé?	Eh? Disappeared?
A--hái douh.	Oh--they're here.
nàhı	here!
Nàh, nídouh chāt hòuhjí.	Here, here's 70¢.

(The two get out of the taxi)

Agō

yuhng	use
Néih yiu chín yuhng.	You'll need some money to use.
je	lend
-jyuh	temporarily, for a short time
jejyuh béi néih	lend to you
Ngóh nídouh jejyuh béi néih sín lā.	I'll lend you some (of what I have) here.
Yiu géidō a?	How much do you need?

Saimúi

Sahp mān gau laak.	Ten dollars will be enough.

Agō

baak	hundred
baak mān	hundred dollars
jí	paper. here, paper money, i.e. $ bill
baak mān jí	hundred dollar bill
jèung	measure for bank notes
jèung yāt baak mān jí	a one-hundred-dollar bill
dāk	have only, only have
ja	jō + a = ja
Ngóh dāk jèung yāt baak mān jí ja.	I only have a hundred dollar bill.
cheunghòi	break (a large note for ones of smaller denomination)

242

Dáng ngóh cheunghòi béi néih
    lā.

I'll get it changed and give
    you (the money).

(They stop in at a bank to change the $100
bill. The elder brother addresses a teller:)

Agō

cheunghoi jèung yāt baak mān jí
    tùhng ngóh

split a hundred dollar bill
    for me, on my behalf

Ńhgòi néih tùhng ngóh cheunghòi
    jèung yāt baak mān jí lā.

Would you please change a
    hundred dollar bill for me.

Síujé

dāk

OK, sure

Dāk. Sahp jèung sahp mān jí
    hóu ṁhhóu a?

Sure. Are 10 ten's OK?

Agō

Hóu aak.

Fine.

B. Recapitulation:

Saimúi

Aiyà! Ngóh ṁhgeidāk daai chín
    tìm!

Aiya! I forgot to bring my
    money!

Ńhgányiu--ngóh yáuh.

Never mind--I have some.

(He hands $3.00 to the driver)

Jáaufāan sāam hòuh dāk laak.

Give me 30¢ change, that'll
    be OK.

Sīgēi

Ngóh móuhdāk jáau. Néih yáuh
    móuh sáan ngán a?

I don't have any change. Do
    you have any small coins?

Agō

Yáuh, yáuh. Yí! Ńhginjó gé?
    A--hái douh. Nàh, nīdouh
    chāt hòuhjí.

Yes, I have. Eh? Disappeared?
    Oh, they're here. Here,
    here's 70¢.

(They get out of the taxi)

Agō

Néih yiu chín yuhng. Ngóh nīdouh
    jejyuh béi néih sīn lā. Yiu

You'll need some money to use.
    I'll lend you some. How much

géidō a?   do you need?

Saimúi

Sahp mān gau laak.   Ten dollars will be enough.

Agō

Ngóh dāk jèung yāt baak mān   I only have a hundred dollar
    jí ja. Dáng ngóh cheunghòi   bill. I'll get it changed
    béi néih lā.   and give you (the money).

        (They stop in at a bank to change the $100
        bill. The elder brother addresses a teller:)

Agō

Mhgòi néih tùhng ngóh cheunghòi   Would you please change a
    jèung yāt baak mān jí lā.   hundred dollar bill for me.

Siujé

Dāk. Sahp jèung sahp mān jí   Sure. Are ten 10's OK?
    hóu mhhóu a?

Agō

Hóu aak.   Fine.

II. NOTES

1. sìn, 'first,'

    sìn, 'first,' attaches to the end of a clause sentence, or a minor
sentence consisting of a timeword, with the implication that something
else is to follow.

        Ex: 1. Dáng ngóh ló jí bāt   1. Let me get a pencil first--
                 sìn lā.   (and then I can write
                                                   down the number.)

            2. Ngóh nīdouh jejyuh   2. I'll lend you (some money)
                 béi néih sìn lā.   first--(and then you can
                                                   get through the day.)

            3. A: Dāk meih a?   3. A: Ready yet?

               B: Meih--dáng jahn sìn   B: Not yet--wait a minute
                    lā.   first--(then I'll be
                                                   ready.)

                    (See BC)

    Students of Mandarin will recall that the Mandarin equivalent of sìn,
syān, occupies a different sentence position. In Mandarin syàn comes before the verb, rather than coming at the end of the clause.

        Ex: Děng wǒ syān ná (yì) jř bǐ lái.   Let me first get a pen.

2. **Dāk** = OK, will do, all right

    a. Forms:

        aff: dāk   That's OK, that'll do, all right, can do.

        neg: m̀hdāk   That's not OK, that won't do, can't.

          q: dāk m̀hdāk a?   Will that be all right?

      Ex: 1. Ngóh séung yìhgā   1. I'd like to eat now, OK?
              sihk faahn, dāk
              m̀hdāk a?

         2. M̀hdāk. Yiu dáng yāt- 2. Not OK. We have to wait awhile.
           jahn sìn.

         3. Dāk. Sihk faahn lā.   3. Sure. Eat!

                  (See BC)

    b. **Dāk** joins with **laak** in the affirmative and **meih** in the negative and question forms to form fixed phrases:

        aff: dāk laak.   It's OK now (change from before) It's ready.

        neg: meih dāk   Not OK yet, it's not ready, it's not right yet.

          q: dāk meih a?   Is it ready yet? Is it OK yet?

      Ex: 1. Ngóh gihn chèuhng-   Is my dress ready yet?
              sāam dāk meih a?

         2. Meih dāk.   Not OK yet.

         3. Dāk laak. Néih   It's ready. Try it on!
           sihāh sìn lā.

3. **Dāk** + quantity phrase = have only, get only, obtain only:

    dāk in this sense has a quantity phrase as its object, with the implication that the quantity is insufficient. It contrasts with yáuh, 'have,' which does not have the connotation of insufficiency.

        1. Ngóh dāk léuhng   I have only two shirts.
           gihn sēutsāam.

        2. Ngóh yáuh léuhng   I have two shirts.
           gihn sēutsāam.

              (See BC and Drill 11)

    dāk, as 'have insufficient amount,' is a defective verb--that is, it does not have all three forms: affirmative, negative, and question. It is not used in the negative form, and does not form the choice question regularly:

Forms:

aff: Dāk jèung yāt baak   Have only a $100 bill.
     mān jí.

neg: -- --   -- --

  q: Haih m̀hhaih dāk   Do you have only a $100 bill?
     jèung yāt baak
     mān jí a?

4. yáuhdāk + verb = 'have available to ..Y..,' 'have available for .Y.ing.'

    dāk used between the verb yáuh (or its negative móuh) and a
second verb, forms a verb phrase (VP) 'have (or not have) available
for .Y.ing.'

    The basic meaning of dāk in a yáuhdāk V is 'can.'

    Ex: aff: yáuhdāk maaih   have-can-sell, have for sale

        neg: móuhdāk maaih   don't have-available for sale

          q: yáuh móuh dāk maaih are there any available for
             a?   sale?

             (See BC and Drills 7, 8)

5. tìm! sentence suffix indicating that the speaker has been taken by
   surprise.

    tìm! adds the connotation that the situation expressed in the
sentence is different from what the speaker expected.

    This tìm! perhaps is derived from tìm, 'more,' 'in addition,'
which you encountered before in Lesson 4, but differs both in implication and in expressive intonation.

    tìm! expressing surprise is a stressed syllable in its sentence,
but tìm, 'in addition' does not receive heavy sentence stress.
Further, tìm, 'in addition' can be followed by another sentence
suffix, but tìm!, expressing surprise, cannot.

    Ex: 1. Joi dáng ngóh géi   'Please wait for me a few
           fānjūng tìm lā.   minutes more.'

        2. M̀géidāk tìm!   I forgot it! (having just
                                 realized it)

             (See BC and Drill 3)

246

6. -dò and -síu phrases of indefinite amounts

   a. -dò 'large amount' and -síu 'small amount' combine with preceding
      hóu- and others to form phrases of indefinite amounts.

   Ex: 1. hóudò   a lot, many, much

       2. géidò   quite a lot

       3. móuhgéidò   not very much

       4. hóusíu   very little, very few

       5. sèsíu   a little

       6. síusíu   just a little, just a few

   b. These -dò/-síu phrases can be used as modifier to a following
      nominal construction or as head in a nominal construction.

      Ex:

      as modifier:

      Ngóh yáuh hóudò chín.   I have a lot of money.

      as head:

      Kéuih dōu yáuh hóudò.   He has a lot too.

   c. sèsíu and síusíu modify mass nouns only, directly preceding the
      noun. As head structures they are used only in connection
      with mass nouns.

      Ex: 1. Béi sèsíu tòhng ngóh   Please give me a little sugar.
             lā.

          2. Béi síusíu tòhng   Please give me just a tiny
             ngóh lā.   bit of sugar.

          3. Sèsíu hóu lā.   A little bit is fine.
                             (Someone asked how much sugar
                             you want in your coffee.)

          4. Síusíu hóu lā.   Just a tiny bit is fine.

   d. The following -dò/-síu phrases can modify individual and mass
      nouns directly:

-dò/-síu	Ind/Mass Noun	
1. hóudò	⎫ sēutsāam	1. many shirts; much sugar
2. géidò	⎬ tòhng	2. quite a few shirts; quite a bit of sugar
3. móuhgéidò		3. not many shirts; not much sugar
4. (QW) géidō	....?	4. how many shirts?; how much sugar?
5. hóusíu	⎭	5. very few shirts; very little sugar

           (See Drills 11, 12)

e. The following can precede a Measure (+ Noun):

-dò	M	N	
hóudò	gihn	sēutsāam	many [M] shirts
móuhgéidò	"	"	not many [M] shirts
géidò (& géidō?) "		"	quite a few [M] shirts (how many [M] shirts?)

7. <u>cheung</u> and <u>cheunghòi</u> 'to change money into smaller denomination'

These both form VO phrases with a following money phrase.

<u>cheung</u> = change into (what you want) (followed by denomination wanted)

<u>cheunghòi</u> = change, i.e., break (a big bill) (followed by denomination held.)

        Ex: cheung sahp mān jí   = change into $10 bills

            cheunghòi jèung sahp mān jí = break a $10 bill

8. Sentence suffix <u>gé</u>

    <u>gé</u> represents sentence suffix <u>ge</u>, 'that's the way it is'
plus rising intonation for uncertainty and doubt.

        Ex: Yí-m̀hgìnjó gé?   Eh? (They're) lost?

                    (See BC)

                    248

III. DRILLS

1. Alteration Drill

    Ex: 1. T: Nī go haih cháang   T: This is an orange.
           làih ge.

         S: Nàh--nīdouh yáuh S: Here--here's an orange.
           go cháang.

1. Nī dī haih ngàuhyuhk làih ge.
    1. Nàh--nīdouh yáuh dī ngàuh-yuhk.

2. Nī jī haih heiséui làih ge.
    2. Nàh--nīdouh yáuh jī heiséui.

3. Nī dī haih tòhng làih ge.
    3. Nàh--nīdouh yáuh dī tòhng.

4. Nī go haih pìhnggwó làih ge.
    4. Nàh--nīdouh yáuh go pìhnggwó.

5. Nī jèung haih sahp mān jī làih ge.
    5. Nàh--nīdouh yáuh jèung sahp mān jī.

+ 6. Nī go haih ńgh hòuhjí ngán làih ge. (ngán = coin)
    6. Nàh--nīdouh yáuh go ńgh hòuhjí ngán.

7. Nī go haih yāt mān ngán làih ge.
    7. Nàh--nīdouh yáuh go yāt mān ngán.

    a. Repeat, in reverse, teacher cueing with yáuh sentences, students responding with haih sentences.

———

2. Substitution Drill

    Ex: T: Béi ńgh hòuhjí   T: Give me 50¢. /give back change/
         ngóh. /jáaufàan/

        S: Jáaufàan ńgh hòuhjí S: Give me back 50¢ change.
         ngóh.

1. Béi sahp mān ngóh. /je/
   Give me ten dollars.
    1. Je sahp mān ngóh.
      Lend me ten dollars.

2. Béi jī bāt ngóh. /ló/
    2. Ló jī bāt ngóh.
      Bring me a pen(cil).

3. Béi gihn sēutsāam ngóh. /máaih/
    3. Máaih gihn sēutsāam ngóh.
      Buy me a shirt. (Buy a shirt to give me.)

4. Béi go dihnwá ngóh. /dá/
   Give me a phone call.
   (also: Give me a phone.)
    4. Dá go dihnwá ngóh.

+ 5. Béi jèung sahp mān jī ngóh. /wuhn/
   Give me a ten-dollar bill. /Change (into)/
    5. Wuhn jèung sahp mān jī ngóh. Change (this) into a ten-dollar bill for me. (The speakers is holding small

                              change and bills that
                              he wants converted into a
                              larger bill.)

      Comment: <u>wuhn</u> 'exchange,' 'change (into)' in reference to
               money, is usually used when you have small denomina-
               tions that you want to change for larger. When you
               have a large bill you want to break into smaller
               denominations you use the verb <u>cheunghòi</u> 'break
               (a bill into smaller denominations)', 'change.'
               (See BC). <u>wuhn</u> also means to exchange one currency
               for another, as exchange HK money for US money.

      a. Repeat the above drill as expansion drill thus:

            T: Jáaufàan ńgh hòuhjí ngóh.
               Give me back 50¢ change.

            S: Ṁhgòi néih jáaufàan ńgh hòuhjí ngóh lā.
               Please give me back 50¢ change.

                    _____

3. Substitution Drill

      Ex: T: Ṁhngāamjeuk bo.   It doesn't fit, that's for sure.

            S: Ṁhngāamjeuk tìm!   It doesn't fit, shucks!
                                           (<u>tìm</u> here carries the im-
                                           plication that you are dis-
                                           appointed. I like it, but
                                           it doesn't fit - shucks.)

      1. Maaihsaai bo.   1. Maaihsaai tìm!

    + 2. Ṁhhái douh bo.((He's) not here.)2. Ṁhhái douh tìm! (douh=place)

      3. Chēutjó gāai bo.   3. Chēutjó gāai tìm!

      4. Ṁhgau chín bo.   4. Ṁhgau chín tìm!

      5. Tèng ṁhdóu bo.   5. Tèng ṁhdóu tìm!
         I can't hear it.

      6. Wán ṁhdóu bo.   6. Wán ṁhdóu tìm!
         (I) can't find (it).

      7. Dáṁhdóu bo.   7. Dáṁhdóu tìm!
         I can't reach him by phone.
         <u>or</u>
         He can't be reached by phone.
         (ambiguous as to whether
         he has no phone or his phone
         is busy.)

      8. Ṁhgeidāk bo.   8. Ṁhgeidāk tìm!
         (I) forgot.

a. Reverse roles, teacher cueing with sentences in right hand
   column, students responding with those at the left.

---

4. Expansion Drill

Ex: T: Yāt baak māan jí.   T: This is a $100 bill.

    S: M̀hgòi néih cheunghòi   S: Please break this $100 bill
       jèung yāt baak   for me.
       māan jí ngóh lā!

1. /ńgh hòuhjí ngán/   1. M̀hgòi néih cheunghòi go
                                     ńgh hòuhjí ngán ngóh lā!

2. /yāt māan ngán/   2. M̀hgòi néih chèunghòi go
                                     yāt māan ngán ngóh lā!

3. /sahp māan jí/   3. M̀hgòi néih chèunghòi jèung
                                     sahp māan jí ngóh lā!

4. /ńgh māan jí/   4. M̀hgòi néih chèunghòi jèung
                                     ńgh māan jí ngóh lā!

5. /ńgh baak māan jí/   5. M̀hgòi néih chèunghòi jèung
                                     ńgh baak māan jí ngóh lā!

6. /yāt baak māan jí/   6. M̀hgòi néih chèunghòi jèung
                                     yāt baak māan jí ngóh lā!

   a. Repeat, teacher writing visual cues ($100, 50¢, etc.)
      on the blackboard, students responding chèunghòi sentence.

      T: Write: $100

      S: M̀hgòi néih chèunghòi jèung yāt baak māan jí ngóh lā!

---

5. Expansion Drill

Ex: T: Kéuih yámsaai dī   T: He drank up all the soft
       heiséui.   drinks.

    S: Kéuih yámsaai dī   S: He drank up all the soft
       heiséui. Gám,   drinks. So I don't have
       ngóh móuhdāk yám   any [available to drink],
       tìm.   blast it!

1. Kéuih yuhngsaai dī chín.   1. Kéuih yuhngsaai dī chín.
   He used up all the money.   Gám, ngóh móuhdāk yuhng
                                     tìm.

2. Kéuih sihksaai dī faahn.   2. Kéuih sihksaai dī faahn.
                                     Gám, ngóh móuhdāk sihk tìm.

251

3. Kéuih lósaai dī chín.

3. Kéuih lósaai dī chín.
   Gám, ngóh móuhdāk ló tìm.

4. Kéuih yámsaai dī gafē.

4. Kéuih yámsaai dī gafē.
   Gám, ngóh móuhdāk yám tìm.

---

6. Expansion Drill

Ex: 1. T: Yīnggwok yáuh
        Yahtbún bējáu
        maaih. /nod/
        Méihgwok/

T: In England there is Japanese
   beer for sale. /nod/America/

S: Méihgwok dōu
   yáuhdāk maaih.

S: In America also they have it
   for sale. [America also have-
   can-sell.]

2. T: Yīnggwok yáuh
      Yahtbún bējáu
      maaih. /shake/
      Méihgwok/

T: England has Japanese beer for
   sale. /shake/America/

S: Yīnggwok yáuh
   Yahtbún bējáu
   maaih, daahn-
   haih Méihgwok
   móuhdāk maaih.

S: England has Japanese beer for
   sale but in America they
   don't have it for sale.
   [America not have-can-sell.]

1. Ngóh yáuh chín yuhng.
   /nod/ngóh pàhngyáuh/

1. Ngóh yáuh chín yuhng, ngóh
   pàhngyáuh dōu yauhdāk
   yuhng.

2. Kéuih yáuh chàh yám.
   /shake/ngóh/

2. Kéuih yáuh chàh yám, daahnhaih ngóh móuhdāk yám.

3. Chāansāt yáuh chàh yám.
   /nod/chàhlàuh/

3. Chāansāt yáuh chàh yám,
   chàhlàuh dōu yáuhdāk yám.

4. Kéuih yáuh yúhlāu jeuk.
   /shake/Léih Sàang/

4. Kéuih yáuh yúhlāu jeuk,
   daahnhaih Léih Sàang móuhdāk jeuk.

5. Hèunggóng yáuh Jùngmàhn syù
   maaih. /nod/Yahtbún/

5. Hèunggóng yáuh Jùngmàhn syù
   maaih, Yahtbún dōu yáuhdāk maaih.

252

7. Follow Drill

      Ex: T: Ngóh séung hohk   T: I'm thinking of studying
            Gwóngdùngwá.   Cantonese.

         S: Bīndouh yáuhdāk   S: Where can one study (it)?
            hohk a?   [Where have-can-study?]

1. Ngóh séung hohk Gwokyúh.   1. Bīndouh yáuhdāk hohk a?

2. Ngóh yiu dá dihnwá.   2. Bīndouh yáuhdāk dá a?

3. Ngóh séung sihk faahn.   3. Bīndouh yáuhdāk sihk a?

4. Ngóh séung yám gafē.   4. Bīndouh yáuhdāk yám a?

5. Ngóh séung máaih lāangsāam. 5. Bīndouh yáuhdāk maaih a?
   /maaih/

6. Ngóh séung máaih chē. /maaih/ 6. Bīndouh yáuhdāk maaih a?

---

8. Alteration Drill

      Ex: T: Gó júng chē, bīn-   T: That kind of car--where is it
            douh yáuhdāk   available for sale?
            maaih a?   /Hongkong/
            /Hèunggóng/

         S: Gó júng chē, Hèung- S: That kind of car--is it for
            góng yáuh móuhdāk   sale in Hongkong? <u>or</u>
            maaih a?   Can you buy that kind of car
                                   in Hongkong?

1. Nī júng bīu, bīndouh yáuhdāk 1. Nī júng bīu, Yahtbún yáuh
   maaih a? /Yahtbún/   móuhdāk maaih a?

2. Nī júng pìhnggwó, bīndouh   2. Nī júng pìhnggwó, Jùnggwok
   yáuhdāk maaih a? /Jùnggwok/   yáuh móuhdāk maaih a?

3. Nī júng gafē, bīndouh yáuhdāk 3. Nī júng gafē, chāansāt
   yám a? /chāansāt/   yáuh móuhdāk yám a?

4. Nī júng béng, bīndouh yáuhdāk 4. Nī júng béng, Màhnwàh Jáudim
   sihk a?/Màhnwàh Jáudim/   yáuh móuhdāk sihk a?

5. Nī júng bāt, bīndouh yáuhdāk 5. Nī júng bāt, Hèunggóng yáuh
   maaih a? /Hèunggóng/   móuhdāk maaih a?

9. Expansion Drill

Ex: T: Jáaufàan ńgh hòuhjí   T: **Give me back 50¢**
    béi ngóh lā.

    S: Jáaufàan ńgh hòuhjí   S: It'll be OK to give me back 50¢.
       béi ngóh dāk laak.   (You can keep the rest)
                                 [Give me back 50¢, then it
                                 will be OK.]

1. Ṁhgòi néih wah kéuih jí ngóh   1. Ṁhgòi néih wah kéuih jí ngóh
   ṁhfàanlàih sihk faahn lā.   ṁhfàanlàih sihk faahn
                                        dāk laak. (i.e. you don't
                                        need to do anything fur-
                                        ther)

2. Ṁhgòi néih giu kéuih hái chē   2. Giu kéuih hái chē jaahm
   jaahm dáng ngóh lā.   dáng ngóh dāk laak.
                                        (i.e. doesn't need to come
                                        all the way to the house)

3. Giu kéuih hái jógán máaih lā.   3. Giu kéuih hái jógán máaih
                                        dāk laak. (i.e. doesn't
                                        have to go to town)

4. Daai yih baak mān lā.   4. Daai yih baak mān dāk laak.

5. Jejyuh baak lèhng mān béi   5. Jejyuh baak lèhng mān béi
   ngóh lā.   ngóh dāk laak.

6. Béi sáanjí ngóh lā.   6. Béi sáanjí ngóh dāk laak.

7. Ló béi kéuih lā.   7. Ló béi kéuih dāk laak.

8. Yuhng yùhnbāt sé lā.   8. Yuhng yùhnbāt sé dāk laak.

---

10. Response Drill

Ex: 1. T: Néih gau ṁhgau chín máaih bējáu a? /nod/

        S: Gau. Ngóh ngāamngāam gau chín máaih.

    2. T: Néih gau ṁhgau chín máaih hàaih a? /shake/

        S: Ṁhgau. Ngóh ṁhgau chín máaih.

1. Néih gau ṁhgau chín máaih   1. Gau. Ngóh ngāamngāam gau
   yùhnbāt a? /nod/   chín máaih.

2. Néih gau ṁhgau chín máaih   2. Ṁhgau. Ngóh ṁhgau chín
   pìhnggwó a? /shake/   máaih.

3. Néih gau ṁhgau chín máaih   3. Gau. Ngóh ngāamngāam gau
   yīnjái a? /nod/   chín máaih.

4. Néih gau ṁhgau chín máaih   4. Gau. Ngóh ngāamngāam gau
   cháang a? /nod/   chín máaih.

254

5. Néih gau m̀hgau chìn máaih   5. M̀hgau. Ngóh m̀hgau chìn máaih.
   sēutsāam a? /shake/

6. Néih gau m̀hgau chìn máaih   6. M̀hgau. Ngóh m̀hgau chìn máaih.
   hàaih a? /shake/

---

11. Expansion & Substitution Drill

+ Ex: 1. T: Ngóh dāk hóusíu   T: I have very little money.
+   chìn. /hóudò/   /a lot/
         (very little)

      S: Ngóh dāk hóusíu   S: I have very little money, but
         chìn, daahnhaih   he has a lot.
         kéuih yáuh
         hóudò.

   2. T: Kéuih yáuh hóudò   T: He has a lot money. /very
         chìn. /hóusíu   little/
         ja/

      S: Kéuih yáuh hóudò   S: He has a lot of money, but I
         chìn, daahnhaih   have very little.
         ngóh dāk hóusíu
         ja.

 1. Kéuih yáuh hóudò chìn.   1. Kéuih yáuh hóudò chìn,
+   /móuhgéidò ja/   daahnhaih ngóh móuhgéidò
     /not much/   ja.
                                     He has a lot of money,
                                     but I don't have much.

 2. Ngóh móuhgéidò chìn.   2. Ngóh móuhgéidò chìn, daahn-
+   /géidò ga/   haih kéuih yáuh géidò ga.
     /quite a lot/   I don't have much money,
                                     but he has quite a lot.

 3. Kéuih yáuh géidò chìn.   3. Kéuih yáuh géidò chìn, daahn-
     /sèsíu ja/   haih ngóh dāk sèsíu ja.

 4. Ngóh yáuh sèsíu chìn.   4. Ngóh yáuh sèsíu chìn, daahn-
     /hóudò ga/   haih kéuih yáuh hóudò ga.
     /much, a lot/   I have a little money,
     I have a little money.   but he has a lot.

 5. Kéuih yáuh hóudò chìn.   5. Kéuih yáuh hóudò chìn, daahn-
     /hóusíu ja/   haih ngóh dāk hóusíu ja.

 6. Ngóh yáuh hóusíu chìn.   6. Ngóh yáuh hóusíu chìn, daahn-
     /géidò/   haih kéuih yáuh géidò ga.

7. Kéuih yáuh géidò chín.
   /sèsiu ja/
   /just a little/

7. Kéuih yáuh géidò chín, daahnhaih ngóh dāk sèsiu ja.

8. Ngóh yáuh sèsiu chín.
   /hóudò ga/

8. Ngóh yáuh sèsiu chín, daahnhaih kéuih yáuh hóudò ga.

9. Kéuih yáuh géidò pàhngyáuh.
   /móuhgéidò ja/
   /not many/

9. Kéuih yáuh géidò pàhngyáuh,
   daahnhaih ngóh dāk móuhgéidò ja.
   He has quite a few friends,
   but I have not many.

10. Ngóh móuhgéidò pàhngyáuh.
    /hóudò/
    /many, a lot/

10. Ngóh móuhgéidò pàhngyáuh,
    daahnhaih kéuih yáuh hóudò.

11. Kéuih yáuh hóudò pàhngyáuh.
    /hóusiu ja/
    /just a few/

11. Kéuih yáuh hóudò pàhngyáuh,
    daahnhaih ngóh dāk hóusiu
    ja.

Comment: 1) ja (pronounced [jə] is a fusion of jē and a, and
implies 'not much,' 'merely.'

2) ga is a fusion of final ge, indicating matter-of-
fact statement, and final a, the sentence softener.
Here ga is pronounced [gə].

---

12. Substitution Drill

Ex: T: Kéuih sihk hóudò
       ngàuhyuhk ga.
       /géidò ga/

T: He eats a lot of beef.
   /quite a lot/

S: Kéuih sihk géidò
   ngàuhyuhk ga.

S: He eats quite a lot of beef.

1. Kéuih sihk géidò ngàuhyuhk
   ga. /faahn/

1. Kéuih sihk géidò faahn ga.

2. Kéuih sihk géidò faahn.
   /jyùyuhk ga/

2. Kéuih sihk géidò jyùyuhk.

3. Kéuih sihk géidò jyùyuhk ga.
   /yám chàh/

3. Kéuih yám géidò chàh.

4. Kéuih yám géidò chàh.
   /hóusiu ge ja/

4. Kéuih yám hóusiu chàh ge ja.

5. Kéuih yám hóusiu chàh ge ja.
   /bējáu/

5. Kéuih yám hóusiu bējáu.

6. Kéuih yám hóusiu bējáu.
   /ngàuhnáaih/

6. Kéuih yám hóusiu ngàuhnáaih.

7. Kéuih yám hóusiu ngàuhnáaih
   ge ja. /sihk faahn/

7. Kéuih sihk hóusiu faahn ge
   ja.

256

8. Kéuih sihk hóusíu faahn ge ja.
/móuhgéidò/

8. Kéuih sihk móuhgéidò faahn.

9. Kéuih sihk móuhgéidò faahn
ge ja. /ló chìn/

9. Kéuih ló móuhgéidò chìn ge
ja.

---

13. Substitution Drill:

Ex: T: Yi, ngóh jì bāt
mhginjó gé.
/yùhnbāt/

S: Yí, ngóh jì yùhnbāt mhginjó gé.

1. Yí, ngóh go bīu mhginjó gé.
/sàam/

1. Yí, ngóh gihn sàam mhginjó
gé.

2. /dáifu/

2. Yí, ngóh tiuh dáifu mhginjó
gé.

3. /kwàhn/

3. Yí, ngóh tiuh kwàhn mhginjó
gé.

4. /jē/

4. Yí, ngóh bá jē mhginjó gé.

+ 5. /fu ngáhngéng/
(M. + eyeglasses)

5. Yí, ngóh fu ngáhngéng mhginjó gé.

+ 6. /go ngáhngéngdói/
(eyeglass case)

6. Yí, ngóh go ngáhngéngdói
mhginjó gé.

+ 7. /go sáudói/
((woman's) handbag)

7. Yí, ngóh go sáudói mhginjó
gé.

8. /gihn dáisāam/

8. Yí, ngóh gihn dáisāam
mhginjó gé.

---

14. Money Drill: For class practice: teacher writes on the blackboard.

Ex: T: 2 (50¢)

S: Béi léuhng go ńgh
hóuhjí ngàn ngóh
lā!

T: 2 50¢ coins

S: Please give me 2 50¢ [5 dime]
coins.

1. 10 $ 10

1. Béi sahp jèung sahp mān jí
ngóh lā!

2. 1 $ 10

2. Béi jèung sahp mān jí ngóh
lā!

3. 1 $ 100

3. Béi jèung yāt baak mān jí
ngóh lā!

4. 5 $ 10

4. Béi ńgh jèung sahp mān jí
ngóh lā!

5. 2 | $ 500 |

     5. Béi léuhng jèung ńgh baak
        māan jí ngóh lā!

6. 5 (50¢)

     6. Béi ńgh go ńgh hòuhjí ngán
        ngóh lā!

7. 3 (10¢)

     7. Béi sàam go yāt hòuhjí ngán
        ngóh lā!

8. 10 ($1⁰⁰)

     8. Béi sahp go yāt māan ngán
        ngóh lā!

9. 2 (50¢)

     9. Béi léuhng go ńgh hòuhjí
        ngán ngóh lā!

10. 10 (10¢)

     10. Béi sahp go yāt hòuhjí ngán
         ngóh lā!

Comment: jí 'bill', and ngán 'coin', can be omitted from the
          sentences above without changing meaning or emphasis.

———

15. Money Exchange Drill: For class practice. Teacher writes on
    blackboard, or holds up actual or pretend money.

    Ex: T: 10 | $ 10 | → 1 | $ 100 |

        S1: Nīdouh yáuh sahp
            jèung sahp māan
            (jí).

                       S1: Here's ten $10 bills.

        S2: Ḿhgòi néih wuhn
            jèung yāt baak
            māan (jí) ngóh lā!

                       S2: Please change into a $100
                            bill for me. [give me.]

1. 5 ($1⁰⁰) → 1 | $ 5⁰⁰ |

                       1. A. Nīdouh yáuh ńgh go yāt
                          māan (ngán).
                          Ḿhgòi néih wuhn jèung
                          ńgh māan (jí) ngóh lā!

2. 10 ($1⁰⁰) → 1 | $ 10 |

                       2. A. Nīdouh yáuh sahp go yāt
                          māan (ngán).
                          Ḿhgòi néih wuhn jèung
                          sahp māan (jí) ngóh lā!

3. 5 | $ 100 | → 1 | $ 500 |

                       3. A. Nīdouh yáuh ńgh jèung yāt
                          baak māan (jí).
                          Ḿhgòi néih wuhn jèung
                          ńgh baak māan (jí) ngóh
                          lā!

4. 2 | $ 5⁰⁰ | → 1 | $ 10 |

                       4. A. Nīdouh yáuh léuhng jèung
                          ńgh māan (jí).
                          Ḿhgòi néih wuhn jèung
                          sahp māan (jí) ngóh lā!

5. 10 (10¢) → 1 ($1⁰⁰)

5. A. Nīdouh yáuh sahp go yāt
      hòuhjí (ngán).
      Mhgòi néih wuhn go yāt
      mān (ngán) ngóh lā!

6. 2 (50¢) → 1 ($1⁰⁰)

6. A. Nīdouh yáuh léuhng go ńgh
      hòuhjí (ngán).
      Mhgòi néih wuhn go yāt
      mān (ngán) ngóh lā!

16. Money Change Drill: Teacher draws on board, or holds up real or
    pretend money.

    Ex: T: 1 $ 10   10 $ 1⁰⁰

    S1: Nīdouh yáuh jèung   S1: Here's a $10 bill.
        sahp mān (jí).

    + S2: Mhgòi néih cheung   S2: Please change (this) for me
          sahp go yāt man   into 10 on-dollar coins.
          (ngán) (béi)
          ngóh lā!

1. 1 [$ 500] → 5 [$ 100]

1. A. Nīdouh yáuh jèung ńgh
      baak mān jí.

   B. Mhgòi néih cheung ńgh
      jèung yāt baak mān jí
      ngóh lā!

2. 1 [$ 100] → 10 [$ 10]

2. A. Nīdouh yáuh jèung yāt
      baak mān jí.

   B. Mhgòi néih cheung sahp
      jèung sahp mān jí ngóh
      lā!

3. 1 [$ 5⁰⁰] → 10 (50¢)

3. A. Nīdouh yáuh jèung ńgh
      mān jí.

   B. Mhgòi néih cheung sahp
      go ńgh hòuhjí ngán
      ngóh lā!

4. 1 [$ 10] → 10 ($1⁰⁰)

4. A. Nīdouh yáuh jèung sahp
      mān jí.

   B. Mhgòi néih cheung sahp
      go yāt mān ngán ngóh
      lā!

Comment: cheung 'change money into smaller denomination'
         (followed by denomination desired)

17. Number Drill I: Classroom practice.

    A. Teacher writes examples on board, calls them out, students listen.

        Example:

1. 10		1. sahp	
2. 100		2. yāt baak	
+ 3. 1000		3. yāt chĭn (chĭn = thousand)	
4. 20		4. yihsahp	
5. 200		5. yih baak	
6. 2000		6. yih chĭn	

    B. Teacher says number in Cantonese, students write it down. Teacher then writes figure on board. At end of section, teacher points to numbers on board at random, students say them.

1. 40	6. 700	11. 900
2. 80	7. 6000	12. 3000
3. 800	8. 500	13. 600
4. 9000	9. 4000	14. 5000
5. 300	10. 30	15. 100

(answers)

1. seisahp	6. chāt baak	11. gáu baak
2. baatsahp	7. luhk chĭn	12. sàam chĭn
3. baat baak	8. ńgh baak	13. luhk baak
4. gáu chĭn	9. sei chĭn	14. ńgh chĭn
5. saam baak	10. sàamsahp	15. yāt baak

---

18. Number Drill II: Numbers with final zeroes.

    A: Teacher writes example numbers on board, calls them out. Students listen.

        Example:

1. 11	=	sahpyāt
2. 110	=	baak yāt or yāt baak yātsahp
3. 1100	=	chĭn yāt or yāt chĭn yāt baak
4. 21	=	yihsahpyāt or yahyāt
5. 210	=	yih baak yāt or yih baak yāt sahp

6. 2100   = yih chīn yāt or yih chīn yāt baak

Comment: In numbers with a final zero (or zeroes), the Cantonese favor not calling the measure of the last number. It is of course predictable from the Measure preceding.

B. Teacher says number, students write it down (without looking at book). Teacher then writes figure on board. At end of section, teacher points to numbers on board at random, students say the numbers.

1. 340	9. 880	17. 38
2. 680	10. 480	18. 280
3. 7500	11. 170	19. 85
4. 9900	12. 990	20. 140
5. 440	13. 52	21. 14
6. 78	14. 540	22. 1400
7. 190	15. 180	23. 5900
8. 830	16. 710	24. 460

19. Number Drill III: Numbers with internal zeroes.

A. Teacher writes the numbers on the board and calls them out, pointing to them as he does so. Students listen.

Example:

1. 1   = yāt
2. 101   = yāt baak lìhng yāt
3. 1,001   = yāt chīn lìhng yāt
4. 1,010   = yāt chīn lìhng yātsahp
5. 4   = sei
6. 404   = sei baak lìhng sei
7. 4,004   = sei chīn lìhng sei
8. 4,040   = sei chīn lìhng seisahp

Comment: In saying a number, Cantonese marks the presence of an internal zero (or zeroes) by lìhng.

B. Teacher says number, students write it down; teacher then writes figure on blackboard. At end of section, teacher points to numbers on board at random, students say them.

1. 1018	3. 1101	5. 8008
2. 1029	4. 808	6. 8080

7. 209	12. 5008	17. 3303
8. 2029	13. 6708	18. 5804
9. 2008	14. 9009	19. 701
10. 2202	15. 307	20. 7406
11. 508	16. 708	21. 805
		22. 908

IV. CONVERSATIONS FOR LISTENING

(On tape. Refer to the wordlist below as you listen to the tape.)
Unfamiliar terms, in order of occurrence:

1) oi = here: to have in your possession

2) gàmyaht = today

3) yātján = dángyātjahn = 'in a little while'

V.   SAY IT IN CANTONESE

A. You say to the person sitting next to you:

B. And he responds:

1. I forgot to bring money!

1. I'll lend you some--how much do you need?

2. Do you have enough money to buy beer?

2. I have just enough to buy six bottles, but I'd like to buy a dozen.

3. I don't have enough money to buy a dozen bottles.

3. You want some money, huh?-- I'll lend you $20, OK?

4. What the...? I can't find my glasses.

4. They're here by me.

5. Please break this $10 bill for me.

5. OK. One five and five ones, is that all right?

6. How much is US$10 in Hong Kong dollars?

6. About $60.00.

7. How much is HK$100.00 in American money?

7. About $16.60.

8. Does Hong Kong have that kind of car for sale?

8. Sure, you can buy them in H.K. (Hongkong-available-sell)

9. You can't buy English beer in Japan--can you buy Japanese beer in England?

9. I don't know, probably so.

262

10. I have very few sweaters, but my younger sister has a lot.

10. Not so! You have quite a lot too!

11. Keep the change! (Don't need to give back.)

11. Thanks.

Vocabulary Checklist for Lesson 11

1. agō	n:	elder brother
2. baak	nu:	hundred
3. cheung	v:	change money into smaller denomination
4. cheunghòi	v:	split, break up large banknote or coin to exchange for ones of lesser denomination.
5. chīn	nu:	thousand
6. daai	v:	carry
7. daai...heui	v:	take...along
8. daai...làih	v:	bring...along
9. dāk	v:	all right, OK, will do
10. -dāk-	bf:	in yáuhdāk .V. = available, can
11. dāk...	v:	only have ...
12. fu	m:	M. for eyeglasses
13. géidò	Ph:	quite a lot
14. hái douh	Ph:	(he, she, it, etc.) is here; is at (this) place
15. hóudò	Ph:	a lot
16. housíu	Ph:	very little
17. jáau	v:	give change
18. jáaufàan	v:	give back change
19. je	v:	lend, borrow
20. jejyuh	v:	lend or borrow temporarily
21. jèung	m:	M. for banknotes
22. jí	n:	banknote; paper
23. -jyuh	Vsuf:	temporarily, for a short time
24. m̀hgeidāk	VP:	forget (not remember)
25. m̀hginjó	VP:	lose, lost; 'nowhere to be seen'
26. móuhdāk .V.	VP:	not have available for .V.-ing
27. móuhgéidò	Ph:	not much, not many

263

28. Nàh!   ex: Here!

29. ngáhngéng   n: eyeglasses

30. ngáhngéngdói   n: eyeglasses case

31. ngán   n: coin

32. sáanngán   n: small coins

33. saimúi   n: younger sister

34. sáudói   n: (woman's) handbag

35. sīgēi   n: taxi driver

36. tǐm   ss: sen. suf. indicating speaker has been taken by
                          surprise.

37. tùhng   coV: on behalf of, for

38. wuhn   v: in ref. to money, change small denomination for
                          larger one (followed by denomination desired);
                          exchange one currency for another.

39. yáuhdāk   VP: have available to .V.., have available for .V.ing.

40. Yí!   ex: exclamation of distress:'Oh-oh!'

41. yuhng   v: use; spend (money)

I. BASIC CONVERSATION

  A. Buildup:

                    (Two friends meet at the bus stop)
                         Chàhn Táai

      heui   go
      heui bîndouh a?   where are you going?
    A, Wòhng Táai, heui bîndouh a?   Ah, Mrs. Wong, where are you
                                            going?

                         Wòhng Táai

    Ngóh heui ngàhnhòhng ló chín.   I'm going to the bank to get
      Néih nē?   some money. And you?
                         Chàhn Táai

      hohkhaauh   school
    Ngóh heui hohkhaauh.   I'm going to school.
                         Wòhng Táai

    Heui gódouh yáuh mēyéh sih a?   What is it you're going there
                                            to do?

                         Chàhn Táai

      néui   daughter
      ngóh gó néui   my daughter
      jip   meet, fetch, pick up (a
                                            person)
      heui jip ngóh go néui   go to get my daughter
    Ngóh heui jip ngóh go néui.   I'm going to get my daughter.
    Kéuih yihgā hái hohkhaauh dáng   She's at school now waiting
      ngóh.   for me.
      màhmā   mother
      ngóh màhmā   my mother
      taam   visit
      taam ngóh màhmā   visit my mother
      daai kéuih   take/bring him along
    Ngóh daai kéuih heui taam   I'm taking her to visit my
      ngóh màhmā.   mother.
                         Wòhng Táai

      jyuh   live
    Néih màhmā hái bîndouh jyuh a?   Where does your mother live?
                            265

<u>Chàhn Táai</u>

Gáulùhng   Kowloon

Kéuih hái Gáulùhng jyuh.   She lives in Kowloon.

   (Mrs. Wong looks down the street and sees a bus coming)

<u>Wòhng Táai</u>

  làih   come

  ga chē   a car

A, yáuh ga chē làih laak. Haih   Oh, there's a bus [car] coming.

  m̀hhaih baat houh a?   Is it a Number 8?

   tái m̀hchìngchó   not see clearly

Ngóh tái m̀hchìngchó.   I can't see clearly.

<u>Chàhn Táai</u>

M̀hhaih baat houh, haih sàam   It's not a Number 8, it's a

  houh.   Number 3.

  hauhbihn   in back, behind

Hauhbihn yáuh ga baat houh.   There's a Number 8 behind it.

<u>Wòhng Táai</u>

  móuh cho   right! correct! [not have
                                            mistake]

A, móuh cho--   Ah, that's right--

  sàam houh hauhbihn   behind the Number 3

  gànjyuh   follow

Sàam houh hauhbihn gànjyuh   Behind the Number 3, following

  yáuh ga baat hauh.   there is a Number 8.

B. Recapitulation:

<u>Chàhn Táai</u>

A, Wòhng Táai, heui bīndouh a?   Ah, Mrs. Wong, where are you
                                            going?

<u>Wòhng Táai</u>

Ngóh heui ngàhnhòhng ló chín.   I'm going to the bank to get

  Néih nē?   some money. And you?

<u>Chàhn Táai</u>

Ngóh heui hohkhaauh.   I'm going to school.

<u>Wòhng Táai</u>

Heui gódouh yáuh mēyéh sih a?

What is it you're going there for?

<u>Chàhn Táai</u>

Ngóh heui jip ngóh go néui. Kéuih yihgā hái hohkhaauh dáng ngóh. Ngóh daai kéuih heui taam ngóh māhmā.

I'm going to get my daughter. She's at school now waiting for me. I'm taking her to visit my mother.

<u>Wòhng Táai</u>

Néih màhmā hái bīndouh jyuh a?

Where does your mother live?

<u>Chàhn Táai</u>

Kéuih hái Gáulùhng jyuh.

She lives in Kowloon.

<u>Wòhng Táai</u>

A, yáuh ga chē làih laak. Haih m̀hhaih baat houh a? Ngóh tái m̀hchìngchó.

Oh, there's a bus coming. Is it a Number 8? I can't see clearly.

<u>Chàhn Táai</u>

M̀hhaih baat houh, haih sàam houh. Hauhbihn yáuh ga baat houh.

It's not a Number 8, it's a Number 3. There's a Number 8 behind it.

<u>Wòhng Táai</u>

A, móuh cho--
Sàam houh hauhbihn gànjyuh yáuh ga baat houh.

At, that's right--
Behind the Number 3, following there's a Number 8.

II. NOTES

A. Culture Notes

1. <u>Greetings</u>.

In Lesson 4 we touched on the matter of differences in the way Americans and Cantonese greet each other. One very common form of greeting between Cantonese who run into each other on the street is <u>Heui bīndouh a?</u> or <u>Heui bīn a?</u> 'Where are you going?' This isn't being nosey, it's just a greeting form, just as in English 'How are you?' is a greeting form and doesn't call for a

detailed description of your health. To answer Heui bīndouh a?,
you say where you're going, or, if you don't want to tell, simply
say Chēut gāai or Heui gāai 'I'm going out' (said as you emerge
from your house) or Chēutlàih hàahngháh 'I've come out for a walk'
(if you're already out).

Other greetings are Fàan gùng a? (Going to work?' Chēut gāai a?
'You're out?' Fàan hohk a? 'Going to school?' You can respond to
all of these by nodding you head, saying an A of assent, and
greeting the person by name: A, Hòh Táai!

Around noontime or dinnertime if two acquaintances meet, a
common greeting form is Sihk faahn meih a? 'Have you eaten yet?'
Responses are: Meih a, néih nē? 'Not yet, and you?' and Sihkjó
laak, 'I've eaten.'

2. Counting system of numbering the floors of a building.

The Chinese system of numbering floors of a building is the
same as the American system, but different from the British system.
The floor above the ground floor is called yih láu [two-storey]
in Cantonese, 'the second floor' in American English, and 'the
first floor' in British English.

The British system of numbering floors is used in Hong Kong
when one speaks English. This, of course, means referring to the
floor above the ground floor as the first floor, the floor two
storeys up as the second floor, and so on.

> Ex: Ngóh jyuh hái sàam   I live on the second floor.
>   láu.   (British counting system)
>   I live on the third floor.
>   (American counting system)

(See Drill 2.8)

B. Structure Notes

1. Sentence type: Subordinate clause-primary clause sentence.

In Cantonese sentences, subordinate clauses precede the
primary clause.

> Ex: Kéuih fàanlàih, m̀hgòi   When she comes back, please tell
>   néih giu kéuih dá   her to phone Mrs. Cheung.
>   dihnwá béi Jèung
>   Táai lā.

268

The order is fixed. This contrasts with the situation in
the English counterpart, in which subordinate-primary clauses are
reversible:

Ex: Subordinate   Primary

When she comes home   please tell her to call Mrs.
                           Cheung.

or   Primary   Subordinate

Please tell her to call Mrs. Cheung   when she comes
                                         home.

2. Sentence type: Multi-verb sentence.

The term multi-verb sentence refers to single-clause sentences
containing a series of verb phrases. Whereas English typically
expands a single clause sentence by retaining one principle verb
and adding on such adjuncts as prepositional phrases (with me),
participles (waiting for me), infinitive phrases (to fetch his
girlfriend), adverbial nouns of place (home), Chinese typically
expands a simple sentence into a series of verbal expressions,
so that an expanded single clause sentence in Chinese has the
shape: S + V(O) + V(O) (+ V(O)).

Ex: 1. Kéuih hái hohkhaauh   He's at school waiting for
       dáng ngóh.   me [at-school+await-me]

    2. Kéuih je chín béi   He lent me money.
       ngóh.   [lend-money+give-me]

    3. Mhgòi néih gàn ngóh   Please come with me. Please
       làih.   follow me. [follow-me+
                                   come]

    4. Kéuih heui ngàhn-   He's going to the bank to
       hòhng ló chín.   get some money. [go-bank+
                                   get-money]

    5. Kéuih sung ngóh fàan   He took me home. [deliver-me+
       ngūkkéi.   return-home]

    6. Kéuih séung maaih   He wants to buy a shirt.
       gihn sēutsāam.   [wish+buy-shirt]

    7. Kéuih heui tái hei.   He went to see a movie. [go+
                                   see-movie]

    8. Kéuih heui Gáuluhng   He's going to Kowloon to fetch
       jip néuihpàhngyáuh.   his girlfriend.

    9. Kéuih jip kéuih go   He's fetching his son to take
       jái heui Gáuluhng   him to Kowloon to see a movie.
       tái hei.   [fetch-son+go-Kowloon+see-
                                   movie]

269

3. Auxiliary verbs.

Auxiliary verbs cannot serve as the only verb in a sentence, but require another verb as their object. The negative and question forms attach to the auxiliary verb.

      Ex: séung = be of a mind to..., want to..., think (I'll)...

          aff: Ngóh séung sihk   I think I'll eat dinner.
               faahn.

          neg: Ngóh m̀hséung sihk   I don't think I'll eat.
               faahn.

           q: Séung m̀hséung sihk Do you want to have dinner?
               faahn a?

4. Co-verbs.

There is a category of verb in Cantonese which cannot serve as the only verb in a sentence, and which takes a noun as its object. This category is given the name co-verb (companion verb). A co-verb phrase precedes the verb it is companion to. Co-verbs ordinarily translate into English as prepositions, and the co-verb and its object as a prepositional phrase; but in Cantonese co-verbs are verbs, since they can occur in the three basic verb forms: affirmative, negative, and choice question.

      Ex: Co-V + Noun object + Verb

        aff: Gàn   sīnsàang   góng.   Repeat after the teacher.
                                        [Follow-teacher speak.]

        neg: M̀hgàn   sīnsàang   góng.   Don't repeat after the
                                        teacher.

        q: Gàn m̀hgàn sīnsàang   góng   (Should we) repeat
                                    a?   after the teacher?

                (See Drills 11, 12)

5. Verb sequence: Aux V + Co-V + V

Auxiliary verb precedes Co-Verb phrase in a sentence in which both occur:

      Ex: Ngóh séung gàn kéuih   I think I'll follow him.
          heui.

6. tùhng 'with' (Co-V) compared with tùhng 'and' (Cj)

tùhng 'with' and tùhng 'and' both stand between two nouns (N tùhng N), but since otherwise they pattern differently in a sentence, they are classed as different parts of speech.

tùhng 'with' may take negative and question forms as well as
the affirmative, and may be preceded by an auxiliary verb. It is
therefore a verb. But as it cannot stand as the only verb in a
sentence, and requires another verb following its noun object, it
is classed as a Co-Verb.

Ex: Ngóh m̀hséung tùhng   I don't want to go with Mrs.
Léih Táai heui.   Lee.

tùhng, 'and' does not take the negative and question forms,
therefore it cannot be called a verb. It cannot be preceded by an
auxiliary verb. It joins two nouns which then act as a compound
unit in subject or object position.   tùhng, 'and' is classed as a
conjunction.

Ex: Léih Táai tùhng ngóh   Mrs. Lee and I are going.
heui. Máh Sàang   Mr. and Mrs. Ma aren't going.
tùhng Máh Táai
m̀hheui.

Làuh Sàang tùhng Làuh   Mr. and Mrs. Lau don't wish
Taaitáai m̀hséung   to go.
heui.

Ngóh m̀hsīk Làuh Síujé   I don't know Miss Lau and her
tùhng kéuih màhmā.   mother.

(See Drills 12.5 and 6)

7. gànjyuh, gàn, 'to follow'

These two are alike in meaning, but different in use. gànjyuh
is a full verb, can serve as the only verb in a sentence. gàn is
a co-verb, cannot serve as the only verb in a sentence. It is
limited to multi-verb sentences in which it precedes another verb.
phrase.

Ex: M̀hgòi néih gàn ngóh làih. Please follow me.

M̀hgòi néih gànjyuh ngóh   Please follow me.
làih.

Gànjyuh gó ga chē!   Follow that car!

(-) Gàn gó ga chē!   (doesn't occur)

Gàn (jyuh) gó ga chē   Follow that car!
heui!

271

In the Basic Conversation of this lesson gànjyuh is used as the subject of a clause, the clause itself being predicate in the larger topic: comment sentence:

Subject (topic)	Predicate (Comment)	
	Subject	Predicate
Sàam houh hauhbihn	gànjyuh	yáuh ga baat houh.
[Three-number behind	following	there is [M] eight-number]

'Behind the Number 3 there's a Number 8 following.'

(See Drills 6, 7)

8. sung 'deliver (someone or something),' 'take (someone/something) to destination and leave him/it there.'

sung, 'deliver,' can be the only verb in a sentence, or it can be the verb of a VO expression which is followed by heui or some other verb indicating movement.

Ex: Ngóh sung néih.	I'll see you to your destination.
Ngóh sung dī jáinéui heui taam pàhngyáuh.	I took the children to visit friends.
Gàan gūngsī sung dī yéh làih.	The department store delivered the goods (to speaker's place).

(See Drill 10)

9. daai, 'to bring, take along'

daai, 'bring/take someone/something along' can serve as the only verb in the sentence, usually with an impersonal object:

Ex: Kéuih daai chín.	He's brought money along.

daai can also serve as the verb of a VO expression which is followed by heui or some other verb indicating movement.

Ex: Ngóh daai ngóh go néui heui tái yīsāng.	I'm taking my daughter to see the doctor.

(See BC)

10. jip = 'fetch (someone),' 'meet (someone) and take him someplace else.'

Ex: Ngóh heui Gáuluhng jip ngóh go néui.	I'm going to Kowloon to get my daughter.
Ngóh jip ngóh go néui heui Gáuluhng.	I'm meeting my daughter to take her to Kowloon.

(See BC)

Ordinarily, the grammatical object of <u>jip</u> is a personal noun (<u>jip yàhn</u> = go fetch someone), but the grammatical object can be a vehicle (<u>jip chē</u> = meet the bus [car] and fetch someone away). In such a case the vehicle is the grammatical object but a person is the underlying object.

11. <u>hái</u> phrase in a multi-verb clause.

With most verbs a <u>hái</u> phrase precedes the other verb phrase, but with verbs of thrust (put, place) it follows the other verb phrase, and with verbs of station (live, sit, stand) it can precede or follow the other verb phrase. In all cases <u>hái</u> has a placeword object.

Ex: (before other V) Kéuih hái chāansāt sihk faahn.	He's eating (<u>or</u> he ate) at the restaurant.
(after other V) Jài dĬ chàh hái nĬdouh.	Put the tea here.
(before or after) Kéuih hái Géuluhng jyuh.	He lives (<u>or</u> lived) in Kowloon.
Kéuih jyuh hái Gáuluhng.	

(See Drill __4__)

12. Possessive modification with family names: <u>ngóh màhmā</u>, 'my mother' and others.

Some family names function irregularly with respect to possessive modification, not using either the general possessive <u>ge</u> or the individual measures <u>go</u> and <u>dĬ</u> between modifier and head noun. In such cases the modifier precedes the noun directly. With other family names either <u>ge</u> or <u>go/dĬ</u> is required in modification structure; with still other family names filling the <u>ge/go</u> position is optional.

(Examples are on following page)

Ex:

modifier	go/dĭ/ge or/--/	Noun		Eng. equivalents
ngòh	--	màhma	my your Mrs. Lee's Mr. Lee's	mother
néih	--	bàhbā		father
Léih Táai	--	sīnsāang		husband
Léih Sàang	--	taaitáai		wife
	/go/dĭ/ge/	jái		son(s)
	go/dĭ/ge/	néui		daughter(s)
	dĭ/ge/	jáinéui		children
	go/dĭ/ge	múi		younger sister
	/-/go/dĭ/ge	sáimúi		younger sister
	/-/go/dĭ/ge	gājē		elder sister
	/-/go/dĭ/ge/	sáilóu		younger brother
	/-/go/dĭ/ge/	agō		elder brother

(See Drill 3)

13. Chinese response to questions negatively phrased.

(You're not going, are you? type):

Negatively phrased questions in Cantonese are tricky from the English speaking student's point of view, because where the English answer would be 'No,' the Cantonese answers seem to be 'yes,' and where the English answer is 'yes,' the Cantonese answer sounds like 'no.'

Ex: 1. A. Néih ūkkéi móuh dihnwá àh.

   Your house doesn't have a phone, does it.

   B. Haih a. Móuh dihnwá.

   That's right. There's no phone.
   (Idiomatic English answer: No, it doesn't.)

2. A. Kéuih m̀hfàanlàih sihk aan àh.

   He's not coming home for lunch, is he.

   B. Móuh cho. M̀hfàanlàih.

   That's right. He's not coming home.
   (Idiomatic English answer: No, he's not.)

3. A. Néih ūkkéi móuh dihnwá àh.

   You don't have a phone at your house, do you.

   B. M̀hhaih. Yáuh dihnwá.

   Not so! We do have one.
   (Idiomatic English: Yes, we do.)

4. A. Kéuih m̀hfàanlàih   He's not coming home for lunch,
      sihk aan àh.   is he.

   B. M̀hhaih. Kéuih   Not so. He is.
      fàanlàih.   (Idiomatic English: Yes,
                              he is.)

   (See Drill 14)

III. DRILLS

1. Question & Answer Drill

Ex: T: Hèunggóng.
    A: Néih hái bĭndouh jyuh a?
    B: Ngóh hái Hèunggóng jyuh.

1. Gáulùhng.

2. Méihgwok.

3. Jùngwàahn.

4. Hohkhaauh.

5. Hèunggóng.

1. A. Néih hái bĭndouh jyuh a?
   B. Ngóh hái Gáulùhng jyuh.

2. A. Néih hái bĭndouh jyuh a?
   B. Ngóh hái Méihgwok jyuh.

3. A. Néih hái bĭndouh jyuh a?
   B. Ngóh hái Jùngwàahn jyuh.

4. A. Néih hái bĭndouh jyuh a?
   B. Ngóh hái hohkhaauh jyuh.

5. A. Néih hái bĭndouh jyuh a?
   B. Ngóh hái Hèunggóng jyuh.

---

2. Expansion Drill: Repeat after the teacher.

+ 1. a. jái
     b. ngóh go jái
     c. Ngóh go jái heui
     d. Ngóh go jái heui Gáulùhng.
     e. Ngóh go jái yĭhgā heui Gáulùhng.

+ 2. a. jáinéui

     b. dĭ jáinéui
     c. daai dĭ jáinéui
     d. daai dĭ jáinéui heui
     e. daai dĭ jáinéui heui Wòhng Táai douh.

   + f. Ngóh sĭnsàang daai dĭ jáinéui heui Wòhng Táai douh. Note the new meaning for sĭnsàang: 'husband.'

1. a. son
   b. my son
   c. My son is going
   d. My son is going to Kowloon.
   e. My son is going to Kowloon now.

2. a. children (of a family), sons and daughters (of a family)

   b. the children
   c. bring/take the children
   d. take the children.
   e. take the children to Mrs. Wong's.

   f. My husband is taking the children to Mrs. Wong's (Though sĭnsàang may also mean 'teacher'

the context usually
makes the meaning
clear.)

+ 3. a. jouh

   b. jouh mēyéh

   c. heui Gáulùhng jouh mēyéh a?

   d. Kéuih heui Gáulùhng jouh mēyéh a?

   e. Kéuih heui Gáulùhng taam pàhngyáuh.

+ 4. a. yīsāng

   b. tái yīsāng

   c. heui tái yīsāng

   d. jip kéuih go néui heui tái yīsāng.

   e. Kéuih jip kéuih go néui heui tái yīsāng.

+ 5. a. ngóh taaitáai

   b. tùhng ngóh taaitáai

   c. tùhng ngóh taaitáai heui

   d. m̀htùhng ngóh taaitáai heui

   e. Wòhng Táai m̀htùhng ngóh taaitáai heui.

+ 6. a. máaih yéh (yéh = things, stuff)

   b. heui máaih yéh

   c. bīngo heui máaih yéh a?

   d. tùhng bīngo heui máaih yéh a?

   e. Néih tùhng bīngo heui máaih yéh a?

7. a. sih

+   b. jouh sih

   c. hái bīndouh jouh sih a?

   d. Néih hái bīndouh jouh sih a?

   e. Ngóh hái Jùngwàahn jouh sih.

+ 8. a. douh

3. a. do

   b. do what?

   c. go to Kowloon to do what?

   d. What is he going to Kowloon to do?

   e. He's going to Kowloon to see a friend.

4. a. doctor

   b. see a doctor

   c. go to see a doctor

   d. meet her daughter and go to see the doctor.

   e. She's meeting her daughter to take her to the doctor.

5. a. my wife

   b. with my wife

   c. go with my wife

   d. not go with my wife

   e. Mrs. Wong isn't going with my wife.

6. a. buy things, do shopping

   b. go shopping

   c. who is going shopping?

   d. go shopping with whom?

   e. Who are you going shopping with?

7. a. affairs, business

   b. work, have a job

   c. work where?

   d. Where do you work?

   e. I work in the Central District.

8. a. road

277

+	b.	Nèihdēun Douh	b.	Nathan Road
+	c.	Nèihdēun Douh ńgh baak luhk-sahpyih houh (houh = number)	c.	Number 562 Nathan Road
+	d.	Nèihdēun Douh ńgh baak luhk-sahpyih houh sàam láu (láu = floor, story of a building)	d.	562 Nathan Road 3rd floor (2nd floor British counting system)
	e.	Ngóh jyuh hái Nèihdēun Douh ńgh baak luhksahpyih houh sàam láu.	e.	I live at 562 Nathan Road, on the 3rd floor.

Comment: In Hongkong, when speaking English, the British system of counting the floors of a building is used: ground floor, 1st floor, 2d floor, etc. In speaking Cantonese, the Chinese (which is also the American) system is used: the ground floor is called 1st floor the floor above the 1st floor is called the 2d floor, etc.

---

3. Substitution Drill: Repeat the first sentence after the techer, then substitute as directed.

1. Ngóh sīnsàang m̀hhái ngūkkéi. My husband is not at home.	1. Ngóh sīnsàang m̀hhái ngūkkéi.
2. /ngóh go jái/	2. Ngóh go jái m̀hhái ūkkéi.
3. /ngóh go néui/	3. Ngóh go néui m̀hhái ūkkéi.
4. /ngóh ge jái/	4. Ngóh ge jái m̀hhái ūkkéi.
5. /ngóh ge jáinéui/	5. Ngóh ge jáinéui m̀hhái ūkkéi.
6. /ngóh ge néui/	6. Ngóh ge néui m̀hhái ūkkéi.
7. /ngóh taaitáai/	7. Ngóh taaitáai m̀hhái ūkkéi.
+ 8. /ngóh bàhbā/	8. Ngóh bàhbā m̀hhái ūkkéi. My father is not at home.
+ 9. /ngóh ge néuihpàhngyáuh/	9. Ngóh ge néuihpàhngyáuh m̀hhái ūkkéi. My girl friend is not at home.
10. /ngóh ge nàahmpàhngyáuh/	10. Ngóh ge nàahmpàhngyáuh m̀hhái ūkkéi. My boy friend is not at home.

278

4. Transformation Drill

    Ex: T: Ngóh hái Hèunggóng   T: I live in Hong Kong.
           jyuh.

       S: Ngóh jyuh hái Hèung-   S: I live in Hong Kong.
          góng.

1. Ngóh màhmā hái Gáulùhng jyuh.   1. Ngóh màhmā jyuh hái Gáu-
                                   lùhng.

2. Néih hái bīndouh jyuh a?   2. Néih jyuh hái bīndouh a?

3. Ngóh néuihpàhngyáuh hái   3. Ngóh néuihpàhngyáuh jyuh
   Hèunggóng jyuh.   hái Hèunggóng.

4. Kéuih bàhbā hái Yīnggwok jyuh.   4. Kéuih bàhbā jyuh hái
                                  Yīnggwok.

5. Gó go yàhn hái douh jyuh.   5. Gó go yàhn jyuh hái douh.

5. Expansion Drill

    Ex: T: Hòh Sàang heui   T: Mr. Ho is going to Kowloon.
          Gáulùhng.

       S: Hòh Sàang heui   S: What's Mr. Ho going to Kowloon
          Gáulùhng jouh māt-   to do? or
          yéh a?   What's Mr. Ho going to Kow-
                                   loon for?

1. Ngóh heui hohkhaauh.   1. Néih heui hohkhaauh jouh
                                 mātyéh a?

2. Ngóh sīnsàang heui gaaklèih.   2. Néih sīnsàang heui gaaklèih
                                 jouh mātyéh a?

3. Kéuih nàahmpàhngyáuh heui Dāk   3. Kéuih nàahmpàhngyáuh heui
   Fu Douh Jùng.   Dāk Fu Douh Jùng jouh
                                 mātyéh a?

4. Léih Sàang néuihpàhngyáuh heui   4. Léih Sàang néuihpàhngyáuh
   Jùngwàahn.   heui Jùngwàahn jouh
                                 mātyéh a?

5. Ngóh màhmā heui ngàhnhòhng.   5. Néih màhmā heui ngàhnhòhng
                               jouh mātyéh a?

6. Ngóh bàhbā heui Hèunggóng   6. Néih bàhbā heui Hèunggóng
   Chāansāt.   Chāansāt jouh mātyéh a?

Comment: Note that néuihpàhngyáuh and nàahmpàhngyáuh accept
        possessive modifiers with or without ge or go:

      Ex: Léih Síujé } - } nàahmpàhngyáuh   Miss Lee's boy-
                 { ge {   friend
                 } go }

6. Transformation Drill

Ex: T: Ṁhgòi néih gànjyuh   T: Please follow me.
        ngóh làih lā.

    S: Ṁhhóu gànjyuh ngóh   S: Don't follow me, please.
        làih lā.

1. Ṁhgòi néih gànjyuh kéuih heui   1. Ṁhhóu gànjyuh kéuih heui lā.
    lā.
    Please follow him.

2. Ṁhgòi néih gànjyuh ngóh góng   2. Ṁhhóu gànjyuh ngóh góng lā.
    lā.
    Please repeat after me.

3. Ṁhgòi néih gànjyuh gó ga hāak   3. Ṁhhóu gànjyuh gó ga hāak
    chē heui lā.   chē heui lā.

4. Ṁhgòi néih gànjyuh gó go yàhn   4. Ṁhhóu gànjyuh gó go yàhn
    heui lā.   heui lā.

5. Ṁhgòi néih gànjyuh ngóh làih lā.   5. Ṁhhóu gànjyuh ngóh làih lā.

---

7. Response Drill

Ex: T: Ṁhgòi néih gànjyuh   T: Please follow me.
        ngóh heui lā.

  + S: Sái ṁhsái gàn néih   S: Should I follow you?
        heui a?   [Should I following you, go?]

1. Ṁhgòi néih gànjyuh kéuih   1. Sái ṁhsái gàn kéuih heui a?
    heui lā.

2. Ṁhgòi néih gànjyuh Wòhng Táai   2. Sái ṁhsái gàn Wòhng Táai
    heui lā.   heui a?

3. Ṁhgòi néih gànjyuh gó go Méih-   3. Sái ṁhsái gàn gó go Méihgwok-
    gwokyàhn heui lā.   yàhn heui a?

4. Ṁhgòi néih gànjyuh ngóh màhmā   4. Sái ṁhsái gàn néih màhmā
    heui lā.   heui a?

5. Ṁhgòi néih gànjyuh ngóh pàhng-   5. Sái ṁhsái gàn néih pàhngyáuh
    yáuh làih lā.   làih a?

Comment: gànjyuh and gàn both mean 'follow' and in some cases
         may be used interchangeably; but gàn cannot be used
         as the only verb in a sentence, whereas gànjyuh can.

---

8. Substitution Drill: Repeat the first sentence after the teacher, then substitute as directed.

1. Ngóh heui Yìnggwok.
   I'm going to England.

1. Ngóh heui Yìnggwok.

2. /ngóh go jái/

2. Ngóh go jái heui Yìnggwok.

3. /tòuhsyùgwún/

3. Ngóh go jái heui tòuhsyùgwún.

4. /kéuih taaitáai/

4. Kéuih taaitáai heui tòuhsyùgwún.

5. /séjihlàuh/

5. Kéuih taaitáai heui séjihlàuh.

6. /kéuih sìnsàang/

6. Kéuih sìnsàang heui séjihlàuh.

7. /Méihgwok/

7. Kéuih sìnsàang heui Méihgwok.

8. /ngóh màhmā/

8. Ngóh màhmā heui Méihgwok.

---

9. Conversation Exercise

Ex: A: Hòh Sàang heui
    bìndouh a?

A: Where is Mr. Ho going?

B: Kéuih heui Gáulùhng.

B: He's going to Kowloon.

A: Heui Gáulùhng jouh
   mātyéh a?

A: What's he going to do there?

B: Heui máaih yéh.

B: He's going shopping.

A: A, heui máaih yéh.

A: Oh, he's going shopping.

1. A. Wòhng Síujé..........?

1. A. Wòhng Síujé heui bìndouh
      a?

B. ....Hèunggóng.

B. Kéuih heui Hèunggóng.

A. ....?

A. Heui Hèunggóng jouh
   mēyéh a?

B. ....taam pàhngyáuh.

B. Heui taam pàhngyáuh.

A. ....

A. A, heui taam pàhngyáuh.

2. A. Néih taaitáai ....?

2. A. Néih taaitáai heui
      bìndouh a?

B. ....ngàhnhòhng.

B. Kéuih heui ngàhnhòhng.

A. ....?

A. Heui ngàhnhòhng jouh
   mēyéh a?

B. ....ló chín.

B. Heui ló chín.

A. ....

A. A, heui ló chín.

3. A. Néih.............?   3. A. Néih heui bīndouh a?

   B. ....Tīnsīng Máhtàuh.   B. Ngóh heui Tīnsīng Máhtàuh.

   A. ....?   A. Heui Tīnsīng Máhtàuh
                                      jouh mēyéh a?

   B. ......jip ngóh ge jáinéui.   B. Heui jip ngóh ge jáinéui.

   A. ....   A. A, heui jip néih ge
                                      jáinéui.

Comment: To let the other person know you've been paying
         attention in English, we have such phrases as 'I see'
         and 'Is that so?'. On the telephone we signal we're
         still listening by such phrases as 'unhuh', 'yes',
         'I see,' during pauses in the flow of speech from
         the person at the other end of the phone. A favorite
         way to signal such information in Cantonese is for
         the listener to repeat the speaker's last sentence,
         or a portion of it.

10. Question and Answer Drill

    + Ex: T: Néih sung néih go   T: Where are you <u>taking</u> your
             néui heui bīndouh   daughter? /school/
             a? /hohkhaauh/
             (Sung = deliver)

          S: Ngóh sung ngóh go   S: I'm taking my daughter to
             néui heui hohkhaauh.   school.

1. Néih sung néih go néui heui   1. Ngóh sung ngóh go néui heui
   bīndouh a? /Tīnsīng Máhtàuh/   Tīnsīng Máhtàuh.

2. Néih sung néih go néui heui   2. Ngóh sung ngóh go néui heui
   bīndouh a? /Màhnwàh Jáudim/   Màhnwàh Jáudim.

3. Néih sung néih go jái heui   3. Ngóh sung ngóh go jái heui
   bīndouh a? /Chàhn Yīsāng   Chàhn Yīsāng douh.
   douh/   I'm taking my son to Dr.
                                      Chan's.

4. Néih sung néih go jái heui   4. Ngóh sung ngóh go jái heui
   bīndouh a? /hohkhaauh/   hohkhaauh.

5. Néih sung néih go jái heui   5. Ngóh sung ngóh go jái fàan
   bīndouh a? /fàan hohk/   hohk.

6. Néih sung néih ge néuihpàhng-   6. Ngóh sung ngóh ge néuih-
   yáuh heui bīndouh a?   pàhngyáuh fàan gùng.
   /fàan gùng/

7. Néih sung néih màhmā heui bīn-   7. Ngóh sung ngóh màhmā fàan
   douh a? /fàan ngūkkéi/   ngūkkéi.

Comment: <u>sung</u> 'deliver,' to accompany someone to a destination
         and leave him there, contrasts with <u>daai</u> 'take

along,': take someone along with you and he stays
with you.

———————

11. Response Drill

+ Ex: T: Néih <u>tùhng</u> bīngo   T: Who are you going shopping <u>with</u>?
heui māaih yéh a?   /Miss Wong/
/Wòhng Síujé/

S: Ngóh tùhng Wòhng   S: I'm going with Miss Wong.
Síujé heui.

1. Néih tùhng bīngo heui sihk   1. Ngóh tùhng ngóh taaitáai
faahn a? /ngóh taaitáai/   heui.

2. Wòhng Sàang tùhng bīngo heui   2. Wòhng Sàang tùhng Wòhng Táai
ngàhnhòhng a? /Wòhng Táai/   heui.

3. Kéuih tùhng bīngo heui tái   3. Kéuih tùhng kéuih sīnsàang
yīsāng a? /kéuih sīnsàang/   heui.

4. Jèung Síujé tùhng bīngo heui   4. Jèung Síujé tùhng kéuih
yám chàh a? /kéuih bàhbā/   bàhbā heui.

5. Néih tùhng bīngo làih a?   5. Ngóh tùhng ngóh màhmā làih.
/ngóh màhmā/

Repeat, as Alteration Drill, thus:

T: Néih tùhng bīngo heui máaih yéh a? /Wòhng Síujé/
Who are you going shopping with? /Miss Wong/

S: Néih tùhng m̀htùhng Wòhng Síujé heui maaih yéh a?
Are you going shopping with Miss Wong?

———————

12. Transformation Drill

Ex: T: Ngóh tùhng kéuih   T: I'm going with him to the
heui tái yīsāng.   doctor's.

S: Ngóh m̀htùhng kéuih   S: I'm not going with him to the
heui tái yīsāng.   doctor's.

1. Kéuih daai ngóh heui máaih   1. Kéuih m̀hdaai ngóh heui
yéh.   máaih yéh.

2. Kéuih jip ngóh heui hohkhaauh.   2. Kéuih m̀hjip ngóh heui
hohkhaauh.

3. Kéuih dáng ngóh sihk faahn.   3. Kéuih m̀hdáng ngóh sihk faahn.

4. Ngóh sung kéuih fàan ūkkéi.   4. Ngóh m̀hsung kéuih fàan ūkkéi.

5. Ngóh jùngyi tùhng kéuih heui   5. Ngóh m̀hjùngyi tùhng kéuih
gāai.   heui gāai.

283

I like to go out with him.   I don't like to go out
                                              with him.

6. Ngóh tùhng kéuih dōu jùngyi   6. Ngóh tùhng kéuih dōu m̀hjùng-
   heui gāai.   yi heui gāai.
   We both like to go out.   Neither one of us likes
                                            to go out.

7. Ngóh gàn kéuih heui Méihgwok.   7. Ngóh m̀hgàn kéuih heui
                                           Méihgwok.

8. Ngóh séung gàn kéuih heui   8. Ngóh m̀hséung gàn kéuih heui
   Yahtbún.   Yahtbún.

+ 9. Ngóh yiu daai kéuih heui jouh   9. Ngóh m̀hsái daai kéuih heui
     sāam.   jouh sāam.
     (jouh sāam =   I don't have to take her
     make clothes, have clothes   to have clothes made.
     made)
     I have to take her to have
     clothes made.

10. Kéuih tùhng ngóh heui máaih   10. Kéuih m̀htùhng ngóh heui
    sáudói.   máaih sáudói.

---

13. Expansion Drill

         Ex: T: Kéuih heui hohkhaauh.   T: He's going to school.
                /baat dim bun/   /8:30/

             S: Kéuih baat dim bun   S: He's going to school at 8:30.
                heui hohkhaauh.

1. Kéuih heui sihk faahn.   1. Kéuih tùhng ngóh heui sihk
   /tùhng ngóh/   faahn.

2. Kéuih heui chàhlàuh. /yám chàh/   2. Kéuih heui chàhlàuh yám
                                           chàh.

3. Kéuih tùhng kéuih sīnsàang   3. Kéuih m̀htùhng kéuih sīnsàang
   heui Gáulùhng. /m̀htùhng/   heui Gáulùhng.

4. Kéuih daai kéuih go jái heui   4. Kéuih daai m̀hdaai kéuih go
   tái yīsāng. /daai m̀hdaai a?/   jái heui tái yīsāng a?

5. Kéuih heui jip kéuih sīnsàang.   5. Kéuih heui séjihlàuh jip
   /séjihlàuh/   kéuih sīnsàang.

6. Kéuih gàn màhmā heui chāansāt.   6. Kéuih gàn màhmā heui chāan-
   /yám chàh/   sāt yám chàh.

7. Kéuih sung néuihpàhngyáuh fāan   7. Kéuih sung kéuih ge néuih-
   ūkkéi. /kéuih ge/   pàhngyáuh fàan ūkkéi.

8. Kéuih hái chāansāt dáng ngóh.   8. Kéuih yīhgā hái chāansāt
   /yìhgā/   dáng ngóh.

---

14. Response Drill

    Ex: 1. T: Kéuih yám gafē àh.   T: He's drinking coffee. isn't he.

         S: Haih a, yám gafē.   S: That's right--drinking coffee.

       2. T: Kéuih m̀hsīk góng   T: She doesn't know how to speak
           Yìngmahn àh.   English, does she?

         S: Haih a, m̀hsīk góng.   S: That's right; she doesn't.

1. Kéuih chēutjógāai àh.
   She's gone out, hasn't she.

      1. Haih a, chēutjógāai.
         That's right, gone out.

2. Néih ūkkéi móuh dihnwá àh.

      2. Haih a, móuh dihnwá.

3. Hòh Sàang heui yám chàh àh.

      3. Haih a, heui yám chàh.

4. Chàhn Síujé séung máaih hàaih àh.

      4. Haih a, séung máaih hàaih.

5. Néih sīnsàang m̀hfàanlàih sihk
   faahn àh.

      5. Haih a, m̀hfàanlàih sihk
         faahn.

6. Gó go yàhn hái Méihgwok Ngàhnhòhng jouh sih àh.

      6. Haih a, hái Méihgwok Ngàhn-
         hòhng jouh sih.

7. Kéuihdeih heui Gáulùhng máaih
   yéh àh.

      7. Haih a, heui Gáulùhng máaih
         yéh.

8. Néih m̀hjùngyi yám bējáu àh.

      8. Haih a, m̀hjùngyi yám bējáu.

9. Kéuih taaitáai heui jip kéuih
   go néui àh?

      9. Haih a, heui jip kéuih go
         néui.

---

15. Expansion Drill

1. Hauhbihn yáuh go chē jaahm.
   /Ngóh séjihlàuh/
   There's a car stop in back.

      1. Ngóh séjihlàuh hauhbihn
        yáuh go chē jaahm.
        Behind my office there's
        a car stop.

+ 2. Chìhnbihn yáuh gàan ngàhnhòhng.
    /Chàhn Síujé ūkkéi/
    (in front;
    front side)

      2. Chàhn Síujé ūkkéi chìhnbihn
        yáuh gàan ngàhnhòhng.
        In front of Miss Chan's
        house there's a bank.

3. Hauhbihn yáuh gàan jáudim.
   /Hèunggóng Ngàhnhòhng/

      3. Hèunggóng Ngàhnhòhng hauh-
        bihn yáuh gàan jáudim.

4. Hauhbihn yáuh gàan gūngsī.
   /Hèunggóng Chāansāt/

      4. Hèunggóng Chāansāt hauhbihn
        yáuh gàan gūngsī.

5. Chìhnbihn yáuh mēyéh a?
   /Jùnggwok Chàhlàuh/

      5. Jùnggwok Chàhlàuh chìhnbihn
        yáuh mēyéh a?

    Comment: chìhnbihn and hauhbihn literally mean 'front side' and
       'back side' and are not specific as to whether the
       positions designated are inside/outside the front/
       back side. Only very rarely, though, is the meaning
       unclear in context.

IV: CONVERSATIONS FOR LISTENING

> (On tape. Refer to wordlist below as you listen.)
>
> Unfamiliar terms, in order of occurrence:
>
> 1) bīn? = bīndouh?
>
> 2) Mēyéh sih a? = What's the matter?
>
> 3) lòh = sen. suf. expressing sympathy
>
> 4) ngāamngāam = just now, just on the point of, just
>
> 5) Yáuh mēyéh sih a? = What's going on?
>
> 6) Móuh mēyéh sih.= Nothing special.
>
> 7) ngāamngāam séung heui = just thinking of going
>
> 8) yātján = in a little while

V.   SAY IT IN CANTONESE

A. You say to the person sitting next to you:

1. A, Mr. Lau, where are you going?

2. I'm going to Kowloon to buy something.

3. Where do you live?

4. I'm taking my daughter to see the doctor.

5. Who are you going shopping with?

6. You don't have a phone at home, do you. (confident that he doesn't)

7. She doesn't drink alcoholic beverages, does she. (confident that she doesn't.)

8. What are you going over to Kowloon to do?

9. Where is the Number 8 car stop?

10. I can't make out what bus that is over there.

11. Your office is behind the Mandarin Hotel, isn't it?

B. And he responds:

1. I'm going to work, how about you?

2. I'm going to Kowloon too.

3. I live in the Central District.

4. Which doctor are you going to?

5. I'm going with Miss Lee.

6. That's right, we don't have one.

7. Not so! She does drink alcoholic beverages.

8. I'm going to visit my father.

9. It's in front of the bank.

10. Over there where?

11. No, it's in the vicinity of the Central Market.

12. I take my son to school at eight.

13. Where are you going?

14. I'm going to Kowloon to go shopping.

15. My boy friend is not going shopping with me.

16. Should I follow you?

12. What time does your daughter go?

13. I'm going to my girl friend's house to meet her.

14. Is your boy friend going with you?

15. He told me he wanted to go with you.

16. Yes, please follow me.

Vocabulary Checklist for Lesson 12

1.	bàhbā	n:	father
2.	chìhnbihn	PW:	front (front side)
3.	chìngchó	adj:	clear, vivid, clearly
4.	daai	V/coV:	take/bring (someone/something) along
5.	douh	bf:	road, restricted to use following named road
6.	ga	m:	M. for vehicle
7.	gàn	coV:	follow, come behind
8.	gànjyuh	v:	follow, come behind
9.	Gáulùhng	PW:	Kowloon
10.	hauhbihn	PW:	back (back side); behind
11.	heui	v:	go
12.	hohkhaauh	n/PW:	school
13.	houh	m:	number
14.	jái	n:	son
15.	jáinéui	n:	children (of a family), sons and daughters
16.	jip	v:	meet, fetch, pick up (a person)
17.	jouh	v:	do, work
18.	jouh sāam	vo:	make clothes, have clothes made
19.	jouh sih	vo:	to work, have a job
20.	jyuh	v:	live
21.	làih	v:	come
22.	láu	m:	floor, storey of a building
23.	màhmā	n:	mother
24.	Móuh cho.	Ph:	That's right.

25.	nàahmpàhngyáuh	n:	boy-friend
26.	Nèihdēun Douh	PW:	Nathan Road
27.	néui	n:	daughter
28.	néuihpàhngyáuh	n:	girl-friend
29.	sih	n:	piece of business, affair, matter
30.	sīnsàang	n:	husband
31.	sung	coV/V:	deliver
32.	taaitáai	n:	wife; married woman
33.	taam	v:	to visit
34.	tái yīsāng	vo:	see the doctor
35.	tùhng	coV:	with
36.	yéh	n:	things, stuff
37.	yīsāng	n:	doctor

I. BASIC CONVERSATION

A. Buildup:

<u>Sīgēi</u>

Heui bīndouh a?	Where to?
daaphaak	passenger

<u>Daaphaak</u>

gāai	street
gó tiuh gāai	that street
méng	name
mēyéh méng	what name?
giujouh, <u>or</u> giu	called, be called
giujouh mēyéh méng a?	what's its name?
gó tiuh gāai giujouh mēyéh	what's the name of that
méng a?	street?
Ngóh m̀hgeidāk gó tiuh gāai	I don't remember the name of
giujouh mēyéh méng.	the street.
hàahng	go; walk; drive
yātjihk	straight
Néih yātjihk hàahng sīn.	Go straight first.
dou	arrive
wah néih tèng	tell you
Dou gamseuhnghá, ngóh wah	I'll tell you as we go along.
néih tèng.	
yauh	right
jyun	turn
jyun yauh	turn right
Hái nīdouh jyun yauh.	Turn right here.
jó	left
jyun jó	turn left
gwodī	a little farther on
Gwodī, jyun jó.	Just a little farther on,
	turn left.

<u>Sīgēi</u>

Haih m̀hhaih nīdouh a?	Is this the place?

289

Daaphaak

Ṁhhaih--gwodī tīm.	No--still farther.
gwo	pass, cross by
gwo géi gàan	pass a few buildings
jauh	clause connector: then; and
Gwo géi gàan, jauh haih laak.	Pass a few buildings (more) and that's it.
Dou laak!	Arrived! (i.e.: Here it is!)
jósáubihn or jóbihm	left hand side, left side
Hái jósáubihn gó gàan.	It's that building on the left.

Sīgēi

tihng	stop
tihng chè	stop the car
hóyíh	be permitted, can
Nīdouh ṁhhóyíh tihng chè.	You can't stop here.

Daaphaak

(pointing to the driveway:)

yahp-	in
yahpheui	go in
Jyun yahpheui lā.	Turn in (the driveway).
wái	place; seat
paak	park
yáuh wái paak chè	there's a place to park
yahpbihn	inside
Yahpbihn yáuh wái paak chè.	Inside there's a place to park.

(The car goes into the driveway)

Daaphaak

Hóu laak. Hái nīdouh tihng chè lā.	OK. Stop here.
Ṁhgòi néih dáng jahn--	Please wait--
jauh	immediately, soon
Ngóh jauh fàanlàih.	I'll be right back.

B. <u>Recapitulation:</u>

<u>Sīgēi</u>

Heui bīndouh a?   Where to?

<u>Daaphaak</u>

Ngóh m̀hgeidāk gó tiuh gāai   I don't remember the name of
  giujouh mēyéh méng.   the street.

Néih yātjihk hàahng sīn.   Go straight first.

Dou gamseuhnghá, ngóh wáh néih   I'll tell you as we go along.
  tèng.

Hái nīdouh jyun yauh.   Turn right here.

Gwodī, jyun jó.   Just a little farther on, turn
                                            left.

<u>Sīgēi</u>

Haih m̀hhaih nīdouh a?   Is this the place?

<u>Daaphaak</u>

M̀hhaih--gwodī tīm.   No--still farther.

Gwo géi gàan, jauh haih laak.   Pass a few buildings more and
                                            that's it.

Dou laak!   Here it is!

<u>Sīgēi</u>

Nīdouh m̀hhóyíh tìhng chè.   You aren't allowed to stop here.

<u>Daaphaak</u>

      (pointing to the driveway:)

Jyun yahpheui lā.   Turn in (the driveway).

Yahpbihn yáuh wái paak chè.   Inside there's a place to
                                            park.

      (The car goes into the driveway:)

<u>Daaphaak</u>

Hóu laak. Hái nīdouh tìhng chè lā.   OK--stop here.

M̀hgòi néih dáng jahn--ngóh jauh   Please wait--I'll be right
  fàanlàih.   back.

_____

291

II. NOTES

1. (yāt)jihk 'straight,' 'straight-away'

In combination with following heui, the portion yāt can be omitted.

(Yāt)jihk heui lā!   go straight.

In combination with following hàahng, yātjihk is preferred:

yātjihk hàahng: go (or walk) straight

(See BC)

(yāt)jihk may have the meaning 'straight-away,' 'without being interrupted or diverted'

Ex: Nī ga chē jihk heui Jùng-   This bus goes straight to the
    wàahn ga.   Central District.

2. jauh = (1) ..., then....

(2) immediately

a. jauh in a two-clause sentence = ..., then ....

jauh connects subordinate clause and main clause in a sentence of sequential relationship:

(When or After) _A_ , then _B_ .

As clause connector jauh comes in the second clause (the main clause), following the subject of the clause (if any) and preceding the verb.

Ex: 1. Gwo géi gàan, jauh   (After we) pass a few buildings,
       haih laak.   then there it is.

    2. Gwo géi fānjūng, néih After a few minutes pass, you
       jauh hóyíh fàan-   can come back.
       làih.

(See BC and Drill _10_)

b. jauh in a single clause sentence = 'right away, immediately'

In this jauh acts as an adverb, positioned immediately before the verb it concerns:

Ex: Ngóh jauh fàanlàih.   I'll be right back.

    Ngóh jauh tùhng kéuih   I'll be right back with him. or
    fàanlàih.   I'll bring him right back.

    Ngóh tùhng kéuih jauh   He and I will be right back.
    fàanlàih.

    Ngóh sàam dímjūng jauh   I'll be back at 3 o'clock.
    fàanlàih.   (an early hour from the
                                 speaker's point of view)

(See BC)
292

3. hóyìh = 'can,' in the sense of 1) 'permitted to'

                             2) 'willing and able,' 'can do a favor'

hóyìh is an auxiliary verb, which takes another verb as its object. The colloquial English equivalent is usually 'can,' but it may have one of two different underlying meanings.

    a. 'can' in the sense of 'permitted to'

        Nīdouh m̀hhóyìh paak chē.   You can't park here.
                                      [Here it is not allowed to
                                      park]

              (See BC and Drills 1, 4)

    b. 'can' in the sense of 'can do a favor,' 'able and willing

       to...' In the negative = 'willing but unable'

        1. Ngóh hóyìh je yāt baak   I can lend you $100.
          mān (béi) néih.

        2. Néih hó m̀hhóyìh je yāt   Can you lend me $100?
          baak mān (béi) ngóh
          a?

        3. Deuim̀hjyuh--ngóh m̀h-   I'm sorry, I can't come get
          hóyìh làih jip   you, I have some work (I
          néih--yáuh dī sih.   have to attend to.)

4. tìhng, 'stop' with hái phrases.

    tìhng, 'stop' is one of a group of verbs which a hái phrase can either precede or follow. (See note on hái with verbs of station, p273.)

       Hái nīdouh tìhng chē lā.   Here stop. (i.e. Stop here.)

              (See BC)

     Tìhng hái bīndouh a?   Stop where?

           (See Drill 7)

    paak, 'park (a car)' also belongs to the group of verbs which a hái phrase can either precede or follow. Abstracting a common characteristic of this group of verbs, we say that they are 'standing still' verbs, or verbs of station. The verbs for stand, sit, lie down, stop, park and others are members of this group.

    As for which comes first, the hái phrase or the other verb, it goes according to the Chinese language characteristic of making what you're talking about the subject of the sentence and putting it at the beginning of the sentence. If you're concerned about 'where' you put the hái phrase first; if you're most concerned about stopping, you put that part first.

(See BC and Drill __7_)

5. Sentence suffix <u>la</u> for friendly advice or persuasion.

An imperative sentence with sentence suffix <u>la</u> at mid pitch on the intonation scale adds the connotation of friendly advice or persuasion.

Ex: M̀hhóu fàanjyun tàuh la.   Don't turn and go back =
                                 Better not turn and go back.
                                 (Said as friendly advice
                                 rather than command)

(See Drill _12_)

6. jó and yauh, 'left' and 'right.'

<u>jó</u> and <u>yauh</u> are boundwords which may be bound to a preceding verb to form a VO phrase, or to a following boundword of place to become a PW, or to a following noun as a modifier.

Ex: VO: jyun jó   turn left
    PW: jóbihn   left side, left, to the left
mod+N: jó sáu   left hand

(See BC)

III. DRILLS

1. Expansion Drill

+ 1. a. <u>fàanjyuntàuh</u>

1. a. <u>turn</u> (the car) <u>around</u>
and go back the other
way

b. hái nǐdouh fàanjyuntàuh

b. turn around here and go
back

c. hóyǐh hái nǐdouh fàanjyuntàuh

c. you may turn around and
go back here <u>or</u>
it is permitted to turn
around and go back from
here

d. m̀hhóyǐh hái nǐdouh fàanjyuntàuh

d. it's not allowed to turn
around and go back here

e. Hó m̀hhóyǐh hái nǐdouh fàanjyuntàuh a?

e. May I turn around and go
back here?

Comment: <u>fàanjyuntàuh</u> [return-turn-head] is used when you
have overshot the place you intend to go and want
to direct the driver to turn the car around and
go back.

+ 2. a. <u>tanhauh</u>

2. a. <u>back up, reverse</u> (a car)

b. tanhauh lā

b. back up please

c. tanhauh lā, gódouh yáuh
go wái

c. back up, there's a place

d. tanhauh lā, gódouh hauhbihn
yáuh go wái

d. back up, behind us
there's a place

e. Tanhauh lā, gódouh hauhbihn
yáuh go wái paak chē.

e. Back up, behind us there's
a place to park.

+ 3. a. <u>Wǐhng Ōn Gūngsǐ</u>

3. a. <u>Wing On Company.</u> (a
department store in
Hong Kong)

b. hái Wǐhng Ōn Gūngsǐ

b. at Wing On

c. hái Wǐhng Ōn Gūngsǐ tìhng chē

c. stop the car at Wing On

d. m̀hgòi néih hái Wǐhng Ōn
Gūngsǐ tìhng chē lā

d. please stop the car at
Wing On

e. M̀hgòi néih hái Wǐhng Ōn
Gūngsǐ gwodǐ tìhng chē lā.

e. Please stop the car a
little beyond Wing On.

4. a. yahpheui

4. a. enter, go in.

b. jyun yahpheui

b. turn in (there)
[turn, go in]

c. gànjyuh jyun yahpheui.

c. follow (that car) in

295

d. gànjyuh gó ga chē jyun
   yahpheui

d. follow that car in
   [follow that car, turn
   in]

e. gànjyuh gó ga hāak chē jyun
   yahpheui

e. follow that black car in
   [follow that black car
   there turn in]

f. Gànjyuh chìhnbihn gó ga hāak
   chē jyun yahpheui.

f. Follow that black car
   ahead in. or
   Turn where that black
   car up there is.
   [Follow that black car
   over there, turn in.]

5. a. yáuh wái

5. a. there is space

   b. yáuh go wái

   b. there is a space

   c. yáuh go wái paak chē

   c. there is a place to
      park cars

   d. hauhbihn yáuh go wái paak chē

   d. in the back there is a
      place to park cars

   e. ga hāak chē hauhbihn yáuh go
      wái paak chē

   e. behind the black car
      there is a parking
      place

   f. gó ga hāak chē hauhbihn yáuh
      go wái paak chē

   f. behind that black car
      there is a parking
      place

   g. Nē! Gó ga hāak chē hauhbihn
      yáuh go wái paak chē.

   g. There! Behind the black
      car there is a parking
      place.

---

2. Substitution Drill: Repeat the first sentence, then substitute
   as directed.

   1. Hàaih, Yìngmán giujouh mēyéh a?
      How do you say "shoes" in
      English?

   1. Hàaih, Yìngmán giujouh
      mēyéh a?

   2. /pìhnggwó/

   2. Pìhnggwó, Yìngmán giujouh
      mēyéh a?

   3. /tòhng/

   3. Tòhng, Yìngmán giujouh
      mēyéh a?

   4. /bīu/

   4. Bīu, Yìngmán giujouh mēyéh
      a?

   5. /jūng/

   5. Jūng, Yìngmán giujouh mēyéh
      a?

   6. /gāi/

   6. Gāi, Yìngmán giujouh mēyéh
      a?

7. /gāai/   7. Gāai, Yĭngmán giujouh mēyéh
                                       a?

Comment: giu may substitute for giujouh in all sentences above.

---

3. Response Drill

    Ex: 1. T: Gó gàan gūngsĭ   T: What's the name of that depart-
           giu mēyéh méng   ment store? /Wing On Company/
           a? /Wĭhng Ŏn
           Gūngsĭ/

        S: Giujouh Wĭhng Ŏn   S: It's called the Wing On Company.
          Gūngsĭ.

      2. T: Gó gàan gūngsĭ   T: What's the name of that depart-
           giu mēyéh méng   ment store? /shake/
           a? /shake/

        S: Deuim̀hjyuh, ngóh   S: Excuse me, I don't know what
          m̀hjĭdou giujouh   it's called.
          mēyéh méng.

1. Gaaklèih gàan chàhlàuh giu   1. Deuim̀hjyuh, ngóh m̀hjĭdou
  mēyéh méng a? /shake/   giujouh mēyéh méng.

2. Jógán gó gàan ngàhnhòhng giu   2. Giujouh Méihgwok Ngàhnhòhng.
  mēyéh méng a? /Méihgwok
  Ngàhnhòhng/

3. Gó bihn gàan jáudim giu mēyéh   3. Giujouh Màhnwàh Jáudim.
  méng a? /Màhnwàh Jáudim/

4. Daaih Douh Jùng gó gàan chāan- 4. Deuim̀hjyuh, ngóh m̀hjĭdou
  sāt giu mēyéh méng a?   giujouh mēyéh méng.
  /shake/

5. Deuimihn go máhtàuh giu mēyéh   5. Giujouh Tĭnsĭng Máhtàuh.
  méng a? /Tĭnsĭng Máhtàuh/

6. Nĭ tíuh gāai giu mēyéh méng a? 6. Giujouh Daaih Douh Jùng.
  /Daaih Douh Jùng/

7. Gó gàan gūngsĭ giu mēyéh méng   7. Deuim̀hjyuh, ngóh m̀hjĭdou
  a? /shake/   giujouh mēyéh méng.

  a. Repeat: Omitting 'méng' in question and answer.

---

4. Alteration Drill

Ex: T: M̀hgòi néih hái nīdouh   T: Please stop (the car) here.
       tìhng chē lā.

    S: Hó m̀hhóyíh hái nīdouh   S: May one stop here? or
       tìhng chē a?   Is it permitted to stop here?

1. M̀hgòi néih gwodī jyun jó lā.   1. Hó m̀hhóyíh gwodī jyun jó a?

2. M̀hgòi néih jyun yahpheui lā.   2. Hó m̀hhóyíh jyun yahpheui a?

+ 3. M̀hgòi néih jyun yahp yauhsáu-   3. Hó m̀hhóyíh jyun yahp
     bihn lā.   yauhsáubihn a?
     (yauhsáubihn =
     right hand side)
     Please turn in on the right
     hand side.

4. M̀hgòi néih hái nīdouh jyun   4. Hó m̀hhóyíh hái nīdouh jyun
   yahp heui lā.   yahp heui a?

5. M̀hgòi néih tanhauh lā.   5. Hó m̀hhóyíh tanhauh a?

---

5. Substitution Drill: Students gesture where appropriate. Repeat
   first sentence, then substitute as directed.

1. Nīdouh m̀hhóyíh jyun yauh.   1. Nīdouh m̀hhóyíh jyun yauh.
   It's not allowed to turn
   to the right here.

+ 2. diuhtàuh   2. Nīdouh m̀hhóyíh diuhtàuh.
     (turn around (a car))

3. jyun yahpheui   3. Nīdouh m̀hhóyíh jyun yahpheui.

4. tanhauh   4. Nīdouh m̀hhóyíh tanhauh.

5. yāt jihk heui   5. Nīdouh m̀hhóyíh yāt jihk
                                             heui.

6. jyun jó.   6. Nīdouh m̀hhóyíh jyun jó.

Comment: Compare word order of:

1. Nīdouh m̀hhóyíh jyun jó.   ⎫
2. M̀hhóyíh hái nīdouh jyun jó.   ⎬ You can't turn left
3. Hái nīdouh m̀hhóyíh jyun jó.   ⎭ here.

These are interchangeable. Note absence of hái
   before nīdouh in first sentence. Omission of hái
   before PW is permitted when PW begins the sentence.

---

6. Substitution Drill: Repeat the first sentence, then substitute as
   directed.

1. Yiu hái nídouh tanhauh.   1. Yiu hái nídouh tanhauh.
   (We) want to back up here. or
   Back up here.

2. mhsái   2. Mhsái hái nídouh tanhauh.

3. diuhtàuh   3. Mhsái hái nídouh diuhtàuh.

4. yiu   4. Yiu hái nídouh diuhtàuh.

5. jyun yahpheui   5. Yiu hái nídouh jyun yahpheui.

6. hóyíh   6. Hóyíh hái nídouh jyun yahp-
                                         heui.

7. jyun yauh   7. Hóyíh hái nídouh jyun yauh.

8. hóu mhhóu   8. Hóu mhhóu hái nídouh jyun
                                         yauh a?
                                         Is it OK to turn right
                                         here?

9. yātjihk heui   9. Hóu mhhóu hái nídouh yāt-
                                         jihk heui a?

10. fàanjyun tàuh   10. Hóu mhhóu hái nídouh fàan-
                                          jyuntàuh a?

---

7. Response Drill: Students gesture where appropriate.

   Ex: T: Tīnsīng Máhtàuh   T: Star Ferry
       S1: Tìhng hái bíndouh a? S1: Where should I stop?
       S2: Tìhng hái Tīnsīng   S2: Stop at the Star Ferry.
           Máhtàuh lā.

1. Tìhng hái bíndouh a?   1. Tìhng hái Màhnwàh Jáudim
   /Màhnwàh Jáudim mùhnháu/   mùhnháu lā.

2. Tìhng hái bíndouh a?   2. Tìhng hái Wìhng Ōn Gūngsī
   /Wìhng Ōn Gūngsī deuimihn/   deuimihn lā.

3. Tìhng hái bíndouh a?   3. Tìhng hái Méihgwok Ngàhn-
   /Méihgwok Ngàhnhòhng gaaklèih/   hòhng gaaklèih lā.

4. Tìhng hái bíndouh a?   4. Tìhng hái Jùnggwok Chàh-
   /Jùnggwok Chàhlàuh chìhnbihn/   làuh chìhnbihn lā.

5. Tìhng hái bíndouh a?   5. Tìhng hái tòuhsyùgwún
   /tòuhsyùgwún mùhnháu/   mùhnháu lā.

6. Tìhng hái bíndouh a?   6. Tìhng hái Tīnsīng Màhtàuh
   /Tīnsīng Máhtàuh gwodī/   gwodī lā.

299

7. Tȋhng hái bȋndouh a?
   /Mèihgwok Jáudim yauhsáubihn/

7. Tȋhng hái Mèihgwok Jáudim
   yauhsáubihn lā.

8. Tȋhng hái bȋndouh a?
 + /ngàhnhòhng yauhbihn/
   (right side)

8. Tȋhng hái ngàhnhòhng yauhbihn lā.

Comment: Tȋhng, 'stop' is one of a group of verbs which accepts
a hái phrase in either pre-verb position or post-
verb position.

Ex: A: Tȋhng hái bȋndouh a?⎫
    Hái bȋndouh tȋhng a?⎰ Where should I stop?

B: Tȋhng hái Tȋnsȋng Máhtàuh lā.⎫Stop at the
   Hái Tȋnsȋng Máhtàuh tȋhng lā.⎰Star Ferry.

---

8. Substitution Drill: Repeat the first sentence, then substitute
   as directed.

1. Jùnggwok Chàhlàuh gwodȋ, jyun
   yauh.
   A little beyond the China
   Teahouse, turn right.

1. Jùnggwok chàhlàuh gwodȋ,
   jyun yauh.

2. jyun jó

2. Jùnggwok Chàhlàuh gwodȋ,
   jyun jó.

3. chē jaahm

3. Chē jaahm gwodȋ, jyun jó.

4. jyun yauh

4. Chē jaahm gwodȋ, jyun yauh.

5. Hèunggóng Chāansāt

5. Hèunggóng Chāansāt gwodȋ,
   jyun yauh.

6. Màhnwàh Jáudim

6. Màhnwàh Jáudim gwodȋ,
   jyun yauh.

7. Dāk Fuh Douh

7. Dāk Fuh Douh gwodȋ, jyun
   yauh.

8. hohkhaauh

8. Hohkhaauh gwodȋ, jyun yauh.

9. Daaih Douh Jùng

9. Daaih Douh Jùng gwodȋ, jyun
   yauh.

10. jyun jó

10. Daaih Douh Jùng gwodȋ, jyun
    jó.

a. Do #1-4 as expansion drill, incorporating hàahngdou 'walk
   to, go to,' thus:

T: Jùnggwok Chàhlàuh
   gwodȋ, jyun yauh.

A little beyond the China
Teahouse, turn right.

S: Hàahngdou Jùnggwok
   Chàhlàuh gwodȋ,
   jyun yauh.

Go a little beyond the China
Teahouse, and turn right.

Note that <u>hàahng</u> is not limited to the meaning 'walk,' but
is used as a verb of locomotion for cars as well.

---

9. Expansion Drill: Students should gesture to indicate directions.

Ex: T: Wíhng Ōn Gūngsí
gwodí, jyun jó.

S: Wíhng Ōn Gūngsí
gwodí, jyun jó,
m̀hhaih jyun yauh.

T: Turn left a little beyond Wing
On Department Store.

S: Turn left a little beyond Wing
On Department Store; not
right.

1. Méihgwok Ngàhnhòhng gwodí,
jyun jó.

2. Chē jaahm gwodí, jyun yauh.

3. Jùnggwok Chàhlàuh gwodí,
jyun yauh.

4. Hèunggóng Chāansāt gwodí,
jyun jó.

5. Màhnwàh Jáudim gwodí, jyun
yauh.

1. Méihgwok Ngàhnhòhng gwodí,
jyun jó, m̀hhaih jyun yauh.

2. Chē jaahm gwodí, jyun yauh,
m̀hhaih jyun jó.

3. Jùnggwok Chàhlàuh gwodí,
jyun yauh, m̀hhaih jyun jó.

4. Hèunggóng Chāansāt gwodí,
jyun jo, m̀hhaih jyun yauh.

5. Màhnwàh Jáudim gwodí, jyun
yauh, m̀hhaih jyun jó.

---

10. Substitution Drill: Repeat first sentence, then substitute as
directed.

1. Gwo léuhng go chē jaahm, jauh
haih laak.
Pass two bus stops, and
there you are.

2. yāt tìuh gāai

3. sàam go chē jaahm

4. léuhng gàan gūngsí

5. léuhng tìuh gāai

6. yāt gàan

7. géi gàan

1. Gwo léuhng go chē jaahm,
jauh haih laak.

2. Gwo yāt tìuh gāai, jauh
haih laak.

3. Gwo sàam go chē jaahm, jauh
haih laak.

4. Gwo léuhng gàan gūngsí,
jauh haih laak.

5. Gwo léuhng tìuh gāai, jauh
haih laak.

6. Gwo yāt gàan, jauh haih
laak.

7. Gwo géi gàan, jauh haih laak.

---

11. Response Drill

      Ex: .T: Kéuih hái bīn gàan   Which teahouse is he in?
          chàhlàuh a?   /next door, adjacent/
          /gaaklèih/

        S: Kéuih hái gaaklèih   He's in the one next door.
          gó gàan.

1. Kéuih hái bīn gàan ngàhnhòhng   1. Kéuih hái deuimihn gó gàan.
   a? /deuimihn/

2. Néih heui bīn gàan gūngsī a?   2. Ngóh heui chìhnbihn gó gàan.
   /chìhnbihn/

3. Néih màhmā hái bīn gàan séjih-   3. Ngóh màhmā hái yauhbihn gó
   làuh a? /yauhbihn/   gàan.

4. Néih séung heui bīn gàan   4. Ngóh séung heui nī bihn
   chāansāt a? /nī bihn/   gó gàan.

5. Kéuih hái bīn gàan hohkhaauh a? 5. Kéuih hái jósáubihn gó gàan.
   /jósáubihn/

     Comment: Compare the structure and meaning above with one you
         have studied previously:

        1. Kéuih hái gaaklèih gó gàan chàhlàuh.
          He's at the teahouse next door. [next-door teahouse]

        2. Kéuih hái gó gàan chàhlàuh gaaklèih.
          He's next door to the teahouse.

----

12. Transformation Drill: Affirmative to Negative.

      Ex: T: Kéuih heui Tīnsīng   T: He's going to the Star Ferry.
          Máhtàuh.

        S: Kéuih m̀hheui Tīnsīng S: He's not going to the Star
          Máhtàuh.   Ferry.

1. Kéuih jip ngóh heui tái   1. Kéuih m̀hjip ngóh heui tái
   yīsāng.   yīsāng.

2. Hái nīdouh hóyíh tanhauh.   2. Hái nīdouh m̀hhóyíh tanhauh.

3. Ngóh yáuh sahp mān.   3. Ngóh móuh sahp mān.

4. Ngóh gau chín máaih bīu.   4. Ngóh m̀hgau chín máaih bīu.

5. Chàhn Táai deui hàaih géi leng. 5. Chàhn Táai deui hàaih
                         m̀hhaih géi leng.

6. Wòhng Sàang jùngyi tùhng ngóh 6. Wòhng Sàang m̀hjùngyi tùhng
   bàhbā heui yám chàh.   ngóh bàhbā heui yám chàh.

+ 7. Sihk yīn lā!   7. M̀hhóu sihk yīn la!
                      (friendly advice)

8. Wòhng Táai tùhng ngóh màhmā   8. Wòhng Táai tùhng ngóh màhmā
   hóu jùngyi jouh sāam.   m̀hjùngyi jouh sāam.

9. Ngóh táidóu Léih Síujé hái   9. Ngóh táim̀hdóu Léih Síujé
   deuimihn gàan chàhlàuh.   hái deuimihn gàan chàhlàuh.

10. Fàanjyun tàuh lā!   10. M̀hhóu fàanjyun tàuh la. or
                                           M̀hsái fàanjyun tàuh la.

    Comment: in #7 and #10 above note that the sentence suffix
             on the negative sentences is la and not lā. The mid-
             pitched final la gives the imperative sentence a
             connotation of friendly advice, contrasting to the high
             pitch lā, polite but more urgent.

---

13. Transformation Drill: Change the sentence from a question-word
    question to a choice type question, following the pattern of
    the example.

        Ex: T: Bīn tìuh haih Dāk   T: Which street is Des Voeux
               Fuh Douh Jùng a?   Central?

            S: Nī tìuh haih m̀hhaih   S: Is this Des Voeux Road Central?
               Dāk Fuh Douh Jùng
               a?

    1. Bīn gàan haih Jùnggwok   1. Nī gàan haih m̀hhaih Jùng-
       Ngàhnhòhng a?   gwok Ngàhnhòhng a?

    2. Bīn gàan haih Wíhng Ōn Gūngsī   2. Nī gàan haih m̀hhaih Wíhng
       a?   Ōn Gūngsī a?

    3. Bīn gàan haih Méihgwok Jáudim   3. Nī gàan haih m̀hhaih Méih-
       a?   gwok Jáudim a?

    4. Bīn tìuh haih Daaih Douh Jùng   4. Nī tìuh haih m̀hhaih Daaih
       a?   Douh Jùng a?

    5. Bīn gàan haih Màhnwàh Jáudim   5. Nī gàan haih m̀hhaih Màhnwàh
       a?   Jáudim a?

---

14. Substitution Drill: Repeat the first sentence, then substitute as
    directed.

    1. Chìhnbihn yáuh móuh wái paak   1. Chìhnbihn yáuh móuh wái paak
       chē a?   chē a?
       Is there a place to park the
       car in front?

    2. /yahpbihn/   2. Yahpbihn yáuh móuh wái
                                          paak chē a?

    3. /deuimihn/   3. Deuimihn yáuh móuh wái
                                          paak chē a?

303

4. /mùhnháu/

5. /gaaklèih/

6. /nǐjógán/

7. /jóbihn/

8. /yauhbihn/

4. Mùhnháu yáuh móuh wái paak chē a?

5. Gaaklèih yáuh móuh wái paak chē a?

6. Nǐjógán yáuh móuh wái paak chē a?

7. Jóbihn yáuh móuh wái paak chē a?

8. Yauhbihn yáuh móuh wái paak chē a?

---

15. Response Drill:

+ Ex: T: Néih sǐk m̀hsǐk jà chē a? /m̀hsǐk/

Do you know how to drive? [drive car] /not know how/

S: Ngóh m̀hsǐk jà chē.

I don't know how to drive.

1. Bǐngo gaau néih jà chē ga? /Hòh Sàang/

1. Hòh Sàang gaau ngóh jà chē ge.

2. Hèunggóng yáuh móuh hohkhaauh gaau jà chē ga? /dāk géi gàan...ge ja/

2. Hèunggóng dāk géi gàan hohkhaauh gaau jà chē ge ja.

3. Néih hái bǐndouh hohk jà chē ga? /Gáulùhng/

3. Ngóh hái Gáulùhng hohk jà chē ge.

4. Nǐ tiuh gāai hó m̀hhóyǐh hohk jà chē ga? /m̀hhóyǐh bo/++ Is this a street that you can learn to drive on?

4. Nǐ tiuh gāai m̀hhóyǐh hohk jà chē bo.

5. Néih jùngyi jà bǐn gwok ge chē a? /Méihgwok chē/ Which country's cars do you like to drive?

5. Ngóh jùngyi jà Méihgwok chē.

6. Néih jùng m̀hjùngyi jà chē a? /m̀hhaih géi jùngyi ge ja/

6. Ngóh m̀hhaih géi jùngyi jà chē ge ja.

++ Access to some streets in Hong Kong is prohibited to learner drivers.

---

16. Expansion Drill

Ex: T: M̀hgòi néih, faaidī   T: Faster please. /drive/
    lā! /jà/

    S: M̀hgòi néih jà faaidī   S: Please drive faster.
    lā!

1. M̀hgòi néih, maahndī lā! /góng/   1. M̀hgòi néih góng maahndī lā!

2. M̀hgòi néih, faaidī lā! /hàahng/   2. M̀hgòi néih hàahng faaidī lā!

3. M̀hgòi néih, chèuhngdī lā!
   /jouh/
   Longer please. (said to a
   tailor)
                  3. M̀hgòi néih jouh chèuhngdī
                    lā!
                    Make it longer please.

4. M̀hgòi néih, dyúndī lā! /jouh/   4. M̀hgòi néih jouh dyúndī lā!

5. M̀hgòi néih, pèhngdī lā! /maaih/   5. M̀hgòi néih maaih pèhngdī lā!
   Cheaper! (said to shopkeeper)   Sell it cheaper!

6. M̀hgòi néih, daaihdī lā! /jouh/   6. M̀hgòi néih jouh daaihdī lā!

7. M̀hgòi néih, faaidī lā! /sé/   7. M̀hgòi néih sé faaidī lā!

8. M̀hgòi néih, saidī lā! /sé/   8. M̀hgòi néih sé saidī lā!

9. M̀hgòi néih, futdī lā. /jouh/   9. M̀hgòi néih jouh futdī lā!
   Wider please. (said to a   Please make (it) a bit
   tailor)   wider.

10. M̀hgòi néih, jaakdī lā. /jouh/   10. M̀hgòi néih jouh jaakdī lā!
    A bit narrower, please.   Please make (it) a bit
                    narrower.

---

17. Classroom Conversation Drill: Teacher asks, students answer,
    giving their actual Cantonese names. Students should learn to
    react appropriately to the different questions.

1. Gwaising a? (polite)   1. Síu sing <u>Surname</u>. or
                           Ngóh sing _____.

2. Sing mēyéh a? (ordinary)   2. Ngóh sing <u>Surname</u>.

+ 3. Gwaisingmìhng a? (polite)   3. <u>Surname Given name</u>.
    <u>Your family name and given</u>
    <u>name?</u>

4. Mēyéh méng a?   4. <u>Surname Given name</u>.

5. Néih giu mēyéh méng a?   5. <u>Surname Given name</u>.

6. Néih mēyéh méng a?   6. <u>Surname Given name</u>.

    Comment: The response to #4 <u>mēyéh méng a?</u> may be simply the
          given name if the surname is not in question.

Comment: An expanded form of the responses to #3-6 is:

Ngóh sing _____ giu(jouh) _____.

———————————

IV. CONVERSATIONS FOR LISTENING

(On tape. Refer to wordlist below as you listen.)

Unfamiliar terms, in order of occurrence:

1) yātján = in a little while

2) dīksí = taxi

3) gāaiháu = intersection [street-mouth]

4) hóu chìh = very likely ..., most likely ...

5) Ei! = mild exclamation

6) gwojó la = here: we've overshot it, we've passed it.
   gwo = pass by

7) sái = drive

———————————

V. SAY IT IN CANTONESE

A. Say to the classmate next to you:

1. Could you please tell me which building is the Wing On Company?

2. What's the name of this street?

3. Is this Nathan Road?

4. Here it is! Please stop here. (as if said to taxi-driver)

5. Is it OK to park here?

6. What street is your school on?

7. Can you drive a car?

8. Turn right just beyond the library.

B. And he responds:

1. It's that one on the right hand side.

2. This is Queens Road Central.

3. No--Nathan Road is on the Kowloon side.

4. It's not permitted to stop here--a little further down it's OK to stop.

5. No. Go in there to the right--there's a place inside to park.

6. I forget the name of the street--

7. Yes, I can--do you want me to teach you to drive?

8. You can't turn in to the right on that street. Should I stop here?

9. Is that the Mandarin Hotel
   there on the right?

9. No, that building is the
   Hilton Hotel.

Vocabulary Checklist for Lesson 13

1.	daaphaak	n:	passenger
2.	diuhtàuh	vo:	turn (a car) around [reverse head]
3.	dou	v:	arrive
4.	fàanjyun tàuh	vp:	turn (the car) around and go back [return-turn head]
5.	gāai	n:	street
6.	giu(jouh)	v:	is called, is named
7.	gwaisingmìhng?	Ph:	what is your surname and given name? (polite)
8.	gwo	v:	pass by (a point); cross (a street); go over to (a place)
9.	gwodī	Ph:	beyond; a little farther on
10.	Gwodī tìm.	Ph:	Go further on; Keep going (said to taxi driver)
11.	hàahng	v:	go; walk; drive
12.	hóyìh	auxV:	can, as (1) be permitted, allowed to; (2) be willing to
13.	jà chē	vo:	to drive a car
14.	jauh	adv:	immediately, soon; as clause connector = then; and
15.	jihk	bf:	straight
16.	jó	bf:	left (direction)
17.	jóbihn	PW:	left side
18.	jósáubihn	PW:	lefthand side
19.	jyun	v:	turn
20.	la	ss:	as sen. suf. to imperative sentence, gives connotation of friendly advice
21.	méng	n:	name; given name
22.	paak (chē)	v(o):	park a car
23.	tanhauh	v:	back (a car) up, move back
24.	tìhng	v:	stop
25.	wái	n:	place, seat
26.	WìhngŌn Gūngsī	PW:	Wing On Department Store
27.	yahp	bf:	enter

28. yahpbihn   PW: inside
29. yahpheui   v: go in; enter
30. yātjihk   adv: straight a) direction
                            b) without being diverted: straight-
                            away
31. yauh   bf: right (direction)
32. yauhbihn   PW: right side
33. yauhsáubihn   PW: right hand side

I. BASIC CONVERSATION

A. Buildup:

(A Hong Kong native and a foreign friend have lunch in a Chinese restaurant:)

Búndeihyàhn

fógei	waiter
A: Fógei!	Waiter!
choipáai	menu, bill of fare
nǐng	carry
nǐnglàih; nǐngheui	bring; take
nǐng go choipáai làih lā	bring the food list please
nǐng go choipáai làih béi ngóh lā	please bring me a menu
táiháh	have a look
béi ngóh táiháh lā	please let me have a look
Ṁhgòi néih nǐng go choipáai làih béi ngóh táiháh lā.	Please bring me a menu to have a look at.

Fógei

Hóu aak, jauh làih.	Yes sir; coming right away.
ngoihgwokyàhn	foreigner

Ngoihgwokyàhn

dǐm	order (food from a list)
choi	food, dishes
Ngóh ṁhsǐk dǐm choi ga.	I don't know how to order food.
gaaisiuh	recommend, introduce
Ṁhgòi néih gaaisiuhháh lā.	Please make a recommendation.

Búndeihyàhn

Gám, dáng ngóh dǐm lā.	Well then, I'll choose.
yùhjyū	suckling pig
gwo	verb-suffix: indicates experience; to have done something before.
meih	not yet
sihkgwo meih?	have (you) eaten (it) before?

	question formula: Verbed before, or not yet?
Néih sihkgwo yúhjyū meih a?	Have you ever eaten roast suckling pig?

Ngoihgwokyàhn

Meih a.	Not yet.
yāt chi dōu meih ...	not yet even one time
Yāt chi dōu meih sihkgwo.	I haven't eaten it even once.

Búndeihyàhn

hóu ma?	OK?
ma?	sen. suf. which makes a question of the sentence it is attached to.
Siháh lā, hóu ma?	Let's try it, OK?

Ngoihgwokyàhn

Hóu ā.	Fine.

Búndeihyàhn

hā	shrimp
yíkwaahk?	... or ...?
Néih jùngyi sihk hā yíkwaahk sihk yú nē?	Do you like to eat shrimp, or eat fish?

Ngoihgwokyàhn

Sihdaahn lā.	As you wish. i.e., Either one.
jùngyi sihk hā	like to eat shrimp
dōuhaih jùngyi sihk hā	really like to eat shrimp
bātgwo	however, but, although
Bātgwo ngóh dōuhaih jùngyi sihk hā.	Although I really like shrimp. (i.e., I really like shrimp better.)
juhng	still, in addition, also (precedes verbal expression)
juhng oi dī mēyéh a?	also want some what?
juhng séung oi dī mēyéh a?	also want to have some what?

310

Ngóhdeih juhng séung oi dĪ   What else do we want to have?
  mēyéh a?

Búndeihyàhn

tòng   soup
Juhng séung oi go tòng tĬm.   In addition let's have a soup
                                      too.

  (Later the local resident calls the waiter again:)

Búndeihyàhn

-dò-   additional; another; more
                                      (precedes Measure expres-
                                      sion)

béi dò jĬ bējáu ngóh   give me another bottle of
                                      beer

-dò léuhng jĬ bējáu   two more bottles of beer
Fógei! Béi dò léuhng jĬ bējáu   Waiter! Please give us two
  ngóhdeih tĬm lā.   more bottles of beer.

Ngoihgwokyàhn

m̀hcho   good [not wrong]
DĪ yúhjyù jànhaih m̀hcho.   The suckling pig is really good.

Búndeihyàhn

dōdĪ   more
Sihk dōdĪ lā!   Have some more!

Ngoihgwokyàhn

dòjeh   thank you (for the gift)
Gau laak. Dòjehsaai.   I've had plenty. Thanks a lot.

Búndeihyàhn

màaihdāan   check please! [together-
                                      list]

Fógei! Màaihdāan!   Waiter! The check please!

B. Recapitulation:

            (A Hong Kong native and a foreign friend
            have lunch in a Chinese restaurant:)

Búndeihyàhn

A! Fógei!   Waiter!

311

Ḿhgòi néih níng go choipáai
    làih béi ngóh táiháh lā.

Fógei

Hóu aak, jauh làih.

Yes sir, coming right away.

Ngoihgwokyàhn

Ngóh ṁhsìk dím choi ga. Ḿhgòi
    néih gaaisiuhháh lā.

I don't know how to order food.
    Please make a recommendation.

Búndeihyàhn

Gám, dáng ngóh dím lā.

Well then, I'll choose.

Néih sihkgwo yúhjyū meih a?

Have you ever eaten roast
    suckling pig?

Ngoihgwokyàhn

Meih a--yāt chi dōu meih
    sihkgwo.

Not yet--I've not eaten it
    even once.

Búndeihyàhn

Siháh lā, hóu ma?

Let's try it, OK?

Ngoihgwokyāhn

Hóu ā.

Fine.

Búndeihyàhn

Néih jùngyi sihk hā yìkwaahk
    sihk yú nē?

Do you prefer shrimp, or fish?

Ngoihgwokyàhn

Sihdaahn lā.

As you wish. i.e., Either one.

Bātgwo ngóh dōuhaih jùngyi
    sihk hā.

Although I really like shrimp.
    (i.e., I really like shrimp
    better.)

Ngóhdeih juhng séung oi dī
    mēyéh a?

What else do we want to have?

Búndeihyàhn

Juhng séung oi go tòng tìm.

In addition, let's have a
    soup, too.

(Later the Hong Kong native calls the waiter again:)

Fógei! Béi dò léuhng jì
    bējáu ngóhdeih tìm lā.

Waiter! Please give us two
    more bottles of beer.

Ngoihgwokyàhn

Dī yùhjyū jànhaih mhcho.   The suckling pig is really
                                          good!

Bùndeihyàhn

Sihk dōdī lā!   Have some more!

Ngoihgwokyàhn

Gau laak. Dòjehsaai.   I've had plenty. Thanks a lot.

Bùndeihyàhn

Fógei! Màaihdāan!   Waiter! The check please!

II. NOTES

   A. Culture notes

      1. Styles of cooking Chinese food.

            Different areas of China have different styles of cooking and
      different specialties, making use of the foods particular to each
      area. For an interesting discussion of the hows and whats of
      Chinese food, see How to Cook and Eat in Chinese, by Buwei Yang
      Chao, (NY: John Day, 1949)

      2. choi. 'a dish (of food),' 'food'.

            The Chinese style of informal eating is for each person to
      have a bowl of rice (if it's in the South--in the North they eat
      bread more) for himself, and for there to be several dishes on the
      table which are communal property for everyone to eat from. The
      eater uses his chopsticks or a spoon to take food from the center
      dishes. The center dishes are called choi.

            A choi can be a fish dish, a meat dish, or a vegetable dish.
      choi is also the general term for 'vegetable.' Finally, choi may
      mean 'cooking style,' or 'food,' as in Seuhnghói choi, 'Shanghai
      cooking,' 'Shanghai food'; Jùngchoi 'Chinese cooking,' 'Chinese
      food.'

            (In this book we use the term Jùngchoi as the general term
      for Chinese food. There is another term sometimes used having
      the same meaning: Tòhngchoi = Chinese food.)

313

3. choipáai and choidāan, 'menu'.

choipáai, 'menu,' 'bill of fare,' is the list you choose from
in a restaurant.

choidāan, 'menu' is the written-down account of a particular
meal.

B. Structure Notes:

1. directional verb compounds. Ex: nìnglàih, 'bring (something) here;
   and nìngheui, 'take (something) there'

a. Directional verbs use -làih and -heui as suffixes to indicate
   direction towards and away from the speaker (or other point
   of reference).

   Ex: nìng   carry
       nìnglàih carry towards the speaker--i.e., bring here
       nìngheui carry away from the speaker--i.e., take there
   We give the directional verb plus the heui/làih suffix
   the name directional verb compound.

b. The noun object of a directional verb compound comes between
   the verb and the suffix. In the absence of a noun object, the
   verb and suffix come together, since a pronoun object is not
   stated:

   Ex: A: Nìng jì bējáu làih   Please bring a bottle of beer.
          la.
       B: Hóu, jauh nìnglàih.   Right--bringing it right away.
       (See BC and Drills 1.3, 10)

c. Another way of forming sentences with directional verb compounds
   is to put the logical object of the verb into subject position.
   Ex: DÌ bējá yìhgìng nìng-   The beer (I've) already
         làih laak.   brought.

2. gwo 'pass,' used as verb suffix

gwo, a verb with the basic meaning 'pass,' 'pass by,' 'pass
through,' is used as a verb suffix indicating 'have passed through
(experienced)' the action expressed by the verb.

   Ex: sihkgwo, 'pass through the experience of eating,'
         'have eaten,' 'ate.'

       (See BC and Drills 7, 8, 9, 13)

3. **meih** 'not yet.'

    The negative **meih** 'not yet' precedes the verb in a negative sentence. In a choice question, it follows the verb:

        Ex: 1. Meih sihkgwo.   (I) haven't had the experience
                                       of eating (it).

            2. Sihkgwo meih?   Have (you) had the experience
                                       of eating (this)?

          (See BC and Drills 3, 8, 9. 13)

    meih 'not yet,' indicates that the action expressed by the verb is one which the speaker contemplates doing--'I haven't eaten it yet,' (but I'd like to.)

4. **mēyéh**, (**mātyéh**) as mass noun.

    mēyéh functions as a mass noun, in taking the mass measure **dī**:

        Ex: dī mēyéh?   Some what?

           Sihk dī mēyéh a?   What will you have to eat?
                              [eat-a little-what?]

5. ...,**yìkwaahk**...... = '....., or .....?'

    yìkwaahk 'or' can be called an interrogative conjunction. It connects two verb phrases, indicating: .^A.. or .^B.., which one?

        Ex: Néih jùngyi sihk hā,   Which do you prefer, to eat
           yìkwaahk sihk yú nē?   shrimp, or to eat fish? **or**
                               Do you want shrimp, or would
                               you rather have fish?

          (See BC and Drills 2, 3)

    The English possibility of:

        A: Do you want coffee or tea?

        B: No thanks.

is not covered by **yìkwaahk**. In Chinese you would have to rephrase the sentence to say something like 'Would you like something to drink? We have coffee and tea.'

6. **dōuhaih** 'really'

    In the following sentence taken from the Basic Conversation,

        Bātgwo ngóh dōuhaih   Although I really like shrimp.
        jùngyi sihk hā.

    dōuhaih is said with very light stress, and has very little content meaning. It serves as an intonation marker, lightening an otherwise blunt statement.   The same function is served by 'really' in the English translation. The situation is: you'd rather have shrimp than fish but you don't want to insist upon it.

7. sentence suffix <u>ma</u>?

    <u>ma</u>? is an interrogative sentence suffix which makes a question of the affirmative or negative sentence it attaches to. It is not used with a sentence which is already in question form--i.e., it is not used with choice-type and question-word questions.

(See BC)

8. sentence suffix <u>ā</u>

    In the Basic Conversation there is the following exchange:

        A: Siháh lā, hòu ma?   Let's try it, OK?

        B: Hóu ā.   Fine.

    The raised intonation on the final <u>ā</u> expresses liveliness.

(See BC)

9. <u>juhng</u> 'still,' 'in addition,' 'also'

    <u>juhng</u> is an adverb which positions before a verb.

      Ex: 1. Juhng séung oi dī   Also think you want some what? meyéh a?   i.e. What else would you like to have?

        2. Juhng séung oi dī   We also think we want some soup tòng tìm.   too.

(See BC and Drills <u>6,11</u>)

10. <u>dò</u> 'additional;' 'more'

    <u>dò</u> with the above meanings is bound to a following number-measure phrase. When the number is <u>yāt</u> 'one,' the number part may be omitted. Before mass nouns the measure <u>dī</u> follows <u>dò</u>, with the number <u>yāt</u> omitted.

      Ex: 1. dò (yāt)dī   another bottle, one more bottle, an additional bottle

        2. dò léuhng go   two more, an additional two

        3. dò (yāt) dī tòng   more soup, additional soup

(See BC and Drills <u>1.3, 1.4, 5, 10</u>)

11. <u>bātgwo</u> however, but, although

    <u>bātgwo</u> is a conjunction joining two clauses. Its sentence position is first word in the second clause.

      Ex: Yú tùhng hā dōu hóu   Fish and shrimp are both good-- housihk, bātgwo   but I really prefer shrimp. ngóh dōuhaih jùngyi sihk hā.

III. DRILLS

  1. Expansion Drill

+ 1. a.   Wún   a.   bowl
     b.   Wún tòng.   b.   bowl of soup
     c. Yám   wún tòng.   c.   have a bowl of soup
     d. Yám   wún tòng lā.   d. Please have a bowl of soup.
     e. Yám dò wún tòng lā.   e. Have another bowl of soup.
     f. Yám dōdī   tòng lā.   f. Have some more soup.

     Comment: In this group of sentences wún, 'bowl' is used as a
              Measure. wún may also be used as a Noun, as in
              sàam jek wún, '3 bowls.' (also sàam go wún, '3
              bowls.')

+ 2. a.   Bùi   a.   cupful
     b.   Bùi chàh   b.   a cup of tea
     c.   Béi bùi chàh   c. Please give me a cup of tea.
           ngóh lā.
     d. Ṁhgòi néih béi bùi chàh   d. Please give me a cup of tea.
           ngóh lā.

+ 3. a.   Būi.   a.   cup
     b.   Jek būi.   b.   a   cup
     c. Nìng   jek būi làih.   c. Bring   a   cup.
     d. Nìng dò jek būi lāih.   d. Bring another   cup.
     e. Nìng dò léuhng jek būi làih.   e. Bring two more cups.
     f. Nìng dò léuhng jek būi làih   f. Bring two more cups too.
           tīm.

+ 4. a.   Baahk faahn.   a.   white rice.
                                            (i.e. plain boiled or
                                            steamed rice)
     b.   Wún baahk faahn.   b.   a bowl of rice.
     c. Béi   wún baahk faahn ngóh.   d. Give me   a bowl of rice.
     d. Béi dò wún baahk faahn ngóh.   d. Give me another bowl of rice.
     e. Ṁhgòi néih   e. Please
           béi dò wún baahk faahn ngóh lā. give me another bowl of rice.

+ 5. a.   Cháau mihn   a.   fried noodles
     b.   Sihk cháau mihn   b.   eat fried noodles
     c.   Jùngyi sihk cháau mihn   c. like to eat fried noodles
     d.   Jùngyi sihk cháau mihn   d. like to eat fried noodles or
+   yìkwaahk tòng mihn a?   soup noodles?

317

e. Néih jùngyi sihk cháau mihn
   yíkwaahk tòng mihn a?

e. Would you like to eat fried
   noodles or soup noodles?

---

2. Transformation Drill

Ex: T: Néih yám mātyéh a?
    /chàh/gafē/

T: What will you have to drink?
   /tea/coffee/

S: Néih yám chàh yík-
   waahk gafē nē?

S: Would you like tea, or coffee?
   (i.e., Which would you like,
   tea or coffee?)

1. Néih yám mātyéh a?
   /heiséui/bējáu/

1. Néih yám heiséui yíkwaahk
   bējáu a?

2. Néih oi mātyéh a?
   /jyùyuhk/ngàuhyuhk/

2. Néih oi jyùyuhk yíkwaahk
   ngàuhyuhk a?

3. Néih heui bíndouh a?
   /Jùngwàahn/Gáulùhng/

3. Néih heui Jùngwàahn yíkwaahk
   Gáulùhng a?

4. Néih wán bíngo a?
   /Hòh Sàang/Hòh Táai/

4. Néih wán Hòh Sàang yíkwaahk
   Hòh Táai a?

+ 5. Néih jùngyi bíndí a?
     /cháau faahn/cháau mihn/
     (cháau faahn =
     fried rice)

5. Néih jùngyi cháau faahn
   yíkwaahk cháau mihn a?
   Would you prefer fried
   rice, or fried noodles?

6. Néih jùngyi bíndí a?
 + /Seuhnghói choi/Gwóngdùng
   choi/
   (/Shanghai food/Cantonese
   food/)

6. Néih jùngyi Seuhnghói choi
   yíkwaahk Gwóngdùng choi nē?
   Would you prefer Shanghai
   food or Cantonese food?

7. Néih jùngyi bíndí a?
 + /Jùng choi/Sàichāan/
   (/Chinese food/Western food/)

7. Néih jùngyi Jùng choi yíkwaahk Sàichāan nē?
   Would you prefer Chinese
   food, or Western food?

318

3. Response Drill

Ex: T: /chaau faahn/ chaau mihn/	T: /fried rice/fried noodles/
S1: Néih jùngyi sihk cháau faahn yìhwaahk sihk cháau mihn a?	S1: Do you want to have fried rice, or fried noodles.
S2: <u>Sihdaahn lā</u>. Cháau faahn tùhng cháau mihn dou dāk.	S2: Either one. Fried rice and fried noodles are both fine.

1. /jyùyuhk/ngàuhyuhk/

       1. S1: Néih jùngyi sihk jyùyuhk yìkwaahk ngàuhyuhk a?

           S2: Sihdaahn lā. Jyùyuhk tùhng ngàuhyuhk dōu dāk.

2. /Jùngchoi/Sāichāan/

       2. S1: Néih jùngyi sihk Jùngchoi yìkwaahk Sāichāan a?

           S2: Sihdaahn lā. Jùngchoi tùhng Sāichāan dōu dāk.

3. /Seuhnghói choi/Gwóngdùng choi/

       3. S1: Néih jùngyi sihk Seuhnghói choi yìkwaahk Gwóngdùng choi a?

           S2: Sihdaahn lā. Seuhnghói choi tùhng Gwóngdùng choi dōu dāk.

4. /ngàuhnáaih/heiséui/

       4. S1: Néih jùngyi yám ngàuhnáaih yìkwaahk heiséui a?

           S2: Sihdaahn lā. Ngàuhnáaih tùhng heiséui dōu dāk.

5. /chàh/gafē/

       5. S1: Néih jùngyi yám chàh yìkwaahk gafē a?

           S2: Sihdaahn lā. Chàh tùhng gafē dōu dāk.

------

4. Expension Drill

Ex: T: /jì bējáu/	T: /a bottle of beer/
S: Béi jì bējáu ngóh lā.	S: Give me a bottle of beer.

1. /jì heiséui/

     1. Béi jì heiséui ngóh lā.

+ 2. /jek gāng/
     (a spoon)

     2. Béi jek gāng ngóh lā.
       Please give me a spoon.

3. /bùi chàh/

     3. Béi bùi chàh ngóh lā.

4. /bùi gafē/

     4. Béi bùi gafē ngóh lā.

5. /go cháau mihn/

     5. Béi go cháau mihn ngóh lā.

6. /go cháau faahn/

     6. Béi go cháau faahn ngóh lā.

7. /go tòng mihn/
8. /wún baahk faahn/
9. /wún tòng mihn/
10. /tìuh kwàhn/
11. /jek jīu/

7. Béi go tòng mihn ngóh lā.
8. Béi wún baahk faahn ngóh lā.
9. Béi wún tòng mihn ngóh lā.
10. Béi tìuh kwàhn ngóh lā.
11. Béi jek jīu ngóh lā.

Comment: The sentences in the right hand column are appropriate
said by a diner in a restaurant to a waiter.

Note that tòng mihn may be either go tòng mihn, 'an
order of soup noodles' (see #7) or wún tòng mihn,
'a bowl of soup noodles' (see #9).

———

5. Expansion Drill: Expand the sentences by adding dò.

Ex: 1. T: Béi bàau yīnjái
ngóh lā!

S: Béi dò bàau yīn-
jái ngóh lā!

2. T: Béi léuhng gihn
sēutsāam ngóh
lā!

S: Béi dò léuhng gihn
sēutsāam ngóh lā!

T: Give me a pack of cigarettes.

S: Give me another pack of
cigarettes.

T: Give me two shirts.

S: Give me two more shirts.

+ 1. Béi deui faaijí ngóh lā!
(chopsticks)

2. Béi go tòng ngóh lā!
3. Béi bá jē ngóh lā!
4. Béi jek gāng ngóh lā!
5. Béi léuhng bàau yīnjái ngóh lā!

1. Béi dò deui faaijí ngóh lā!
Please give me another
pair of chopsticks.

2. Béi dò go tòng ngóh lā!
3. Béi dò bá jē ngóh lā!
4. Béi dò jek gāng ngóh lā!
5. Béi dò léuhng bàau yīnjái
ngóh lā!

———

6. Substitution Drill: Repeat the first sentence after the teacher,
then substitute as directed.

1. Juhng séung yiu dī mēyéh nē?
What else do you want?

2. /yám/

3. /sihk/

1. Juhng séung yiu dī mēyéh
nē?

2. Juhng séung yám dī mēyéh nē?

3. Juhng séung sihk dī mēyéh
nē?

320

4. /oi/

4. Juhng séung oi dī mēyéh nē?

5. /si/

5. Juhng séung si dī mēyéh nē?
   What else would you like
   to try? (in restaurant,
   ordering food)

6. /ló/

6. Juhng séung ló dī mēyéh nē?
   What else do you want to
   get?

7. /máaih/

7. Juhng séung máaih dī mēyéh
   nē?

---

7. Response Drill

Ex: T: Néih jeukgwo nī júng   T: Have you worn this kind of
       yùhlāu meih a?   raincoat before? /nod/
       /nod/

    S: Jeukgwo.   S: Yes.

    T: Néih jeukgwo gó deui   T: Have you worn that pair of
       hàaih meih a?   shoes yet?
       /shake/

    S: Meih.   S: No, not yet.

1. Néih sihkgwo hā meih a?   1. Meih.
   /shake/

2. Néih yámgwo nī júng bējáu   2. Yámgwo.
   meih a? /nod/

3. Néih làihgwo Hèunggóng meih   3. Meih.
   a? /shake/

4. Néih heuigwo Méihgwok meih   4. Heuigwo.
   a? /nod/

5. Néih jyuhgwo Gáulùhng meih a? 5. Meih.
   /shake/

6. Néih yuhnggwo faaijí meih a? 6. Meih.
   /shake/

7. Néih yámgwo nī dī tòng meih   7. Meih.
   a? /shake/

+ 8. Néih jouhgwo nī dī yéh meih a? 8. Jouhgwo.
     /nod/
     Have you done this kind of work
     before?
     (jouh yéh =
     do chores; have a job)

321

8. Transformation Drill

      Ex: T: Ngóh sihkgwo cháau   I've eaten fried noodles before.
            mihn.

         S: Ngóh meih sihkgwo cháau   I've never eaten fried noodles
            mihn.   before.

1. Ngóh jàgwo chē.   1. Ngóh meih jàgwo chē.

2. Ngóh heuigwo Méihgwok.   2. Ngóh meih heuigwo Méihgwok.

3. Ngóh jyuhgwo Gáulùhng.   3. Ngóh meih jyuhgwo Gáulùhng.

4. Ngóh yámgwo nī júng bējáu.   4. Ngóh meih yámgwo nī júng
                                   bējáu.

5. Ngóh yuhnggwo faaijí.   5. Ngóh meih yuhnggwo faaijí.

+ 6. Ngóh làihgwo nī gàan jáugā.   6. Ngóh meih làihgwo nī gàan
    (Chinese style restaurant)   jáugā.

---

9. Expansion Drill

      Ex: T: Ngóh meih sihkgwo hā.   I've never eaten prawns.

         S: Ngóh meih sihkgwo hā,   I've never eaten prawns; have
           néih sihkgwo meih a?   you?

1. Ngóh meih sihkgwo yùhjyū.   1. Ngóh meih sihkgwo yùhjyū.
                            Néih sihkgwo meih a?

2. Ngóh meih yámgwo nī júng tòng. 2. Ngóh meih yámgwo nī júng
                            tòng. Néih yámgwo meih a?

3. Ngóh meih sihkgwo gó júng   3. Ngóh meih sihkgwo gó júng
    yījái.   yījái. Néih sihkgwo
                            meih a?

4. Ngóh meih heuigwo gó gàan   4. Ngóh meih heuigwo gó gàan
    jáugā.   jáugā. Néih heuigwo
                            meih a?

5. Ngóh meih dímgwo nī júng choi. 5. Ngóh meih dímgwo nī júng
                            choi. Néih dímgwo meih a?

---

10. Expansion Drill

  Ex: T: Ṁhgòi néih nǐng jǐ   Please bring a bottle of beer.
     bējáu làih.

    S: Ṁhgòi néih nǐng dǒ jǐ Please bring another bottle of
     bējáu làih.   beer.

 1. Ṁhgòi néih nǐng deui faaijí 1. Ṁhgòi néih nǐng dǒ deui
  làih.   faaijí làih.

 2. Ṁhgòi néih nǐng jek gāng làih. 2. Ṁhgòi néih nǐng dǒ jek gāng
              làih.

 3. Ṁhgòi néih nǐng jek būi làih. 3. Ṁhgòi néih nǐng dǒ jek būi
              làih.

+ 4. Ṁhgòi néih nǐng go wúnjái làih. 4. Ṁhgòi néih nǐng dǒ go wún-
  /small bowl/   jái làih.

+ 5. Ṁhgòi néih nǐng jek séui būi 5. Ṁhgòi néih nǐng dǒ jek séui
  làih. /water glass/   būi làih.

  a. Repeat, teacher giving cue only, students responding with
   sentences in left hand column, thus:

    T: jǐ bējáu

    S: Ṁhgòi néih nǐng jǐ bējáu làih.

---

11. Expansion Drill

  Ex: T: Néih sihksaai dǐ hā Have you eaten up all the
     meih a?   shrimp

    S: Sihksaai laak, ngóh I've eaten (them all) up, and
     juhng séung yiu dǐ   I still want some more.
     tǐm.   [in addition, want to have
              some more]

 1. Néih sihksaai dǐ yú meih a? 1. Sihksaai laak, ngóh juhng
              séung yiu dǐ tǐm.

 2. Néih sihksaai dǐ cháau faahn 2. Sihksaai laak, ngóh juhng
  meih a?   séung yiu dǐ tǐm.

 3. Néih yám saai dǐ chàh meih a? 3. Yám saai laak, ngóh juhng
              séung yiu dǐ tǐm.

 4. Néih yuhngsaai dǐ chǐn meih a? 4. Yuhngsaai laak, ngóh juhng
              séung yiu dǐ tǐm.

 5. Néih sihksaai dǐ cháau mihn 5. Sihksaai laak, ngóh
  meih a?   juhng séung yiu dǐ tǐm.

 6. Néih yámsaai dǐ tòng meih a? 6. Yámsaai laak, ngóh juhng
              séung yiu dǐ tǐm.

---

12. Response Drill

Ex: T: Yú tùhng hā, néih
jùngyi bīn yeuhng
a? (type, kind)

S: Yú tùhng hā, ngóh
léuhng yeuhng dōu
jùngyi.

T: Which do you like better, fish
or prawns? [fish and prawns,
you like which kind more?]

S: Fish and prawns, I like both.

1. Jùngchoi tùhng Sāichāan, néih
jùngyi bīn yeuhng a?

2. Gwóngdùng choi tùhng Seuhnghói
choi, néih jùngyi bīn yeuhng
a?

3. Cháau mihn tùhng tòng mihn,
néih jùngyi bīn yeuhng a?

4. Cháau faahn tùhng baahk faahn,
néih jùngyi bīn yeuhng a?

+ 5. Jùnggwok choi tùhng Yahtbún
choi, néih jùngyi bīn yeuhng a?
(Chinese food)
(Japanese food)

1. Jùngchoi tùhng Sāichāan,
ngóh léuhng yeuhng dōu
jùngyi.

2. Gwóngdùng choi tùhng Seuhnghói choi, ngóh léuhng
yeuhng dōu jùngyi.

3. Cháau mihn tùhng tòng mihn,
ngóh léuhng yeuhng dōu
jùngyi.

4. Cháau faahn tùhng baahk
faahn, ngóh léuhng yeuhng
dōu jùngyi.

5. Jùnggwok choi tùhng Yahtbún
choi, ngóh léuhng yeuhng
dōu jùngyi.

13. Response Drill

Ex: T: Néih heuigwo géidō
chi a?

S: Yāt chi dōu meih
heuigwo.

T: How many times have you been
there?

S: I've never been even once.

1. Néih làihgwo géidō chi a?
2. Néih yuhnggwo géidō chi a?
3. Néih heuigwo géidō chi a?
4. Néih sihkgwo géidō chi a?
5. Néih fàangwo Seuhnghói géidò
chi a?

1. Yāt chi dōu meih làihgwo.
2. Yāt chi dōu meih yuhnggwo.
3. Yāt chi dōu meih heuigwo.
4. Yāt chi dōu meih sihkgwo.
5. Yāt chi dōu meih fàangwo.

14. Expansion Drill

       Ex: T: Kéuih yáuh léuhng   T: He has two cars.
            ga chē.

         S: Kéuih yáuh léuhng   S: He has two cars, but I don't
           ga chē, daahnhaih   even have one.
           ngóh yāt ga dōu
           móuh.

1. Gó go hohkwàang yáuh géi jí   1. Gó go hohksàang yáuh géi jí
   yùhnjíbāt.   yùhnjíbāt, daahnhaih ngóh
                             yāt jí dōu móuh.

2. Kéuih yáuh léuhng go taaitáai. 2. Kéuih yáuh léuhng go taai-
                               tàai, daahnhaih ngóh yāt
                             go dōu móuh.

3. Kéuih yáuh léuhng go sáudói. 3. Kéuih yáuh léuhng go sáudói,
                               daahnhaih ngóh yāt go dōu
                             móuh.

4. Gó go sīgēi yáuh léuhng ga   4. Gó go sīgēi yáuh léuhng ga
   chē.   chē, daahnhaih ngóh yāt
                             ga dōu móuh.

5. Kéuih yáuh léuhng go jái.   5. Kéuih yáuh léuhng go jái,
                               daahnhaih ngóh yāt go
                             dōu móuh.

---

15. Transformation Drill

      Ex: T: Sihk dōdī lā.   T: Have some more.

        S: Mhhóu sihk gam dò a. S: Don't eat so much.

1. Jà maahndī lā!   1. Mhhóu jà gam maahn a.

2. Dím dōdī lā!   2. Mhhóu dím gam dò a.

3. Sihk dōdī lā!   3. Mhhóu sihk gam dò a.

4. Jà faaidī lā!   4. Mhhóu jà gam faai a.

5. Hàahng faaidī lā!   5. Mhhóu hàahng gam faai a.

6. Yám dōdī lā!   6. Mhhóu yám gam dò a.

7. Jouh chèuhngdī lā!   7. Mhhóu jouh gam chèuhng a.

8. Jouh dyúndī lā!   8. Mhhóu jouh gam dyún a.

IV. CONVERSATIONS FOR LISTENING

(On tape. Refer to wordlist below as you listen.)

Unfamiliar terms, in order of occurrence:

1) ngāamngāam = just now

2) fòng gùng = leave work, get off from work

3) yìhm guhk gāi = salt-roasted chicken

4) gaailáan cháau ngàuhyuhk = stir fried beef and broccoli

5) taai - too, excessively

6) sài yèuhng choi tòng = watercress soup

7) giu = order, call for (without having to look at a listed menu)

8) Yèuhngjàu cháau faahn = Yangchow fried rice

9) Sàiyèuhngchoi tòng = watercress soup

10) faai = soon, almost, approaching (preceding a time expression)

11) yáuh méng = famous

12) gù lòu yuhk = sweet & sour pork

13) dōu yiu sai ge = want both to be small portions

V. SAY IT IN CANTONESE

A. Say to the classmate sitting next to you:

1. Have you eaten fried noodles before?

2. Which do you like better, fried noodles or fried rice?

3. (deciding on a restaurant:) Which would you prefer-- Shanghai food or Cantonese food?

4. I don't know how to order-- would you suggest something?

5. What else shall we have?

6. Waiter, would you please bring two bottles of beer?

7. Waiter, please bring another glass.

B. And he answers:

1. Yes, many times.

2. Fried rice.

3. Either one, I like both.

4. Let's have fried noodles and a soup, OK?

5. Shall we have some beer?

6. Yes, sir, right away.

7. All right--shall I bring another bottle of beer?

8. Can you use chopsticks?

8. No--please show me (intro-duce).

9. The soup noodles are not bad!

9. I think so too.

10. Have some more!

10. I've had enough, thanks.

11. Have you eaten in this (Western style) restaurant before?

11. No, I've never been here even once.

12. Have you ever eaten roast suckling pig?

12. Yes, several times.

13. Have you drunk up all your beer?

13. Yes, and I think I'd like some more.

14. Mr. Chan has 10 sons.

14. Is that so! I don't even have one.

15. Don't eat so much!

15. Don't drink so much!

Vocabulary Checklist for Lesson 14

1.	baahk faahn	n:	boiled or steamed rice [white rice]
2.	bātgwo	cj:	however; but; although
3.	būi	n:	cup, glass
4.	bùi	m:	M. for cup, glass
5.	cháau	v:	to toss-fry in small amt of oil, as in scrambling eggs.
6.	cháau faahn	n:	fried rice
7.	cháau mihn	n:	fried noodles
8.	choi	n:	food; a particular food, a dish
9.	choipáai	n:	menu, bill of fare
10.	dím	v:	to order (food)
11.	dò	bf:	additional, as modifier in Noun phrase
12.	dōdī	adv:	more (in addition) (follows V)
13.	Dòjeh.	Ph:	Thank you. (for a gift)
14.	Dòjehsaai.	Ph:	Thank you very much.
15.	dōuhaih	adv:	always, really
16.	faaijí	n:	chopsticks
17.	fógei	n:	waiter in restaurant
18.	gaaisiuh	v:	recommend; introduce
19.	gāng	n:	spoon

20.	-gwo	Vsuf:	indicates experience; to have done something before
21.	Gwóngdùng choi	n:	Cantonese food
22.	hā	n:	shrimp
23.	Hóu ma?	Ph:	Is that OK?
24.	jáugā	n/PW:	Chinese style restaurant
25.	jek	m:	M. for spoon
26.	jouh yéh	vo:	do chores; have a job
27.	juhng	adv:	still, in addition, also (+ verb)
28.	Jùngchoi	n:	Chinese food
29.	Jùnggwok choi	n:	Chinese food
30.	ma?	ss:	sen. suf. making a question of the sentence it attaches to
31.	Màaihdāan!	Ph:	The check please!
32.	meih	adv:	negative, 'not yet'
33.	m̀hcho	Ph:	good [not-wrong], 'not bad!'
34.	ngoihgwokyàhn	n:	foreigner(s)
35.	nìng	v:	carry (something)
36.	nìng...heui	v:	take, carry off (something)
37.	nìng...làih	v:	bring (something)...here
38.	Sāichāan	n:	Western meal
39.	Seuhnghói choi	n:	Shanghai food
40.	séui būi	n:	water glass
41.	Sihdaahn lā.	Ph:	Either one. No preference. As you wish. (when offered a choice)
42.	táiháh	VP:	have a look
43.	tòng	n:	soup
44.	tòng mihn	n:	soup noodles
45.	wún	m:	M. a bowl of...
46.	wún	n:	bowl
47.	wúnjái	n:	small bowl
48.	Yahtbún choi	n:	Japanese food
49.	yāt chi dōu meih...	VP:	not even once...
50.	yāt..M..dōu .Neg.V.	Ph:	Not even one...; can't V. even one __M__.
51.	yéh	n:	work (as in __jouh yéh__) (with restricted use)
52.	yeuhng	m:	kind, type

53. yìkwaahk...?   cj: or?

54. yúhjyū   n: roast suckling pig

I. BASIC CONVERSATION

A. **Buildup:**

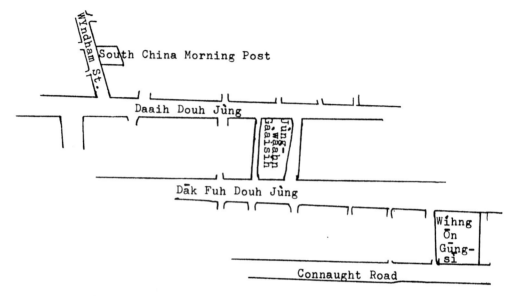

(Mr. Wong approaches another pedestrian
on the street in front of the South China
Morning Post building on Wyndham Street)

Wòhng Sàang

dím heui?   how go?, how (do you) go
                                         (to)?

dím heui Wíhng Ōn Gūngsī a?   how do you go to the Wing
                                         On Company?

yàuh   from

yàuh nīdouh   from here

yàuh nīdouh dím heui Wíhng   how do you get to the Wing
    Ōn Gūngsī a?   On Company from here?

Chéng mahn néih, yàuh nīdouh   Could you please tell me how
    dím heui Wíhng Ōn Gūngsī a?   to get to the Wing On
                                          Company from here?

louhyàhn   pedestrian

Louhyàhn

lohk   down

330

lohkheui   go down [down go]

hàahng lohkheui   walk down (to)

hàahng lohkheui Daaih   go down to Queen's Road
  Douh Jūng   Central

hàahng lohkheui Daaih   first go down to Queen's
  Douh Jūng sìn   Road Central

yìhn(jì)hauh   then, after that

Hàahng lohkheui Daaih Douh   First go down to Queen's Road
  Jūng sìn, yìhnhauh jyun jó.   Central, then turn left.

Wòhng Sàang

Jyun jó.   Turn left.

Louhyàhn

  gàaisìh   food market

  Jùngwàahn Gàaisìh   Central Market

  hàahngdou Jùngwàahn Gàaisìh   walk to Central Market

  -dou   verb suf. to verbs of
                                    action indicates arrival
                                    at goal.

Gám, yātjihk hàahngdou   Then, go straight till you get
  Jùngwàahn Gàaisìh, jyun yauh.   to Central Market, and turn
                                    right.

  gwojó gàaisìh   get past the market

Gwojó gàaisìh, jauh haih Dāk   When you get past the market,
  Fuh Douh Jùng laak.   you are on Des Voeux Road
                                    Central.

  mahn yàhn lā   ask someone

Heuidou gódouh, joi mahn   When you get there, ask again.
  yàhn lā.

(Mr. Wong arrives at Wing On and approaches a salesclerk:)

Wòhng Sàang

  bouhfahn   department (in a store)

  gó go bouhfahn   that department

  maaih lāangsāam gó go   the sweater department
    bouhfahn   [the department that
                                    sells sweaters]

Maaih lāangsāam gó go bouh-
    fahn hái bǐndouh a?

Where is the sweater
    department?

Sauhfoyùhn

séuhng

séuhng sàam láu

go up

go up to the third floor
    (Chinese and American
    style of counting; 2nd
    floor British style of
    counting)

chéng

Chéng séuhng sàam láu lā.

invite; please

Please go up to the second
    (or third) floor.

B.   Recapitulation:

Wòhng Sàang

Chéng mahn néih, yàuh mǐdouh
    dǐm heui Wǐhng Ōn Gūngsǐ a?

Could you please tell me how
    to get to the Wing On
    Company from here?

Louhyàhn

Hàahng lohkheui Daaih Douh
    Jùng sìn, yìhnhauh jyun jó.

First go down to Queen's Road
    Central, then turn left.

Wòhng Sàang

Jyun jó.

Turn left.

Louhyàhn

Gám, yātjihk hàahngdou
    Jùngwàahn Gàaisíh, jyun yauh.

Then go straight till you get
    to Central Market, and turn
    right.

Gwojó gàaisíh, jauh haih Dāk
    Fuh Douh Jùng laak.

When you get past the market,
    you are at Des Voeux Road
    Central.

Heuidou gódouh, joi mahn yàhn
    lā.

When you get there, ask again.

    (Mr. Wong gets to the store and asks a clerk:)

Wòhng Sàang

Maaih lāangsāam gó go beuhfahn
    hái bǐndouh a?

Where is the sweater
    department?

<u>Sauhfoyùhn</u>

Chéng séuhng sàam láu là!   Please go up to the second
                                   floor.

II. NOTES

1. Paired conjunctions:

...sìn, yìhnhauh (or yìhnjìhauh).... = 'first..., then....'

This set of paired conjunctions connects two primary clauses in
a sentence of sequential relationship.

    Ex: Hàahng lohkheui Daaih Douh   Go down to Queen's Road
        Jùng sìn, yìhnhauh   Central first, then turn left.
        jyun jó.

        (See BC and Drills 10, 11)

2. <u>Directional verbs</u>.

    a. Examples of directional verbs are:

        1. séuhng = up

        2. lohk   = down

        3. yahp   = in

        4. chēut = out

        5. gwo   = over, across

    b. In Cantonese these words pattern as verbs. They can be preceded by
    m̀h, and form a question on the <u>Vm̀hV</u> pattern.

        Ex: A: Néih lohk m̀hlohk a?   Are you going down? (Said at
                                       top of escalator)

            B: M̀hlohk.   No, I'm not going down.

    c. These directional verbs can be followed by either a placeword
    object, or one of the two directional suffixes, <u>-làih</u> and <u>-heui</u>,
    or both.

        Ex: 1. Kéuih séuhng sàam láu.   He went up to the 2nd floor.

            2. Ngóh dōu séuhngheui.   I went up too.

            3. Kéuih séuhng(làih)   He came up to the 2nd floor.
               sàam láu.

            4. Kéuih chēutheui Daaih   He went out to Queen's Road
               Douh Jùng.   Central.

        (See Drills 13, 14)

d. The directional verbs may combine with a preceding verb of movement, such as hàahng 'walk,' jyun 'turn,' nĭng 'carry.'

        Ex: 1. Kéuih hàahng lohk-   He walked down to the second
               (heui) sàam láu.   floor.

            2. Kéuih jyun yahp(heui)   He turned into Des Voeux Road
               Dāk Fuh Douh Jùng.   Central.

            3. Ṁhgòi néih nĭng   Please bring it out.
               chēutlaih.

                        (See Drill 12)

3. deihhá, làuhhah, hahbihn differentiated.

   1. deihhá simply means 'ground floor.'

   2. làuhhah [floor-below] is a pronoun of place whose meaning derives
      from position in relationship to another location. If you are on
      the 3d floor làuhhah is a floor below the 3d floor. If you are
      on the ground floor làuhhah is the basement.

   3. hahbihn [below-side] is also a locative whose meaning derives from
      position in relationship to another position. It can mean
      'downstairs' in relation to upstairs, 'under' something, 'below'
      something.

4. Two-part Verb forms: performance and achievement. Chinese verbs are
   often in two parts, with the first part telling of the performance
   and the second part telling of the achievement. For example:

        tái + dóu   = look + successful = see

        wán + dóu   = search + successful = find

        heui + dou   = go + arrive = reach (a place)

        gwo + jó   = pass + accomplish = get past (a place)

        chéng + dóu = invite + successful = invite (someone) and have
                                            him accept

   The second part of these two-part verbs we regard as suffix to the
   first part.

5. -dou as verb suffix, indicates reaching the destination or goal.

        Ex: 1. heuidou = arrive [go-arrive]

               Kéuih heuidou gódouh,...   When he got there,... or
                                          When he gets there,...

            2. duhkdou = read to [read-arrive]

               Kéuih duhkdou sa'ahsei   He read to page 34.
               yihp.

                    (See BC and Drills 3,4)

6. -jó verb suffix = accomplish the performance: 'get/got it done'

> Ex: Gwojó Jùngwàahn Gàaihsih,   When you get past the Central
>   jyun jó.   Market, turn left.

The -jó indicates that the action of the verb to which it is attached is viewed from the standpoint of its being accomplished.

> Ex: gwojó X = 'accomplish going past X'

> (See BC and Drill _9_)

7. daih- = ordinal prefix.

a. daih- prefixed to a number makes it an ordinal number:

> Ex: sàam fo = 3 lessons
>   daih sàam fo = the 3d lesson

> (See Drill _3_)

b. daihyih- is ambiguous.

> daihyih-, bound to a following measure, may mean 'the second'; 'the next'; or 'another, some others   Only rarely is there any mixup in an actual situation.

> Ex: 1. daihyih ga chē   the second car
>   2. daihyih tìuh gāai   the next street, the second
>   street. (i.e. the first one
>   after the place you're
>   talking about)
>
>   3. daihyih go gùngyàhn   another servant
>   4. daihyih dī gùngyàhn   other servants

In this lesson we practice only the first two meanings.

daihyih as 'other' you will meet in Lesson 16.

8. yàuh (and hái) as 'from ..PW..'

> yàuh (or alternately, hái) serves as 'from' in the PW phrase:
>   yàuh .PW.. + .Verb.of.movement. = go/come/etc. from .PW..

Though similar to co-verbs in having an object, yàuh differs from co-verbs in not normally being preceded by mh, but using the verb haih between mh and itself.

> Ex: Mhhaih yàuh nīdouh chēut-   Don't exit from here.
>   heui.

Occasionally you may hear someone say Mhyàuh nīdouh chēutheui or some other phrase with mhyàuh, but it is not common usage. Therefore we class yàuh (and hái used in this position) not as a co-verb but as a preposition.

> (See BC and Drill _6_)

9. <u>yihp</u> 'page' and <u>fo</u> 'lesson' classed as measures.

Note that in the grammatical sense <u>yihp</u> and <u>fo</u> are measures, inasmuch as they can follow numbers directly. From the point of view of having substantive meaning, they are like nouns.

(See Drills <u>3,4</u>)

10. <u>chéng</u>... = invite (someone to do something); Please .Ꮩ.

<u>chéng</u> basically means 'invite.' <u>chéng</u> + Verb is used as a polite imperative:

  Ex: Chéng séuhng sàam láu. Please go up to the 3d floor
                 [invite you to go up]

(See BC)

As polite imperative it is only used affirmatively. To say 'Please don't.Ꮩ.' with <u>chéng</u>, the negative attaches to the following verb.

  Ex: Chéng m̀hséuhng sàam láu. Please don't go up to the 3d
                 floor.

III. DRILLS

1. Substitution Drill: Repeat the first sentence after the teacher,
   then substitute as directed.

    1. Kéuih hái douh dáng néih.   1. Kéuih hái douh dáng néih.
       He's waiting for you here.

    2. /hauhbihn/   2. Kéuih hái hauhbihn dáng néih.

  + 3. /yahpbihn/   3. Kéuih hái yahpbihn dáng néih.
                                             He's waiting for you
                                             <u>inside</u>.

  + 4. /deihhá/   4. Kéuih hái deihhá dáng néih.
       <u>ground floor</u>   He's waiting for you on
                                             the ground floor.

  + 5. /seuhngbihn/   5. Kéuih hái seuhngbihn dáng
       <u>above; upstairs; on top</u>   néih.
       [up-side]   He's waiting for you
                                             upstairs.

  + 6. /hahbihn/   6. Kéuih hái hahbihn dáng néih.
       <u>downstairs; below; under</u>   He's waiting for you
       [down-side]   downstairs.

  + 7. /làuhseuhng/   7. Kéuih hái làuhseuhng dáng
       <u>upstairs</u> [floor-above]   néih.
                                             He's waiting for you
                                             upstairs.

  + 8. /làuhhah/   8. Kéuih hái làuhhah dáng néih.
       <u>downstairs</u> [floor[below]   He's waiting for you down-
                                             stairs.

    9. /sei láu/   9. Kéuih hái sei láu dáng néih.

  + 10. /chēutbihn/   10. Kéuih hái chēutbihn dáng
        <u>outside</u>   néih.

---

2. Response Drill: Students gesture the directions.

       Ex: 1. T: Màhnwàh Jáudim   T: The Mandarin Hotel is in
              hái chìhnbihn,   front, isn't it?
              haih m̀haih a?   /behind, in the back/
              /hauhbihn/

           S: M̀haih, hái hauh-   S: No, it's in the back.
              bihn.

         2. T: Màhnwàh Jáudim   T: The Mandarin Hotel is in
              hái chìhnbihn,   front, isn't it?
              haih m̀haih a?   /in front, ahead/
              /chìhnbihn/

                              337

S: Haih. Hái chìhn-   S: That's right, it's in front.
   bihn.

1. Méihgwok Ngàhnhòhng hái jósáu-   1. M̀hhaih, hái yauhsáubihn.
   bihn, haih m̀hhaih a?
   /yauhsáubihn/

2. Néih sīnsàang (ge) séjihlàuh   2. M̀hhaih, hái hauhbihn.
   hái chìhnbihn, haih m̀hhaih
   a? /hauhbihn/

3. Wòhng Sàang hái chēutbihn, haih   3. Haih, hái chēutbihn.
   m̀hhaih a? /chēutbihn/

4. Léih Táai hái yahpbihn, haih   4. M̀hhaih, hái chìhnbihn.
   m̀hhaih a? /chìhnbihn/

5. Tīnsīng Máhtàuh hái yauhsáubihn,   5. Haih, hái yauhsáubihn.
   haih m̀hhaih a? /yauhsáubihn/

6. Maaih hàaih gó go bouhfahn hái   6. M̀hhaih, hái deihhá.
   yih láu, haih m̀hhaih a?
   /deihhá/

7. Maaih syù gó go bouhfahn hái   7. M̀hhaih, hái làuhhah.
   làuhseuhng, haih m̀hhaih a?
   /làuhhah/

Comment: Note (#2 above) that ge can be omitted in everyday
         speech in modification structure before séjihlàuh.

    a. Repeat, students taking both parts, teacher
       cueing thus:

       1. /Màhnwàh Jáudim/chìhnbihn/hauhbihn/

    or 2. /Màhnwàh Jáudim/chìhnbihn/

_____

3. Expansion Drill

+ 1. a. yihp   1. a. page

     b. sei'ah yihp.   b. 40 pages

+   c. duhk sei'ah yihp   c. read 40 pages

+   d. duhkdou sei'ah yihp   d. read to page 40

+   e. seuhngchi duhkdou sei'ah yihp   e. last time read to page
                                            40

+   f. seuhngchi duhkdou daih sei'ah   f. last time read to the
        yihp   40th page.
        (ordinal number marker,
        -st, -nd, -rd, etc.)

     g. Ngóhdeih seuhngchi duhkdou   g. Last time we read to
        daih sei'ah yihp.   the 40th page.

338

+ 2. a. <u>fo</u>

   b. géi fo a?

   c. daih géi fo a?

   d. duhk daih géi fo a?

   e. seuhngchi duhk daih géi fo a?

   f. Ngóhdeih seuhngchi duhk daih géi fo a?

 3. a. daih sahp yihp

+   b. <u>dáhòi</u> bún syù daih sahp yihp

   c. dáhòi bún syù daih sei'ah sàam yihp

   d. Dáhòi bún syù daih sàam baak sei'ah sàam yihp.

2. a. <u>lesson</u>

   b. how many lessons?

   c. which[th] lesson?

   d. read which lesson?

   e. last time read which lesson?

   f. What lesson did we do last time?

3. a. the 10th page

   b. <u>open</u> your book to page 10

   c. open your books to the 43rd page (page 43)

   d. Open your books to page 343.

---

4. Response Drill

Ex: 1. T: Ngóhdeih seuhngchi duhkdou daih géi yihp a? /43/

S: Duhkdou daih sei'ahsàam yihp.

T: What page did we get to last time?

S: We got to page 43.

2. T: Ngóhdeih seuhngchi duhk daih géi fo a? /3/

S: Daih sàam fo.

T: What lesson did we do last time?

S: We did lesson 3.

1. Ngóhdeih seuhngchi duhkdou daih géi yihp a? /86/

2. Ngóhdeih seuhngchi duhk daih géi fo a? /7/

3. Ngóhdeih seuhngchi duhk daih géi fo a? /15/

4. Ngóhdeih seuhngchi duhkdou daih géi yihp a? /254/

5. Ngóhdeih seuhngchi duhk daih géi fo a? /26/

1. Duhkdou daih baatsahpluhk yihp.

2. Daih chāt fo.

3. Daih sahpńgh fo.

4. Duhkdou daih yih baak ńgh-sahpsei yihp.

5. Daih yahluhk fo.

---

5. Substitution Drill: Repeat the first sentence after the teacher, then substitute as directed.

1. Sàam láu yáuh dī mēyéh maaih
   a?
   What's for sale on the 2nd
   floor? What do they have
   (for sale) on the 2nd floor?

1. Sàam láu yáuh dī mēyéh
   maaih a?

2. /sei láu/

2. Sei láu yáuh dī mēyéh
   maaih a?

3. /làuhhah/

3. Làuhhah yáuh dī mēyéh maaih
   a?

4. /làuhseuhng/

4. Làuhseuhng yáuh dī mēyéh
   maaih a?

5. /yahpbihn/

5. Yahpbihn yáuh dī mēyéh
   maaih a?

6. /seuhngbihn/

6. Seuhngbihn yáuh dī mēyéh
   maaih a?

7. /hahbihn/

7. Hahbihn yáuh dī mēyéh
   maaih a?

Comment: Note in #1 and #2 above the absence of ordinalizing
prefix daih in connection with láu, 'floor, story'.

Compare: sàam láu = the third floor.
           daih sàam fo = the third lesson.

           daih is not used before numbers when modifying
           láu.

---

6. Substitution Drill: Repeat the first sentence after the teacher,
then substitute as directed.

1. Yáuh nīdouh, dím heui Tīn-
   sīng Máhtàuh a?
   How do you get to the Star
   Ferry from here?

1. Yáuh nīdouh, dím heui Tīnsīng Máhtàuh a?

2. /Màhnwàh Jáudim/

2. Yáuh nīdouh, dím heui
   Màhnwàh Jáudim a?

3. /Méihgwok Ngàhnhòhng/

3. Yáuh nīdouh, dím heui
   Méihgwok Ngàhnhòhng a?

4. /Jùngwàahn Gàaisíh/

4. Yáuh nīdouh, dím heui
   Jùngwàahn Gàaisíh a?

5. /Hèunggóng Chāansāt/

5. Yáuh nīdouh, dím heui
   Hèunggóng Chāansāt a?

Comment: <u>hái</u> is used in place of <u>yàuh</u> by some speakers, with no difference in meaning.

Ex: Hái nîdouh, dím heui
   Tīnsīng Máhtàuh a?
<u>or</u> Yàuh nîdouh, dím
   heui Tīnsīng Máhtàuh
   a?
	How do you get to the
	Star Ferry from here?

---

7. Expansion Drill

Ex: T: /WíhngŌn Gūngsī/	T: The WingŌn Company

S: Chéng mahn néih, dím
   heui WíhngŌn Gūng-
   sī a?
	S: Can you please tell me how to
	   get to the WingŌn Company?

1. /Jùnggwok Jáugā/	1. Chéng mahn néih, dím heui Jùnggwok Jáugā a?
2. /Jùngwàahn Gàaisíh/	2. Chéng mahn néih, dím heui Jùngwàahn Gàaisíh a?
3. /Tīnsīng Máhtàuh/	3. Chéng mahn néih, dím heui Tīnsīng Máhtàuh a?

4. /Gáulùhng WíhngŌn Gūngsī/	4. Chéng mahn néih, dím heui
	   Gáulùhng Wíhng Ōn Gūngsī
	   a?

5. /Nèihdēun Douh/	5. Chéng mahn néih, dím heui Nèihdēun Douh a?

---

8. Alteration Drill

Ex: T: Gwo sàam gàan,
    jauh dou laak.
	T: Pass three buildings, then
	   (you) arrive. (i.e., It's
	   just 3 buildings away.)

S: Gwojó daih sàam gàan,
   jauh dou laak.
	S: When you've passed the third
	   building, then you're there.

+ 1. Gwo sàam go <u>gàaiháu</u>, jauh
   dou laak.
   Pass three <u>intersections</u>
   [<u>street-mouth</u>], and there
   it is.
	1. Gwojó daih sàam go gàaiháu,
	   jauh dou laak.
	   When you've passed the
	   third intersection, it's
	   right there.

2. Gwo yāt gàan, jauh haih laak.	2. Gwojó daih yāt gàan, jauh haih laak.
3. Gwo sàam gàan, jauh jyun jó.	3. Gwojó daih sàam gàan, jauh jyun jó.

4. Gwo sei go gàaiháu, jauh
   jyun yauh.

4. Gwojó daih sei go gàaiháu,
   jauh jyun yauh.

5. Gwo léuhng gàan, jauh táidóu
   laak.

5. Gwojó daih yih gàan, jauh
   táidóu laak.

6. Gwo sàam go gàaiháu, jauh tìhng
   lā.

6. Gwojó daih sàam go gàaiháu,
   jauh tìhng lā.

Comment: -jó may be added to gwo in left hand column, but not
         subtracted from right hand. Instead of gwojó on
         right, hàahngdou is permissable.

---

9. Alteration Drill

   Ex: T: Gwojó Méihgwok Jáu-   T: After you pass the Hilton,
          dim, jauh jyun yauh.   turn right.

       S: Méihgwok Jáudim   S: Beyond the Hilton, turn right.
          gwodl, jyun yauh.

   1. Gwojó Jùngwàahn Gàaisíh, jauh   1. Jùngwàahn Gàaisíh gwodl,
      jyun yauh.   jyun yauh.

   2. Gwojó WìhngŌn Gūngsī, jauh   2. WìhngŌn Gūngsī gwodl, jauh
      haih laak.   haih laak.

   3. Gwojó Màhnwàh Jáudim, jauh   3. Màhnwàh Jáudim gwodl, jyun
      jyun jó.   jó.

   4. Gwojó Nèihdēun Douh, jauh   4. Nèihdēun Douh gwodl, jauh
      haih laak.   haih laak.

   5. Gwojó daih sàam go gàaiháu,   5. Daih sàam go gàaiháu gwodl,
      jauh jyun yauh.   jyun yauh.

---

10. Substitution Drill: Repeat the first sentence after the teacher,
    then substitute as directed.

    1. Mhgòi néih heui Jùngwàahn sìn,   1. Mhgòi néih heui Jùngwàahn
       yìhnhauh heui Gáulùhng.   sìn, yìhnhauh heui Gáu-
       Please go to the Central   lùhng.
       District first, and after
       that go to Kowloon.

    2. /Méihgwok Ngàhnhòhng/   2. Mhgòi néih heui Méihgwok
       /Jùngwàahn Gàaisíh/   Ngàhnhòhng sìn, yìhnhauh
                                             heui Jùngwàahn Gàaisíh.

    3. /Màhnwàh Jáudim/   3. Mhgòi néih heui Màhnwàh
       /WìhngŌn Gūngsī/   Jáudim sìn, yìhnhauh heui
                                             WìhngŌn Gūngsī.

342

4. /Jùnggwok Jáugā/
   /Tīnsīng Máhtàuh/

4. Mhgòi néih heui Jùnggwok
   Jáugā sīn, yìhnhauh heui
   Tīnsīng Máhtàuh.

5. /séjihlàuh/fàan ūkkéi/

5. Mhgòi néih heui séjihlàuh
   sīn, yìhnhauh fàan ūkkéi.

---

11. Expansion Drill

   1. /heui máaih yéh/
      /fàan hohk/

1. Ngóh séung heui máaih yéh
   sīn, yìhnhauh fàan hohk.
   I think I'll go shopping
   first, and after that go
   to school.

   2. /heui yám chàh/fàan gùng/

2. Ngóh séung heui yám chàh
   sīn, yìhnhauh fàan gùng.

   3. /heui taam Wòhng Táai/
      /heui wán Léih Síujé/

3. Ngóh séung heui taam Wòhng
   Táai sīn, yìhnhauh heui
   wán Léih Síujé.

   4. /heui Jùngwàahn Gàaisíh/
      /fàan ūkkéi/

4. Ngóh séung heui Jùngwàahn
   Gàaisíh sīn, yìhnhauh
   fàan ūkkéi.

   5. /yám bùi chàh/
      /chēutheui mùhnháu dáng kéuih/

5. Ngóh séung yám bùi chàh sīn,
   yìhnhauh chēutheui mùhnháu
   dáng kéuih.

++ 6. /wuhn sāam/dá dihnwá giu chē/
      /change clothes/phone for
      a cab/

6. Ngóh séung wuhn sāam sīn,
   yìhnhauh dá dihnwá giu
   chē.
   I'll change clothes first,
   and after that call for
   a cab.

---

12. Expansion Drill

   Ex: 1. T: /deihhá/yih láu/   T: /ground floor/lst floor/

        S: Ngóh yàuh deihhá   S: I walked from the ground floor
           hàahng séuhng   up to the lst floor.
           (heui) yih láu.

      2. T: /sàam láu/yih láu/   T: /2nd floor/lst floor/

         S: Ngóh yàuh sàam   S: I walked from the 2nd floor
            láu hàahng lohk   down to the lst floor.
            (heui) yih láu.

   1. /yih láu/deihhá/

1. Ngóh yàuh yih láu hàahng
   lohk (heui) deihhá.

343

2. /sàam láu/ńgh láu/

2. Ngóh yàuh sàam láu hàahng séuhng (heui) ńgh láu.

3. /luhk láu/sei láu/

3. Ngóh yàuh luhk láu hàahng lohk (heui) sei láu.

4. /chāt láu/baat láu/

4. Ngóh yàuh chāt láu hàahng séuhng (heui) baat láu.

5. /baat láu/luhk láu/

5. Ngóh yàuh baat láu hàahng lohk (heui) luhk láu.

---

13. Expansion Drill: Students should gesture the directions.

Ex: T: Ngóh hái sàam láu. /sei láu/

I am on the 2nd floor. /3rd floor/

S: Ngóh hái sàam láu, yìhgā séuhng sei láu.

I am on the 2nd floor, now I'm going up to the 3rd floor.

1. Ngóh hái yih láu. /sàam láu/

1. Ngóh hái yih láu, yìhgā séuhng sàam láu.

2. Ngóh hái sàam láu. /yih láu/

2. Ngóh hái sàam láu, yìhgā lohk yih láu.

3. Ngóh hái deihhá. /yih láu/

3. Ngóh hái deihhá, yìhgā séuhng yih láu.

4. Ngóh hái yih láu. /deihhá/

4. Ngóh hái yih láu, yìhgā lohk deihhá.

5. Ngóh hái deihhá. /sei láu/

5. Ngóh hái deihhá, yìhgā séuhng sei láu.

---

14. Expansion Drill

Ex: T: Ngóh hái Dākfuh Douh Jùng. /Wìhng Ōn Gūngsī/

T: I am at Des Voeux Road Central. /Wing On Company/

S: Ngóh hái Dākfuh Douh Jùng, yìhgā ngóh yahpheui Wìhng Ōn Gūngsī dáng néih.

S: I'm at Des Voeux Road Central, now I'm going into Wing On Company to wait for you.

1. Ngóh hái Dākfuh Douh Jùng. /Jùngwàahn Gàaisíh/

1. Ngóh hái Dākfuh Douh Jùng, yìhgā ngóh yahpheui Jùngwàahn Gàaisíh dáng néih.

2. Ngóh hái Wǐhng Ōn Gūngsī.
   /Dākfuh Douh Jùng/

2. Ngóh hái Wǐhng Ōn Gūngsī,
   yǐhgā ngóh chēutheui
   Dākfuh Douh Jùng dáng néih.

3. Ngóh hái Méihgwok Ngàhnhòhng.
   /Daaih Douh Jùng/

3. Ngóh hái Méihgwok Ngàhnhòhng,
   yǐhgā ngóh chēutheui Daaih
   Douh Jùng dáng néih.

4. Ngóh hái Daaih Douh Jùng.
   /Méihgwok Ngàhnhòhng/

4. Ngóh hái Daaih Douh Jùng,
   yǐhgā ngóh yahpheui Méihgwok Ngàhnhòhng dáng néih

---

15. Response Drill: Do the right hand column of this drill first as a
    Listen & Repeat drill, teacher writing picture on blackboard &
    pointing to appropriate section as he speaks, students repeating
    after him.

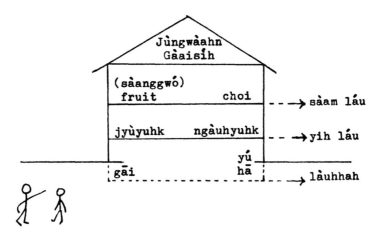

1. Maaih gāi gó go bouhfahn hái
   bǐndouh a?

1. Làuhhah jósáubihn.

2. Maaih choi gó go bouhfahn hái
   bǐndouh a?

2. Sàam láu yauhsáubihn.

3. Bǐndouh yáuh pìhnggwó tùhng
   cháang maaih a?

3. Sàam láu jósáubihn.

4. Bǐndouh yáuh jyùyuhk maaih a?

4. Yih láu jósáubihn.

5. Maaih hā gó go bouhfahn hái
   bǐndouh a?

5. Làuhhah yauhsáubihn.

6. Bǐndouh yáuh yú maaih a?

6. Làuhhah yauhsáubihn.

7. Bǐndouh yáuh ngàuhyuhk maaih a?

7. Yih láu yauhsáubihn.

Comment: Central Market has three floors, the lowest of which
         is below the level of the street on the Queen's Road

Central side. Thus <u>làuhhah</u> instead of <u>deihhá</u>.

---

16. Response Drill

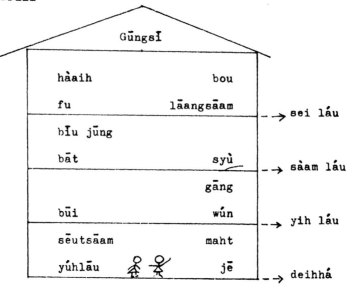

Ex: 1. T: Máaih hàaih   T: What floor do I go up to
       séuhng géi   buy shoes?
       láu a?

    S: Séuhng sei láu   S: Go up to the 3rd floor.
       lā.

    2. T: Máaih jē hái géi   T: What floor do you buy umbrellas
       láu a?   on?

    S: Hái deihhá.   S: On the ground floor.

1. Máaih lāangsāam séuhng géi   1. Séuhng sei láu lā!
   láu a?

2. Máaih bāt séuhng géi láu a?   2. Séuhng sàam láu lā!

3. Máaih jē hái géi láu a?   3. Hái deihhá.

4. Máaih syù hái géi láu a?   4. Hái sàam láu.

5. Máaih hàaih séuhng géi láu a?   5. Séuhng sei láu lā!

6. Máaih bīu séuhng géi láu a?   6. Séuhng sàam láu lā!

7. Máaih sēutsāam hái géi láu a?   7. Hái deihhá.

8. Máaih bou hái géi láu a?   8. Hái sei láu.

9. Máaih būi hái géi láu a?   9. Hái yih láu.

10. Máaih fu séuhng géi láu a?   10. Séuhng sei láu lā!

11. Máaih maht hái géi láu a?   11. Hái deihhá.

12. Máaih gāng séuhng géi láu a?   12. Séuhng yih láu lā!

13. Máaih wún séuhng géi láu a?   13. Séuhng yih láu lā!

14. Máaih yúhlāu hái géi láu a?   14. Hái deihhá.

15. Máaih jūng séuhng géi láu a?   15. Séuhng sàam láu lā!

IV. CONVERSATIONS FOR LISTENING

(On tape. Refer to wordlist below as you listen.)

Unfamiliar terms, in order of occurrence:

     1) yáuh yuhng = useful

V. SAY IT IN CANTONESE

A. Say to the classmate sitting next to you:

B. And he responds:

1. Where did we read to last time?

1. We read to page 300.

2. What lesson did we read last time?

2. Lesson 14.

3. Could you please tell me how to get to the Mandarin Hotel?

3. Go straight, and when you get to the 3d intersection, turn left. Go two blocks and you'll be there.

4. How do you get to the Central Market from here?

4. Turn left at the next intersection and it's two blocks down.

5. (in a dept store:) Where is the umbrella department?

5. On the ground floor.

6. Where is the shoe department?

6. Go up to the 1st floor.

7. I'm going down to the ground floor to buy a raincoat I'll wait for you there, OK?

7. Wait just a sec, and I'll go with you.

8. Turn left just beyond the library.

8. You can't turn in there-- I'll stop at the intersection, OK?

9. What's for sale on the 4th floor?

9. Sweaters and shoes and fabrics.

10. Go up to the 3d floor first, then go down to the 1st floor.

10. OK, want to come with me?

11. Could you please tell me how
to get to the Wing On Company
from here?

11. From here you go straight,
after you pass the 2d
intersection, it's the
1st building on the right.

12. When you get to Queens Road
Central, turn left.

12. Thanks a lot.

13. Your father is waiting for
you upstairs.

13. What does he want, do you
know?

14. My glasses are downstairs--
would you go down and get
them for me?

14. OK. Downstairs where?

15. Your boy friend is outside
waiting for you.

15. Please ask him to come in.

Vocabulary Checklist for Lesson 15

1. bouhfahn   n: department (in a store)
2. chéng...   v: please (+ verb); invite
3. chēut   v: out
4. chēutheui   v: go out
5. chēutlàih   v: come out
6. chēutbihn   PW: outside, exterior
7. dá dihnwá giu chē   VP: phone for a cab
8. dáhòi   v: open (as of a book)
9. daih-   bf: ordinal number marker: -st, -nd, -rd, -th.
10. daihyāt   Ph: the first
11. deihhá   PW: ground, ground floor
12. -dou   Vsuf: suffix to verbs of motion, indicating
                              arrival at goal
13. duhk   v: read
14. duhkdou...   v: read to...
15. fo   m: lesson
16. gàaiháu   n/PW: street opening, i.e. intersection
17. gàaisíh   n/PW: food market
18. hàahng   v: walk; go
19. hahbihn   PW: below; under
20. hái   prep: from

348

21.	-héui	Vsuf:	attaches to verbs of motion, indicating direction away from speaker
22.	-jó	Vsuf:	verb suf. indicating 'accomplish the performance'
23.	Jùngwàahn Gàaisíh	PW:	Central Market
24.	-làih	Vsuf:	attaches to verbs of motion, indicating direction towards the speaker
25.	làuhhah	PW:	[floor-below] downstairs
26.	làuhseuhng	PW:	[floor-above] upstairs
27.	lohk	v:	descend
28.	lohkheui	v:	go down
29.	louhyàhn	n:	pedestrian
30.	séuhng	v:	ascend
31.	seuhngbihn	PW:	above; on top
32.	seuhngchi	TW:	last time
33.	...sìn, yìhnhauh...	PCj:	...first, then...
34.	wuhn sāam	VO:	change clothes
35.	yàhn	n:	someone
36.	yàuh	prep:	from
37.	yìhn(jì)hauh	Cj:	afterwards, then
38.	yihp	m:	page

IV. CONVERSATIONS FOR LISTENING

Lesson Two

1. At a party:

Man : Síujé gwaising a?

Woman: Ngóh sing Chàhn. Sīnsàang gwaising a?

Man : Síusing Hòh. Chàhn síujé haih m̀hhaih Gwóngdùngyàhn a?

Woman: M̀hhaih a. Ngóh haih Seuhnghóiyàhn. Néih nē? Néih haih m̀hhaih
         Méihgwokyàhn a?

Man : Haih a. Ngóh haih Méihgwokyàhn.

2. At the first day of school, students are getting acquainted:

First student: Néih sing mēyéh a?

Second student: Ngóh sing Wòhng.

First student: Néih pàhngyáuh nē?

Second student: Kéuih dōu haih sing Wòhng ge.

First student: Néih haih m̀hhaih Gwóngdùngyàhn a?

Second student: Haih.

First student: Néih pàhngyáuh haih m̀hhaih dōu haih Gwóngdùngyàhn a?

Second student: M̀hhaih a. Kéuih haih Seuhnghóiyàhn.

Lesson Three

The following conversations take place among
some university students between classes.

1. A: Léih Sàang sīk m̀hsīk góng Yahtbúnwá a?

   B: Sīk sèsíu.

   A: Gám, kéuih sīk m̀hsīk góng Yìngmán nē?

   B: Dōu sīk sèsíu.

   A: Bīngo gaau kéuih góng Yìngmán ge nē?

   B: Haih Wòhng Sàang gaau kéuih ge.

2. A: Néih sīk m̀hsīk góng Gwokyúh a?

   B: Deuim̀hjyuh. Ngóh tèng m̀hchìngchó - m̀hgòi néih joi góng yātchi.

   A: Néih sīk m̀hsīk góng Gwokyúh a?

   B: Sīk sèsíu jē.

   A: Gám, néih sīk m̀hsīk Yìngmàhn nē?

   B: Sīk góng, m̀hsīk sé. Néih nē?

   A: Ngóh dōu m̀hsīk. 'Yāt yih sàam' dōu m̀hsīk góng.

3. A: Néih gaau bīngo Gwóngdùngwá a?

   B: Ngóh gaau Wòhng Táai.

   A: Kéuih haih m̀haih Méihgwokyàhn a?

   B: M̀haih. Kéuih haih Yìnggwokyàhn.

   A: Kéuih sīk m̀sīk sé Jùngmàhn nē?

   B: M̀sīk. Kéuih hohk góng, daahnhaih m̀hohk sé.

   A: Kéuih hohk m̀hohk Gwokyúh a?

   B: Ngóh m̀jídou a.

Lesson Four

1. Man   : Ngóh go bīu maahn sèsíu. Néih go haih m̀haih a?

   Woman: M̀haih. Ngóh go haih jéun ge.

   Man   : Gám, yìhgā géidímjūng a?

   Woman: Yìhgā ngāamngāam sahpyih dím.

   Man   : Ngóh go bīu yìhgā haih sahpyāt dím daahp sahp.

   Woman: Gám, néih go maahn léuhnggojih.

2. Woman: Yìhgā haih m̀haih baat dím sàamgogwāt a?

   Man   : M̀haih. Ngóh go bīu yìhgā haih baat dím daahp baat jē.

   Woman: Néih go bīu jéun m̀jéun a?

   Man   : Jéun. M̀faai m̀maahn.

   Woman: Gám, ngóh go faai yāt go jih.

   Man   : Waahkjé haih.

3. Woman: Jóusàhn, Wòhng Sàang. Néih jī m̀jī yìhgā géidímjūng a?

   Man   : A, jóusàhn, Chàhn Síujé. Ngóh go bīu yìhgā haih gáu dím daahp yāt.

   Woman: Néih go bīu haih m̀haih faai sèsíu a?

   Man   : Waahkjé haih. Ngóh m̀jī.

   Woman: Néih jī m̀jī Léih Táai géidímjūng hohk Gwóngdùngwá a?

   Man   : Ngóh jídou. Haih sahp dím bun.

Lesson Five

1. Two friends in a coffee shop deciding what to have for a mid-after-noon tea:

   A: Néih yám mēyéh a?

   B: Ngóh yám gafē. Néih nē?

A: Ngóh yám chàh. Sihk m̀hsihk béng a?

B: Hóu aak.

A: Néih géidímjūng yiu jáu a?

B: Sei dím.

A: Jànhaih gam faai yiu jáu mē?

B: Haih a, jànhaih.

2. A hostess is entertaining a new acquaintance at tea:

Hostess: Yám chàh lā.

Guest: Hóu, m̀hgòi.

Hostess: Sihk béng lā.

Guest: Hóu aak, m̀hgòi.

Hostess: Sihk yín lā.

Guest: Síu sihk. M̀hsái haakhei.

Hostess: Néih haakhei jó.

3. At lunchtime Mrs. Wong instructs her servant about the work for the rest of the day:

Mrs. Wong: Ngóh tùhng Wòhng Sàang sàam dím bun yiu yám chàh.

Servant : Sihk m̀hsihk béng a?

Mrs. Wong: Sèsíu lā.

Servant : Gám, géidímjūng sihk faahn a?

Mrs. Wong: Baat dím lā.

Servant : Hóu aak.

Lesson Six

1. In a department store:

Clerk: Jóusàhn, séung máaih mēyéh a?

Customer: Ngóh séung máaih tiuh fu. Nī léuhng tiuh yiu géidò chín a?

Clerk: Nī tiuh sahpbaat mān, gó tiuh yahyih mān.

Customer: Gám, ngóh máaih nī tiuh lā.

2. In a department store:

Customer: Nī gihn sēutsāam haih m̀hhaih yahsei mān a?

Clerk   : M̀hhaih. Haih yahgáu mān.

Customer: Gó gihn dōu haih yahgáu mān, haih m̀hhaih nē?

Clerk   : Haih. Néih haih m̀hhaih léuhng gihn dōu máaih nē?

Customer: M̀hhaih. Ngóh máaih nī gihn, m̀hmáaih gó gihn.

352

3. In a department store:

    Clerk   : Máaih mēyéh a?

    Customer: Ngóh séung máaih sēutsāam. Nī gihn géidò chín a?

    Clerk   : Nī gihn sahpyih mān jē. Máaih géidò gihn nē?

    Customer: Béi yāt gihn ngóh lā.

Lesson Seven

The following conversations take place between clerk and customer:

1. Clerk   : Máaih mēyéh a?

    Customer: Ngóh séung máaih bējáu. Géidō chín jī a?

    Clerk   : Go baat ngàhnchín. Oi géidō jī a?

    Customer: Oi léuhng jī.

    Clerk   : Sái m̀hsái máaih yīnjái a?

    Customer: Hóu, béi bāau ngóh lā!

2. Customer: Nī dī bou géidō chín máh a?

    Clerk   : Yahsāam go bun. Néih yiu géidō máh a?

    Customer: Ngóh m̀hyiu laak. Gó dī nē? Géidō chín máh a?

    Clerk   : Gó dī sahpsāam go bun ngàhnchín máh. Néih máaih m̀hmáaih a?

    Customer: Hóu. Ngóh oi léuhng máh.

    Clerk   : Yahchāt mān léuhng máh lā.

3. Clerk   : Máaih mēyéh a?

    Customer: Ngóh séuhng máaih dī ngàuhyuhk. Dím maaih nē?

    Clerk   : Nī dī sei go baat ngàhnchín gàn. Gó dī chāt go bun
                 ngàhnchín gàn.

    Customer: Béi sàam gàn gó dī ngóh lā.

    Clerk   : Sàam gàn yahyih go bun.

    Customer: Ngóh dōu séung oi léuhng gàn nī dī.

    Clerk   : Hóu aak, gán go luhk ngàhn chín lā.

Lesson Eight

1. In a department store:

    Clerk   : Jóusàhn. Séung máaih mēyéh a?

    Customer: Yáuh móuh baahk sēutsāam a?

    Clerk   : Haih m̀hhaih néih jeuk ga?

Customer: Haih.

Clerk   : Néih jeuk géidō houh a?

Customer: Sàamsahp luhk, waahkjé sàamsahp baat.

Clerk   : Nǐ gihn haih sàamsahpluhk.

Customer: Nǐ gihn m̀hgau daaih. Yáuh móuh sàamsahpbaat ge nē?

Clerk   : Deuim̀hjyuh - sàamsahpbaat ge maaihsaai laak.

2. In a department store:

Customer: Yáuh móuh baahk hàaih maaih a?

Clerk   : Yáuh. Néih jùng m̀hjùngyi nǐ deui nē?

Customer: Géi leng. Géi(dō) chín deui a?

Clerk   : Nǐ deui haih Méihgwok hàaih. Chāt'ahgáu mān deui.

Customer: Yáuh móuh pèhngdǐ ge nē?

Clerk   : Yáuh. Gó deui haih Yahtbún hàaih. Yahńgh mān deui jē.

Customer: M̀hgòi néih béi deui Yahtbún ge ngóh lā.

Clerk   : Hóu aak.

3. In a department store:

Customer: Yáuh móuh maht a?

Clerk   : Yáuh. Nǐ dǐ néih jùng m̀hjùngyi nē?

Customer: Géi jùngyi. Dǐm maaih a?

Clerk   : Luhk go bun ngàhnchǐn deui. Néih jeuk géi houh a?

Customer: M̀hjǐ - Ngóh jeuk luhk houh ge Méihgwok hàaih.

Clerk   : Gám, gáu houh lā. Néih séung máaih géidō deui a?

Customer: Béi sàam deui ngóh lā.

Clerk   : Hóu aak. Oi m̀hoi hàaih nē?

Customer: M̀hoi laak. M̀hgòi.

4. At a grocery store:

Customer: Yáuh móuh tòhng maaih a?

Clerk   : Yáuh. Máaih géidō bohng nē? Ǹgh bohng gau m̀hgau a?

Customer: M̀hsái gam dò. Léuhng bohng gau laak. A! Ngóh séung oi dǐ
          ngàuhyuhk, dǐm maaih a?

Clerk   : Sei go baat ngàhnchǐn gàn.

Customer: Béi yāt gàn ngóh lā.

Clerk   : Hóu.

Lesson Nine

1. Mr. Wong phones Mrs. Ho:

    Amah   : Wéi.

    Caller : Haih m̀hhaih chāt-sàam-lìhng-sei-ńgh-lìhng a?

    Amah   : M̀hgòi néih daaihsēngdī. Ngóh tèng m̀hchìngchó.

    Caller : Chāt-sàam-lìhng-sei-ńgh-lìhng, haih m̀hhaih a?

    Amah   : Haih. Wán bīngo a?

    Caller : M̀hgòi néih giu Hòh Táai tèng dihnwá lā.

    Amah   : Hóu. Dáng (yāt)ján.

    Mrs. Ho: Wéi.

    Caller : Hòh Táai, jóusàhn.

    Mrs. Ho: Jóusàhn.

    Caller : Ngóh haih Wòhng Sàang a. Néih jì m̀hjì Chàhn Sīnsàang ge
             dihnwá géidò houh a?

    Mrs. Ho: A! Jì. Kéuih ge dihnwá haih ńgh sei sàam yih yāt lìhng.

    Caller : Hóu, m̀hgòi.

    Mrs. Ho: M̀hsái m̀hgòi.

2. Mr. Wong calls a businessman at his office:

    Secretary: Wái.

    Caller   : Wái. Haih m̀hhaih sàam baat luhk lìhng ńgh gáu a?

    Secretary: Haih. Wán bīnwái nē?

    Caller   : Ngóh séung wán Léih Sàang tèng dihnwá.

    Secretary: Deuim̀hjyuh laak. Kéuih chēutjó gāai bo.

    Caller   : Gám, kéuih géidímjūng fàanlàih nē?

    Secretary: Léuhng dím lèhng jūng gamseuhnghā lā.

    Caller   : Hóu. M̀hgòi néih.

    Secretary: M̀hsái m̀hgòi.

3. Mr. Ho telephones Mr. Chan:

    Amah : Wéi. Wán bīngo a?

    Caller: Wái. M̀hgòi néih giu Chàhn Sīnsàang tèng dihnwá lā.

    Amah : Kéuih fàanjó gùng bo. Gwaising wán kéuih a?

    Caller: Sing Hòh ge. Kéuih géisìh fàanlàih nē?

    Amah : M̀hjì bo.

    Caller: Dáng kéuih fàanlàih m̀hgòi néih giu kéuih dá dihnwá béi ngóh
            lā. Ngóh ge dihnwá haih....

Amah : M̀hgòi néih dáng yātján; ngóh ló jī bāt sīn. Wéi, néih ge
          dihnwá haih....

Caller: Chāt-yāt-yāt-yih-lìhng-chāt.

Amah : Hóu lā. Kéuih fàanlàih, ngóh giu kéuih dá béi néih lā.

Lesson Ten

1. Asking directions:

   A: Chéng mahn Tīnsīng Máhtàuh hái bīndouh a?

   B: Hái Màhnwàh Jáudim deuimihn.

   A: Ngóh m̀hjī Màhnwàh Jáudim hái bīndouh bo.

   B: Nē -- hái gó bihn gó gàan - néih tái m̀htáidóu a?

   A: A, táidóu. M̀hgòisaai.

   B: M̀hsái m̀hgòi.

2. Two friends discuss restaurants:

   A: Néih séjihlàuh hái m̀hhái Hèunggóng nī bihn a?

   B: Hái. Hái Daaih Douh Jūng.

   A: Gódouh jógán yáuh móuh hóu ge chàhlàuh a?

   B: Yáuh. Ngóh séjihlàuh gaaklèih yáuh gàan hóu hóu ga. Ngóh hóu
      jungyi hái gódouh yám chàh ga.

   A: Ngóh séjihlàuh jógán ge chàhlàuh dōu m̀hhaih géi hóu, daahnhaih
      yáuh gàan géi hóu ge chāansāt. Ngóh jùngyi hái gódouh sihk
      ngaan.

3. Mrs. Ho compliments Miss Wong on her sweater:

   Mrs. Ho : Néih gihn lāangsāam hóu leng. Hái bīndouh máaih ga?

   Miss Wong: Hái Jùngwàahn yāt gàan gūngsī máaih ge.

   Mrs. Ho : Bīn gàan nē?

   Miss Wong: Hái ngóh séjihlàuh gaaklèih gó gàan.

   Mrs. Ho : Haih m̀hhaih hái chējaahm deuimihn a?

   Miss Wong: Haih. Haih gó gàan.

4. Mr. Ho calls Mr. Lee on the phone:

   Léih Sàang: Wéi.

   Hòh Sàang : Léih Sàang àh.

   Léih Sàang: Haih a, bīn wái a?

   Hòh Sàang : Ngóh haih Hòh Yaht-sīn a. Néih jī m̀hjī Méihgwok Jáudim

hái bīndouh a? Yáuh go pàhngyáuh yātjàn sàam dím hái
gódouh dáng ngóh. Kéuih wáh ngóh jī Méihgwok Jáudim
hái Seuhnghói Ngàhnhòhng gàaklèih, daahnhaih ngóh
wán m̀hdóu.

Léih Sàang: Méihgwok Jáudim m̀hhaih hái Seuhnghói Ngàhnhòhng gaaklèih.
Hái Jùnggwok Ngàhnhòhng deuimihn. Néih jī m̀hjī Jùnggwok
Ngàhnhòhng hái bīndouh a?

Hòh Sàang : O. Gám, ngóh jī laak. M̀hgòisaai. Joigin.

    1) yātjàn = dángyātjahn = 'in a little while'

    2) wán m̀hdóu = can't find it, search but not success-
       ful

Lesson Eleven

1. A clerk totals the bill for a customer at a grocery store:

    Clerk   : Sei jī bējáu, luhk jī heiséui, sahp go cháang...sahpsàam
          go yih lā.

    Customer: Nàh, nīdouh yāt baak mān.

    Clerk   : Hóu, dáng ngóh jáaufàan béi néih lā. Aiya, deuim̀hjyuh,
          m̀hgau sáanjí tìm. Néih yáuh móuh sáanjí a?

    Customer: Ngóh dōu móuh bo.

    Clerk   : Gám, m̀hgòi néih dáng jahn, ngóh wán yàhn cheunghòi kéuih
          lā.

    Customer: Hóu lā.

    Clerk   : Nīdouh jáaufàan baatsahpluhk go baat béi néih.

    Customer: Néih yáuh móuh yāt mān ngán a?

    Clerk   : Yáuh, néih séung yiu géidō nē?

    Customer: M̀hgòi néih cheung sahp mān ngóh lā.

    Clerk   : Hóu.

    Customer: M̀hgòisaai.

2. At the teller's window in the bank Mr. Wong puts down a $500 bill
   and says:

    Mr. Wòhng: M̀hgòi néih tùhng ngóh cheunghòi kéuih lā!

    Teller   : Cheung géidō a? Haih m̀hhaih ngoisaai sahp mān jí a?

    Mr. Wòhng: M̀hhaih. Oi sei jèung yāt baak mān jí, sahp jèung sahp
          mān.

    Teller   : M̀hgau sahp mān jí bo. Oi gáu jèung sahp mān jí, sahp go
          yāt mān ngán, hóu m̀hhóu a?

    Mr. Wòhng: Hóu, oi dī sáangán dōu hóu.

        1) oi = here: to have in your possession

3. Talking about a borrowed book:

A: Néih <u>gàmyaht</u> m̀hgeidāk daai gó bún syù fàanlàih béi ngóh a?

B: Aiya! M̀hgeidāk tìm! Jànhaih deuimhjyuh laak! Néih géisìh (géisí) yiu yuhng a?

A: Ngóh dáng jahn yiu ga. <u>Yātján</u> ngóh hohk Yīngmán móuh syù tái, m̀hdāk ge bo!

B: Gám, ngóh yìhgā fàan ūkkéi ló béi néih lā.

A: Yiu fàan ūkkéi ló àh. M̀hhóu laak. Néih jí m̀hjí nīdouh bīngo yáuh nī bún syù hóyíh jejyuh béi ngóh sìn ga?

B: A! Chàhn Sàang dōu yuhng gó bún syù hohk Yīngmán, dáng ngóh giu kéuih je béi néih lā.

A: Hóu aak! M̀hgòisaai.

    1) gàmyaht = today

    2) yātján = dángyātjahn = 'in a little while'

Lesson Twelve

1. Two women meet in the elevator of their apartment building. One woman has her daughter with her:

Wòhng Táai: A, Léih Táai, tùhng gó néui heui <u>bīn</u> a?

Léih Táai : Ngóh daai kéuih heui tái yīsāng a.

Wòhng Táai: <u>Mēyéh sih a?</u>

Léih Táai : Kéuih m̀hséung sihk faahn <u>lòh</u>.

Wòhng Táai: Néih daai kéuih heui tái bīn go yīsāng a?

Léih Táai : Ngóh sīnsàang giu ngóh daai kéuih tái Jèung Yīsāng. Kéuih haih ngóhdeih gè pàhngyáuh.

Wòhng Táai: Bīn go Jèung Yīsāng a? Haih m̀hhaih Seuhnghói Ngàhnhòhng gó go a?

Léih Táai : Móuh cho, haih kéuih laak.

Wòhng Táai: Gám, ngóh sung néihdeih heui lā. Ngóh <u>ngāamngāam</u> yiu heui ngàhnhòhng ló chín.

Léih Táai : Hóu aak. M̀hgòisaai bo.

    1) bīn = bīndouh?

    2) Mēyéh sih a? = What's the matter?

    3) lòh = sen. suf. expressing sympathy

    4) ngāamngāam = just now, just on the point of; just

2. Two men on their way to the bus stop. They have just finished work:

A: Néih haih m̀hhaih fàan ūkkéi a?

B: M̀hhaih, ngóh yìhgā yiu heui ngóh néuipàhngyáuh ūkkéi taam kéuih màhmā.

A: Kéuih màhmā yáuh mēyéh sih a?

B: Móuh mēyéh sih. Kéuih giu ngóh heui kéuihdeih douh sihk faahn jē.

A: O--kéuihdeih jyuh hái bīn a?

B: Kéuihdeih ngāamngāam jyuh hái néih hauhbihn.

A: Haih mē? Gám, ngóh sung néih heui lā.

B: Mhgòisaai.

    1) Yáuh mēyéh sih a? = What's going on?

    2) Móuh mēyéh sih = Nothing special.

3. Mr. and Mrs. Lee at home:

   Léih Táai : Ngóh yātján yiu heui gūngsī máaih yéh. Néih yáuh móuh
          chín a?

   Léih Sàang: Ngóh dāk sèsíu ja. Ngóh ngāamngāam séung heui ngàhnhòhng
          ló chín. Néih géidímjung cheutgaai a?

   Léih Táai : Hmmm...Ngóh yiu dáng Hòh Táai dihnwá bo.

   Léih Sàang: Gám...Ngóh yìhgā heui ngàhnhòhng ló chín sìn. Néih
          yātján làih ngóh séjihlàuh ló chín, hóu mhhóu a?

   Léih Táai : Hóu! ...A, ...néih yáuh móuh yéh yiu máaih a?

   Léih Sàang: Móuh laak.

          1) ngāamngāam séung heui = just thinking of going

          2) yātján = in a little while

Lesson Thirteen

1. Two girls driving in a car talk about a young man they see:

   A: Hái hāak sīk gó ga chē hauhbihn gó go yàhn haih mhhaih néih
      pàhngyáuh a?

   B: Haih bo! Mhgòi néih fàanjyuntàuh lā. Ngóh yáuh dī yéh séung wah
      kéuih jī ge.

   A: Hóu aak. Kéuih haih mhhaih sing Jèung ga?

   B: Mhhaih, kéuih sing Chàhn ge.

   A: Kéuih giujouh mēyéh méng a?

   B: Kéuih giujouh Gwok-wàh.

   A: Chàhn Gwok-wàh...Hmm...Gám, mhhaih laak.

   B: Mhhaih mēyéh a?

   A: Kéuih mhhaih Léih Síujé ge nàahmpàhngyáuh laak.

2. A young girl calls home:

   Wòhng Táai: Wéi!

359

Síu-Yìng : Wéi, màhmā àh? Ngóh haih Síu-Yìng a. Ngóh yìhgā hái
  Màhnwàh Jáudim yám chàh. Néih làih m̀hlàih a?

Wòhng Táai: Néih tùhng bīngo yám chàh a?

Síu-Yìng : Ngóh tùhng Hòh Méi-Wàh. Nīdouh dī béng hóu leng ga.
  Néih làih lā.

Wòhng Táai: Néih yáuh pàhngyáuh hái douh, ngóh m̀hlàih la.

Síu-Yìng : Làih lā, màhmā, ngóh séung néih <u>yātján</u> tùhng ngóh heui
  máaih yéh a.

Wòhng Táai: Gám àh, sái m̀hsái ngóh jà chē làih ā?

Síu-Yìng : Nījógán hóu síu wái paak chē ge bo. Néih giu <u>dīksí</u> làih
  lā.

Wòhng Táai: Hóu lā, ngóh jauh làih laak.

        1) yātján = in a little while

        2) dīksí = taxi

3. Asking directions:

A: Chéng mahn nī tiuh haih m̀hhaih Daaih Douh Jùng a?

B: M̀hhaih, néih hái nīdouh yātjihk heui, haahng dou daih sàam go
  <u>gàaiháu</u> gó tiuh jauh haih laak.

A: O, m̀hgòi.

                (He goes on...)

A: Chéng mahn, Daaih Douh Jùng n̄gh baak lìhng sei houh hái m̀hhái
  nījógán a?

C: N̄gh baak lìhng sei houh àh. Nē, chìhnbihn yauhsáubihn daih sàam
  gàan jauh haih laak.

A: Gó douh yáuh móuh wái paak chē ga?

C: <u>Hóu chíh</u> móuh bo.

A: Hóu. M̀hgòisaai.

        1) gàaiháu = intersection [street-mouth]

        2) hóu chíh = very likely..., most likely...

4. Passenger and taxi driver:

A: M̀hgòi Néih Dēun Douh, n̄gh baak yihsahp sei houh.

B: Hóu.

              (They ride for awhile)

A: Gwojó daih yih go gàaiháu yauhbihn, tìhng chē lā.
  Ei! <u>Gwojó la</u>, m̀hgòi néih tanhauh sēsíu lā.

B: O, m̀hdāk bo, hauhbihn yáuh chē làih, m̀hhóyíh tanhauh.

        1) Ei! = mild exclamation

        2) gwojó la = here: we've overshot it, we've passed it. gwo =
  pass by

A: Gám, joi <u>sái</u> gwodī, fàanjyuntàuh lā.

B: Dāk.

        The driver makes a U-turn at the
        intersection and goes back)

A: Hóu. Hái douh tìhng.

      (He pays the driver $3 for the $2.70 ride)

  Mhsái jáau la.

B: Dòjeh.

     1) sái = drive

Lesson Fourteen

  1. Lunchtime:

Wòhng Sàang: A, Léih Síujé. Heui bīndouh a?

Léih Síujé : O, Wòhng Sàang. Ngóh <u>ngāamngāam</u> <u>fòng gùng</u>. Néih nē?

Wòhng Sàang: Ngóh ngāamngāam hái ngàhnhòhng ló chín fàanlàih. Sihk
        faahn meih a?

Léih Síujé : Meih a! Néih nē?

Wòhng Sàang: Ngóh dōu meih a, ngóh chéng néih heui sihk faahn lā,
        hóu mhhóu a?

Léih Síujé : Hóu aak, heui bīn gàan nē?

Wòhng Sàang: Gwóngjàu Jáugā dī <u>yihm guhk gāi</u> hóu leng ga, néih
        sihkgwo meih a?

Léih Síujé : Meih sihkgwo.

Wòhng Sàang: Gám, ngóhdeih heui siháh lā.

      (They arrive at the restaurant)

Wòhng Sàang: Fógei! Ngóhdeih séung yiu jek yihm guhk gāi, mm...Léih
        Síujé, juhng yiu meyéh choi tìm nē?

Léih Síujé : <u>Gaailáan cháau ngàuhyuhk</u> lā, mm...yāt jek gāi <u>taai</u> dò,
        ngóhdeih sihk mhsaai, yiu bun jek jauh gau la, joi
        dím go <u>sài yèuhng choi tòng</u>, hóu mhhóu a?

Wòhng Sàang: A. Hóu, Léih Síujé jànhaih sīk dím choi ge laak. Fógei
        mhgòi néih faai dī bo.

        1) ngāamgnāam = just now

        2) fòng gùng = leave work, get off from work

        3) yihm guhk gāi = salt-roasted chicken

        4) gaailáan cháau ngàuhyuhk = stir fried beef and
                                  broccoli

        5) taai = too

        6) sài yèuhng choi tòng = watercress soup

Léih Síujé : Nídouh dī choi jànhaih m̀hcho, ngóh dōu yiu daai ngóh
             māhmā làih siháh.

             (They finish eating)

Wòhng Sàang: Fógei, màaihdāan.

Fógei   : Sīnsàang, yahsāam mān lā!

Wòhng Sàang: Nídouh yah ńgh mān, m̀hsái jáau laak.·

Léih Síujé : Wòhng sīnsàang, dòjehsaai bo.

Wòhng Sàang: M̀hsái haakhei.

2. Miss Lee takes her foreign friend to a restaurant for lunch:

A: Nī gàan jáugā m̀hcho ga. Dī yéh yauh pèhng yauh leng.

B: O. Haih mē?

A: Wai, fógei! M̀hgòi néih nīng go choipáai làih táiháh lā.

W: Hóu. Jauh làih.

A: Nídouh yáuh Gwóngdùng choi, Seuhnghói choi. Néih séung sihk bīn
   yeuhng nē?

B: Ngóh séung siháh Gwóngdùng choi. M̀hgòi néih gaaisiuhháh lā.

A: Gám, dím go yúhjyù, joi yiu go daaih hā. Hóu m̀hhóu a?

B: Hóu aak. <u>Giu go Yèuhngjàu cháau faahn</u> siháh lā.

A: Mmm...Néih séung oi go mēyéh tòng tīm nē?

B: <u>Sàiyèuhngchoi tòng</u> lā.

A: A, fógei, m̀hgòi ló dò léuhng jì heiséui làih lā.

B: Mmm, dī cháau faahn tùhng daaih hā jànhaih m̀hcho laak.

A: Sihk dōdī tīm lā! M̀hhóu haakhei a.

B: Gau la! Dòjehsaai.

A: Fógei! Màaihdāan!

    1) giu = order, call for (without having to look at a listed
       menu)

    2) Yèuhngjàu cháau faahn = Yangchow fried rice

    3) Sàiyèuhngchoi tòng = watercress soup

3. Deciding where to eat:

A: Néih jùngyi sihk mēyéh nē?

B: Néih wah lā, ngóh mēyéh dōu sihk gé.

A: Gám, néih séung sihk Jùngchoi yīkwaahk sāichāan nē?

B: Dōu dāk; néih wah lā.

A: Gam, ngóhdeih heui sihk Gwóngdùng choi, hóu m̀hhóu a?

B: Hóu! Néih jì m̀hjì bīndouh ge Gwóngdùng choi hóusihk a?

362

A: Jùnggwok Chàhlàuh ge géi hóu. Heui gódouh, hóu m̀hhóu a?

B: Hóu aak. Jà m̀hjà chē heui nē?

A: M̀hsái la. Jùnggwok Chàhlàuh hái deuimihn jē. Ngóhdeih hàahng heui lā.

4. Time for lunch. Two women friends:

A: A! Yìhgā jauh <u>faai</u> sahp-yih dím la. Ngóhdeih heui sihk aan sin, hóu m̀hhóu a?

B: Hóu aak!

A: Nīdouh jógán yáuh gàan hóu <u>yáuh méng</u> ge Gwóngdùng jáugā. Ngóh daai néih heui siháh lā.

B: Hóu a.

(In the restaurant a waiter
gives them a menu card:)

Waiter: Léuhng wái séung dím dī mēyéh choi nē?

A   : Wòhng Táai, néih jùngyi sihk dī mēyéh a?

B   : Ngóh m̀hsīk dím ga. Néih gaaisiuh géi yeuhng jauh dāk la.

A   : Gám, ngóh dím géi yeuhng nīdouh yáuh méng ge béi néih siháh lā. Fógei, yiu go <u>gùlòu yuhk</u>, yāt go daaih hā, <u>dōu yiu sai ge</u>.

B   : Joi yiu yāt go jyùhuhk tòng, hóu m̀hhóu a?

A   : Hóu aak! Fógei, juhng yiu yāt go jyùyuhk tòng tìm. Faaidī bo.

Waiter: Hóu.

A   : Wòhng Táai, sihk dōdī lā.

B   : Gau la--nīdouh dī choi jànhaih m̀hcho bo!

A   : Haih a. A! Yìhgā jauh faai yāt dím bun la, ngóhdeih jáu la, hóu ma?

B   : Hóu aak.

A   : Fógei! Màaihdāan. (She pays the check, leaving a tip.)

Waiter: Dòjehsaai.

1) faai = soon, almost, approaching (preceding a time expression)

2) yáuh méng = famous

3) gùlòu yuhk = sweet & sour pork

4) dōu yiu sai ge = want both to be small portions

363

Lesson Fifteen

1. Asking directions:

    A: Chéng mahn néih, Méihgwok Gūngsī hái bīndouh a?

    B: Hái Dāk Fuh Douh Jùng.

    A: Yàuh nīdouh dím heui a?

    B: Hái nīdouh yātjihk hàahng, gwojó daih yih go gàaiháu, yìhnhauh
        jyun yauh.

    A: Jyun yauh jíhauh nē?

    B: Joi yātjihk hàahng, gwojó gàaisíh, jauh haih Dāk Fuh Douh Jùng.
        Heuidou gódouh, néih jauh táidóu ga laak.

    A: Hóu, m̀hgòi.

    B: M̀hsái m̀hgòi.

2. At a department store, looking for a friend who works there:

    A: Chéng mahn, Léih Síu-lìhng Síujé hái bīndouh a?

    B: Léih Síu-lìhng, kéuih hái bīn go bouhfahn jouh sih ga?

    A: Hái maaih lāangsāam gó go bouhfahn.

    B: O, haih laak. Kéuih wah ngóh jī yáuh wái sīnsàang yiu wán kéuih,
        yìhgā kéuih hái yahpbihn dáng néih.

    A: Gám, ngóh hái bīndouh yahpheui a?

    B: Hmm...Néih hái nīdouh yātjihk hàahng, yìhnhauh jyunchēut jósáubihn,
        Léih Síujé jáuh hái gódouh laak.

    A: M̀hgòisaai.

    B: M̀hsái m̀hgòi.

3. Mr. Cheung has rung the bell of apt. 12-A. A servant answers the door,
   and Mr. Cheung says:

    A: Chéng mahn néih, Wòhng Sīnsàang hái m̀hhái douh a?

    B: Bīn wái Wòhng Sīnsàang a?

    A: Wòhng Wíhng-yihp Sīnsàang.

    B: M̀hhái nīdouh bo. Chéng néih séuhngheui sei láu mahnháh lā.

                        (Goes up)

    A: Chéng mahn, Wòhng Wíhng-yihp Sīnsàang hái m̀hhái douh a?

    C: Néih wán bīngo a? Ngóhdeih nīdouh móuh sing Wòhng ge bo.

    A: Haih mē? Deuim̀hjyuh bo. Daahnhaih ngóh ngāamngāam mahngwo yih
        láu yāt go yàhn, kéuih wah Wòhng Wíhng-yihp jyuh hái sei láu
        ge bo.

    C: Oh! Wòhng Wíhng-yihp! Kéuih haih m̀hhaih gaau Gwóngdùngwá ga?

    A: Móuh cho, haih kéuih laak.

                        364

C: Kéuih jyuh hái sàam láu, néih hàahng fàan lohk heui lā.

A: Hóu, mhgòisaai.

4. Discussing Cantonese lessons:

A: Yìhgā bĭngo gaau néih góng Gwongdùngwá a?

B: Dōu haih Jèung Sàang.

A: Hohkdou daih géi fo a?

B: Daih sahpńgh fo ge la.

A: Daih sahpńgh fo góng mēyéh ga?

B: Haih góng heui gūngsī máaih yéh gé, nī fo jànhaih hóu <u>yáuh yuhng</u>. Hohkjó nī fo ngóh jauh hóyíh tùhng gūngsī ge fógei góng Gwóng-dùngwá laak.

A: Haih àh.

B: Haih a! Go fógei juhng wah ngóh ge Gwóngdùngwá hóu hóu tìm.

A: Haih ā. Néih ge Gwóngdùngwá haih mhcho aak.

B: Néih gám góng, ngóh jauh jànhaih mhhóu yisi la.

  1) yáuh yuhng = useful

GRAMMATICAL INDEX

Numbers to the left of the period refer to
lesson numbers, and those to the right, to
page numbers.

ǎ, ss: a (QV) + raised intonation
    for liveliness, 14.316

a, ss: sen. softener, 2.40-41

àh, ss: 'I suppose,' indicating
    rhetorical question, 8.186

aak, ss: a (QV) + -K (QV), 5.114

adjectives, 4.92; 8.183-85; as
    modifier to nouns, 8.187

adverbs, 1.25

auxiliary verbs, 3.68; compared with
    co-verbs, 12.270

bātgwo, 14.316

bīn-M?, 'which?', 8.177, 8.188

bīnwái?, substituting for gwaising?,
    9.214

bo, ss: for definiteness, 9.207

boundwords, 6.136

chéng V , 'please V ', polite
    imperative, 15.336

chìhnbihn, 12.285

co-verbs, 12.270

daai, 'bring/take along', 12.272;
    'take/bring along', contrasted
    with sung, 12.282-83

daih-, ordinal prefix, 15.335

daihyih-, 1) the second, 2) the
    next, 15.335

dāk, 'OK', 11.245; 'ready', 11.245;
    with quantity phrase object,
    = 'have only X amount', have
    sufficient amount, 11.245; in
    yáuhdāk V ', 'have available
    to V ', 11.246

deihhá, differentiated from làuhhah
    and hahbihn, 15.334

dī, as adj. suffix, 8.185; general
    measure for mass nouns, 7.159;
    plural measure, 7.158; substi-
    tute for noun in a follow
    sentence, 7.158

dialect variations, hl tone substi-
    tuted for hf tone, 1.6; initial
    consonant l substituted for n,
    3.63; ng before words beginning
    with /a/o/u/, 4.94

directional verbs, 15.333; preceded
    by verbs of movement, 15.334

directional verb compounds, 14.314;
    position of noun object, 14.314

dò, 'additional,' 'more', bound to
    following Nu-M phrase; nominal
    construction, 14.316; patterning
    like adj., patterning like N,
    patterning like Nu, 8.188;
    'large amount' in phrases of
    indefinite amounts, 11.247-48

-dò/-síu phrases, with following
    Measure, 11.248; with following
    N, 11.247

dōu, also, both, all, 3.68; even,
    3.68

dōuhaih, 'really' as intonation
    marker lightening a blunt
    statement, 14.315

-dōu, Vsuf indicating reaching desti-
    nation or goal, 15.334

-douh, PW formant, 10.226

-dóu, Vsuf, indicating successful accomplishment of performance of the verb, 10.228

fo, 'lesson', classed as Measure, 15.336

Free words, 6.136

ga, fusion of ge, noun-forming bound-word (QV) + ss. a (QV), 2.43

ga, ss: fusion of ss. ge, 'that's the way it is,' and ss. a, sentence softener, 11.256

gàn, 'follow', compared with gànjyuh, 12.271

gànjyuh, (follow', compared with gàn, 12.271

-ge, noun-forming boundward, 2.43

ge, as nominal, adj + ge = Noun Phrase, 8.185; suffix to adj in modification structure, 8.187; as nominal, substituting for noun, 8.187

ge, ss., matter-of-fact 'that's the way it is' connotation, 3.64

ge, as possessive marker, 9.207-08; overlap with Measure, 9.208

gé, ss. ge, 'that's the way it is' + rising intonation for uncertainty, 11.248

géi(dō)?, as interrogative number, 6.137

géi?, how many?, compared with géi, several, 6.137; compared w. géidō?, 6.137

géi, several, compared with géi? 'how many?', 6.137

go jih, omission of in time phrases, 9.210

gó, 'that', 6.136

-gwo, Vsuf, experiential verb suffix, 14,314

hahbihn, differentiated from deihá and làuhhah, 15.334

-háh, Vsuf for casualness, 5.115

haih, as first verb in series, 3.64

haih..X..laih ge, phrase frame for nouns, 7.160

hái, location verb, 10.22; in multi-verb clauses follows verbs of thrust (ex: jài, 'put,' 'place'), precedes or follows verbs of station (ex: jyuh, 'live'), 12.273; as preposition 'from', interchangeable with yàuh, 15.341

hauhbihn, back side, 12.285

hóyih, 'can' in the sense of 'can do a favor', 'willing and able', 13.293

hóyih, 'can', in the sense of 'permitted to', 13.293

indirect object, 6.137

ja, ss: fusion of ss. jē (QV) and ss. a (QV), implies 'not much', 11.256

jauh, 'then', in two-clause sentence, 13.292

jauh, 'right away,' 'immediately', in single-clause sentence, 13.292

jē, ss: 'merely', 3.64

jip, 'fetch,' 'meet', 12.272-73

-jó, Vsuf accomplishment of intended action, 9.207; 'accomplish the performance', 15.335

juhng, still, in addition, also, 14.316

jùngyi, differentiated from séung, 9.209

-k, word suffix, suffixed to certain sentence suffixes, indicating liveliness, 5.114

lā, ss: for polite suggestion in imperative sentence, 4.93; for polite imperative, 5.114

la, ss: indicating change, 4.93; in imperative sentence, conveying attitude of friendly advice, 13.294 and 13.303

laak, ss: for change, 5.113

léh, ss: for definiteness, 5.114

làih ge see haih...X...làih ge, 7.160

làuhhah, differentiated from deihhá and hahbihn, 15.334

léuhng and yih, '2', 4.93

locatives, 10.225

Mhjì...a?, as polite question, 6.137

mhsái, 6.135

ma?, ss: interrogative sentence suffix, 14.316

mē?, ss: for surprised question, 3.64

Measures, 4.91-9; as word class, 6.133; individual measures, 6.133; group measures, 6.134; standard measures, 6.134; substituting for noun, 6.135; without preceding number, 6.135

Measure, overlap with possessive ge, 9.208

meih, 14.315

mēyéh, as mass noun, 14.315

money expressions, 7.160-162

nē?, interrogative ss, How about___?, 2.41; ss: to a question sentence continuing the same topic, 8.186

nē, ss: used more by women than men, suffix to clause sentence, 8.186

negative questions, responses to, 12.274

nī, 'this', 6.136

noun modification structures, 8.187

Nouns, absence of singular/plural distinction, 2.39; modification of nouns, 2.40; as word class, 6.135; individual nouns, 6.133; mass nouns, 7.159; mass nouns, how counted, 7.159; individual and mass nouns compared, 7.159

Nouns as modifiers to Nouns, 8.187

Numbers, 1-19, 4.92; 20-29, 6.132; abbreviated forms, 6.132; numbers with internal zeroes, 11.261; numbers with final zeroes, 11.261

paired conjunctions, ...sīn, yìhnhauh...., 15.333

Phrases, 1.25-26

Phrase frame, 7.160

Placewords (PW), 10.224-26; ordinary nouns which are also PWs, 10.225; -douh as PW formant for non-PWs, 10.226

Possessive with -ge, in head structures, 9.207-08

Possessive modification, with -ge, 9.207-08; without -ge, 9.208; without ge or M, for some family names, 12.273-74; with without ge or M, 12.279; with without ge or M, 15.338

Predicates, verbal predicate, 3.66; nominal predicate, 3.66; sentence predicate, 3.67

Pronouns, personal pronouns, 2.39; plural marker for personal pronouns, 2.39-40; absence of pronoun object, 3.67

Question sentences with N nē?, 2.41; choice type, 2.42; word order of question-word sentences, 2.43; with ss. mē?, 3.64; with ss. àh for rhetorical question, 8.186; with VP nē?, 8.186; with _ hjì....a? (or....nē?), 6.13 ; choice type Q for 2 syllable adjs Vsuf, 8.185; responses to questions negatively phrased, 12.274; with ss. ma?, 14.316

Question words (QW): bīn-M?, 8.177, 8.188; bīndouh?, 10.222; bīngo?, 3.75; géi-?, 4.90, 6.137; géidím(jūng)?, 4.90; géidō?, 6.127, 6.137; géisí?(var:géisìh?), 9.201 dím? 3.59; mātyéh? (var:mēyéh?, mīyéh?), 2.32, 2.42.

sèsíu, 'a little,' modifies mass nouns only, 11.247

Sentence suffixes: as means to signal feelings, 2.40; tone marks inappropriate, 2.41; intonational, 4.93, 11.248, 2.41, 14.316.

Sentence suffixes, list of:
    ā, 14.316
    a, 2.40-41
    āh, 8.186
    aak, 5.114
    bo, 9.207
    ge/ga, 3.64; 11.256
    ja [j], 11.257
    jē, 3.64
    lā, 4.93; 5.114
    la, for change, 4.93
    la, for friendly advice, 13.294, 13.303
    laak, 5.113
    lēh, 5.114
    ma?, 14.316
    mē?, 3.64
    nē?, 2.41; 8.186
    tìm, 'in addition', 4.84
    tìm!, for taken by surprise, 11.246
    wá?, 4.91

Sentence types: full sentence, 1.25; minor sentence, 1.25; SP sentence, 1.25; lead sentence, 1.26; follow sen., 1.26; choice-type question, 2.42; QW question, 2.42; loose relationship of Subject and Predicate, 3.65; Topic:Comment sentence, 3.65; sentence w. verbal predicate, 3.66; sentence w. nominal predicate, 3.66; sentence w. sentence predicate, 3.67; SVO sentence 3.67; subjectless sentence 3.67; subordinate clause, primary clause sentence, 12.268-69; multi-verb single clause sentence, 12.269

séung, 'plan to,' 'am considering', 3.58; differentiated from jùngyi, 9.209; differentiated from yiu, 9:209

sīk, 'know (how to);' 'know (someone),' 3.69

sìn, 'first,' implies something else to follow, 11.244

-síu, 'small amount,' in phrases of indefinite amounts, 11.247-48

siusíu,'a tiny bit,' 'very little,' modifies mass nouns only, 11.247

Specifiers, 6.136

sung, 'deliver,' 12.272; contrasted with daai, 12-282-83

tìm , s.s.: 'in addition,' 4.84

tìm!, s.s.: indicating speaker has been taken by surprise, 11.246

Time When expressions, 4.90

Time Spent expressions, 4.91

tùhng, 'and,' 3.68

tùhng, 'with,' 12.283; compared with tùhng, 'and,' 12.270-71

Verb suffixes, list of:
    -dou, 15.334
    -dóu, 10.228
    -gwo, 14.314
    -hàh, 5.115
    -jó, 9.207;15.335

Verbs: preceded by mh, 1.25; modification by adverbs, 1.25; absence of subject-verb concord, 2.39; verbs in series, 3.63, 12.269; uninflected verb forms, 3.63; haih as first verb in series, 3.64; two-part verbs of performance and achievement, 15.334

wá?, interrogative sen.suf., 4.91

word class, multiple membership:7.162

yāt, 'one,' ommsion in certain 'one dollar' phrases, 7.162; omission in certain 'one o'clock' phrases, 9.210

yātjihk, 'straight'; 'straightaway', 13.292

yauh, 'and,' 3.68

yàuh PW, 'from PW'. 15.335;

yáuh, 'to have; there is/are', 8.183; in pivotal construction, 10.227

<u>yáuhdāk</u> <u>V</u> , 'have available for <u>V-ing</u>,
     11.246

<u>yih</u>, '2,' compared with <u>léuhng</u>, 4.93

<u>yìkwaahk</u>, '...., or...?, 14.315

<u>yihp</u>, 'page,' 15.336

<u>yiu</u>, 'must,' 5.115; relationship with
     <u>m̀hsái</u>, 5.115, 6.136; with follow-
     ing money expression='wants,'
     'costs,' 6.140; 'intends to,'
     9.209; contrasted with <u>séung</u>,
     9.209

CUMULATIVE VOCABULARY LIST

LESSONS 1-15

Entries are arranged in alphabetical order by syllable, with h indicating lower register disregarded alphabetically. When words having the same syllable but different tones are listed, the sequence of tone listing is: high level, mid level, low level, high falling, low falling, high rising, low rising. Numbers in the right hand column refer to the lesson in which the item first appears, thus:

12 = Lesson 12 Basic Conversation

12.1 = Lesson 12, Drill 1

1CP = Lesson 1, Classroom Phrases

1N = Lesson 1, Notes

Items which appear for the first time in the Classroom Phrases and Notes are listed again when appearing for the first time in the main body of the text. Measures for the nouns follow the noun entries in brackets.

ā	啊	sen. suf. a (QV) + raised intonation for liveliness	14
A	呀	oh, ah. (a mild exclamation)	1
a	呀	sen. suf., to soften abruptness	2
agō [go]	阿哥	elder brother	11
àh	呀	sen. suf. with force of 'I suppose.'	8
aak	呃	sen. suf. a (QV) + -k (QV)	5.7
āam (var: ngāam)	啱	fitting, proper, right	2CP
āamāam (var: ngāamngāam)	啱啱	exactly	4.5
āamjeuk (var: ngāamjeuk)	啱著	well-fitting (for clothes), fits well	8.2
aan (var: ngaan)	晏	noon, midday	9
Aiya!	哎吔	exclamation of consternation	5
bá	把	Measure for things with handles, such as umbrellas	6.1
baak	百	hundred	11
baahk	白	white	8
baahk faahn [wún] [dī]	白飯	boiled or steamed rice	14.1
baat	八	eight	4.0
bāau	包	package, Measure for cigarette pack	7.1
bàhbā [go]	爸爸	father	12.3
bāt [jī]	筆	writing implement, either pen or pencil	6.1
bātgwo	不過	however; but; although	14

béi	俾	give	6
béi	俾	let, allow	7CP
bējáu [jì] [bùi] [jēun]	啤酒	beer	5.2
béng [go] [dì] [faai]	餅	cake	5
bīn-?	邊	which?	8
bīnbihn?	邊便	which side?	10.8
bīndouh?	邊度	where? [which place?]	4CP;10
bīngo	邊個	whomever, whoever, whichever	3CP
bīngo?	邊個	who?; which person?	3.12
-bihn	便(邊)side		10
bīu [go]	錶[個]	watch, wristwatch	4
bo	噃	sen. suf. expressing certainty	4
bohng	磅	pound (weight)	7
bou [fàai] [fāt]	布	cloth	7.1
bouhfahn [go]	部分[個]	department (in a store)	15
būi [jek] [go]	杯[隻][個]	a cup, glass	14.1
bùi	杯	cupful, glass-full (measure of volume)	14.1
bun	半	half	4.3
bún	本	Measure for book	1CP;7.1
búndeihyàhn [go]	本地人[個]	a native of the place under discussion [this-place-person]	10
chàmhdō	差唔多	approximately	2CP;4
chàh [bùi] [wùh]	茶[杯][壺]	tea	5
chàhlàuh [gàan]	茶樓[間]	Cantonese style tea-house	10.2
chāansāt [gàan]	餐室[間]	Western style restaurant	10.2
cháang [go]	橙[個]	orange (fruit)	5.1
cháau	炒	to toss-fry in a small amount of oil, as in scrambling eggs	14.2
cháau faahn [wún] [dihp]	炒飯[碗][碟]	fried rice	14.2
cháau mihn [wún] [dihp]	炒麵[碗][碟]	fried noodles	14.1
Chàhn	陳	Chan (sur.)	1
chāt	七	seven	4.0
chē [ga]	車[架]	vehicle: car, bus, or tram	10.9
chē jaahm [go]	車站[個]	car stop (bus or tram stop)	10.3
chéng...	請	please (+ Verb). polite preface to imperative sentence.	15

Chéng mahn	請問	'May I ask...?' Polite form used to preface a question equivalent to English 'Could you please tell me...?'	10
chèuihbín	隨便	As you wish. At your convenience.	5
Chèuihbín chóh lā.	隨便坐啦	'Sit anywhere you like.' Polite phrase used by host to guest.	5
cheung	暢(唱)	change money into smaller denomination (followed by denomination desired)	11.16
cheunghòi	暢(唱)開	split, break up a large banknote or coin for ones of lesser denomination (followed by denomination held)	11
chèuhng	長	long (in length)	8.1
chèuhng sāam [gihn]	長衫[件]	cheongsaam. Chinese style dress for women, with high collar and slit skirt	8.7

chēut
  chēutheui
  chēutlàih
	出
	出去
	出嚟
		out, emerge
		go out
		come out
			15

chēutbihn	出便(邊)	outside, exterior	15.1
chēut gāai	出街	to go out (from one's own house)	9.3
chi	次	time, occasion	1CP;3
chīn	千	thousand	11.17
chìhnbihn	前便(邊)	front side, in front, at the front	12.15
chín [dī]	錢[啲]	money	6
chìngchó	清楚	clear	3
chìhngyìhng	情形	circumstances, conditions	7CP
cho	錯	mistake (v/n)	9
chóh	坐	sit	5
choi [dihp] [go]	菜[碟][個]	food; a particular food, a dish	14
choidāan [jèung]	菜單[張]	menu of a specific dinner	14N
choipáai [go]	菜牌[個]	menu, bill of fare	14
dā	打	dozen	8
dá	打	hit	9
dá dihnwá	打電話	make a telephone call	9
dá dihnwá giu chē	打電話叫車	phone for a cab	15.11
dáhòi	打開	open (as of book)	1CP;15.3
daai	帶	carry; bring/take something along; bring/take someone along	11;12

-dóu	到	verb suf., indicating successful accomplishment of what is attempted	10
duhk	讀	read aloud; recite; read	3CP;15.3
duhkdou	讀到	read to...	15.3
duhk syù	讀書	to study	18
dyún	短	short	8
faahn [wún] [túng]	飯[碗][桶]	rice (cooked)	5.1
fàan	返	return (to/from a place you habitually go to)	9.3
fàan gùng	返工	go [return] to work	9.3
fàanheui	返去	go back, return	17
fàan hohk	返學	go to school	9.3
fàanjyuntàuh	返轉頭	turn (the car) around and go back in the direction you had been coming. [return-turn-head]	13.1
fàanlàih	返嚟	come back, return (here)	9
fàan (ng)ūkkéi	返屋企	go [return] home	9.3
faai	快	fast	4
faaijí [deui] [jek] [sēung]	筷子[對][隻][雙]	chopstick(s)	14.5
fānjūng 分鐘	分鐘	minute(s)	4
fànbiht	分別	difference	7CP
fo	課	lesson	4CP;15.3
fógei [go]	伙記[個]	clerk in a grocery store	6
fógei [go]	伙記[個]	waiter in a restaurant	14
fu [tìuh]	褲[條]	trousers, slacks, long pants	6.1
fu	副	pair; M. for eyeglasses	11.13
fut	潤	wide	8.3
ga	㗎	sen. suf: a fusion of noun-forming boundword ge and sen.suf. a (QV)	2.9
ga (var: ge, [gə])	㗎	sen. suf. for matter of fact assertion: 'that's a fact'	3
ga	架	M. for vehicles	12
gāai [tìuh]	街[條]	street	13
gaaisiuh	介紹	recommend; introduce	14
gàaiháu [go]	街口[個]	street opening; i.e., intersection	15.8
gàaisíh [go]	街市[個]	food market	15
gáai(sīk)	解(釋)	explain	7CP

daaih	大	large	8
Daaih Douh Jùng	大道中	Queen's Road Central	10.3
daaihsēng	大聲	loud (voice)	2CP
Daaihsēngdī!	大聲的	Speak louder!	9
daahnhaih	但係	but	3
daap	答	to answer	2CP
Daap cho sin.	搭錯線	Wrong number. [connected the wrong line] (said over the phone)	9.3
daaphaak [dī]	搭客(的)	passenger	13
daahp	搭	tread on. in time expression daahp combines with the numbers on the clock face to indicate the 5-minute subdivisions of the hour. Thus, daahp yāt = 5 after, daahp yih = 10 after, etc.	4
daahp bun	搭半	half past (the hour)	4.4
daahp géi?	搭幾	how many five minutes past the hour? [tread on-which number?]	4.4
daih	第	ordinal number marker: -st, -nd, -rd, -th, etc.	3CP;15.3
daihyāt	第一	the first	15
dáifu [tìuh]	底褲(條)	underpants, undershorts	6.3
dáikwàhn [tìuh]	底裙(條)	slip, petticoat	6.1
dáisāam [gihn]	底衫(件)	underwear	8.13
dāk	得	OK, all right	7CP;11
dāk...	得....	have only..., only have .X.quantity. (dāk with a quantity phrase as object implies that the quantity is insufficient.)	11
yáuh -dāk-	有-得-	available, can. (used between the verb yáuh (or its negative móuh) and a second verb, forms a phrase: 'have (or not have) available for .V.-ing'; 'can .V.'	11
Dākfuh Douh Jùng	德輔道中	Des Veoux Road Central	10.5
Dāk meih?	得未	Are you (Is he, etc.) ready?	4
dáng	等	wait (for)	4
dáng Person.Verb	等	allow, let Person do something; wait while Person does something	9
dáng (yāt)ján or dang yātjahn	等(一)陣 等一陣	wait awhile; in a little while	9.3

deihhá	地下	ground, ground floor	15.1
deui	對	pair; group measure for shoes, socks, chopsticks, things that come in two's	6.1
Deuimhjyuh.	對唔住	Excuse me; I beg your pardon; I'm sorry.	1
deuimihn	對面	opposite side, facing; across the street	10
dī	的	the; some. (plural M for individual nouns)	1CP;7
dī	啲	a little, some; the. (general M for mass nouns)	3;7
-dī	啲	suffixed to Adj. to mean: a little Adj, somewhat Adj, Adj-er. Attached to predicate Adj. means: a little too Adj.	2CP;8
dihnwá [go]	電話(個)	telephone	9
dím	點	to order (food, by pointing out your choice from a list.)	14
dím?	點	how?	3
dím bun	點半	1:30 o'clock	9.7
dím(jūng)	點(鐘)	o'clock. (represents the hour place in a time phrase)	4
diuhtàuh	掉頭	turn (a car) around [turn-head]	13.4
dōdī	多啲	more (in addition). (follows Verb)	14
dò	多	much, many	8
dò	多	additional, another, more. (precedes Number + M phrase)	14
Dòjeh.	多謝	Thank you (for gift)	14
Dòjehsaai.	多謝晒	Thank you very much.	14
dōu	都	also	2
dōu	都	both; and	3
dōuhaih	都係	really	14
dōu + neg:.V.	都	not even ...V.	3.16
dou	到	arrive	13
-dou	到	verb suf. to verbs of motion, indicating arrival at goal	15
Douh	道	Road (restricted to use following named road)	12.2
-douh	度	place. also see: hái douh	11

gaaklèih	隔離	next door, adjacent	10
gàan	間	M. for buildings	10
gaau	教	teach	3.3
gaaudou	教到	teach to...	4CP
gafē [bùi] [wùh]	㗎啡杯(壺)coffee		5.2
gāi [jek]	雞(隻)	chicken	7.1
gaijuhk	繼續	continue	2CP
gam	咁	so (+ Adj.)	5
gamseuhnghá	咁上下	approximately	9.7
gám	咁	that way, this way, thus, such a way	2CP;3CP
Gám,...	咁	'Well then,....' 'Say,...' (Sen. preface, resuming the thread of previous discussion)	3
gàn	斤	catty. unit of weight equalling 600 gms., ca. 1 lb 5 oz.	7
gàn	跟	follow, come behind	12.7
gànjyuh	跟住	follow, come after	1CP; 3CP 12.7
gāng [jek]	羹(隻)	spoon	14.4
gau	夠	enough	6
gauh	舊	old (not new)	8.1
gáu	九	nine	4.0
Gáulùhng	九龍	Kowloon	12
-ge	嘅	noun-forming boundword. added to Verb Phrase makes it a Noun Phrase	2
-ge	嘅	as noun substitute	8.8
ge	嘅	possessive marker, joins with preceding personal noun or pronoun to form possessive.	9.10
gèibún	基本	basic; foundation	4CP
géi	幾	several	4
géi-?	幾	which number?; how many?	4 ; 6
géi	幾	rather, quite	8
géidím? (var: géidímjūng?)	幾點 (幾點鐘)	what time is it? [which number - o'clock?]	4
géidō?	幾多	how much?, how many?	6
géidò	幾多	quite a lot	11.11

géidō houh?	幾多號	what number?	9
géisí? (var: géisih?)	幾時	when?	9
geui	句	sentence	3CP;3.14
géui	舉	give (an example)	7CP
gihn	件	M. for clothes, such as shirt, dress, raincoat	6
giu	叫	instruct, tell (someone to do something); order; call	9
giu chē	叫車	call a cab	15.11
giu(jouh)	叫(做)	is called, is named	13
go	個	general M. for many nouns	1CP;4
go	個	M. for dollar; represents the dollar place in a money phrase	7
gó-	嗰	that; those	6
gó bihn	嗰便(邊)	over there, on that side	10
gódí	嗰的	those (in reference to unit nouns); that (in reference to mass nouns)	7
gódouh	嗰度	there [that-place]	10.1
góng	講	speak	1CP;2CP; 3
góng Person jī	講.....知	tell Person	9.8
góng Person tèng	講.....聽	tell Person	9.8
guhaak [dí]	顧客	customers	6
gūngsī [gàan]	公司[間]	department store; office (of a commercial company)	10
gùngyàhn [go]	工人[個]	servant, laborer	9
gwai	貴	expensive	8.1
gwaising?	貴姓	what is (your) surname? (polite)	2
gwaisingmìhng?	貴姓名	what is your surname and given name? (polite)	13.17
gwāt	骨	quarter (hour)	4
gwo	過	pass by (a point); cross (a street); go over (to a place)	13
-gwo	過	V. suf. indicating experience; to have done something before.	14
gwodí	過的	beyond; a little farther on	13
Gwodí tìm.	過的添	Go further on; i.e. Keep going. (said to taxi driver)	13
Gwokyúh	國語	Mandarin spoken language [National-language]	3

Gwóngdùng	廣東	Kwangtung, province in SE China	2
Gwóngdùng choi	廣東菜	Cantonese food	14.2
Gwóngdùngwá	廣東話	Cantonese spoken language	3.1
Gwóngdùngyàhn [go]	廣東人[個]	Cantonese person, person from Kwangtung province	2
hā [jek]	蝦[隻]	shrimp	14
hahbihn	下便(邊)	below, downstairs	15.1
-háh	吓	verb suf. giving casual effect to the verb it is joined to.	5
hàaih [deui] [jek]	鞋[對][隻]	shoes	6.2;7.1
hāak	黑	black	8
haakhei	客氣	polite	5
hàahng	行	go; walk; drive	13
haih	係	am, is, are, was, were, etc.	1
haih...làih ge	係...嚟嘅	is...; grammatical structure emphasizing enclosed noun	7
hái PW	喺	from PW	15.6
hái PW	喺	location verb, translated as '(is) in/on/at' (requires PW following)	7CP;10
hai douh	喺度	(he, she, it) is here; is at (this) place	11
hauhbihn	後便(邊)	back side; behind, in the back, at the back	12
heiséui [jí] [jèun] [būi]	汽水[支][樽][杯]	soft drink	5.2
heui	去	go	12
-heui	去	attaches to verbs of motion, indicating direction away from the speaker	15
heui gāai	去街	go out (from one's own house)	9.3
Hèunggóng	香港	Hong Kong	10.3
Hòh	何	Ho (sur.)	1
hóyíh	可以	be permitted, allowed to	13
hohk	學	study, learn	3
hohkhaauh [gāan]	學校[間]	school	12
hohksāang [go]	學生[個]	student	1
houh	號	number; 'size' (for some articles of clothing)	8
houh	號	number (for street number in giving an address)	12.2

hòuh(jí)	毫子	dime (represents the dime place in a money expression when the figure is less than a dollar)	7
hóu	好	very, quite	2CP;8
hóu	好	well, good	2CP;8
Hóu	好	OK, All right, Fine, Agreed. (Response phrase indicating agreement.)	4
Hóu aak.	好呃	OK. Agreed. (Lively response phrase indicating agreement.)	5.7
hóudò	好多	a lot	11.11
Hóu ma?	好嗎	Is that OK?	14
hóu m̀hhóu a?	好唔好呀	OK?, is (that) all right?	8
hóusihk	好食	good to eat; tasty	8.2
hóusíu	好少	very little	11.11
hóuyám	好飲	good to drink; tasty	8.2
ja	喳	sen. suf: a fusion of sen. suffixes jē and a, implying not much, merely	11.11
jà	揸	to clutch in the hand(s), grab	13.15
jà chē	揸車	to drive a car	13.15
jaak	窄	narrow	8.3
jaahm	站	stop, station, as in 'bus stop,' 'train station'	10.3
jáau	找	give change	11
jáaufàan	找翻	give back change [change-return]	11
jái [go]	仔(個)	son	12.2
jáinéui [dī]	仔女(的)	children of a family, sons and daughters of a family	12.2
jànhaih	真係	really, indeed	5
jauh	就	then; and; immediately; soon	3CP;13
jáu	走	leave, depart	5
jáu [jèun] [bùi]	酒(樽)(杯)	alcoholic beverage	5.2
jáudim [gàan]	酒店(間)	hotel	10
jáugā [gàan]	酒家(間)	Chinese style restaurant	14.8
jē	嗻	sen. suf: only, merely; that's all	3
jē [bá]	遮	umbrella	6.1
je	借	lend, borrow	11
jejyuh	借住	lend or borrow temporarily	11

jek	隻	M. for shoe, sock, ship, cup, spoon, chicken and others.	7.1
jeuk	著	wear; put on (clothes)	8
jéun	準	accurate, right	2CP;4
Jèung	張	Cheung (sur.)	1.1
jèung	張	M. for banknote, table, chair, newspaper, and other sheet-snaped objects	11
jih [go]	字[個]	written figure; word; used in telling time, indicates the 5-minute divisions of the hour, thus: <u>yāt go jih</u> = 5 minutes; 5 min. past the hour.	4;7CP
jihgéi	自己	my-, your-, him-self; our-, your-, them-selves	2CP
jí	支	M. for pens, pencils, bottles, and other things that are small thin and striplike in size	6.1
jí(dou)	知	to know (something)	3
jí [jèung]	紙[張]	banknote; paper	11
jídou	知道	point to	3CP
jip	接	meet, fetch, pick up (a person)	12
jíu [jek] [sō]	蕉[隻][梳]	banana	5.1
-jó	咗	verb suf. indicating accomplish-ment of performance undertaken	**9**
jó	左	left (direction)	13
jóbihn	左便(邊)	left side	13
-jógán	左近	nearby,(t)hereabouts	10
jósáubihn	左手便(邊)	lefthand side	13
joi	再	again	1CP;3
joi dá làih	再打嚟	call back (on the phone)	9.3
Joigin.	再見	Goodbye.	1
joi góng yātchi	再講一次	say it again	3
jouh	做	do; work; act as	2CP;3CP; 12.2
jouh sāam	做衫	make clothes, have clothes made	12.12
jouh sih	做事	to work, have a job	12.2
jouh yéh	做野	do chores, have a job	14.7
Jóusàhn.	早晨	Good morning.	1
jūng [go]	鐘[個]	clock	6.1

juhng	重	still, in addition, also (+ verb)	14
Jùngchoi	中菜	Chinese food	14.2
Jùnggwok choi	中國菜	Chinese food	14.13
Jùnggwokyàhn	中國人	Chinese person	2.1
Jùngmàhn	中文	Chinese (written) language	3.3
Jùngwàahn	中環	Central District (in Hong Kong)	10.3
Jùngwàahn Gàaihsíh	中環街市	Central Market (in Hong Kong)	15
jùngyi	鍾意	like; prefer; like to	8
júng	種	type, kind	8
jyuh	住	live, reside	12
-jyuh	住	V. suf. indicating temporarily, for a short time	11
jyùuhk [gàn] [bohng] [dī] 豬肉(斤)(磅)(的)		pork	7
jyúyàhn [wái] [go] 主人(位)(個)		host, hostess	5
jyun	轉	turn	13
-k		glottal stop ending to certain sen. suffixes, giving sentence a lively air	5
kàhmyaht	琴日	yesterday	4CP
kámmàaih	冚埋	to close, shut (as of books)	1CP
kéuih	佢	he/him, she/her, it	2
kéuihdeih	佢地	they, them, their	2.1
kwàhn [tìuh]	裙(條)	skirt	6.1
lā	啦	sen. suf. for polite imperative, polite suggestion.	4
lā	啦	sen. suf. la for change + raised intonation for casualness	4
la	啦(嘛)	sen. suf. indicating change-- (that change has occurred, or is about to occur, or may occur)	4CP;4; 5
la	啦(嘛)	sen. suf. to imperative sentence, giving connotation of friendly advice	13.12
laak	嘞	sen. suf. la indicating change or potential change + suffix -k indicating lively mood (la + -k = laak)	2CP;5
lāangsāam [gihn]	冷衫(件)	sweater	8.1
laih	例	example	7CP
laihgeui	例句	example, example sentence	3CP

làih	嚟	for the purpose of	7CP
làih	嚟 (來)	come	12
-làih	嚟	attaches to verbs of motion, indicating direction towards the speaker	15
...làih ge	嚟嘅	see: haih...làih ge	7
Làuh	劉	Lau (sur.)	1.1
làuhhah	樓下	downstairs [floor-below]	15.1
làuhseuhng	樓上	upstairs [floor-above]	15.1
láu	樓	floor, story of a building	12.2
léh	咧	sen. suf. for definiteness	5
Léih	李	Lee (sur.)	1
leng	靚	pretty, good-looking; good, nice (for edibles)	8
lèhng	零	'-and a little bit' in a time phrase following dím, thus: -dím lèhng jūng = a little after the hour	9
léuhng	兩	two	4.1
lihnjaahp [go]	練習 [個]	exercise, drill	3CP
lìhng	零	zero	9
ló	攞	fetch, go get (something)	9
ló chín	攞錢	withdraw money (from bank)	10.9
lohk	落	descend	15
lohkheui	落去	go down	15
louhyàhn [go]	路人 [個]	pedestrian	15
luhk	六	six	4.0
ma?	嗎	sen. suf. making a question of the sentence it attaches to	14
màhmā	媽媽	mother	12
Máh	馬	Ma (sur.)	1.1
máh	碼	yard (in length)	7.1
máhtàuh [go]	碼頭 [個]	pier	10
maaih	賣	sell	7
Maaihsaai laak.	賣哂嘞	All sold out.	8
-màaih	埋	V. suf. meaning together, close	1CP
Màaihdāan!	埋單	The check please! (said to a waiter in restaurant)	14

máaih	買	buy	6
maahn	慢	slow	4.8
mān	蚊	dollar	6
mahn	問	ask	2CP;10
mahntàih [go] [dī]	問題[個][啲]	question	3CP
Màhnwàh Jáudim	文華酒店	Mandarin Hotel	10
mātyéh?	乜嘢	what?	2
maht [deui] [jek]	襪[對][隻]	socks	6.1;7.1
mē?	咩	interrogative sen. suf. indicating surprise	3
mēyéh?	咩嘢	what?	2
meih	未	neg: not yet	4
Méihgwok Jáudim	美國酒店	American Hotel (in HK, another name for the Hong Kong Hilton)	10.3
Méihgwok Ngàhnhòhng	美國銀行	Bank of America	10.3
Méihgwokyàhn	美國人	American person	2.1
méng [go]	名[個]	name; for persons = given name (in contrast to surname)	13
m̀h-	唔	not	1
m̀hcho	唔錯	good, 'not bad' [not-mistake] (said in commenting favorably about something)	14
M̀hgányiu.	唔緊要	That's all right; It doesn't matter; Never mind.	1
m̀hgeidāk	唔記得	forget (not remember)	11
m̀hginjó	唔見咗	lose, lost; 'nowhere to be seen'	11
m̀hgòi	唔該	Thank you (for a service)	5
M̀hgòi néih...	唔該你	Please..., Would you please... (sen. preface preceding a request)	3
m̀hhaih géi Adj	唔係幾...	not very Adj, not Adj	8.1
m̀hhaih hóu Adj	唔係好...	not very Adj	8.4
m̀hhóu .V.	唔好...	don't .V. (as a command) [not good to .V.]	1CP;3CP; 5
V.dāk m̀hhóu	得唔好	badly, not well	2CP
M̀hhóu haakhei.	唔好客氣	'Don't be polite.' Polite phrase used by host to urge guest to have something that he has just politely declined.	5

M̀hhóu yisi.	唔好意思	I'm sorry; It's embarrassing. (used in apologizing for social gaffe)	4
M̀hjì(dou)...a?	唔知(道)..呀	I wonder...?	6.1
m̀hsái	唔使	no need to, not necessary	5
M̀hsái haakhei.	唔使客氣	[don't need to be polite.] 'No thanks!' (to an offer) 'You're welcome.' (when someone thanks you)	5
M̀hsái la.	唔使啦	[Not necessary] No thanks. polite phrase used in declining a courtesy or a gift.	5
M̀hsái m̀hgòi.	唔使唔該	[Not necessary to (say) thanks] Polite response when someone thanks you for something you have done for him.	5
mĭyéh?	乜嘢	what?	
móuh	冇	not have, there isn't (aren't)	3CP;8
Móuh cho.	冇錯	That's right.	
móuhdāk ...	冇得...	not have available for V-ing, there's none to V.., not have available to ... (used in combination with following verb)	11
móuhgéidò	冇幾多	not much, not many	11.11
mùhnháu [go]	門口(個)	doorway	10.6
nàahmpàhngyáuh [go]	男朋友(個)	boyfriend	12.3
Nàh!	嗱	Here! (expression accompanying giving something to someone)	11
nē?	呢	interrogative sen. suf.	2
Nē!	呢	There! (expression accompanying pointing out something to someone)	10
Nèihdēun Douh	彌敦道	Nathan Road	12.2
néih	你	you, your	2
néihdeih	你哋	you (plu.)	1CP;2
néui [go]	女(個)	daughter	12
néuihpàhngyáuh [go] [wái]	女朋友(個)(位)	girlfriend	12.3
ńgh 五		five	3
ngāam	啱	fitting, proper, right	2CP
ngāamjeuk	啱著	well-fitting (for clothes), fits well	8.2

ngāamngāam(var:āam āam)	啱啱	exactly, just	4.5
ngaan (var:aan)	晏	noon, midday	9
ngàhnchín [go]	銀錢[個]	money [silver-money]	7
ngàhnhòhng [gàan]	銀行[間]	bank	10
ngán	銀	coin	11.1
ngáhngéng [fu]	眼鏡[副]	eyeglasses	11.13
ngáhngéngdói [go]	眼鏡袋[個]	eyeglasses case	11.13
ngahp táu	頷頭	nod the head	3CP
ngàuhnáaih [dī]	牛奶 [的]	milk [cow-milk]	5.2
ngàuhyuhk [gàn] [bohng] [dī]	牛肉 [斤] [磅] [的]	beef	7
ngóh	我	I, me, my	1
ngóhdeih	我哋	we, our, us	2.1
ngoi (var: oi)	愛	want, want to have, want to possess	7
ngoihgwokyàhn [go]	外國人[個]	foreigner [outside-country-person] (in practice, this word refers to Caucasians only)	14
ngūk (var: ūk) [gàan]	屋 [間]	house	10.3
ngūkkéi (var: ūkkéi)	屋企	home	9.3
nī	呢	this	6
nī bihn	呢便	this side	10.3
nī dī	呢的	these (in reference to individual nouns), this (in reference to mass nouns)	7
nīdouh	度	here [this-place]	10.1
nījógán	左近	close by, hereabouts	10.3
nihng táu	擰頭	shake the head	3CP
níng	拎	carry (something)	14
níngheui, níng...heui	拎去拎去	take, carry something away	14
nínglàih, níng...làih	拎嚟拎嚟	bring something here	14
oi (var: ngoi)	愛	want, want to have, want to possess	7
paak	泊	park (a car)	13
paak chē	泊車	to park a car	13
pàhngyáuh [go]	朋友[個]	friend	2
pèhng	平	cheap	8
pìhnggwó [go]	蘋果[個]	apple	5.1
-saai	嗮	completely	8

sàam	三	three	3
sàam go gwat	三個骨	three quarters after the hour	4.6
sáanngán [dī]	散銀(啲)	small coins, small change	11
Sàang	生	Mr.	1
Sāichāan [go]	西餐(個)	Western meal	14.2
sai	細	small	8.2
saimúi [go]	細妹(個)	younger sister	11
sàn	新	new	8.1
sahp	十	ten	4.0
sahpyāt	十一	eleven	4.1
sahpyih	十二	twelve	4.1
sauhfoyùhn [go]	售貨員(個)	salesclerk [sell-goods-personnel]	6
sáudói [go]	手袋(個)	(woman's) handbag	11.13
sèsíu	些少	a little	3
sé	寫	write	3
séjihlàuh [gàan]	寫字樓(間)	office [write-words-building]	10.2
sei	四	four	3
seuhngbihn	上便(邊)	above, upstairs	15.1
seuhngchi	上次	last time, the previous time	4CP;15.3
Seuhnghói	上海	Shanghai	2
Seuhnghói choi	上海菜	Shanghai food	14.2
Seuhnghóiwá	上海話	Shanghai dialect (spoken language)	3
Seuhnghóiyàhn [go]	上海人(個)	person from Shanghai	2
séung	想	be of a mind to, wish to, would like to, want to, considering. (always followed by Verb)	3
séuhng	上	ascend	15
séui [bùi] [dī]	水(杯)(啲)	water	5.2
séui būi [jek]	水杯(隻)	water glass	14.10
sēutsāam [gihn]	恤衫(件)	shirt	6
sīgēi [go]	司機(個)	taxi driver; chauffeur	11
si	試	try	5
siháh	試吓	give it a try	5
sih	事	business, affair, matter	9
Sihdaahn lā.	是但啦	Phrase used when offered a choice, meaning: As you wish; Either one; Both equally preferable.	14

sihhauh	時候	time	7CP
sīk	識	know how (to do something)	3
sīk	識	know someone	3.11
sīk	色	color (n.)	8
sihk	食	eat	5
sihk (ng)aan	食晏	eat lunch	2.1
sihk yīn	食烟	to smoke [eat-tobacco]	5
sīnsàang [go]	先生[個]	husband	12.2
sīnsàang [go] [wái]	先生[個][位]	man, gentleman	1N;2
SĪnsàang	先生	Mr.	1N
SĪnsàang	先生	'Sir,' polite term of direct address	2
sīnsàang [go]	先生[個]	teacher	1
sin	線	line, thread (n.)	9
sin	先	first	3CP;9
...sin, yihnhauh...	...先,然後...	...first, then...	15
sinji	先至	then	7CP
sing	姓	be surnamed, have the surname; surname	1
síujé [wái] [go]	小姐[位][個]	unmarried woman; woman, lady	1N;2
Síujé	小姐	Miss (polite term of direct address; also, title following surname)	1
Síu sihk.	少食	Thanks, I don't smoke. [seldom-smoke] (response by non-smoker when offered a cigarette.)	5.8
Síusing...	小姓	My surname is... (polite)	2
suhk	熟	ripe (in regard to speech = smoothly and with understanding of the content)	2CP
sung	送	deliver	12.10
-syu	處	place (PW boundword)	10N
syù [bún]	書[本]	book	1CP;3CP; 7.1
tāai [tiuh]	呔[條]	tie	6.2
Taaitáai	太太	Mrs.	1N;1
taaitáai [go] [wái]	太太[個][位]	married woman; wife	1N;12.2
Taai	太	Mrs. (title to surname)	1
taam	探	to visit	12
tái	睇	look, look at	1CP;3CP; 10

táidóu	睇倒	see (look-successfully)	10
táiháh	睇吓	have a look	14
tái syù	睇書	read (a book)	10.14
tái yīsāng	睇醫生	see a doctor	12.2
tanhauh	踉後	back (a car) up, move back, reverse [move-back]	13.1
táu = tàuh	頭	head	3CP
tèng	聽	hear, listen (to)	1CP;3CP; 3
tèng dihnwá	聽電話	talk [listen] on the telephone	9
tìm	添	sen. suf. indicating speaker is taken by surprise by a situation contrary to his expectation	11
tìm	添	in addition, also, more	4
Tīnsīng Màhtàuh	天星碼頭	Star Ferry Pier	10
tìhng	停	to stop	13
tìuh	條	M. for trousers, ties, and certain other objects long and narrow in shape	6.1
Tòihsāan	台山	Taishan, a county in Southern Kwangtung about 100 mi. west of Hong Kong	2.1
Tòihsāanwá	台山話	Taishan dialect	3.7
Tòihsāanyàhn	台山人	person from Taishan	2.1
tòng [go] [wún]	湯個碗	soup	14
tòng mihn [go] [wún]	湯麵個碗	soup noodles	14.1
tòhng	糖	sugar	7
Tòhngchoi	唐菜	Chinese food	14N
tòuhsyùwún [gàan]	圖書館間	library	10.2
tùhng	同	and (connects nouns)	3
tùhng	同	on behalf of, for	11
tùhng	同	with	12.11
ūk (var: ngūk) [gàan]	屋間	house	10.3
ūkkéi (var: ngūkkéi)	屋唶	home	9.3
wá	話	spoken language; dialect	3
wá?	話	interrogative sen. suf. calling for repeat of the preceding sentence	4
waahkjé	或者	maybe	4

wah	話	say; opine	8.3
wah yàhn jī	話人知	tell someone (any personal noun or pronoun can fill yàhn position)	9
wah yàhn tèng	話人聽	tell someone	9.8
wái	位	polite M. for persons	6.1
wái [go]	位(個)	a place, seat	13
wānjaahp	温習	to review	4CP
wán	搵	look for, search	9
Wán bīnwái a?	搵邊位呀	(on telephone:) Who do you wish to speak to?	9
wán yàhn	搵人	look someone up	9.9
làih wán person	嚟搵...	come/go see someone	9.9
heui wán person	去搵...		
Wéi!	喂	Hello! (telephone greeting)	9
WìhngŌn Gūngsī	永安公司	Wing On Department Store	13.1
Wòhng	黃(王)	Wong (sur.)	1.1
wuihwá	會話	conversation	4CP
wuhn	換	to change. re money, to change into... (followed by denomination of money desired); to exchange one national currency for another (followed by currency desired)	11
wuhn sāam	換衫	change clothes	15.11
wún [go] [jek]	碗(個)(隻)	bowl (n.)	14.1
wún	碗	a bowl of... (m)	14.1
wúnjái [go] [jek]	碗仔(個)(隻)	small bowl	14.10
yám	飲	to drink	5
yàhn [go]	人(個)	person	2,6
yàhn [go]	人(個)	someone	15
yàhnhaak [wái]	人客(位)	guest	5
yahp	入	enter	13
yahpbihn	入便(邊)	inside	13
yahpheui	入去	go in; enter	13
yāt	一	one	1CP;3
yātchàih	一齊	together	1CP
yātchi	一次	once, one time	3
yāt chi dōu meih...	一次都未...	not even once	14

yāt .M. dōu .Neg:.V.	一..都...	not even one...	14
yāt go gwāt	一個骨	a quarter after the hour	4.6
yāt go jih	一個字	five minutes; five minutes after the hour	4.7
yāt go yāt go	一個一個	one by one	1CP
yātjihk	一直	straight a) in a straight direction b) without being interrupted or diverted.	13
yātyeuhng	一樣	same	7
Yahtbún choi	日本菜	Japanese food	14.12
Yahtbúnwá	日本話	Japanese (spoken) language	3.1
Yahtbúnyàhn	日本人	Japanese person	2.1
Yahtmán	日文	Japanese (written) language	3.6
Yahtmàhn	日文	Japanese (written) language	3.6
yauh	右	right (direction)	13
yauh	又	also (connects Verb Phrases)	3.9
yauh .V.yauh.V.	又..又...	both..., and....	3.9
yauhbihn	右便(邊)	right side	13.7
yauhsáubihn	右手便(邊)	right hand side	13.4
yàuh.PW.	由...	from .PW.	15
yàuhhaak [go]	遊客(個)	tourist	10
yáuh	有	has/have; there is/are	3CP;8
yáuhdāk.V.	有得	to have available to .V., have available for .V-ing. (used in combination with following verb)	11.7
(Yáuh) mēyéh sih a?	(有)咩野事呀	What is it you want? (on the phone: May I take a message?)	9
yáuh sih	有事	have something to attend to; have errand, business	9
yéh	嘢	work; chores	14.7
yéh	嘢	things, stuff	12.2
yeuhng	樣	kind, type	14.12
yīsāng [go]	醫生(個)	doctor	12.2
yih	二	two	3
yìhgā	而家	now, at this moment	1CP;2CP; 3CP;4
Yí!	噫	Exclamation of distress	11

391

...yìkwaahk...?	...抑或...	..., or...? (connects two verbal expressions)	14
yìn [bāau] [dī]	烟(包)(的)	tobacco	5
yìnjái [jì]	烟仔(支)	a cigarette	7.1
yìhn(jì)hauh	然(之)後	then; immediately afterwards	15
Yìngmán	英文	English language	3
Yìngmàhn	英文	English language	3
Yìnggwokyàhn [go]	英國人(個)	Englishman, person from England	2.1
yihp	頁	page	4CP;15.3
yiu	要	want, require	2CP
yiu	要	must; need; have to	5
yiu + money expression	要	want X amount, costs X amount. (i.e., the asking price is X amount)	6.1
yiu	要	going to, intend to	9
yú	魚	fish	7.1
yúhjyū [jek]	乳豬(隻)	roast suckling pig	14
yúhlāu [gihn]	雨樓(件)	raincoat	6.1
yùhnbāt [jì]	鉛筆(支)	pencil	6.1
yùhnjíbāt [jì] [dī]	原子筆	ballpoint pen	6.2
yuhng 用	(支)(的)	use	7CP;11